Eternity Clauses in Democratic Constitutionalism

OXFORD
UNIVERSITY PRESS

Great Clarendon Street, Oxford, OX2 6DP,
United Kingdom

Oxford University Press is a department of the University of Oxford. It furthers the University's objective of excellence in research, scholarship, and education by publishing worldwide. Oxford is a registered trade mark of Oxford University Press in the UK and in certain other countries

First Edition published in 2021

Impression: 3

Published in the United States of America by Oxford University Press
198 Madison Avenue, New York, NY 10016, United States of America

British Library Cataloguing in Publication Data

Data available

Library of Congress Control Number: 2020948225

ISBN 978–0–19–885886–7

DOI: 10.1093/oso/9780198858867.001.0001

Printed and bound by
CPI Group (UK) Ltd, Croydon, CR0 4YY

To my parents

Acknowledgments

This book would not have been possible without the support of mentors, colleagues, and friends. At Edinburgh Law School, I was privileged to benefit from the guidance of my two PhD supervisors, Stephen Tierney and Neil Walker. Their belief in this research project sustained me through the darker times inevitable in any lengthy writing process. They showed me unfailing trust, patience, and respect, all while maintaining a sense of humour about it all, for which I will always be thankful. They are role models both as intellectuals and as individuals and I feel very fortunate to have benefited from their mentorship during my academic journey. My dissertation examiners, Martin Loughlin and Elisenda Casañas Adam, engaged with this research robustly and helped improve it significantly. They have remained sources of inspiration and support ever since.

The academic environment at Edinburgh Law School provided the stimulating context in which I developed a significant portion of this work. The Constitutional Law Discussion Group and Edinburgh Centre for Constitutional Law offered the perfect mix of academic rigour and friendly atmosphere in which to test my thinking, engage with peers, and truly feel part of a research community. The Legal Theory Research Group also afforded me opportunities to pursue research interests beyond the mainstreams of constitutional theory. Members of all these clusters whose insights have helped me refine my ideas include: Tom Gerald Daly, Martin Kelly, Cormac Mac Amhlaigh, Euan MacDonald, Claudio Michelon, and Asanga Welikala. Alongside them, Christine Bell has provided generous feedback on my writing and support for my academic pursuits during and after my time in Edinburgh. Hers remains a model of engaged scholarship.

Since joining UCL's Faculty of Laws in 2016, I was fortunate to benefit from an intellectual home like no other. I am grateful for the lively research environment at UCL, as well as for the friendships I am lucky to have created here. Members of the Public Law Group in particular have provided useful feedback on various strands of my research and deeply enriching conversations, including: Rodney Austin, Paul Burgess, Joe Crampin, Conor Crummey, Aleisha Ebrahimi, Oliver Gerstenberg, Carlos Herrera-Martin, Myriam Hunter-Henin, Jeff King, Daniella Lock, Ronan McCrea, Colm O'Cinneide, Rick Rawlings, Natalie Sedacca, and Eugenio Velasco Ibarra. Two workshops organized with faculty and university support, one on exclusionary constitutionalism in 2018 and one on constitutional identity in 2019, were fantastic opportunities for focused discussion around the trickier arguments in the book. Huge thanks are due to all the participants in both events. Presenting my research as part of our faculty staff seminars further challenged my thinking in a collegial atmosphere. I am indebted to Piet Eeckhout, Richard Moorhead, and Eloise Scotford for making that possible.

Parts of this research were presented at conferences and workshops at institutions throughout the world. These include: the University of Aberdeen, the University of Bristol, Charles University in Prague, the Chinese University of Hong Kong, the University of Copenhagen, the Devolution Club in London, the European University Institute in Florence, the University of Glasgow, the University of Hong Kong, the International IDEA Constitution Building Programme in The Hague, the International Institute for the Sociology of Law in Oñati, the London School of Economics and Political Science, the University of Oxford, New York University, Queen's University Belfast, SungKyunKwan University in Seoul, the University of Trento, and the University of Victoria in Canada. I am grateful to the discussants and participants in all these for their generous engagement with my work. I am thankful also to my colleagues in the Central and Eastern European chapter of the International Society of Public Law and in the UK Constitutional Law Association for stimulating conversations that, directly or indirectly, have helped enrich the ideas in this book.

Richard Albert and Robert Schütze were wonderful stewards of this book as part of Oxford University Press's Comparative Constitutionalism series, believing in the project throughout its various written iterations. Jamie Berezin and Imogen Hill ensured the project stayed on track. The anonymous reviewers provided constructive comments as well as reassurance about the book's distinctive contribution. I am grateful to them all for helping to get this project over the finishing line.

Finally, I owe a great debt of gratitude to friends and family who have stood by me, allowed me to complain (but not too much), and always found a word of reassurance to spare. Kasia Chalaczkiewicz-Ladna, Koto Eristavi, Gigi Jokubauskaite, and Alex Latham-Gambi made our PhD days feel like a fun adventure. I hope we will have many more chances to share each other's joyous occasions, whether in the city of shifting light and changing skies or on the sunny hills of Emilia-Romagna. At UCL Laws, Niamh Connolly, Mark Dsouza, Ugljesa Grusic, Magda Raczynska, Daniela Simone, and Kevin Toh have been partners in crime and caring friends. Ana Cannilla, Ashleigh Keall, and Maria Lee have been true feminist allies. Mara Malagodi and Jenna Sapiano have cheered me on and shared their wise counsel from different corners of the world—they embody the power of scholarly sisterhood. Casiana Ionita has provided constant encouragement and expert advice, not to mention being the best plant mom. Mihai Evoiu lent his designer's eye and feline support system during moments of need. Anica and Victor Titiu welcomed me unreservedly and offered respite, not to mention a fair bit of sustenance. My partner, Bogdan Titiu, has been my champion throughout. His love, patience, and gentleness sustained me. Our laughs together kept me sane. Finally, my parents, Trandafira and Ioan, and my brother Iuliu have been my rock. They have never once doubted I could achieve whatever I set my mind to and so much more. I hope this book makes them proud.

Contents

III. ETERNITY CLAUSES IN CONTEMPORARY CONSTITUTIONAL REFORM PROCESSES: TRANSNATIONAL FORCES, POPULAR PARTICIPATION, AND CONSTITUTIONAL RENEWAL

Table of Cases

UNITED KINGDOM

EUROPEAN COURT OF HUMAN RIGHTS

EUROPEAN COURT OF JUSTICE

AFRICAN COMMISSION ON HUMAN AND PEOPLE'S RIGHTS

CENTRAL AMERICAN COURT OF JUSTICE

INTER-AMERICAN COURT OF HUMAN RIGHTS

ARGENTINA

BANGLADESH

BOLIVIA

BOSNIA AND HERZEGOVINA

COLOMBIA

CZECH REPUBLIC

FIJI

FRANCE

GERMANY

HONDURAS

HUNGARY

INDIA

ISRAEL

ITALY

KENYA

KOSOVO

MALAYSIA

NIGER

PAKISTAN

REPUBLIC OF SOUTH AFRICA

ROMANIA

SINGAPORE

SLOVAKIA

SPAIN

SRI LANKA

THAILAND

TURKEY

Table of Legislation

NATIONAL LEGISLATION

Turkey

Ukraine

United Kingdom

United States

Venezuela

INTERNATIONAL LEGISLATION

Introduction

The Rise of Eternity Clauses in Democratic Constitutionalism

The rise of eternity clauses

Constitutions are drafted to endure. Both symbolic statements of core societal values and blueprints for organizing government, they are meant to provide stability and a sense of identity. How to achieve such longevity, however, is less clear. From constitutionalism's earliest days, constitution-makers have struggled with how best to calibrate basic laws in order to ensure they are not too easily discarded nor ossifying. Jefferson's call for the constitution to be renegotiated once every generation[1] and James Madison's fear that 'a frequent reference of constitutional questions to the decision of the whole society' would engage dangerous passions[2] still capture the two poles of this debate. Whether to allow for constitutional flexibility or, conversely, to shut off certain matters from renegotiation demarcate the choices between which drafters must decide in their pursuit of constitutional durability. They look to constitutional theory and comparative practice to help them ascertain which of these paths is more suited to their own polity.

Along the rigidity end of this spectrum of choices, eternity clauses have gained wide popularity. They are a type of constitutional provision which insulates from amendment certain constitutional values, principles, or institutions. They represent a special mechanism of constitutional entrenchment, one which might be termed indefinite or limitless. Alongside such formal eternity clauses, there has been a rise of doctrines of implicit unamendability, such as basic structure or substantive core doctrines. Their logic is similar to that behind eternity clauses, though they reach beyond a single textual anchor. Unconstitutional constitutional amendment doctrines hold that otherwise procedurally valid constitutional amendments may still infringe fundamental pillars of the constitution or its inviolable core and are thereby invalid. Such amendments may jeopardize the constitution's very identity. This in turn justifies the substantive review of constitutional amendments, whether or not the constitutional text explicitly envisions it.

[1] Thomas Jefferson to James Madison, 6 September 1789.
[2] James Madison, *Federalist No. 49*, 5 February 1788.

Eternity Clauses in Democratic Constitutionalism. Silvia Suteu, Oxford University Press.
DOI: 10.1093/oso/9780198858867.003.0001

Eternity clauses and judicially created doctrines of unamendability are paradoxical from the point of view of democratic constitutionalism. The tense relationship between constitutional precommitment and democracy is further strained if we take eternity clauses to be at the farthest end of a constitutional rigidity continuum. As this study will show, however, it is not just that eternity clauses are the most rigid among amendment rules that is problematic. Unamendability is also qualitatively different from other mechanisms of constitutional entrenchment. Unlike procedural entrenchment rules such as supermajority rules or ratification referendums, unamendability imposes material limitations on constitutional change on the basis of a hierarchy of norms within and sometimes even above the constitution. That hierarchy rests on value commitments that are unavoidably vague and underspecified but that are nonetheless enforced by constitutional review whose reach can be deeply unsettling to committed democrats. The history of constitutional rigidity has shown it to be an instrument of elite entrenchment, not just insulating from change features deemed of higher or constitutive importance, but also protecting privilege and power asymmetries.[3] Democratic participation being limited in the name of elite-favouring values and constitutional change being brought under far-reaching judicial control should thus be deeply unsettling to democratic constitutionalists.[4]

This book makes a critical contribution to the growing literature on constitutional unamendability, as well as to the broader scholarship in the field of comparative constitutional change. It represents a unique analysis of unamendability in democratic constitutionalism that engages critically and systematically with its perils, offering a much-needed corrective to existing understandings of this phenomenon. The book takes seriously the democratic challenge eternity clauses pose and argues that this goes beyond the old tension between constitutionalism and democracy. Instead, when critically assessing unamendability in constitution-making and constitutional interpretation, eternity clauses reveal themselves to be a far more ambivalent constitutional mechanism, one with greater and more insidious potential for abuse than has been hitherto recognized. The book also offers a novel look at unamendability in democratic constitutions by placing the rise of eternity clauses in the context of other significant trends in recent constitutional practice: the transnational embeddedness of constitution-making and of constitutional adjudication; the rise of popular participation in constitutional reform processes; and the ongoing crisis of democratic backsliding in liberal democracies.

The book adopts a contextual approach that allows for more nuanced understandings of constitutional amendment rules and substantive limits on amendments. It looks beyond the usual suspects typically discussed in this literature

[3] Melissa Schwartzberg, *Democracy and Legal Change* (Cambridge University Press 2009).

[4] Allan C. Hutchinson and Joel Colon-Rios, 'Democracy and Constitutional Change', Osgoode Hall Law School Research Paper No. 48/2010 6:11 (2010), 4.

such as Germany and India and brings to the fore a variety of case studies from non-traditional jurisdictions. These insights from the periphery illuminate the prospects of unamendability fulfilling its intended aims, protecting constitutional democracy foremost among them. Its promise most appealing in new, post-conflict, and fragile democracies, unamendability reveals itself to be ironically both less potent and potentially more dangerous in precisely these contexts.

This critical engagement with unamendability offers a paradigm-shifting analysis of the phenomenon of eternity clauses, yielding conclusions that democratic constitutionalists must be aware of. These include: the reality of 'the dark side of unamendability', notably its propensity to insulate majoritarian, exclusionary, and internally incoherent values; the different role played by eternity clauses in transitional contexts, where they often serve as facilitators of political bargaining rather than as statements of high values; and the far-reaching impact of transnational norms on both the content and the interpretation of unamendable norms. These findings together paint a more ambiguous picture of unamendability in democratic constitutionalism than previously thought and caution constitution-makers, practitioners, and scholars to more carefully consider the promise and perils of eternity clauses in the constitutional architecture.

Existing work in the area

There has been a marked growth in the literature on comparative constitutional change in recent years. Works in this area have included edited volumes comparing the mechanisms of constitutional amendment in different countries,[5] as well as more targeted scholarship, notably on the rise of public participation in constitutional reform processes.[6] When it comes to eternity clauses, however, there is both a broad literature with which this book is in conversation, and a narrower one focused specifically on unamendability to which it seeks to make a substantial contribution.

Insofar as the problems raised by unamendability go to the core of legal philosophy and constitutional theory, they can be read in the old key of the constitutionalism versus democracy debates. In this arena, precommitment theories

[5] Mads Andenas, ed., *The Creation and Amendment of Constitutional Norms* (British Institute of International and Comparative Law 2000); Dawn Oliver and Carlo Fusaro, eds., *How Constitutions Change: A Comparative Study* (Hart 2011); Xenophon Contiades, ed., *Engineering Constitutional Change: A Comparative Perspective on Europe, Canada and the USA* (Routledge 2012); Richard Albert, Xenophon Contiades, and Alkmene Fotiadou, eds., *The Foundations and Traditions of Constitutional Amendment* (Hart 2017); Richard Albert, *Constitutional Amendments: Making, Breaking, and Changing Constitutions* (Oxford University Press 2019); Xenophon Contiades and Alkmene Fotiadou, eds., *Routledge Handbook of Comparative Constitutional Change* (Routledge 2020); Bui Ngoc Son, *Constitutional Change in the Contemporary Socialist World* (Oxford University Press 2020).

[6] Xenophon Contiades and Alkmene Fotiadou, eds., *Participatory Constitutional Change: The People as Amenders of the Constitution* (Routledge 2017).

have asked how constitutionalism can defend its democratic credentials in the face of criticism that a will cannot bind itself, nor a generation its successors.[7] Such writings, written in the aftermath of the post-1989 wave of constitution-making, largely ignored the problems posed by eternity clauses and dealt cursorily with constitutional amendment rules. Their main concern was with justifying counter-majoritarian constitutional devices as a means of wise self-binding, wherein generations tie their hands for the future in order to prevent dangerous collective passions.

This body of literature thus shares an affinity with militant democracy writings, anxious as they are to prevent constitutions from becoming suicide pacts. Militant democracy is a democracy consciously 'intolerant' of its enemies, one armed with the necessary tools to prevent totalitarian relapses and legal subversions of the constitutional order.[8] Eternity clauses have been read as just such a tool, insofar as they purport to safeguard the very essentials of constitutional democracy from its enemies. They are, together with mechanisms such as parliamentary thresholds and party bans, the constitutional response to the 'Weimar syndrome'.[9]

The literature on constituent power has also grappled with many of the same tensions raised by unamendability: questions of democratic legitimacy over time and how to conceptualize the constitutional subject, either as rhetorical device, static, symbolic, and external to the constitutional order, or else as a dynamic, ever-present agent of change.[10] Inasmuch as the core concern in the present book is with the place of eternity clauses within democratic constitutionalism, it resonates with constituent power theories as theories of democratic legitimacy. However, I seek to heed calls to revise our constitutional imaginary and its assumed foundations, including of a unified, uncontested, knowable constituent power.[11] To the extent that eternity clauses, or the constitution itself, are taken to be the expression of a single will, this view will be shown to oversimplify the messy, conflictual, and often provisional and incomplete nature of constitution-making processes. Constituent power in such processes is plural, often internationalized, and discordant.

[7] Stephen Holmes, *Passions and Constraint: On the Theory of Liberal Democracy* (University of Chicago Press 1995); Jon Elster, *Ulysses Unbound: Studies in Rationality, Precommitment, and Constraints* (Cambridge University Press 2000).

[8] Gregory H. Fox and Georg Nolte, 'Intolerant Democracies', *Harvard Journal of International Law* 36:1 (1995) 1.

[9] Kieran Williams, 'When a Constitutional Amendment Violates the "Substantive Core": The Czech Constitutional Court's September 2009 Early Elections Decision', *Review of Central and Eastern European Law* 36 (2011) 33; Rivka Weil, 'On the Nexus of Eternity Clauses, Proportional Representation, and Banned Political Parties', *Election Law Journal* 16:2 (2017) 237.

[10] Martin Loughlin and Neil Walker, eds., *The Paradox of Constitutionalism: Constituent Power and Constitutional Form* (Oxford University Press 2008); Joel Colón-Ríos, *Weak Constitutionalism: Democratic Legitimacy and the Question of Constituent Power* (Routledge 2012); Andrew Arato, *The Adventures of the Constituent Power: Beyond Revolutions?* (Cambridge University Press 2017); Joel Colón-Ríos, *Constituent Power and the Law* (Oxford University Press 2020).

[11] Zoran Oklopcic, *Beyond the People: Social Imaginary and Constituent Imagination* (Oxford University Press 2018).

The budding literature on unamendability represents the immediate interlocutor for this project, however. For some time and to an extent still, this body of work has focused on country studies, seeking to highlight the operation of a formal or judicially crafted eternity clause in a given context.[12] With Richard Albert's scholarship on constitutional amendment rules, including formal and constructive unamendability, however, the field progressed significantly in the direction of the systematic study of mechanisms of constitutional change.[13] His work has highlighted not only the importance of taking formal amendment rules seriously—he calls them 'the gatekeepers to a constitution'[14]—but also the myriad design options that exist to give constitutional drafters choices on the continuum between flexibility and rigidity.

Other significant studies of unamendability have primarily been theoretical and classificatory.[15] Yaniv Roznai's work in particular has advanced our understanding of unamendable provisions, mapping their emergence and content, providing a coherent theory to distinguish between amendment power and constituent power, and beginning the work needed for a theory of the judicial enforcement of unamendability. His foremost contributions have been to document the pervasiveness of eternity clauses and judicial doctrines of unamendability around the world, as well as to explain their operation in constitutional theoretical terms. He has found 212 constitutions (or 28 per cent) of 742 constitutions counted between 1789 and 2015 to contain formal eternity clauses, with higher figures for constitutions adopted after 1989: eighty-one (or 54 per cent) out of 149 fundamental laws counted in this period.[16] Theoretically, Roznai distinguishes between original and derived, or primary and secondary, constituent powers, the first belonging to the original constitution-making power and the second the amendment power that is regulated under the constitution both procedurally and materially. The substantive limits on this amendment power are either enshrined in a formal eternity clause or else derived through judicial interpretation from the constitution's core principles or basic structure. It is then only natural for constitutional courts, as guardians of the constitution, to step in and enforce material unamendability in concrete cases of attempted constitutional change. Roznai cautions judicial self-restraint and modulation of this court intervention depending on the democratic credentials of

[12] Richard Albert and Bertil Emrah Oder, eds., *An Unamendable Constitution? Unamendability in Constitutional Democracies* (Springer 2018).

[13] Albert (2019).

[14] Ibid., 2.

[15] Po Jen Yap, 'The Conundrum of Unconstitutional Constitutional Amendments', *Global Constitutionalism* 4:1 (2015) 114; Yaniv Roznai, 'Unconstitutional Constitutional Amendments—The Migration and Success of a Constitutional Idea', *American Journal of Comparative Law* 61 (2013) 657; Yaniv Roznai, *Unconstitutional Constitutional Amendments: The Limits of Amendment Powers* (Oxford University Press 2017); Michael Hein, 'Do Constitutional Entrenchment Clauses Matter? Constitutional Review of Constitutional Amendments in Europe', *International Journal of Constitutional Law* 18:1 (2020) 78.

[16] Roznai (2017), 20–1.

the amendment process. However, he ultimately defends unamendability as a potentially useful 'lock on the door' of constitutionalism, one that may not always prevent intrusion but can at least impede and deter it.[17]

Without taking away from this important achievement, however, the present book seeks to add necessary missing elements to the story of unamendability. First, it adopts a more critical lens in an effort to reveal not just the synergies, but also the tensions between unamendability and democratic constitutionalism. The book reveals that, rather than always safeguarding lofty constitutionalist goals, unamendability not infrequently serves as a tool for entrenching elite interests, majoritarian exclusion, and judicial turf protecting. Moreover, amendment invalidation on material grounds is not always a measure of last resort as defenders of unconstitutional constitutional amendment doctrines often assume. Second, the book more directly engages with democratic justifications for, and objections to, eternity clauses. It does so not in abstract terms but contextually, analysing the distinctive democratic considerations that underpin a particular eternity clause and testing their operation in practice. It highlights the distinctive challenges posed by unamendability in new and fragile democracies, paradoxically both most in need of the promise of eternity and most likely to fall prey to its limitations. This unique focus on conflict-affected case studies recognizes that, rather than the exception, these represent the vast majority of current constitution building processes. Third, the present project also studies eternity clauses against the background of contemporaneous, and potentially contradictory, trends: the rise of direct popular involvement in constitutional change and the growing internationalization of constitution-making and adjudication. Here are two more paradoxes of unamendability: their simultaneity with the participatory turn in constitutional reform processes and their uneasy straddling of the particular and the universal.

A noteworthy turn in the study of unamendability has been interest in its effectiveness as a tool to fight democratic backsliding.[18] Even where the constitutional text lacks an eternity clause, it has been argued that implicit material limits should be recognized to govern constitutional amendment and prevent abusive constitutionalism.[19] The legal guise taken by many of the attacks on democracy, including formal amendment and constitutional replacement, should make unconstitutional constitutional amendment doctrines ripe for deployment in their most militant guise. Indeed, one way to read the history of eternity clauses and basic structure doctrines sees them emerging precisely in contexts where democracy was under threat, such as in response to Nazi Germany's legal descent

[17] Ibid., 133–4.

[18] Gábor Halmai, 'Unconstitutional Constitutional Amendments: Constitutional Courts as Guardians of the Constitution?', *Constellations* 19:2 (2012) 182; Rosalind Dixon and David Landau, 'Transnational Constitutionalism and a Limited Doctrine of Unconstitutional Constitutional Amendment', *International Journal of Constitutional Law* 13:3 (2015) 606.

[19] David Landau, 'Abusive Constitutionalism', *UC Davis Law Review* 47 (2013a) 189.

into totalitarianism and to executive abuse during a state of emergency in Indira Gandhi's India. However, as I show in the book, the reality of democratic backsliding today renders unamendability's promise as a bulwark against it rather illusory. Democratic erosion nowadays often begins with the courts themselves, such as through court packing, judicial replacement, and restriction of constitutional review powers, making them unlikely or else impotent allies against backsliding. It will be far more likely that a constellation of constitutional actors and mechanisms needs to be deployed, and that their chances of success depend on political and not just legal considerations.[20]

The case for a democratic critique of unamendability

The contours of democratic constitutionalism are not fixed, and self-professed democrats themselves differ in their understanding of what it might entail. Indeed, the very question of what version of democracy is to be constitutionalized is itself political and will be negotiated and renegotiated continuously within a polity. In its thinner and more procedural version, democratic constitutionalism demands protection for the preconditions of democratic participation, such as for the institutions and fundamental rights that are constitutive of the democratic process.[21] In its more radical version, democratic constitutionalism as applied to the constitution-making context seeks to retain the central role of ordinary citizens as the drivers of processes of constitutional change, from initiating to deliberating on and ratifying such change.[22] It denies that democratic energies within a polity are to be confined to elections only and values a certain degree of constitutional openness as a means to keep the fundamental law societally responsive. Democratic constitutionalism prioritizes the democratic dimension of constitutional legitimation, seeks to reclaim radical politics, and opposes a view of constitutional democracy that prioritizes order and stability over the possibility of democratic self-rule.[23] Its critique of existing structures is also foundational, seeking as it does novel forms of democratic engagement and legitimation.

This book's approach is closer to the latter understanding of democratic constitutionalism, insofar as it takes seriously democratic constitutions' promise of constitutional *self*-government. This view correlates with a particular understanding

[20] Stephen Gardbaum, 'The Counter-playbook: Resisting the Populist Assault on Separation of Powers', *Columbia Journal of Transnational Law* 59:1 (2020 forthcoming).

[21] John Hart Ely, *Democracy and Distrust: A Theory of Judicial Review* (Harvard University Press 1980); Jeremy Waldron, *Law and Disagreement* (Oxford University Press 1999).

[22] Colón-Ríos (2012), 5.

[23] Paul Blokker, 'Constitutional Reform in Europe and Recourse to the People' in Xenophon Contiades and Alkmene Fotiadou, eds., *Participatory Constitutional Change: The People as Amenders of the Constitution* (Routledge 2017) 31, 40–2.

of constitutions and constitutional amendments informing this project. I view constitutions as contested documents, negotiated products of often fraught processes that are not to be fossilized in the name of an idealized constituent moment. Possibly exclusionary and certainly always perfectible, constitution-making is thus not closed off and immutable but an ever-changing 'process of becoming'.[24] Constitutional amendments, then, are necessary mechanisms to facilitate constitutional responsiveness. And, while the danger of abusive constitutional change is real, opting for extreme constitutional rigidity such as unamendability risks entirely denying the radical democratic potential of constitutional amendment.

This book argues that unamendability's tense relationship with democratic constitutionalism should be recentred as the core concern in studies of eternity clauses and unconstitutional constitutional amendment doctrines. Justifying unamendability on counter-majoritarian grounds *tout court*, as much of the literature has hitherto done, fails to capture the specific democratic challenge it poses. Whether as a tool of precommitment, militant democracy, or a thick understanding of constitutionalism, this way of viewing constitutional unamendability risks missing precisely what makes it special and worthy of study on its own terms. As the book shows, dismissing eternity clauses as merely symbolic is misguided and likely anchored in a bygone era of constitutionalism in which strong judicial review and assertive courts were not yet the norm. Instead, they are vehicles for judicial self-empowerment, even where the constitution explicitly seeks to prevent the material review of constitutional amendments.

Still misguided, however, would be to assume that unamendability is always a neutral instrument defending liberal constitutionalist commitments and liberal democracy itself. Several of the book's chapters show that unamendability is repeatedly employed in exclusionary ways. This is done pragmatically, as in post-conflict contexts where certain compromises reached during peace negotiations are enshrined in the constitution, or intentionally, as part of majoritarian constitution-making processes. What is important to note is that such exclusionary eternity clauses often coexist with liberal democratic constitutional commitments. The exclusionary aims of constitutional entrenchment in general and eternity clauses in particular are thus not relegated to non-democracies, but sometimes take centre stage in constitutional democracies otherwise committed to fundamental rights, equality, and non-discrimination. Thus, this study should be read in conjunction with other work in comparative constitutional law that draws attention to exclusionary constitutionalism.[25] It should also be read as asking who stands to win and who stands to lose from constitutional unamendability, taking the latter as just as if

24 Loughlin and Walker (2008), 4.

25 Mara Malagodi, *Constitutional Nationalism and Legal Exclusion: Equality, Identity Politics, and Democracy in Nepal (1990–2007)* (Oxford University Press 2013); Mazen Masri, *The Dynamics of Exclusionary Constitutionalism: Israel as a Jewish and Democratic State* (Hart 2017).

not more illuminating about the purposes and operation of eternal constitutional pledges.

The book also cautions against reading eternity clauses as the epitome of autochthonous constitutionalism. It situates the emergence of such provisions within trends of transnational engagement in constitution-making and adjudication today.[26] Shifting the focus of existing accounts of unamendability from the abstract to the concrete and contextual, the book also teases out its significance in global perspective. It thus finds that the growing internationalization of contemporary constitution-making has an impact on both the content and the adjudication of unamendability. It is not just that we find a vigorous migration of the notion of rendering certain aspects of the constitution eternal or recognizing a basic structure or substantive core of the constitution that is impervious to change. Nor is it just witnessing a novel instantiation of the diffusion of global constitutional values. Instead, more and more we find international actors as constitutional drafters and advisers; as the initiators, supporters, and guarantors of constitutional documents; and as the external audience on whom constitutional legitimation will depend. Unamendability is thus also a response to this growing chorus of voices and interests in globalized constitution-making processes. The courts tasked with enforcing it are themselves transnationally embedded, whether this means enforcing global values, adjudicating unamendability with a transnational referent, or even developing unconstitutional constitutional amendment doctrines at the supranational level.

By (re)calling our attention to the tension between eternity clauses and democratic constitutionalism, this book in a sense takes us back to the starting point of scholarly engagement with unamendability. Within the flurry of research and doctrinal activity surrounding eternity clauses, there is a risk that we adopt an overly doctrinal, legal constitutionalist reading of unamendability and lose track of the real democratic challenge that it poses. I invite us to retrace our steps to this original puzzle in order to take a different path in trying to solve it: one that takes seriously the constitutional politics surrounding unamendability and seeks a richer understanding of its origins, operation, and intended purposes.

Structure of the book

The book is divided into three parts. Part I is focused on constitution-making processes and the choices available to constitutional designers within them, including the option to adopt an eternity clause. Given this emphasis on drafter intent, Part I primarily explores the design and operation of formal eternity clauses

[26] Vicky Jackson, *Constitutional Engagement in a Transnational Era* (Oxford University Press 2010).

and the interplay between these provisions and the broader constitutional architecture. It seeks to test and then correct several widespread assumptions about eternity clauses. The first of these is that they are easily discernible, in the sense that where the constitutional text itself lists its unamendable elements, the scope of unamendability is more or less straightforward. Instead, not only are these provisions typically drafted in abstract, general language, but they necessarily retain a certain degree of ambiguity in order to perform their intended function. Another assumption holds that eternity clauses are essentially liberal democratic—that they crystallize a core of liberal constitutionalism so deserving of protection as to render them immutable. This goes hand in hand with an exalted reading of constitutional foundings, idealized as rational exercises in coherent constitutional design, where instead we are just as likely to find elite self-interest and pragmatism.

Chapter 1 examines eternity clauses as mechanisms of constitutional precommitment and as tools for defending democracy in the face of anti-democratic forces, strongly justified in democratizing contexts. It looks at two broad categories of eternity clauses: provisions protecting state fundamentals such as the nature of the regime (republican or monarchical), the nature of the country's territorial architecture (federal or unitary), the integrity of the territory as a whole, or the state's secular or religious foundations; and provisions defending democratic pluralism, such as by declaring unamendable the multiparty democratic system and rights of democratic participation, a threshold of protection of fundamental rights, or the principle of the rule of law itself. Looking at the operation of these eternity clauses in practice, the chapter casts a critical eye on understandings of unamendability as either merely descriptive or as preservative of a core of liberal constitutionalism. It finds these provisions to deal in imponderables, enshrining values that are in need of judicial specification. This renders their precommitment and militant promise entirely dependent on other elements of the constitutional architecture, in particular constitutional review, and on constitutional courts' own understanding of their role as guardians of the fundamental law. The chapter shows that this almost always results in court self-empowerment and not infrequently in unduly limiting the scope of permitted constitutional change in the name of democracy.

Chapter 2 analyses eternity clauses as drafting mechanisms that facilitate and later safeguard post-conflict constitution-making. It looks at the constitutional bargaining dynamics specific to conflict-affected settings and teases out a hitherto largely ignored function of unamendability: of political insurance to constitution-makers, reflecting strategic compromises about the contours of the state and alternation in power. This understanding of eternity clauses thus sees them as preservative of a pragmatic political pact, rather than of the essentials of constitutionalism. The chapter highlights three distinctive roles played by post-conflict unamendability: signalling compliance with international norms, notably by placing human rights as a whole or a minimum threshold of their protection beyond amendment; ensuring electoral turnover, such as via executive term limits; and insulating political and military elites, such as by declaring unamendable amnesties and immunities for past acts. The chapter shows how contested and sometimes incoherent the unamendable values in post-conflict constitutions can be, reflecting as they do the messiness of constitution-making processes in these contexts. It also shows the risks associated with expecting too much from eternity clauses in fraught state-building settings, habitually characterized by institutional weakness and shifting political commitments. The recent experience with term limit removal in both Latin America and Africa illustrates this danger.

Part II of the book shifts our focus from constitution-making to adjudication. It investigates more closely how courts have operationalized unamendability in practice, looking at the rise of unconstitutional constitutional amendment doctrines in a large number of jurisdictions. Through deeply contextual analyses of constitutional identity review and basic structure doctrines, Part II corrects a further series of assumptions about unamendability. One such assumption holds that, on the whole, eternity clauses will be interpreted to protect liberal constitutionalism and augment democratic protections. As will be seen, the scope and reach of unamendability doctrines is hugely dependent on factors such as courts' self-understanding of their role as democratic players, their willingness to yield the final word to domestic legislatures or supranational bodies, and their propensity to defend their own competence and jurisprudential lines. Another expectation widely held in the literature and challenged by the case studies in Part II is that unamendability will be relied on as a measure of last resort by courts conscious of discharging their role as guardians of the constitution with self-restraint.

Chapter 3 scrutinizes the literature on constitutional identity, within which eternity clauses are viewed as repositories of the constitution's core values. This understanding of unamendability links together its ostensible expressive function with its protective one: as *the* site of constitutional expression, eternity clauses are to defend against attacks on the integrity and identity of the constitution as a whole. This chapter shows, however, that there are serious problems with importing the sociological concept of identity into constitutional theory's arsenal. I show that the concept relies on particular understandings of both liberal constitutionalism and pluralism, as well as on a presumed pacified and coherent (if sometimes disharmonious) national constitutional ethos. This obscures the deep and continuous contestation of the core constitutional commitments unamendability is meant to safeguard. Moreover, the rise of constitutional identity review to resist supranational integration in Europe highlights possible unintended consequences of unamendability. In some instances, it has come to anchor sovereigntist and even autocratic projects.

Chapter 4 shifts our focus to implicit unamendability, whether supplementing or absent any formal eternity clause in the constitutional text. Illustrated by basic structure or substantive/minimum core doctrines, this understanding of unamendability sees it as a necessary implication of liberal constitutions in general. The chapter proceeds to examine arguments about why courts should recognize an unamendable constitutional core even where the constitution itself is silent on this matter; where to locate the elements of this constitutional core; how to adjudicate any trespass against them; and how to restrain such unamendability doctrines to prevent judicial overreach. The chapter revisits the birth of the basic structure doctrine in India and traces its global influence, as well as calls to develop unconstitutional constitutional amendment doctrines in response to democratic backsliding. Chapter 4 finds that judicially created unamendability is prone to both over- and under-reach in concrete adjudication; that it is likely impossible to delineate a workable standard of review that would mitigate democratic concerns; and that its prospects as bulwark against democratic erosion are more limited than its proponents suggest.

Part III aims, first, to reflect on recent trends in contemporary constitution-making. It asks how unamendability has been affected by two developments in modern constitutionalism: globalization and the transnational embeddedness of constitution-making and constitutional adjudication on the one hand, and the rise of popular participation in processes of constitutional change on the other. Part III also asks, now that we have accrued decades of comparative experience with eternity clauses, what we can say about the full life of formal eternity clauses and basic structure doctrines, specifically about their repeal. It investigates claims that only constitutional revolution can or should do away with eternity clauses and the interplay with arguments about the feasibility of constitutional replacement doctrines and 'domesticating' constituent power within the existing constitutional framework.

Chapter 5 analyses eternity clauses in a transnational context. It acknowledges the internationalized nature of constitution-making processes and notes the growing diffusion of global values in democratic constitutionalism, including those protected through unamendability. The chapter explains this diffusion along two axes: the internationalization of constitutional authorship, with external actors increasingly influencing and even driving constitution-building worldwide, and the rise of international and regional organizations as constitutional norm entrepreneurs. The chapter also examines the adjudication of unamendability as transnationally embedded. This can take the form of national courts relying on international law or a transnational referent (such as comparative constitutional practice or international and regional standards) when developing unconstitutional constitutional amendment doctrines. More unexpectedly, it can also take the form of international courts reviewing the constitutionality of domestic constitutional amendments and thus developing a form of supranational unconstitutional constitutional amendment doctrine. Looking at all these developments through a critical lens, the chapter raises awareness about the impact of the transnational on the content and authorship of eternity clauses, but also cautions against assuming that transnational engagement in the adjudication of unamendability will necessarily rest on norm convergence and good faith cooperation. Mounting backlash against universalistic values and international law means invoking them as anchors to ground and orient unconstitutional constitutional amendment doctrines may exacerbate rather than answer democratic legitimation concerns about unamendability.

Chapter 6 turns our attention to a trend seemingly contradicting the global rise of eternity clauses: the turn to popular participation in constitution-making processes. The chapter asks whether a deeper democratic embeddedness of constitutions as pursued through such processes can help address democratic anxiety about eternity clauses. The chapter maps four processes of constitution-making that can be characterized as participatory, with a view to determining whether unamendability was incorporated into the final constitutional drafts, how it was debated (if at all), and whether and why alternative design choices may have been adopted instead (notably supermajority amendment rules). The chapter thus seeks to test empirically theoretical arguments about eternity clauses as repositories of constituent intent. It also asks, more broadly, whether eternity clauses are the high point of the battle between rigidity and openness in constitutional design today or merely a distraction. The chapter's findings are mixed, identifying a rather ambiguous relationship between popular participation in constitution-making and eternity clauses: while there is no direct link between such popular involvement and more flexible, open constitutions, neither is there clear evidence that constitutional rigidity will be opted for to 'seal in' design choices.

Chapter 7 investigates the possibility of repealing eternity clauses and renouncing doctrines of implicit unamendability. There is now enough comparative experience with constitutional unamendability over time to revisit initial understandings of how it might be done away with. The chapter proceeds from two case studies, Turkey and India, where backtracking from an eternity clause and basic structure doctrine, respectively, were debated and ultimately rejected. It also explores the possibility of placing judicial doctrines of unamendability on formal constitutional footing and the impact this has on constitutional adjudication. The chapter also examines the distinctions upon which unamendability repeal rests, such as between constitutional amendment and constitutional revision, between formal and informal amendments, and between amendment and revolution. The chapter shows that pushback against unamendability is very difficult through formal constitutional change and unlikely through judicial interpretation. In other words, constitutional unamendability increasingly appears to be a one-way street, once adopted itself entrenched at the heart of the constitutional project.

PART I

ETERNITY CLAUSES IN CONSTITUTION-MAKING

Between Militant Democracy and Political Bargaining

1

Eternity and Democratic Precommitment

Unamendability as an Instrument of Militant Democracy

This chapter engages with two of the most widespread readings of eternity clauses: as mechanisms of constitutional precommitment and as tools for defending democracy in the face of anti-democratic forces, strongly justified in contexts where experience has proven the fragility of democracy. Both formal eternity clauses and judicial doctrines of unamendability have been explained on these grounds. By looking at both familiar and less well-known case studies, this chapter aims to better understand the nexus between unamendability, precommitment theories, and militant democracy.

The chapter studies the values and principles insulated by eternity clauses and separates their intended democracy-protecting aims into two broad categories. First, there are provisions that seek to place outside the vagaries of politics certain fundamental building blocks of the state, be it the nature of the regime (republican or monarchical), the nature of the country's territorial architecture (federal or unitary), the integrity of the territory as a whole, or the state's secular or religious foundations. Second, unamendable provisions can aim to protect democracy from anti-pluralistic forces, such as by declaring unamendable the multiparty democratic system, rights of democratic participation, a threshold of protection of fundamental rights, or the principle of the rule of law itself. Occasionally, constitutions will even formally declare the rule of law principle as a whole as inviolable. Drawing on a vast array of case studies, the chapter thus engages seriously with the main promise of eternity clauses: to safeguard the democratic constitutional order for future generations.

However, the chapter retains a critical lens and questions whether and on what grounds eternity clauses are bound to fulfil their precommitment and militant democratic promise. They will unavoidably operate in tandem with, and depend on, other elements of the constitutional architecture such as constitutional review, the federal structure, the electoral system, and rules governing amendment procedures. This renders stand-alone evaluations of unamendability incomplete. More importantly, however, most if not all of the values and principles entrenched in eternity clauses are under-specified. They are neither objective nor procedural

Eternity Clauses in Democratic Constitutionalism. Silvia Suteu, Oxford University Press. © Silvia Suteu 2021.
DOI: 10.1093/oso/9780198858867.003.0002

but highly abstract, which means their enforcement will have to go beyond legal formalism and veer into normative interpretation.[1] Examples in this chapter as well as elsewhere in the book, notably in Part II, will illustrate just how contested such interpretation can be. The chapter therefore aims to critically assess the precommitment and militant democratic aspirations of eternity clauses and to evaluate their promise in the real world, in particular in the new democracies where they are most appealing.

1.1 Eternity clauses as precommitment and militant democracy instrument

The literature on constitutions as instruments of precommitment puts forth a very specific view of the aims and mechanisms of constitutionalism. It sees the people as unpredictable and to be distrusted, threatening insofar as they might show a 'weakness of the will' that will result in their downfall.[2] The purpose of constitutionalism therefore becomes to alleviate this danger, for 'without tying their own hands, the people will have no hands'.[3] Liberal constitutional design, aiming to reduce the power of the people, is tasked with creating a machinery of government that will reduce these popular 'passions' and a machinery of amendment that will be slow and cumbersome.[4] Supermajority rules, for example, are likely to reduce the risk of legislators being 'caught up in the collective frenzy' and unamendable clauses become 'a perfect protection against impulsive rashness'.[5]

Precommitment scholarship has had to defend its democratic credentials in the face of criticism that a will cannot bind itself, nor can one generation bind the next—the so-called 'paradox of precommitment'.[6] Jon Elster has acknowledged the differences between a collective and an individual self-binding but nevertheless has argued that it makes sense to speak of constitutional precommitment.[7] Stephen Holmes has argued that precommitment can be both 'democracy-enabling' and 'democracy-stabilizing' and that it empowers rather than blocks

[1] For similar arguments, see Denis Baranger, 'The Language of Eternity: Judicial Review of the Amending Power in France (or the Absence Thereof)', *Israeli Law Review* 44 (2011) 389; Po Jen Yap, 'The Conundrum of Unconstitutional Constitutional Amendments', *Global Constitutionalism* 4:1 (2015) 114.

[2] Jon Elster, 'Consequences of Constitutional Choice: Reflections on Tocqueville' in Jon Elster and Rune Slagstad, eds., *Constitutionalism and Democracy* (Cambridge University Press 1988) 81, 93.

[3] Stephen Holmes, 'Precommitment and the Paradox of Democracy' in Jon Elster and Rune Slagstad, eds., *Constitutionalism and Democracy* (Cambridge University Press 1988) 195, 231.

[4] Jon Elster, *Ulysses Unbound: Studies in Rationality, Precommitment, and Constraints* (Cambridge University Press 2000), 117–18.

[5] Jon Elster, 'Majority Rule and Individual Rights' in Obrad Savić, ed., *The Politics of Human Rights* (Verso 2002) 120, 146.

[6] Jeremy Waldron, *Law and Disagreement* (Oxford University Press 1999), 261–6.

[7] Elster (2000), 96.

current generations: 'Precommitment is justified because it does not enslave but rather enfranchises future generations.'[8] Furthermore, because of the flexibility afforded by imaginative judicial interpretation, Holmes argues, loyalty to the past is reconciled with responsiveness to the present.[9] Other liberal scholars have also defended the democracy-enabling function of constitutional limits, particularly of those protecting certain political rights.[10] As we will see, however, eternity clauses do not only protect democracy-enabling values and in some instances they may even shield exclusionary values.

Precommitment theories tend to remain at the general level when discussing constitutional entrenchment, concerned primarily with constitutions as mechanisms of self-limitation. Eternity clauses are a logical counter-majoritarian instrument in their repertoire, even while their purpose is supposedly 'mainly symbolic'.[11] In this key, eternity clauses insulating essential state characteristics or core democratic guarantees are a matter of rational constitutional design. They are 'preservative' of the constitutional order itself.[12] However, my project is precisely premised on the insight that 'entrenchment poses different problems from those generated by ordinary constitutionalism'.[13] As will be seen below, even seemingly benign unamendable state characteristics may mask an exclusionary constitutional project or have unintended consequences. Chapter 2 will show that eternity clauses' preservative function may well be in service of elite-driven pacts that have little to do with liberal constitutionalist prerequisites. Chapter 5 will also question the underlying assumption that the will that needs binding is unitary, i.e. that constitutions reflect Ulysses's self-binding will rather than a chorus only partially heard during processes of constitution-making.

Where precommitment and militant democracy theories meet is over their shared premise that democratic constitutions are not meant to be suicide pacts. The latter try to safeguard the democratic constitutional order by imposing limits which would otherwise be seen as illegitimate in a liberal democracy. In post-war Europe, such 'militant', 'disciplined', or 'protected' democracy brought about a new constitutional ethos, with constitutional review, weak parliaments, and European integration as checks on any totalitarian relapses.[14] Eternity clauses are thus a

[8] Holmes (1988), 216.

[9] Ibid., 224–5.

[10] Cass R. Sunstein, 'Constitutions and Democracies: An Epilogue' in Jon Elster and Rune Slagstad, eds., *Constitutionalism and Democracy* (Cambridge University Press 1988) 327, 327–8. See also Judith Squires, 'Liberal Constitutionalism, Identity and Difference' in Richard Bellamy and Dario Castiglione, eds., *Constitutionalism in Transformation: European and Theoretical Perspectives* (Blackwell 1996) 208, 209.

[11] Jon Elster, 'Constitutionalism in Eastern Europe: An Introduction', *University of Chicago Law Review* 58:2 (1991) 447, 471.

[12] Yaniv Roznai, *Unconstitutional Constitutional Amendments: The Limits of Amendment Powers* (Oxford University Press 2017), 26.

[13] Melissa Schwartzberg, *Democracy and Legal Change* (Cambridge University Press 2009), 9.

[14] See discussion in Jan-Werner Müller, *Contesting Democracy: Political Ideas in Twentieth-Century Europe* (Yale University Press 2011), 125–70.

natural fit. Constitutional rigidity generally, and eternity clauses in particular, may be explained as favouring a substantive outcome—the survival of the constitutional democratic order—over mere procedural safeguards. Unamendable provisions, read in this key, are thus the embodiment of a lack of trust in the capacity of the political process to self-regulate so as to avoid sliding into authoritarianism. The spectre of Weimar, where just such a slide happened under the cloak of the law, looms large in these arguments.[15] Such eternity clauses are thus a response to what has been termed 'abusive constitutionalism'—the use of constitutional amendment by would-be autocrats to subvert democracy.[16]

Certain types of eternity clauses are more amenable to militant democracy justifications than others, such as provisions that declare unamendable democracy, the multiparty system, or the rule of law. Germany's might be the most well-known example of such a clause, but there are others. Turkey's eternity clause, discussed in greater depth below, also references democracy and the rule of law among principles not to be touched by amendment. References to democratic pluralism are also not rare. For instance, Article 288 in the Portuguese Constitution includes in a long list of unamendable provisions the '[p]lurality of expression and political organization, including political parties and the right to a democratic opposition'. Angola's protection of 'The state based on the rule of law and pluralist democracy' in Article 236 of its constitution is but one example where such commitments have migrated from one constitutional system to that of a former colony. References to 'multipartyism' also appear in several African constitutions.[17]

Militant democracy justifications do not solely explain formalized eternity clauses, however. As Po Jen Yap has argued, similar reasoning is resorted to when it comes to doctrines of implicit substantive limits on amendment. The idea behind such doctrines is to prevent sliding into totalitarianism even in the absence of formal clauses empowering courts to step in.[18] The language used in several cases by constitutional courts declaring amendments unconstitutional despite not having an eternity clause in the constitution seems to support this view. The Colombian Constitutional Court, in a case involving an extension of presidential terms discussed in greater detail in Chapter 2, stated: 'The power of constitutional reform cannot be used in order to substitute the Social and Democratic State and the Republican form of government (Article 1) with a totalitarian state, a

[15] See Karl Loewenstein, 'Militant Democracy and Fundamental Rights I', *American Political Science Review*, 31:3 (1937) 424; Gregory H. Fox and Georg Nolte, 'Intolerant Democracies', *Harvard Journal of International Law* 36:1 (1995) 1; Svetlana Tyulkina, *Militant Democracy: Undemocratic Political Parties and Beyond* (Routledge 2015), 11–25; Mark Chou, *Democracy Against Itself: Sustaining an Unsustainable Idea* (Edinburgh University Press 2014), 50–76.

[16] David Landau, 'Abusive Constitutionalism', *UC Davis Law Review* 47 (2013a) 189.

[17] See Article 165 of the Constitution of Burkina Faso, Article 118 of the Malian Constitution, and Article 175 of the Constitution of Niger.

[18] Yap (2015), 121.

dictatorship or a monarchy.'[19] As will be seen in Chapter 4, India's Supreme Court was similarly concerned with the erosion of the rule of law when it formulated its basic structure doctrine in the *Kesavananda* case.

The implication of such arguments is that a militant democracy undercurrent exists in all democratic constitutions, even in the absence of an explicit textual crutch. Put differently, the commitment to democracy and the rule of law by their very nature implies an embrace of legal means to safeguard them from subversion. In this reading, militant democracy becomes a tautology as *all* democracy is militant. Of course, the unstated element of such arguments is that the institution meant to give effect to this militancy is a court with the (sometimes self-ascribed) power to judicially review constitutional amendments. If constitutions are not meant to be suicide pacts, the argument would go, neither is the amendment process meant to allow for self-detonation. Eternity clauses are thus meant to operate as the 'lock on the door',[20] or else the 'speed-bump'[21] a democracy may need in order to prevent or forestall its implosion.

1.2 Protecting fundamental characteristics of the state

The aim of eternity clauses that insulate state fundamentals is to ensure the state's survival in a recognizable form. In the same way that militant democracy theory generally aims to address the risk of a democracy voting itself out of existence, so too do certain eternity clauses form part of the state's defence apparatus. This function of constitutions—preventing state disintegration or 'forestall[ing] the destructive capacity of potential constitutional transformations'[22]—is laid bare in conflict-affected situations, discussed in detail in the following chapter. There, the stakes of constitution-making are openly on the table and constitutional subversion can be the death knell of an already weak state. But while it may have become obscured in places with enduring state traditions, protecting the state has always been at the heart of constitutionalism. In its more positive formulation, this is constitution-making as state-building.[23]

[19] Sentencia 551/03, 9 July 2003, para. 33. Po Jen Yap also gives the example of the Bangladesh Supreme Court judgments invalidating the Fifth and Seventh Amendments to the constitution, which had imposed martial law on the country. See Yap (2015), 122 and the discussion inChapter 4 in this book.

[20] Roznai (2017), 132–3.

[21] David Landau, Rosalind Dixon, and Yaniv Roznai, 'From an Unconstitutional Constitutional Amendment to an Unconstitutional Constitution? Lessons from Honduras', *Global Constitutionalism* 8:1 (2019) 40, 47.

[22] Beau Breslin, *From Words to Worlds: Exploring Constitutional Functionality* (Johns Hopkins University Press 2008), 45.

[23] Martin Loughlin, *The Idea of Public Law* (Oxford University Press 2003), 50; Joanne Wallis, *Constitution Making during State Building* (Cambridge University Press 2014).

Unamendable republicanism, unamendable monarchism

Republicanism

The unamendable commitment to republicanism is among the most widespread eternity clauses, with one study counting more than one hundred constitutions having such a clause.[24] Among the most well known are France'sArticle 89 which states: 'The republican form of government shall not be the object of any amendment', and Italy's Article 139: 'The form of Republic shall not be a matter for constitutional amendment.' The origin of such clauses seems to be the fear of a return of the monarchy in the immediate aftermath of the transition to republicanism.[25] Thus, Article 8(3) of France's 1875 Constitution, Article 90(4) of Brazil's 1891 Constitution, and Article 82(2) in Portugal's 1911 Constitution are the earliest examples of such unamendable commitments to republicanism. Even before these, nineteenth-century Latin American constitutions declared their states 'forever' republican (see Article 164 of Colombia's 1830 Constitution, Article 139 of the Dominican Republic's 1865 Constitution, Article 110 of Ecuador's 1843 Constitution, and Article 228 of Venezuela's 1830 Constitution) in what was a wider move in the region towards embracing republican government and empowering legislatures.[26]

For all its influence, both as a colonial power and as a widely imitated constitutional model, France's experience with 'eternal' republicanism does not tell us very much about how such a clause might work in practice. This is because the Conseil Constitutionnel has consistently refused to engage in the review of constitutional amendments.[27] It did so with regard to De Gaulle's 1962 revision of the constitution;[28] in 1992 with regard to the Maastricht Treaty;[29] and again in 2003 in a case involving decentralization.[30] Thus, although this is the sole substantive limitation placed on constitutional reform in the French constitution, the Conseil has refused to make it effective via its refusal to engage in judicial scrutiny of amendments.[31] While reiterating the sacrosanct nature of republicanism, the Conseil decisions

[24] Roznai (2017), 23.

[25] Baranger (2011), 403.

[26] See Roberto Gargarella, 'Towards a Typology of Latin American Constitutionalism, 1810–60', *Latin American Research Review* 39:2 (2004) 141–53.

[27] See discussion in Baranger (2011), 391–8.

[28] Decision No. 62-20 DC, 6 November 1962.

[29] Decision No. 92-308 DC, 9 April 1992 and Decision no. 92-312 DC of 2 September 1992. The Conseil did recognize temporal limits on constitutional amendment, as well as the substantive limit in Article 89, but found that 'the constituent authority is sovereign' otherwise and 'has the power to repeal, amend or amplify constitutional provisions in such manner as it sees fit'. Decision no. 92-312 DC, para. 19.

[30] Decision No. 2003-469 DC, 26 March 2003.

[31] Baranger (2008), 404.

clearly indicate its refusal to substantively review amendments.[32] The absence in the French context of any real threat of a return to monarchy may have encouraged perceptions of this clause as no longer necessary.[33]

Constitutional unamendability should not be confused with universal acceptance, however. The Italian example is instructive, for while the republican choice was endorsed in a 1946 popular referendum, the vote was not only close (a majority of 54.3 per cent of voters opting for republicanism) but also revealed a deep regional division (the south voting in favour of monarchy).[34] Nor should it be assumed that such contestation is entirely quieted by constitutional unamendability. While virtually eradicated in France, monarchism has not fully disappeared from other republics, including some, such as Romania, which also list republicanism among unamendable provisions in their constitutions (Article 152(1)).[35] Republicanism was adopted via executive decree while the 1989 Romanian Revolution was still unfolding and was retained in the 1991 Constitution despite attempts by democratic forces to put the issue to a public referendum.[36] The issue reappeared periodically, such as during a 2013 attempt at participatory constitutional renewal.[37] The then prime minister had also declared, albeit in a likely populist move, that he was prepared to organize a referendum on this issue if public opinion demanded it and that, if successful, it would bring about a new constitution.[38] A return to monarchy in Romania remains unlikely, especially after the 2017 death of its last reigning king, but such open support had made the topic acceptable in public discourse after years of being anathema.

Monarchism

The counterparts to such provisions are clauses which declare the monarchy to be unamendable. Examples include Bahrain's Article 120(c), Cambodia's Article 153,

[32] Eoin Daly, 'Translating Popular Sovereignty as Unfettered Constitutional Amendability', *European Constitutional Law Review* 15 (2019) 619, 624.

[33] Baranger (2008), 404.

[34] Pietro Faraguna, 'Unamendability and Constitutional Identity in the Italian Constitutional Experience', *European Journal of Law Reform* 21 (2019) 329.

[35] Similar debates have also happened in Bulgaria, which does not entrench its republican form of government via an eternity clause, however. See Rossen Vassilev, 'Will Bulgaria Become [a] Monarchy Again?', *Southeast European Politics* 4:2-3 (2003) 157.

[36] Decret Lege nr. 2, 27 December 1989. See also Silvia Suteu, 'The Multinational State That Wasn't: The Constitutional Definition of Romania as a National State', *Vienna Journal on International Constitutional Law* 11:3 (2017a) 413, 419.

[37] An experiment with popular participation in constitution-making in 2013, the Constitutional Forum, produced a report which listed the choice between monarchy and republic as a form of government among the possible topics of constitutional revision. *Raportul Forumului Constituțional 2013*, Asociația Pro Democrația, Bucharest, 2013, 61, http://www.apd.ro/wp-content/uploads/2015/03/Raport-Forumul-Constitutional-2015.pdf.

[38] 'Ponta, despre monarhie: Viitorul şef al statului are obligaţia de a organiza un referendum privind forma de guvernământ', *Mediafax*, 20 October 2014, http://www.gandul.info/politica/ponta-despre-monarhie-viitorul-sef-al-statului-are-obligatia-de-a-organiza-un-referendum-privind-forma-de-guvernamant-13422241.

Morocco's Article 175, or Thailand's Section 255. Some scholars have viewed these as examples of eternity clauses which seek to preserve existing power structures rather than limit power.[39] They see the greater incidence of such provisions in constitutions in certain parts of the world as further evidence of a deficient Arab constitutionalism and thereby distinguish them from provisions on unamendable republicanism.[40] I agree that such provisions are to be distinguished from those declaring republicanism unamendable, insofar as the monarchical principle itself is, at its core, undemocratic. In many instances, drafters retained a commitment to unamendable monarchy to signal continuity rather than radical rupture with the past, and to retain the monarch's rather than the people's constitution-making power.[41]

However, the interplay between eternity clauses entrenching monarchies and democratic constitutionalism is not always straightforward. In some instances, the monarchy is declared unamendable alongside democracy. This is true for both the current, 2017, Thai Constitution and for its former, 2007, fundamental law. In fact, the Thai Constitutional Court in the past ruled unconstitutional several constitutional amendments seeking to modify the 2007 constitution. It struck down amendments seeking to create a Constitutional Drafting Assembly and instituting the direct election of senators, and found that such changes would open up the constitution to total revision, on the one hand, and undermine the principles of democracy and checks and balances, on the other.[42] In so doing, the court ventured into providing its own, anti-majoritarian conception of democracy, in a move that has been explained as masking the persisting disagreements regarding the nature of Thailand's constitutional democratic commitments.[43] At the very least, this example shows that eternity clauses do sometimes protect potentially contradictory constitutional commitments, including with regard to the form of government.

A separate concern is how courts would assess transgressions of republicanism which do not amount to a return to monarchy. The task of judges in such a case would be decidedly more complicated. Examples might include curtailing rights of political participation or altering the separation of powers to such an extent as to de facto extinguish popular sovereignty. Laurence Tribe discusses another—the open-ended delegation of governmental authority—as a potential violation of Article IV, section 4 of the US Constitution ('the United States shall guarantee to every State ... a Republican Form of Government').[44] Evaluating this potential violation

39 Roznai (2017), 28.

40 Roznai describes provisions on the unamendability of monarchical systems of government as 'a manifestation of the more general character of the Arab world's constitutionalism in which written constitutions enhance rather than limit governmental power'. Ibid., fn 104.

41 Nimer Sultany, *Law and Revolution: Legitimacy and Constitutionalism After the Arab Spring* (Oxford University Press 2017), 263–4.

42 Decision 17-22/2555 of 13 July 2012 and Decision 15-18/2556 of 20 November 2013.

43 Ngoc Son Bui, 'Politics of Unconstitutional Constitutional Amendments: The Case of Thailand' in Henning Glaser, ed.., *Identity and Change – The Basic Structure in Asian Constitutional Orders* (Nomos forthcoming).

44 Laurence Tribe, *The Invisible Constitution* (Oxford University Press 2008), 90.

would be trickier. Tribe's conclusion is that the only basis on which such an assessment could be made would be an unwritten principle of democratic accountability, not any precise vision of popular sovereignty or representative government held by the constitution's drafters or ratifiers.[45] He admits that such a principle is 'nowhere written into the text [of the US constitution] or implied by it' but argues that the consent of the governed is 'nonetheless central to its being'.[46] Such reliance on interpretations of constitutional ethos and history may be open to abuse or simply yield very different results elsewhere, not all of them congruent with accepted notions of republicanism and its boundaries.

Unamendable republicanism is thus a seemingly abstract commitment, rooted in fears of monarchical return. However, the practical instantiation of republican commitments may yet be called into question. Courts asked to evaluate such amendments may well find themselves imposing their own ideological commitments onto the meaning of the republican principle.

Unamendable federalism and unitary statehood

Federalism

Federalism as a principle of organization of the state is formally placed beyond the reach of constitutional amendment in a significant number of basic laws. Some of the world's most influential constitutional models in fact protect federalism via unamendable or deeply entrenched provisions. One example is Germany, where Article 20(1) of the Basic Law ('The Federal Republic of Germany is a democratic and social federal state') is among those protected by Article 79(3). Similarly, Article 60(4)(I) in the Brazilian Constitution bans the consideration of any amendment aimed at abolishing 'the federalist form of the National Government'. The earliest concern with the preservation of the equality of territorial units is found in Article V of the US Constitution, which reads in part: 'no State, without its Consent, shall be deprived of its equal Suffrage in the Senate'. Lest one believe this an obsolete method of securing federalism, consider Iraq's 2005 Constitution, which under Article 126(4) declares that amendments taking away regional powers will require 'the approval of the legislative authority of the concerned region and the approval of the majority of its citizens in a general referendum'. I continue here with two examples of federalism unamendability: Germany and Brazil. They highlight, respectively, the potential for an entrenched federal principle to resolve constitutional conflict and bring order to territorial organization, as well as its propensity to throw a spanner in policy reform.

[45] Ibid.
[46] Ibid.

The first case where Germany's *Ewigkeitsklausel* was used was the *Southwest State Case* (1951).[47] This was not only the first case involving the federal aspect of Article 79(3), but also Germany's *Marbury* v. *Madison*: the occasion for the ConstitutionalCourt to claim for itself the power to review the constitutionality of amendments.[48] The case involved territorial reorganization by federal law and was brought by the state of Baden, which challenged redistricting on the basis that it affected the principles of democracy, by diluting votes of constituents, and of federalism, by taking away from the legislative powers of the *Land*. In its judgment, the Constitutional Court spoke of the 'inner unity' of the Basic Law and of its reflecting 'overarching principles and fundamental decisions to which individual provisions are subordinate'.[49] It viewed Article 79(3) as a confirmation of this assumption. The court then announced the 'unconstitutional constitutional amendment' doctrine, whereby even a part of the constitution may be found to be unconstitutional.[50] In other words, a legislative provision is not free of constitutional scrutiny by mere virtue of its incorporation in the constitutional text. The Second Senate of the *Bundesverfassungsgericht* expressed approval of the notion that

> There are constitutional principles that are so fundamental and so much an expression of a law that has precedence even over the Constitution that they also bind the framers of the Constitution and other constitutional provisions that do not rank so high may be null and void because they contravene these principles ... it follows that any constitutional provision must be interpreted in such a way that it is compatible with those elementary principles and with the basic decisions of the framers of the Constitution.[51]

The court found democracy and federalism to be such 'elementary principles' and 'basic decisions of the framers' and as such to prevent the federal government from disenfranchising, via postponed elections, the citizens of some states, or from taking away the legislative power of the states currently in existence. Acknowledging that tensions may exist between democracy and federalism, the court emphasized that in the case of the reorganization of federal territory, 'the people's right to self-determination in a state must be restricted in the interest of the more comprehensive unit'.[52] In the case at hand, therefore, both the bodies

[47] 1 BverfGE 14 (1951). For an assessment of the decision's importance at the time, see Gerhard Leibholz, 'The Federal Constitutional Court in Germany and the "Southwest Case"', *American Political Science Review* 46:3 (1952) 723.

[48] Donald P. Kommers and Russell A. Miller, *The Constitutional Jurisprudence of the Federal Republic of Germany* (Duke University Press 2012), 85. See also Maartje de Visser, *Constitutional Review in Europe: A Comparative Analysis* (Hart 2014), 240.

[49] Cited in Kommers and Miller (2012), 82.

[50] For more on this doctrine, see Gottfried Dietze, 'Unconstitutional Constitutional Norms: Constitutional Development in Postwar Germany', *Virginia Law Review* 42:1 (1956) 1.

[51] Cited in Kommers and Miller (2012), 82.

[52] Cited in ibid., 85.

politic of the federation and of the area to be reorganized were to decide. The new state of Baden-Württenberg came into being the following year after a popular referendum.[53]

The court's decision was 'readily accepted by all parties concerned' and 'had a pacifying influence on the political life of all States involved in the controversy, and ... it cleared the political atmosphere considerably'.[54] This resolution of the conflict endured and was confirmed by a 1970 referendum wherein the state's inhabitants voted to maintain Baden-Württenberg's borders.[55] The federal principle's unamendability in the Basic Law today refers to 'the existence of a plurality of *Länder*, a minimum of substantial autonomy including especially their constitutional autonomy, and substantial participation rights in the legislative process'.[56]

Brazil's federalism is also deeply rooted in a turbulent history, with the degrees of centralization and decentralization varying across different periods and regimes.[57] Unlike elsewhere, however, 'Brazilian federalism was never a response to deep social fissures along ethnic, linguistic and religious lines, and the country's territorial integrity has never been seriously challenged by foreigners or threats of secession'.[58] It has instead been marked by deep regional inequality which has justified central government intervention including, as we shall see, via taxation policies.[59] When it comes to the country's 1988 constitution, this was meant to mark the return to democracy and its eternity clause (or *cláusula pétrea*) unequivocally committed the new regime to democratic principles and to the respect of the federal form of state. Like its German counterpart, the Brazilian Supreme Court has also arrogated for itself the power to review the constitutionality of amendments in the absence of an explicit textual basis for this.[60] As Hübner Mendes points out, in practice, this review of amendment constitutionality 'has become an arena for the discussion of neoliberalism',[61] including as part of tugs of war between the federal government and territorial units.

A relevant example is the involvement of the court in the process of fiscal reform initiated in 1993 by way of a constitutional amendment. The governors of five states

[53] Ibid., 86.
[54] Leibholz (1952), 731.
[55] Kommers and Miller (2012), 86.
[56] Werner Heun, *The Constitution of Germany: A Contextual Analysis* (Hart 2011), 47. See also ibid., 49–84 on the origins and workings of Germany's federal system more generally.
[57] See Celina Souza, 'Brazil: From "Isolated" Federalism to Hybridity' in John Loughlin, John Kincaid, and Wilfried Swenden, eds., *Routledge Handbook of Regionalism & Federalism* (Routledge 2013) 457.
[58] Souza (2013), 459.
[59] Ibid.
[60] See discussion in Conrado Hübner Mendes, 'Judicial Review of Constitutional Amendments in the Brazilian Supreme Court', *Florida Journal of International Law* 17:3 (2005) 449, 456; Juliano Zaiden Benvindo, 'Brazil in the Context of the Debate over Unamendability in Latin America' in Richard Albert and Bertil Emrah Oder, eds., *An Unamendable Constitution? Unamendability in Constitutional Democracies* (Springer 2018) 345, 358.
[61] Hübner Mendes (2005), 455.

filed an injunction request against federal government plans for taxation reform on the grounds that they violated the constitution, including the principle of federalism incorporated in the eternity clause. The Supreme Federal Court quickly issued an injunction suspending the relevant paragraph of the amendment and the collection of tax from states and municipalities. It agreed with the states that 'by authorizing violation of the constitutional principle of "reciprocal taxation immunity" among federal, state, and municipal government, the amendment had undermined an essential element of Brazilian federalism, which the constitution establishes as an unamendable principle'.[62] This was the first time the court ruled on the constitutionality of an amendment to the constitution and it did so by suspending the imposition of a critical tax.[63] The same reforms were implemented the following year, but only after a significant budgetary depletion.[64]

The unitary state

The unitary nature of the state is also declared unamendable in several constitutions. Examples include Angola's Article 236(d), Guinea-Bissau's Article 102(a), Kazakhstan's Article 91(2), and Romania's Article 152(1). The entrenchment of both federalism and the unitary state aim to preserve the territorial status quo, but whereas the former is aimed at preserving equality among states and preventing centralization, the latter is aimed at thwarting any centrifugal forces. Take Romania's example. In a 2014 decision on a proposal for constitutional revision that also contained hard-fought agreement on administrative territorial reorganization, the Romanian Constitutional Court struck down the revision package as a whole, in part for breaching the eternity clause.[65] The court expressed its fear that any such administrative reorganization of territory would lead to territorial autonomy for 'certain population groups', a long-standing bogeyman in Romanian constitutional and political discourse.[66] There was no deeper explanation for how the proposed changes actually breached the unitary character of the state, nor indeed whether the court was implying that any such administrative reorganization would be a priori unconstitutional.

The Romanian case is reminiscent of the constitutional saga surrounding Catalan independence, even while the Spanish Constitution does not contain an eternity clause as such. Instead, the amendment procedure in Spain has been characterized as 'quasi-unamendable' due to its rigidity, even while it formally stops short of outright unamendability.[67] The Spanish Constitution itself contains seemingly contradictory

[62] Diana Kapiszewski, *High Courts and Economic Governance in Argentina and Brazil* (Cambridge University Press 2012), 178.

[63] Ibid.

[64] Ibid., 179.

[65] Decizia nr. 80/2014, 16 February 2014.

[66] Ibid., para. 34. For a lengthier discussion, see Suteu (2017a).

[67] Catarina Santos Botelho, 'Constitutional Narcissism on the Couch of Psychoanalysis: Constitutional Unamendability in Portugal and Spain', *European Journal of Law Reform* 21:3 (2019) 346.

commitments to 'the indissoluble unity of the Spanish Nation, the common and indivisible homeland of all Spaniards' and 'the right to self-government of the nationalities and regions of which it is composed and the solidarity among them all' (Article 2). Thus, it has been noted with regard to the Spanish Constitution that 'while the unity of the state allows national plurality, the unity of the nation renders it impossible'.[68] The Spanish Constitutional Tribunal has repeatedly reinforced this unitary conception of nation, both when it struck down several elements of Catalonia's Statute of Autonomy and when it rendered its decision on the constitutionality of Catalonia's declaration of independence.[69] It did so even while the constitutional text was not as prescriptive in terms of territorial organization and its limits and allowed for more flexible approaches to national pluralism.[70]

These constitutional experiences yield important lessons about the role that precommitment to a particular territorial structure may play, including in processes of constitutional revision. Germany's federalism has been constitutive of the Basic Law in a very real sense: it was *Länder* parliaments which elected members of the Parliamentary Council which drafted it and the *Länder* again which enacted the draft.[71] Constitutionalizing the principle of federalism may thus be seen as recognition for this constitutive role. In Brazil, federalism has been seen as an important counterbalance to a strong executive; at the same time, however, as illustrated above, 'federalism helps explain Brazil's delay in implementing economic reforms'.[72] The capacity of state-based actors to constrain presidential reform initiatives may have kept the executive in check, but it also happened in the context of a constitution which remained vague as to the division of key responsibilities between the centre and units.[73] The intervention of the Brazilian Supreme Federal Court, therefore, left a serious, quantifiable dent in the country's budget at a time when it could ill afford to postpone reform. Unamendable unitary statehood has also on occasion formed the basis for court intervention in processes of constitutional reform. As the Romanian and Spanish examples show, an unamendable unitary state can be interpreted as entrenching a centralized vision of the state that leaves little room for negotiating substate pluralism, or indeed even benign administrative reorganization.

[68] Barbara Guastaferro and Lucía Payero, 'Devolution and Secession in Comparative Perspective: The Case of Spain and Italy' in Robert Schütze and Stephen Tierney, eds., *The United Kingdom and the Federal Idea* (Hart 2018) 123, 126.

[69] Sentencia 31/2010, 28 June 2010 and Sentencia 42/2014, 25 March 2014.

[70] Elisenda Casañas Adam, 'The Constitutional Court of Spain: From System Balancer to Polarizing Centralist' in Nicholas Aroney and John Kinkaid, eds., *Courts in Federal Countries: Federalists or Unitarists?* (University of Toronto Press 2017) 367.

[71] Heun (2011), 51.

[72] David J. Samuels and Scott Mainwaring, 'Strong Federalism, Constraints on Central Government, and Economic Reform in Brazil' in Edward L. Gibson, ed., *Federalism and Democracy in Latin America* (Johns Hopkins University Press 2004) 85, 86.

[73] Ibid., 108.

Unamendable territorial integrity

Another type of eternity clause declares as unamendable territorial 'unity', 'integrity', or 'indivisibility'. Such provisions are found in several postcolonial and postcommunist countries (see, for instance, Article 158 of Azerbaijan's Constitution, Article 91(2) of the Constitution of Kazakhstan, Article 142 of Moldova's and Article 152(1) of Romania's Constitutions, Article 100 of Tajikistan's and Article 157 of Ukraine's), although post-authoritarian constitutions contain them as well—for instance, Article 288 of Portugal's Constitution and Article 248 of El Salvador's. While the justification for such provisions is complex,[74] they can be brought under the state protection umbrella: territory being integral to the life of the nation, its protection becomes coextensive with the state's survival. Crucially, these provisions are not to be conflated with those on the unitary (as opposed to federal) nature of the state: whereas the latter refer to administrative territorial organization, territorial integrity refers to a more fundamental ambition of ensuring the state's survival.[75]

Territorial unamendability has a mixed track record as protection in the face of external and internal forces, however. The principle of territorial integrity has been used to stifle Kurdish separatism in Turkey, which I discuss in the framework of Turkish party bans below. However, as Roznai and I have shown with respect to Ukraine's unamendable commitment to territorial integrity, territorial unamendability was meaningless in the face of Crimea's breaking away. One can hardly imagine a blunter demonstration of the impotence of territorial integrity as a constitutional principle, and perhaps of law more generally, than in this case. Because territory is 'subject to the internal threat of secessionist movements and the external threat of forceful annexation',[76] declaring its integrity unassailable has at most an aspirational function.[77] This is perhaps the instance where Jon Elster's view of eternity clauses as purely symbolic carries most sway.[78] This belief in the enforceability of its constitutionalization has yet to be tested. It may well be that, accompanied by provisions granting a court powers of constitutional review over it, the principle 'moves beyond mere proclamation and into constitutional doctrine'.[79] Once there, however, the task does not become simpler. As Denis Baranger

[74] See discussion in Yaniv Roznai and Silvia Suteu, 'The Eternal Territory? The Crimean Crisis and Ukraine's Territorial Integrity as an Unamendable Constitutional Principle', *German Law Journal* 16:3 (2015) 542.

[75] The Venice Commission has also endorsed this view, declaring: 'The state's indivisibility is not to be confused with its unitary character, and therefore consorts with regionalism and federalism.' European Commission for Democracy Through Law (Venice Commission), 'Self-Determination and Secession in Constitutional Law', CDL-INF (2000) 2, 12 January 2000. See also Roznai and Suteu (2015), 546, fn. 16.

[76] Roznai and Suteu (2015), 580.

[77] Ibid., 570.

[78] Elster (1991), 471.

[79] Roznai and Suteu (2015), 557.

has stated, 'there is nothing objective or merely procedural about such a standard as the "integrity of the territory"' and ruling on it would obviously involve going beyond legal forms.[80]

Unamendable religion or secularism

Religion

Unamendable references to religion come in two guises. The first is the entrenchment of an official religion, such as of Islam in the Constitutions of Algeria (Article 178), Bahrain (Article 120), Iran (Article 177), Morocco (Article 100), and Tunisia (Article 1). The second is the unamendable protection of secularism or the separation of church and state, such as in the Constitutions of Angola (Article 236), Congo (Article 220), Portugal (Article 288), or Turkey (Article 4). Tempted though we might be to see here a correlation to majority Islamic countries, declarations of religious unamendability go back to the nineteenth century, when they were adopted by majority Catholic countries. Examples include Mexico's 1824 or Ecuador's 1854 Constitutions.[81]

Such clauses are often viewed as inherent repositories of constitutional identity, whether by granting and protecting a religion's official status or by its banishment from public life in the form of a commitment to secularism. Richard Albert, for example, lists both official religion and secularism among the elements of preservative eternity clauses, expressing the importance of either religion or non-religion in that constitutional regime.[82] I propose to look at two societies where secularism is one of the core elements of constitutional eternity clauses: India and Turkey. They illustrate how such commitments play not just an expressive role, but a militant one—at times deployed against ideological opponents. This is not to ignore the possibility of unamenable official religion clauses also shifting from declaratory to exclusionary.[83]

Secularism

As will be seen in Chapter 4, the elements of India's basic structure doctrine have not been listed exhaustively and have varied from case to case. The Indian Supreme Court has not wavered, however, in its identification of secularism as one of the key elements of the doctrine. In the case of *Bommai* v. *Union of India*, it thus spoke of 'the objective of secularism which was part of the basic structure of

[80] Baranger (2008), 404.

[81] See Yaniv Roznai, 'Unconstitutional Constitutional Amendments—The Migration and Success of a Constitutional Idea', *American Journal of Comparative Law* 61 (2013) 657, 666.

[82] Richard Albert, 'The Unamendable Core of the United States Constitution' in András Koltay, ed., *Comparative Perspectives on the Fundamental Freedom of Expression* (Wolters Kluwer 2015a) 13.

[83] For a discussion of Tunisia's unamendable constitutional protection of Islam, see Silvia Suteu, 'Eternity Clauses in Post-Conflict and Post-Authoritarian Constitution-Making: Promise and Limits' *Global Constitutionalism* 6:1 (2017b) 63, 79–82.

the Constitution and also the soul of the Constitution'.[84] The Court did so while upholding the president's authority to dismiss the elected Bharatiya Janata Party (BJP)-led governments of three states in the aftermath of the destruction of the Babri Masjid mosque.[85] The judgment is said to have been as much about constitutional principle as about a public emergency.[86] The federal executive's argument had been that failure of the three state governors to ensure constitutional rule and order amounted to an inability to fulfil their mandate and as such rendered them vulnerable to replacement by presidential rule.[87]

The judges in *Bommai* did not seek to avoid ruling in what many saw as a clearly political question. They relied instead on the expressed sympathies and support of the three state governments for the perpetrators of the violence to find a clear violation of the constitution's secular foundations.[88] The judges directly linked secularism to state survival:

> The fact that a party may be entitled to go to people seeking a mandate for a drastic amendment of the Constitution or its replacement by another Constitution is wholly irrelevant in the context. We do not know how the Constitution can be amended so as to remove secularism from the basic structure of the Constitution. Nor do we know how the present Constitution can be replaced by another; it is enough for us to know that the Constitution does not provide for such a course—that it does not provide for its own demise.[89]

This link did not remain at the level of an abstract survival of the state, however, but was integral to the state's socio-economic transformation:

> The Constitution has chosen secularism as its vehicle to establish an egalitarian social order ... Secularism, therefore, is part of the fundamental law and basic structure of the Indian political system to secure to all its people socioeconomic needs essential for man's excellence and of his moral wellbeing, fulfilment of material and [sic] prosperity and political justice.[90]

As Jacobsohn has rightly noted, this view of secularism is 'denoted only partially by its formal constitutional codification' and is better understood in its historical context of the development of the Indian state.[91] Whatever else goes into the basic

[84] *S. R. Bommai* v. *Union of India*, AIR 1975 1994 SC 1918, para. 144.
[85] For a more detailed discussion of the circumstances of this case than is possible here, see Gary J. Jacobsohn, *The Wheel of Law: India's Secularism in Comparative Constitutional Context* (Princeton University Press 2003), 125–38.
[86] Ibid., 131.
[87] Ibid., 130.
[88] Ibid.
[89] *Bommai* v. *Union of India*, para. 310.
[90] Ibid., para. 186.
[91] Gary J. Jacobsohn, *Constitutional Identity* (Harvard University Press 2010), 78.

structure doctrine, therefore, secularism seems to be a principle enjoying universal acceptance. Though not without its critics, the judgment in *Bommai* is a good illustration of how this judicial doctrine could be relied upon to defend secularism in the face of ethnic violence.[92]

Turkey's case is different insofar as its constitutional commitment to secularism has been formally enshrined in the basic law. Thus, it is found not only in the eternity clause in Article 4, but also in the preamble, in Article 2 which lists it as a characteristic of the republic, in Article 13 as a ground for rights limitations, in Article 14 on the abuse of rights, and in numerous other places throughout the Turkish Constitution. Beyond this textual difference, however, Turkey shares with India an understanding of secularism as intrinsically linked to the state's progress to a modernized society. Dicle Koğacıoğlu reconstructed the Turkish Constitutional Court's jurisprudence in this area to uncover a narrative which inextricably binds together notions of unity, democracy, and progress, all seeped into 'a hegemonic republican vision of nationalism and secularism'.[93]

While this jurisprudence is vast,[94] I will focus on only one case: the so-called *Headscarf* decision of 2008.[95] This decision annulled a legislative amendment meant to abolish the ban on headscarves in universities on grounds of equality and the right to education. The court did this on the basis of the secular nature of the Turkish state, which it found to be an essential condition for democracy and 'a guarantor of freedom of religion and of equality before the law'.[96] The judges considered the eternity clause in Article 4 together with Article 175 regulating the amendment procedure and Article 148 on the functions and powers of MPs. In so doing, the justices ascribed themselves the power of substantive review of amendments despite the constitution only explicitly granting them procedural review competence.[97] Exercising this newfound material competence, the court further found a hierarchy of norms within the constitution, topped by the first three articles as entrenched by Article 4.[98] Any amendments infringing upon these articles, therefore, were considered *ultra vires*.

[92] Critics of the judgment saw it as 'represent[ing] the triumph of leftist ideology and rank hypocrisy' given the court's supposed about-turn with respect to state autonomy. See ibid., 131.

[93] Dicle Koğacıoğlu, 'Progress, Unity, and Democracy: Dissolving Political Parties in Turkey', *Law & Society Review* 38:3 (2004) 433, 459 and, generally, 433–62.

[94] See Kemal Gözler, *Judicial Review of Constitutional Amendments: A Comparative Study* (Ekin Press 2008).

[95] Decision of 5 June 2008, E. 2008/16; K. 2008/116, Resmi Gazete, 22 October 2008, No. 27032, 109-52. See a fuller discussion of the case in Yaniv Roznai and Serkan Yolcu, 'An Unconstitutional Constitutional Amendment—The Turkish Perspective: A Comment on the Turkish Constitutional Court's Headscarf Decision', *International Journal of Constitutional Law* 10:1 (2012) 175.

[96] Roznai and Yolcu (2012), 179.

[97] Ibid., 185.

[98] Ibid., 186.

The court went on to define secularism thus:

> The principle of secularism laid down in Article 2 of the Constitution provides that in a Republic, in which sovereignty belongs to the nation, no dogma other than the national will can guide the political system, and legal rules are adopted by considering the democratic national requirements as guided by intelligence and science, rather than religious orders. Freedom of Religion and Conscience is established for everyone, without any discrimination or prerequisites and not subject to any restrictions beyond those provided in the Constitution; misuse and exploitation of religion or religious feelings is prohibited; and the State behaves equally and impartially toward all religions and beliefs in its acts and transactions.[99]

It denounced legal arrangements based on religion rather than national will as incompatible with individual liberties and democracy.[100] They are 'defiant' and make 'protecting social and political peace . . . impossible'.[101]

As will be further discussed below, the court also couched its decision in terms of minority protection: safeguarding the right of the non-religious not to be subjected to the 'instrument of compulsion' which the headscarf represented.[102] Thus, beyond grand pronouncements on Turkey's commitment to secularism since its founding, in practical terms the judgment amounted to a denouncement of a form of religious dress in universities on the grounds that it represented a threat to equality and public order. Coupled with other European jurisprudence on this issue, we can read this case as part of 'the growth of a pan-European legal discourse of religious symbols not only as text, but as a mechanism, however broad and ambiguous, of social control'.[103]

1.3 Eternity clauses protecting pluralist democracy

Eternity clauses have also been relied on to safeguard the democratic sphere. They are part of constitutional design options that seek to protect against the democratic system being undermined from within, whether by anti-democratic political forces or by unbridled majoritarianism. There are three broad examples I will discuss here. The first are party bans, which have been based on unamendable constitutional commitments to multiparty democracy, as in Germany, or on similar

99 Cited inibid.
100 Ibid., 187.
101 Ibid.
102 See ibid., 188.
103 Cindy Skach, 'Şahin v. Turkey. App. no. 44774/98; "Teacher Headscarf". Case no. 2BvR 1436/02', *American Journal of International Law* 100:1 (2006) 186, 190.

commitments to secularism and territorial integrity, as in Turkey.[104] Party bans are a familiar theme in the militant democracy literature, seen by their defenders as an uncomfortable but necessary trade-off for protecting democratic pluralism. The second example is unamendable term limits. I believe the discussion of clauses which declare the number and/or duration of executive mandates unamendable must take into account the distinctive history of term limits as a tool of constitutional design in post-authoritarian contexts. In a sense, they are different from other eternity clauses, more distinctly practical in aim and blunter but therefore more easily recognized as transgressed. The third framework I look at here is that of minority rights, within which eternity clauses serve as immutable commitments to the protection of minorities and safeguards against majoritarian abuse. As discussed in Chapter 3, not all values enshrined in eternity clauses are minority-protecting; some are distinctly majoritarian, such as official religion or language provisions. Examples of both are given here.

Other types of unamendable provisions could have been brought under the umbrella of anti-majoritarianism. Federalism in particular could be seen as a pluralist democratic commitment to preserving territorial subunits. In this light, then, eternity clauses which list federalism among the entrenched values would also be read as minority-protecting, only the minority would be a territorial unit rather than a population. Echoes of such an interpretation exist in German *Ewigkeitsklausel* jurisprudence discussed above.

Protecting democracy through political party bans

Measures against political parties deemed a threat to the constitutional order can take a range of forms. As Samuel Issacharoff has noted, they can include 'the proscription of political parties that fail to accept some fundamental tenet of the social order', 'an electoral code governing the content of political appeals', and 'a ban on electoral participation for some political parties, even if they are permitted to maintain a party organization'.[105] Such bans or restrictions are employed against parties deemed anti-democratic, but also against separatist or ethnic parties.[106] These measures are not necessarily predicated on proof of violence or advocacy of violence by the party in question, but 'directed against the threat of a "legal"

[104] See Rivka Weil, 'On the Nexus of Eternity Clauses, Proportional Representation, and Banned Political Parties', *Election Law Journal* 16:2 (2017) 237, linking unconstitutional constitutional amendment doctrines to party bans as well as to proportional representation electoral rules.

[105] Samuel Issacharoff, *Fragile Democracies: Contested Power in the Era of Constitutional Courts* (Cambridge University Press 2015), 78.

[106] Richard Pildes, 'Political Parties and Constitutionalism' in Tom Ginsburg and Rosalind Dixon, eds., *Comparative Constitutional Law* (Edward Elgar 2011) 254, 260.

anti-democratic takeover of the state apparatus'.[107] However, the evidence indicates that direct involvement in violent acts usually plays a role in a party's ban,[108] while at the same time bans aimed at weakening political opposition have also occurred.[109] Thus, while the militant democracy paradigm cannot fully account for the phenomenon of party bans, constitutional theory has resorted to its logic when attempting to reconcile them with democratic commitments.[110] Party bans are in fact given as *the* example of militant democracy in action.[111] I propose to examine more closely two European states' experience with party bans, though this issue is by no means a solely European one.[112] For example, party bans in Africa have similarly been pursued on militant democratic grounds, with the focus there on ethnic parties in an effort to prevent the politicization of ethnicity.[113]

Anti-democratic parties

In Germany, for instance, Article 79(3) was adopted in conjunction with a vast array of measures based on the drafters' understandings of lessons from the Weimar experience.[114] With regard to the regulation of political parties, the constitution's approach is robust and two-directional. On the one hand, the Basic Law is committed to multiparty democracy and, in Article 21(1), explicitly (and for the first time positively) recognizes political parties as constitutional agents that help form the political opinion of the people.[115] This was a purposeful departure from the Weimar constitution, whose low levels of institutionalization of parties was partially blamed for their abdication of parliamentary responsibility during the Nazi rise to power.[116] On the other hand, Article 21(2) declares unconstitutional parties which 'by reason of their aims or the behaviour of their adherents, seek to undermine or abolish the free democratic basic order or to endanger the existence of the

[107] Matthijs Bogaards, Matthias Basedau, and Christof Hartmann, 'Ethnic Party Bans in Africa: An Introduction', *Democratization* 17:4 (2010) 599, 605.

[108] Angela K. Bourne, 'Democratization and the Illegalization of Political Parties in Europe', *Democratization* 19:6 (2012) 1065, 1080.

[109] Bogaards et al. (2010), 612.

[110] Ibid., 605; Bourne (2012), 1080.

[111] See, among others, Pildes (2011).

[112] For an overview of party bans in Europe, see Angela K. Bourne and Fernando Casal Bértoa, 'Mapping "Militant Democracy": Variation in Party Ban Practices in European Democracies (1945–2015)', *European Constitutional Law Review* 13:2 (2017) 221.

[113] On this, see articles in 'Ethnic Party Bans in Africa' special issue of *Democratization* 17:4 (2010).

[114] Although what, precisely, those lessons were was not uncontested. With regard to measures regulating political parties, for instance, there was disagreement as to whether the lack of thresholds for entry into parliament had been a cause of, or merely impotent in the face of, the rise of political polarisation. See H. W. Koch, *A Constitutional History of Germany* (Longman 1984), 341.

[115] See Elmar M. Hucko, *The Democratic Tradition: Four German Constitutions* (Berg Publishers 1987), 72.

[116] Cindy Skach, *Borrowing Constitutional Designs: Constitutional Law in Weimar Germany and the French Fifth Republic* (Princeton University Press 2005), 38, 52–7, 68; Cindy Skach, 'Political Parties and the Constitution' in Michel Rosenfeld and András Sajó, eds., *The Oxford Handbook of Comparative Constitutional Law* (Oxford University Press 2012) 874, 878.

Federal Republic of Germany'. Moreover, the German Constitutional Court has explained the role of parties as mediators between individuals and the state but not exclusive in their function as facilitators of political opinion, rendering the role of political parties in German democracy more ambiguous and subordinated to the parliamentary system of government.[117]

The case law of the German Constitutional Court includes several instances of calls for party bans, with two successful in the post-war years.[118] They involved Konrad Adenauer's call to prohibit both the Socialist Reich Party (the party-heir to the Nazis) and the Communist Party on the ground of their anti-democratic ideologies.[119] The court decided to ban both parties and established its doctrine in this area: its intervention would involve a detailed investigation of the party's internal structure and of its public actions and statements. It considered itself competent to declare a party unconstitutional, and thus to order its dissolution, 'if, but only if, they seek to topple supreme fundamental values of the free democratic order that are embodied in the Basic Law'.[120] The Court's approach would arguably become more tolerant of anti-democratic parties as German democracy itself consolidated. Attempts to ban the National Democratic Party of Germany (NPD) failed in 2003 and 2017. The 2003 call was dismissed on procedural grounds,[121] while in 2017 the court refused the ban because while undemocratic, the NPD was unlikely to be successful in its endeavour.[122] These are examples of '[p]olitical extremism [being] contained not by militant democracy, but by the orderly political processes, an approach that avoids cloaking extremist political parties as "martyrs of democracy"'.[123] This raises the question of the appropriate timing of party bans, and the careful balancing test courts should engage in when weighing the benefits of such bans against their costs for multiparty democracy.

More significant for my purposes here, however, is the implications of this case law for our understanding of Article 79(3). While the German Constitutional Court did not explicitly rely on the eternity clause given that no constitutional amendments were in play, its decisions did help clarify its interpretation of the commitment to democracy instituted by the Basic Law. Significantly, however, the

[117] See Georg Ress, 'The Constitution and the Requirements of Democracy in Germany' in Christian Starck, *New Challenges to the German Basic Law: The German Contributions to the Third World Congress of the International Association of Constitutional Law* (Nomos Verlagsgesellschaft 1991), 123.

[118] See Kommers and Miller (2012), 300.

[119] 2 BVerfGE 1 (1952) ('*Socialist Reich Party*') and 5 BVerfGE 85 (1956) ('*Communist Party*').

[120] *Socialist Reich Party* case cited in Kommers and Miller (2012), 287.

[121] 107 BVerfGE 339 (2003) ('*NPD Party Ban Dismissal I*'). The dismissal came following the court's concerns that much of the evidence in the case came from state agents having infiltrated the party and thus being potentially compromised.

[122] 2 BvB 1/13 (2017) ('*NPD Party Ban Dismissal II*').

[123] Dieter Oberndörfer, 'Freedom of Speech Through Constitutional Provisions: History and Overall Record' in David Kretzmer and Francine Kershman Hazan, eds., *Freedom of Speech and Incitement Against Democracy* (Kluwer Law International 2000) 240; Michael Minkenberg, 'Repression and Reaction: Militant Democracy and the Radical Right in Germany and France', *Patterns of Prejudice* 40:1 (2006) 25, 29.

court's doctrine in this area cannot be understood without an adequate appreciation of Article 21 and its distinctive background, purpose, and scope. In other words, one must appreciate the complexity of the German constitutional architecture, within which the *Ewigkeitsklausel* interacts with other constitutional provisions in the defence of democracy. This is a useful reminder to countries wishing to emulate the success of Germany's constitutional order that an intricate web of constitutional provisions protect its democracy, and not merely—and possibly not primarily—its unamendability clause.

Separatist and religious parties

A more instructive case for my purposes here is Turkey. There have been twenty-seven party bans in Turkey between 1961 and 2019, twenty-two of which under the 1981 constitution, banning either Kurdish separatist parties (said to breach unamendable territorial integrity) or parties seen to promote political Islam (said to breach unamendable secularism).[124] Article 68 of the Turkish Constitution explicitly requires party statutes and programmes to respect the independence of the state; its indivisible territorial and national integrity; human rights; equality and the rule of law; national sovereignty; and the principles of the democratic and secular republic. The Venice Commission has referred to Turkish legal restrictions as being stricter, including more material limitations on parties, and being applied based on a lower threshold and with fewer procedural obstacles than the rest of Europe.[125] So common have dissolutions become, in fact, that the threat of disbanding has become normalized and Islamic or Kurdish parties, the main targets of these actions, have developed strategies such as setting up 'spare parties' in anticipation of judicial rulings against them.[126] The regulation of political parties, whether by outright bans or via a high parliamentary threshold, has thus been a staple of Turkey's democratization process.[127] Significantly, and contrary to the German case just described, the banned parties have not been politically marginal, but have had parliamentary representation and, in the case of the Welfare Party discussed below, were part of a ruling government coalition.[128]

In discussing two instances of party bans, Dicle Koğacıoğlu reconstructs the discursive and normative steps taken by the Turkish Constitutional Court in its

[124] Gözde Böcü and Felix Petersen, 'Debating State Organization Principles in the Constitutional Conciliation Commission' in Felix Petersen and Zeynep Yanaşmayan, eds., *The Failure of Popular Constitution Making in Turkey: Regressing Towards Autocracy* (Cambridge University Press 2019), 150.

[125] European Commission for Democracy Through Law (Venice Commission), 'Opinion on the Constitutional and Legal Provisions Relevant to the Prohibition of Political Parties in Turkey', CDL-AD (2009) 006, 13 March 2009, para. 65.

[126] See Koğacıoğlu (2004), 440.

[127] See Sabri Sayarı, 'Party System and Democratic Consolidation in Turkey: Problems and Prospects' in Carmen Rodríguez, Antonio Ávalos, Hakan Yılmaz, and Ana I. Planet, eds., *Turkey's Democratization Process* (Routledge 2014) 89, 101.

[128] Koğacıoğlu (2004), 443.

evaluation of threats to the country's democracy. In the case of the prohibition of Halkin Emek Partisi (HEP), the People's Labour Party,[129] the court found the Kurdish party to be separatist and to have threatened the unity of the nation state—a core principle of the Turkish Constitution. The preamble in fact speaks of 'the eternal existence of the Turkish Motherland and Nation and the indivisible unity of the Sublime Turkish State', while unamendable Article 3 declares the state, with its territory and nation, 'an indivisible entity' and the national language Turkish. Other constitutional provisions also mention territorial integrity, such as Article 14 on the prohibition of abuse of fundamental rights. The court invoked this constitutional basis and the history of post-Ataturk Turkey to find that

> in the modern Turkish Republic the granting of minority status on the basis of differences of language or race was incompatible with the unity of the homeland and the nation. The state was unitary, the nation was a whole, and arguments to the contrary could only be seen as unwarranted foreign influences intensified by the rhetoric of human rights and freedoms.[130]

The court dealt with threats to a different but equally foundational constitutional principle in a famous case against *Refah Partisi*, the Welfare Party.[131] In that instance, the Constitutional Court was concerned that the party was bent on replacing the democratic system with one based on sharia law, in contravention to Turkey's express laicism. The latter is protected by another unamendable provision, Article 2, by the preamble which mandates 'that sacred religious feelings shall absolutely not be involved in state affairs and politics as required by the principle of secularism', and by other articles including the aforementioned Article 14. The court proceeded to define secularism as 'a way of life that has destroyed the medieval scholastic dogmatism and has become the basis of the vision of democracy that develops with the enlightenment of science, nation, independence, national sovereignty, and the ideal of humanity'.[132] Based on this definition, the court also accepted a dichotomy between religious states and secular ones, where religion 'is saved from politicization, saved from being a tool of administration and kept in its real respectable place which is the conscience of the people'.[133]

The implications for rights interpretation of similar language used by the Turkish Constitutional Court in cases involving the wearing of the headscarf will be discussed below. What is relevant here is the court's understanding of the democratic ideal it saw itself as tasked with protecting. As Koğacıoğlu has noted, the court's notion of democracy was of 'a formal category, an abstract entity in need

[129] Case No. 1992/1 (Political Party Dissolution), Decision No.: 1993/1, 14 July 1993.
[130] Koğacıoğlu (2004), 447.
[131] Case No. 1997/1 (Political Party Dissolution), Decision No.: 1998/1, 16 January 1998.
[132] Cited in Koğacıoğlu (2004), 450.
[133] Ibid., 451.

of protection'.[134] There was no room left for democracy's inner tensions, only reliance on its presence or absence.[135] In other words, no pluralist notions of democracy motivated the court's decision.[136] Instead, it positioned its rhetoric squarely in the tradition of militant democracy and invoked the right to democratic self-defence.[137] The court did this even while its intervention served to reduce electoral competition.[138]

Of great interest in the Turkish cases of party bans are the transnational elements appealed to in these judicial decisions. In both cases discussed above, both the majority and the minority of judges writing opinions invoked commitments to human rights norms and international treaties in justifying their position.[139] Koğacıoğlu aptly observed that the cases 'were very much an amalgam of nationalist collectivist documents, such as Ataturk's speeches or the problematic 1982 constitution, and international treaties', including the European Convention on Human Rights.[140] But whereas the defence were relying on individual rights to the freedom of thought, expression, and association, 'the Court was emphasizing the element of the right of a democracy to defend itself'.[141] In other words, the Constitutional Court was concerned with providing an international basis for the legitimacy of its rulings, and presented militant democracy, instantiated as the competence to ban political parties which it itself was exercising, as an international norm rooted in democracy and human rights. Interestingly, the European Court of Human Rights would agree with this application of militant democracy aims when reviewing the *Refah* case.[142]

Protecting democracy through minority rights

There are three broad categories of provisions which could be discussed under this umbrella. The first group includes commitments to the unamendability of certain

[134] Ibid., 453.

[135] Ibid., 457. See also Böcü and Petersen (2019), 153, arguing that the Turkish Constitutional Court has not elaborated the core principles of democracy in a systematic manner.

[136] For a discussion of the tensions between the normative commitment to militant versus pluralist democracy as exemplified in the *Refah* case, including at the European Court of Human Rights, see Patrick Macklem, 'Militant Democracy, Legal Pluralism, and the Paradox of Self-determination', *International Journal of Constitutional Law* 4:3 (2006), 488–516.

[137] Koğacıoğlu (2004), 454.

[138] According to some, this was precisely the point, with the Turkish Constitutional Court serving political elite interests. See Böcü and Petersen (2019), 150 and 159.

[139] Ibid., 442, 456.

[140] Ibid., 456.

[141] Ibid.

[142] For a critique of the approach of the European Court of Human Rights in the *Refah Partisi* case and its reliance on militant democracy arguments, see Rory O'Connell, 'Militant Democracy and Human Rights Principles', *Constitutional Law Review* 5:1 (2009) 84.

discrete rights. An example is Germany's Article 79(3) which refers to Articles 1 and 20 of the Basic Law as the entrenched rights. Second are broader commitments to the respect of human rights incorporated in eternity clauses such as Turkey's Article 4. There are provisions which might straddle the two, such as Russia's Article 135(1) which prevents the revision of the entire chapter on rights and liberties. The scope of clauses in this second category in particular is only elucidated via judicial interpretation. The third and seemingly most popular type read more like an unamendable minimum standard of rights protection. Romania's Article 152(2) is an example here: 'Likewise, no revision shall be made if it results in the suppression of the citizens' fundamental rights and freedoms, or the safeguards thereof.' Another is Tunisia's provision which is tellingly incorporated in the constitution's limitation clause (Article 42) and states that 'There can be no amendment to the Constitution that undermines the human rights and freedoms guaranteed in this Constitution.' Such language appears particularly frequently in post-conflict constitutions, which often also refer to international human rights standards (see Bosnia's Article X(2), Kosovo's Article 144(3)). In what follows, I explore examples from the second and third categories. I do so in order to discuss the protection of religious freedom and official language as two instances where minority protection clashes with unamendability.

Religious minorities

The framework of minority rights provides a different lens through which to view the constitutional battles surrounding secularism. As was discussed above, India's Supreme Court has invoked that constitution's secular foundations to protect a religious minority under threat. The Indian court's intervention in this arena has led commentators to call its function '"super" anti-majoritarian'.[143] Other courts interpreting eternity clauses in this area have been less preoccupied with protecting the vulnerable. In Turkey, for instance, secularism has long been at the heart of public battles over constitutional protection of religious identity. The *Headscarf* decision of 2008, also discussed above, made references to the discrimination of the minority non-headscarf-wearing population:

> [I]n Turkey, where the majority of the population is Muslim, the wearing of the Islamic headscarf as a mandatory religious duty would result in discrimination between practicing Muslims, nonpracticing Muslims, and nonbelievers on grounds of dress, with anyone who refused to wear the headscarf undoubtedly being regarded as opposed to religion or as nonreligious.[144]

[143] Manoj S. Mate, 'Two Paths to Judicial Power: The Basic Structure Doctrine and Public Interest Litigation in Comparative Perspective', *San Diego International Law Journal* 12 (2010) 175, 210.
[144] Roznai and Yolcu (2012), 179–80.

In other words, the court turned the tables on those arguing this was a case of religious freedom and rendered a judgment premised on the rights of the secular (but constitutionally entrenched) minority. It did so while at the same time couching its search for constitutional justice in international human rights standards, all while preserving the status quo.[145] Susanna Mancini has noted this same logic being adopted by the European Court of Human Rights in its case reviewing the Turkish decision and found it 'striking that the Court used the margin of appreciation doctrine to protect *minorities* when the majority religion happens to be Islam'.[146] She places this observation in the Turkish context of militant anti-Islamic secularism, but also of the European Court's previous findings that the veil was incompatible with certain fundamental principles.[147] Legislation banning the wearing of the Islamic dress have since spread across European countries and the Strasbourg court has largely upheld state justifications for introducing them.[148]

The Turkish decision is problematic for the protection of rights to religious freedom in a different way as well. The public–private sphere distinction upon which much of the doctrine on the separation of church and state relies was always problematic and has become increasingly so the more constitutionalization encroaches upon hitherto off-limits areas of life.[149] The Turkish Constitutional Court took this as far as to portray its intervention in the *Refah Partisi* case and others as saving religion itself from 'contamination' by politics.[150] In Turkey, therefore, secularism may have relegated Islamic identity and practice to the private sphere, but it was to be followed there by the long arm of state regulation as well.[151]

Linguistic minorities

Another testing ground for eternity clause rights protection are unamendable provisions which incorporate references to an official language. Such provisions exist in Algeria (Article 212(4)), Bahrain (Article 120), Romania (Article 152(1)), Tunisia (Article 1), and Turkey (Article 4). This might seem like a mere declaration

[145] Koğacıoğlu (2004), 459.

[146] Susanna Mancini, 'The Tempting of Europe, the Political Seduction of the Cross: A Schmittian Reading of Christianity and Islam in European Constitutionalism' in Susanna Mancini and Michel Rosenfeld, eds., *Constitutional Secularism in an Age of Religious Revival* (Oxford University Press 2014) 111, 121.

[147] See *Dahlab* v. *Switzerland*, Application No. 42393/98, Decision of 15 February 2001. Mancini wonders whether the European Court finds Islam more generally to be incompatible with democracy, and as such open to regulation: 'Islam, unlike Christianity, even when it is the vast majority's religion, can be restrictively regulated on the ground that it threatens the democratic basis of the state.' Mancini (2014), 121.

[148] Neville Cox, *Behind the Veil: A Critical Analysis of European Veiling Laws* (Edward Elgar 2019). Cox is critical of the Strasbourg court's failure to engage more deeply with these bans, including with the often right-wing populist motivations behind adopting them.

[149] András Sajó, 'Preliminaries to a Concept of Constitutional Secularism' in Susanna Mancini and Michel Rosenfeld, eds., *Constitutional Secularism in an Age of Religious Revival* (Oxford University Press 2014) 54, 62.

[150] Koğacıoğlu (2004), 451.

[151] Ibid., 437.

of fact, but as the cases of Turkey and Romania below demonstrate, it is anything but benign. Indeed, I would argue that just like territorial integrity discussed above, official language unamendability only appears in the constitutions of countries where it is a site of struggle. If unamendable integrity of the territory is more akin to a state's declaration of independence, however, the entrenchment of an official language can and has been used to curtail minority rights in the name of faith to the constitution.

As we have seen, Turkey's eternity clause incorporated in Article 4 of its constitution has been at the heart of constitutional jurisprudence for decades. Less prominent, perhaps, has been the interpretation given by the Turkish Constitutional Court to the provision on official language and its impact upon minority language protection. In the *HEP* case, the court interpreted calls for the use of the Kurdish language as 'a display of separatism'.[152] It thus embraced the prosecution's argument that, while Kurds could speak their language freely, 'attempts to institutionalize the use of Kurdish would amount to attempts to replace the Turkish language as the language of the nation, thereby also amounting to separatism'.[153] Attempts to use a minority language in education and media were ruled a violation of the eternity clause and direct affronts to the unity of the nation and to Ataturk's legacy:

> [T]he Court ruled that in the modern Turkish Republic the granting of minority status on the basis of differences of language or race was incompatible with the unity of the homeland and the nation. The state was unitary, the nation was a whole, and arguments to the contrary could only be seen as unwarranted foreign influences intensified by the rhetoric of human rights and freedoms.[154]

Romania's case is also instructive. Despite early promises that individual and collective minority rights would be protected,[155] the 1991 constitution told a rather different story. Drafted without the inclusion of minority groups, not even the sizeable Hungarian one,[156] the text pays lip service to minority rights while at the same time subjecting them to the rights of the majority. Article 6(2) thus qualifies rights to minority identity protection by stating: 'The protective measures taken by the state to preserve, develop, and express the identity of the members of the

[152] Ibid., 447.
[153] Ibid., 445.
[154] Ibid., 447.
[155] Michael Shafir, 'The Political Party as National Holding Company: The Hungarian Democratic Federation of Romania' in Jonathan Stein, ed., *The Politics of National Minority Participation in Post-Communist Europe: State Building, Democracy and Ethnic Mobilization* (M.E. Sharpe 2000b) 101, 102.
[156] Carmen Kettley, 'Ethnicity, Language and Transition Politics in Romania: The Hungarian Minority in Context' in Farimah Daftary and Francois Grin, eds., *Nation-building, Ethnicity and Language Politics in Transition Countries* (Local Government and Public Service Reform Initiative, Open Society Institute 2003) 243, 251.

national minorities shall be in accordance with the principles of equality and non-discrimination in relation to the other Romanian citizens.' Article 1(1) speaks of a 'unitary and indivisible' state, Article 4(1) of 'the unity of the Romanian people' as the foundation of the state, and Article 13 declares Romanian the official language. Moreover, Article 152(1) lists an array of values and principles which are not to be the object of amendment: 'the national, independent, unitary, and indivisible character of the Romanian state, the Republic as the form of government, territorial integrity, the independence of the judicial system, political pluralism, and the official language'. These were never the elements of a pacified constitutional identity: unitary territory and official language in particular were fiercely contested from the onset by the Hungarian minority.[157]

The Constitutional Court found itself at the centre of Romania's language wars on several occasions. In an early decision, the court was called upon to rule on the constitutionality of education legislation insofar as it affected minority rights.[158] Perhaps the sorest point in this saga has been the quest for a Hungarian-language state-funded university. More than a struggle for minority recognition, this represented a quest for restitution of an institution forcefully taken away during the communist regime.[159] While the constitution guarantees the right of ethnic minorities to learn and be taught in their mother tongue (Article 32(3)), the court unequivocally dismissed all objections of unconstitutionality in that case by virtue of Article 13 and the limitations in Article 6(2). In another case, the court rejected calls for Hungarian to be used in public administration, again invoking Article 13 as the basis.[160] Education in particular has remained the site where language policy controversies have been fought out, with no sign of abating.[161] More recently, in a 2014 ruling on the constitutionality of proposed revisions of the constitution (an exercise of abstract constitutional review), the Constitutional Court analysed a proposed amendment to Article 32 which would have included and defined the scope of a principle of 'university autonomy'.[162] The court found this change unconstitutional on the grounds that it would result in a violation of Article 152(2) ('the elimination of the fundamental rights and freedoms of citizens or of

[157] See also Miklós Bakk, 'Comunitate politică, comunitate națională, comunități teritoriale' in Gabriel Andreescu, Miklos Bakk, Lucian Bojin, and Valentin Constantin, eds., *Comentarii la Constituția României* (Editura Polirom 2010) 87, 110. Bakk argues that the constitutional definition as a national state has limited political debates and the legislative space to negotiate minority status in Romania. See ibid., 111–12.

[158] Decizia nr. 72/1995, 18 July 1995.

[159] See Michael Shafir, 'Mişcările xenofobe şi dilemele "includerii" şi "excluderii": cazul minorității maghiare din România', *Altera* 6:15 (2000a) 159, 172.

[160] Decizia nr. 40/1996, 11 April 1996.

[161] A Hungarian-language state university remains one of the core agenda issues for the country's ethnic Hungarian political party to this day. See ' Kelemen: Trebuie înființată, prin lege şi dialog, o universitate de stat în limba maghiară', *Mediafax*, 23 October 2013, https://www.mediafax.ro/social/kelemen-trebuie-infiintata-prin-lege-si-dialog-o-universitate-de-stat-in-limba-maghiara-11551831.

[162] Decizia nr. 80/2014.

the guarantees of these rights and freedoms').[163] As two minority opinions in this latter case argued, however, the majority judgment did not explain which rights and freedoms would come under attack, nor whether any of the principles contained in the eternity clause were violated and would thus justify a finding of a priori unconstitutionality.[164]

These cases illustrate that even seemingly nonthreatening unamendable provisions such as on official language can have very real consequences for those left out. Relying on apex courts to read ambiguous or discriminatory provisions in these texts in a manner that encourages toleration is not always a successful gamble. I agree therefore with Wojciech Sadurski who cautions against expecting a regime of toleration from constitutional courts in post-communist settings.[165] The reason is not that these courts have not made positive contributions, he says, but instead that they may have been elevated too quickly to a prominent role in the political system which they were perhaps not prepared for.[166] Samuel Issacharoff has made a similar point about courts in all new democracies.[167] The combination of complicated minority relations and potentially weak or inexperienced judicial institutions was not ideal; the entrenchment of exclusionary values could only exacerbate the problem.

Protecting a democracy governed by the rule of law

A by now famous 2009 decision of the Czech Constitutional Court serves as a good illustration of rule of law arguments used to strike down amendments.[168] The decision was handed down in a case involving a constitutional act wherein

[163] Ibid., para. 128.

[164] Decizia nr. 80/2014 Separate Opinion, Judge Petre Lăzăroiu, p. 200 and Separate Opinion, Puskás Valentin-Zoltán, p. 2.

[165] Wojciech Sadurski, 'Transitional Constitutionalism: Simplistic and Fancy Theories' in Adam W. Czarnota, Martin Krygier, and Wojciech Sadurski, eds., *Rethinking the Rule of Law After Communism* (CEU Press 2005) 9, 18–19. He gives the further example of the Ukrainian Constitutional Court, which 'strengthened the constitutional place of the Ukrainian language in Ukraine, and established an affirmative duty on all public bodies to use only Ukrainian throughout the country (even though in the Eastern and Southern regions the Russian language is widely used both in private and public contexts)'.

[166] Ibid., 19.

[167] Samuel Issacharoff, 'Constitutional Courts and Democratic Hedging', *Georgetown Law Journal* 99 (2011) 961, 971.

[168] Decision Pl. ÚS 27/09: Constitutional Act on Shortening the Term of Office of the Chamber of Deputies, 10 September 2009. For analyses of the decision, see: Maxim Tomoszek, 'The Czech Republic' in Dawn Oliver and Carlo Fusaro, eds., *How Constitutions Change: A Comparative Study* (Hart 2011) 41; Kieran Williams, 'When a Constitutional Amendment Violates the "Substantive Core": The Czech Constitutional Court's September 2009 Early Elections Decision', *Review of Central and Eastern European Law* 36 (2011) 33; Yaniv Roznai, 'Legisprudence Limitations on Constitutional Amendments? Reflections on the Czech Constitutional Court's Declaration of Unconstitutional Constitutional Act', *Vienna Journal on International Constitutional Law* 8:1 (2014) 29.

the lower house of parliament had been dissolved ahead of term, with early parliamentary elections already on the way. The proceedings had been initiated by an MP, who charged that his individual right to serve the full duration of his mandate had been violated. Although there was a procedure for early dissolution of parliament in the Czech Constitution (incorporated in Article 35), it had not been resorted to in this instance. Moreover, the petitioner contended, the 'substantive core' of the constitution, which he argued included principles of non-retroactivity, generality, and predictability of laws, had been violated by the constitutional act. The Constitutional Court ignored the rights-based claim but embraced the arguments that the constitutional act represented an affront to the constitution's identity and the integrity of Czech democracy. The decision sought to justify the court's competence to rule on the constitutionality of the law before it, as well as to justify the rule of law principles of generality and non-retroactivity as part of a 'material core' the boundaries of which the court was entrusted to police.

With regard to the latter point, the court went to great lengths to validate its doctrine both by reference to precedent and to history. It sought to 'contextualiz[e] the ... case as the faithful and logical extension of a line of cases running back to the first occasion on which the Court reviewed the constitutionality of a statute'.[169] In this case law, the court had recognized 'popular sovereignty, a right of resistance, and the basic principles of election law' as 'fundamental inviolable values of a democratic society' and as such part of a 'substantive core' of the legal order.[170] The court also relied on the rhetorical force of appeals to history by referencing Czech, but also German and Austrian, experience with democratic subversion, including via the communist semblance of legal order.[171] This rhetoric has been described as necessary for the court to feel empowered to review the constitutional act, even while the threat of the so-called Weimar syndrome might have been exaggerated by the Czech Constitutional Court.[172]

This was the background, the court argued, which helped explain the adoption of Article 9(2) stating: 'Any changes in the essential requirements for a democratic state governed by the rule of law are impermissible'. The practical meaning of this article had previously been disputed, particularly given the lack of an enforcement mechanism attached.[173] Alternative readings saw it as a purely declaratory provision, or else as 'an instruction to the Senate, which is supposed to be the "connecting agent" with responsibility for revising legislation passed by the

[169] Williams (2011), 42.

[170] Ibid.

[171] Ibid.

[172] Ibid. Williams defined the 'Weimar syndrome' with reference to 'states in which authoritarian movements came to power in the past with the help not of foreign armies but of the ballot box'. See also Kieran Williams, 'Judicial Review of Electoral Thresholds in Germany, Russia and the Czech Republic', *Election Law Journal* 4:3 (2005), 191.

[173] Tomoszek (2011), 57.

Chamber of Deputies'.[174] The Constitutional Court took a different view, however, and arrogated for itself the power to review Article 9(2), laying the ground for its 'material structure' doctrine. It emphatically declared this provision as 'non-changeable ... not a mere slogan or proclamation, but a constitutional provision with normative consequences'.[175] In so doing, it believed it was protecting not only core rule of law components such as non-retroactivity and the generality of laws, but also the democratic order, all of which it linked to the identity of the Czech constitutional system.[176]

Thus, not only did the court specify concrete legal principles which make up the unamendable rule of law commitment in Article 9(2) (though crucially, did not provide an exhaustive list), but it also took the more controversial step of declaring itself the guardian of this constitutional 'core'. This move, typical of implicit doctrines of unamendability (discussed in detail in Chapter 4), has been widely criticized in the literature. More sympathetic observers have termed it 'one of the weakest points of the decision' but deemed it unavoidable in the face of a dangerous precedent and bound to remain exceptional.[177] Others accepted the court's move and admitted the problematic aspects of the constitutional act passed by the parliament but maintained that the circumstances of the case had not warranted invalidation.[178] Others still called this an instance of 'undercooked, "fast-food" judging'.[179]

There is an inescapable irony in the court relying on rule of law considerations, including of predictability and legal certainty, while itself making an unprecedented (despite its protestations) move to increase its own review powers and strike down an otherwise constitutionally conforming act.[180] Similar arguments would be at the core of the court's ensuing jurisprudence. In a subsequent ruling on the Treaty of Lisbon, the court was called upon to delineate further the boundaries of its 'material core' doctrine but refused to do so. It declined calls to provide a final list of elements of the doctrine and defended its position as one of 'restraint and judicial minimalism, which is perceived as a means of limiting the judicial power in favour of political processes, and which outweighs the requirement of absolute legal certainty'.[181] It is inherent in the logic of any doctrine of substantive limits on constitutional change that exhaustive lists may unduly constrain the adjudicator and may indeed be inappropriate when dealing with constitutional essentials. At the same time, questions remain over the appropriate dispensation of the judicial

[174] Ibid.
[175] Decision, Part IV.
[176] Ibid., Part VI(a).
[177] Tomoszek (2011), 64–5.
[178] See Roznai (2014), 51.
[179] Williams (2011), 50, using Joseph Weiler's term from his article. 'The "Lisbon Urteil" and the Fast Food Culture', *European Journal of International Law* 20:3 (2009) 505.
[180] See Roznai (2014), 51.
[181] Decision Pl. ÚS 29/09: Treaty of Lisbon II, 3 November 2009, paras. 112–13.

role when defending constitutional fundamentals. Moreover, as discussed further in Chapter 3, the Czech court turned out to be one of several European constitutional courts expanding its unamendability jurisprudence to enforce limits on European integration.

Other arguments in favour of the Czech Constitutional Court's decision of 10 September 2009 seem to be opportunistic, defending it on grounds of the erosion of parliamentary practice in the Czech Republic.[182] These, however, may overstate the danger in the concrete circumstances of this case. The existence of wide parliamentary consensus to shorten rather than extend the mandate raises questions about the proportionality of the court's decision.[183] Although ad hoc, it is doubtful that the act in question would have resulted in the elision of Czech democracy and rule of law. Moreover, the speedy adoption of an amendment to allow precisely the self-dissolution procedure struck down by the court is further evidence that there had been broad consensus behind the act.[184] In other words, the rhetoric of the Czech Constitutional Court, steeped as it was in a history of authoritarianism and reminiscent of militant democracy arguments, was at best only partially convincing. After all, a representative democratic institution willingly relinquishing its mandate so as to escape political crisis may only dubiously be equated with Nazi or communist subversion of democracy by legal means; doing so in an ad hoc manner may raise rule of law concerns, but hardly of a magnitude to affect the constitutional order's very core. This case may therefore be evidence of Europe's 'judicial culture more uniformly anxious for democracy's endurance'.[185] It may also be proof of judicial self-empowerment with a wider reach, as national defence against the encroachment of the supranational. This is after all a court which, like its German counterpart, asserted the 'fundamental core' of the Czech Constitution as delineating the limits of European integration.[186]

1.4 Conclusion

Several conclusions present themselves. The first is that eternity clauses as safeguards of state fundamentals or of democracy are to an extent dealing in

[182] See Tomoszek (2011), 66.

[183] See Radim Dragomaca, 'Constitutional Amendments and the Limits of Judicial Activism: The Case of the Czech Republic' in Willem Witteveen and Maartje de Visser, eds., *The Jurisprudence of Aharon Barak: Views from Europe* (Wolf Legal Publishers 2011) 198.

[184] On the amendment to Article 35 providing for the self-dissolution procedure, see Williams (2011), 46–8.

[185] Williams (2005), 191.

[186] Decisions Pl. ÚS 19/08: Treaty of Lisbon I, 26 November 2008 and Pl. ÚS 29/09: Treaty of Lisbon II, 3 November 2009. See discussion in Petr Bříza, 'The Czech Constitutional Court on the Lisbon Treaty', *European Constitutional Law Review* 5:1 (2009) 143. See further discussion of the rise of constitutional identity review in Europe in Chapter 3.

imponderables.[187] Declaring basic state characteristics as unamendable decidedly serves a symbolic and aspirational function. Just like preambles before them, eternity clauses may here be seen as constitutionalizing a 'yearning for homogeneity'[188]—for a state which will only ever transform within certain ideological boundaries. The main objection to entrenching such state fundamentals in eternity clauses is that it amounts to entrenching a black box of abstract commitments. Constitutions do not come with a lexicon explaining principles such as republicanism, federalism, territorial integrity, or secularism. To the extent that they are enforced at all, these principles will at best reflect a considered interpretation of their significance in their particular society and a reconstruction of the purposes behind their adoption. Not infrequently, however, how these unamendable commitments are interpreted will reflect judicial ideology. Most often, it will be a mix of both. The only way to understand the consequences of such eternity clauses, therefore, is to delve deep into constitutional debates and jurisprudence and evaluate them on a case-by-case basis.

Eternity clauses seeking to protect democracy are similarly neither self-explanatory nor self-enforcing. They do not exist on their own, but tend to be part of a wider militant democratic constitutional architecture. Their operation will therefore interlink with rules of electoral competition and political rights, with the system of government, and with the entrenchment of other rights guarantees. It will also greatly depend on judicial enforcement. On the one hand, there might be relatively uncontroversial cases such as banning fascist parties with known links to violent activity. On the other, however, there might be prohibitions of parties which are not politically marginal but represented in parliament and even in the government, on the grounds of anti-democratic activity contravening unamendable constitutional commitments. Courts' understandings of their own role in such instances will vary. Some will feel confident enough in the political system to allow competition to play itself out. Others, conversely, will take it upon themselves to police the political field based on their own, potentially 'assertive and authoritarian', values.[189] While such interventions may prove more or less controversial, it appears inevitable that they will at least on occasion stifle reasonable disagreement over democratic practice and go beyond the last-resort protection of the constitutional order. In situations where such judicial intervention takes place without explicit constitutional authorization, an additional democratic objection may be raised about their lack of mandate to review amendments.[190]

[187] Yap (2015), 123.

[188] Levinson (2011), 178.

[189] Ergun Özbudun describes the Turkish Constitutional Court's understanding of secularism in these terms. See Ergun Özbudun,'Democracy, Tutelarism and the Search for a New Constitution' in Carmen Rodríguez, Antonio Ávalos, Hakan Yılmaz, and Ana I. Planet, eds., *Turkey's Democratization Process* (Routledge 2014) 274, 306.

[190] This was the case of the Turkish Constitutional Court until 2017, when its self-ascribed jurisdiction to substantively review amendments was removed. A fuller discussion of judicial doctrines of unamendability in the absence of formal eternity clauses may be found in Chapter 4 of this book.

Finally, we saw eternity clauses entrenching rights, whether particular rights such as the overarching right to human dignity or else a non-regression/minimum threshold of rights protection. While such provisions may be less prone to contestation in the abstract, they are also in need of specification through judicial interpretation; moreover, they may coexist alongside other unamendable provisions with which they may come into conflict. Indeed, as the next chapter shows, such tensions are not infrequent in transitional constitutions, especially those emerging from divisive and conflict-affected negotiations.

The cases discussed above have involved courts, often in democratizing settings, having to adjudicate on unamendable provisions directly affecting the electoral arena and the protection of minorities. These examples have shown that courts do not always acquit themselves of this task in a manner that preserves electoral competition, limits executive power, or maximizes minority rights. Thus, the purported militant democratic ethos behind eternity clauses will not always correlate with democracy-enhancing judicial enforcement. It may instead protect (or even foster) a discriminatory status quo. These ideas will be revisited in subsequent chapters.

2
Eternity in Post-Conflict Constitutions

Unamendability as a Facilitator of Political Settlements

This chapter examines the rise of unamendable commitments in constitutions resulting from conflict-affected political transitions and calls attention to the distinctive role they play in these contexts: that of facilitating and later safeguarding a political settlement. In such contexts, a political agreement between rival parties is both hard fought and especially fragile. As such, constitutional unamendability is taken as a guarantee of the terms of the agreement both before and after the adoption of the new fundamental law. This specific role of eternity clauses—as themselves an instrument of political negotiation and conflict resolution—has largely been ignored by the growing literature on unamendability.[1] There has been some acknowledgement of 'reconciliatory' elements such as unamendable amnesties,[2] without considering the different dynamics of conflict-affected constitution-making and the resulting difference in justifications for, expectations from, and operation of unamendability therein.

This chapter fills this gap by investigating the specific bargaining dynamics conditioning political settlements in the contexts where many of today's new constitutions are being written: post-conflict transitions. The chapter investigates the complex bargaining behind several conflict-affected constitution-making processes, finding patterns and novel insights into unamendability's role within them. Declarations of immutability of certain fundamental characteristics of the state (such as religion or language), territorial arrangements (whether federal or unitary), territorial integrity and/or independence, human rights commitments, rights

[1] Silvia Suteu, 'Eternity Clauses in Post-Conflict and Post-Authoritarian Constitution-Making: Promise and Limits', *Global Constitutionalism* 6:1 (2017b) 63. For an exception discussing the US Constitution's Article V in similar terms, see Richard Albert, 'The Expressive Function of Constitutional Amendment Rules', *McGill Law Journal* 59:2 (2013) 225, 245. This function is not to be confused with what Roznai terms 'conflictual unamendability', by which he means eternity clauses acting as gag rules against the renegotiation of contested constitutional values (Yaniv Roznai, *Unconstitutional Constitutional Amendments: The Limits of Amendment Powers* (Oxford University Press 2017), 32–5).

[2] Roznai (2017), 35; Richard Albert, 'Constitutional Handcuffs', *Arizona State Law Journal* 42:3 (2010) 663, 666–7.

Eternity Clauses in Democratic Constitutionalism. Silvia Suteu, Oxford University Press.
DOI: 10.1093/oso/9780198858867.003.0003

of the opposition and/or the plural nature of democracy, and executive term limits are found to be recurrent in fragile and conflict-affected democracies. Amnesties and immunities granted to former warring parties are also sometimes constitutionalized as unamendable and represent a more overt form of elite protection.

Eternity clauses are often read as indicators of what drafters have considered to be the public goods of constitutionalism.[3] However, this chapter shows that they may simultaneously operate to reduce the risk for elites in entering the new dispensation. In this sense, we can understand eternity clauses in post-conflict constitutions analogously to the political insurance reading of constitutional review in new democracies.[4] Just like constitutional courts may help reduce the risks to which political elites may be subject (such as loss of political power or influence), eternity clauses may also perform an insurance role at the time of drafting.[5] Once we view constitution-makers as self-interested actors entering a mutually beneficial bargain, then the nature, content, and expected operation of eternity clauses are also revealed as the product of political deal-making. Presidential term limits, human rights provisions, and guarantees of democratic pluralism appear to give some protection against either party using the new order to reinstate dominance.

Of course, *most* constitutions are the result of political bargaining. Even where they have been imposed—whether by external forces or by internal elites—this imposition is better understood on a continuum rather than as black or white, and may well be corrected sociologically over time.[6] But what constitution-making in conflict-affected societies shows, perhaps more visibly than elsewhere, is that the content of eternity clauses may well be a reflection of strategic compromise, not lofty principles of constitutionalism or democracy. In other words, unamendability may at times play the role of political insurance mechanism at the time of constitution-making, relied on by drafters for reasons more pragmatic than normative. Yes, they are preservative in function, but not necessarily of an inviolable liberal constitutionalist core, instead of a pact that is very much political.[7] This

[3] Christine Bell, 'Introduction: Bargaining on Constitutions—Political Settlements and Constitutional State-Building', *Global Constitutionalism* 6:1 (2017): 13.

[4] Tom Ginsburg, *Judicial Review in New Democracies: Constitutional Courts in Asian Cases* (Cambridge University Press 2003); Ran Hirschl, *Towards Juristocracy: The Origins and Consequences of the New Constitutionalism* (Harvard University Press 2007); Rosalind Dixon and Tom Ginsburg, 'The Forms and Limits of Constitutions as Political Insurance', *International Journal of Constitutional Law* 15:4 (2017) 988.

[5] For two examples of political insurance readings of constitutional amendment rules, see Sergio Verdugo, 'The Fall of the Constitution's Political Insurance: How the Morales Regime Eliminated the Insurance of the 2009 Bolivian Constitution', *International Journal of Constitutional Law* 17:4 (2019) 1098; Dante Gatmaytan, 'Judicial Review of Constitutional Amendments: The Insurance Theory in Post-Marcos Philippines', *Philippine Law and Society Review* 1:1 (2011) 74.

[6] See Xenophon Contiades and Alkmene Fotiadou, 'Imposed Constitutions: Heteronomy and (Un)amendability' in Richard Albert, Xenophon Contiades, Alkmene Fotiadou, eds., *The Law and Legitimacy of Imposed Constitutions* (Routledge 2019) 15.

[7] On the preservative function of unamendable provisions, see Roznai (2017), 26–8. Roznai only briefly mentions the interplay between unamendability and political insurance theories and does not link it specifically to post-conflict settings.

insight will link to my arguments in Chapter 3, where I challenge the idea that eternity clauses are uncontested repositories of constitutional identity.

The chapter examines three types of eternity clauses in post-conflict constitutions, each performing a role *distinctive* to this context: signalling compliance with international norms through entrenched international human rights, ensuring alternation in power through unamendable executive term limits, and insulating elites through unamendable amnesties and immunities. On the basis of these examples, I make four broad propositions for why we should focus on unamendable provisions in post-conflict constitutions as a distinct category of analysis.[8] First, much if not most of constitution-making today takes place in post-conflict societies. It is therefore our responsibility to test and adjust (possibly rethink) our account of unamendability in order to address post-conflict constitutional engineering. Second, constitution building in post-conflict societies is inescapably a matter of political bargaining and compromise. Eternity clauses adopted in such conditions are key to the bargaining and are often necessary in order to ensure a political settlement is reached at all. Third, the political insurance thesis would seem to apply to drafter intent behind adopting eternity clauses in post-conflict constitutions. However, as elsewhere but with specific bearing in conflict-affected contexts, constitutional forms of insurance such as amendment rules and constitutional review will need to be supplemented by—and possibly even depend on—political forms of insurance.[9] Fourth, rather than the exception, eternity clauses containing contested or incoherent values represent a significant percentage of the unamendable provisions adopted today. The often diverging drivers of post-conflict constitutional design make this unavoidable: between signalling commitments to democracy, human rights, and the rule of law and protecting pre-constitutional bargains such as amnesties, immunities, or certain state characteristics, post-conflict unamendability emerges as a far messier and disjointed tool than typically understood. I conclude with a call for replacing our previously largely pacified notions of eternity clauses with a richer, more contextualized understanding of unamnedability, one that better captures the post-conflict settings in which they have become so appealing.

A note on terminology is important. I will refer interchangeably to 'post-conflict' and 'conflict-affected' societies in the coming discussion. By this

[8] I should note that I limit myself in this chapter to a discussion of *formal* unamendability, that is, to unamendable provisions formally incorporated in the constitutional text. This is in keeping with the chapter's focus on negotiations surrounding the adoption of the constitutional text at the time of constitution-making. A discussion of the emergence of judicial doctrines of unamendable constitutional amendment after adoption of a constitution, and especially in the absence of a formal eternity clause, raises somewhat different issues and is discussed in Chapter 4.

[9] Andrew Arato, *The Adventures of Constituent Power: Beyond Revolutions?* (Cambridge University Press 2017), 372. Arato gives electoral rules and bicameralism as examples of political forms of insurance.

I understand societies where a certain degree of violence, whether due to inter- or intra-state clashes, pre-dated and sometimes existed alongside constitution-building. There will invariably be some overlap with analysis of other contexts with deep societal divisions and challenges, notably deeply divided societies and post-authoritarian settings. The former refers to societies in which distinct groups exhibit competing visions of the state and are often differentiated along ethnic, national, or religious lines, divisions which remain politically salient over time.[10] In the case of polities emerging from authoritarianism, the emphasis is on regime change during which dividing lines tend to be between old elites and new political actors. Any definition of post-authoritarianism will inevitably run into the problems identified by 'transitology' literature, wherein it is difficult if not impossible to identify the start and end points of any transitional process, as it is to declare a given democracy consolidated.[11] That said, there will be conceptual overlaps: it often happens that deeply divided societies will also be conflict-affected when those divisions are enmeshed in violent conflict, or that transitions from authoritarianism similarly result in violence. The terminology employed in the chapter, however, retains the focus on conflict in an effort to highlight the specificities of societies grappling with constitution-building in its aftermath.

2.1 Post-conflict constitutions and eternity clauses: correcting core assumptions

The literature on constitutional design and constitution-building has an ambivalent view of post-conflict constitutions. While they have undoubtedly represented a great proportion of constitution-making processes in the past three decades, much of the literature in this field continues to view such documents as exceptional. Whether they adopt a methodology centred on 'prototype' models or even large-N studies, normative accounts of what newly drafted constitutions should contain too often ignore the specific complexities of constitution-making in post-conflict settings.[12] The literature on unamendable provisions is also often guilty of this: pride of place is given to core case studies such as Germany's *Ewigkeitsklausel*

[10] See Hanna Lerner, *Making Constitutions in Deeply Divided Societies* (Cambridge University Press 2011) 31; Sujit Choudhry, ed., *Constitutional Design for Divided Societies: Integration or Accommodation?* (Oxford University Press 2008), 5.

[11] On this, see Juan J. Linz and Alfred Stepan, *Problems of Democratic Transition and Consolidation: Southern Europe, South America, and Post-Communist Europe* (Johns Hopkins University Press, 1996), 3–7.

[12] For more on the different methodological approaches in comparative constitutional law, see Ran Hirschl, *Comparative Matters: The Renaissance of Comparative Constitutional Law* (Oxford University Press 2014).

when it comes to formal unamendability, and to the Indian basic structure doctrine when it comes to judicially created unamendable constitutional amendment doctrines.[13]

My aim here is to indicate several needed correctives to this understanding of constitutions and the place of unamendability within them. It is not just a general call to caution when engaging in normative constitutional advice, as Mark Tushnet has already advised;[14] it is a specific call for contextual, informed, and, yes, careful engagement in analysis of post-conflict unamendability.

The prevalence of post-conflict constitution-making

The first of these has already been hinted at above and has to do with numbers. Statistics show that a great number of recent constitution-making efforts have occurred in conflict-affected settings, with one study counting as many as seventy-five constitutional reform processes taking place 'in the wake of armed conflict, unrest, or negotiated transition from authoritarianism to democracy between 1990 and 2015'.[15] An older study had counted nearly 200 constitutions 'drawn up in countries at risk of conflict, as part of peace processes and the adoption of multi-party political systems' between 1875 and 2003.[16] One study focusing on Africa found that virtually all constitutions on the continent had been rewritten since 1990, often precipitated by shifts to multipartyism or by conflict, whereas forty-four constitutions have been similarly rewritten in sub-Saharan Africa alone.[17] Moreover, despite a change in the nature of conflicts, with a decline of traditional inter-state and rise in intra-state conflicts, the impetus for constitution-building in their aftermath does not appear to be waning.[18] In short, post-conflict constitutions should be central to our analysis for the simple reasons that they form the majority of recent constitution-making instances and that they are not likely to go away.

[13] This is not to deny that both the German and the Indian constitutions could be viewed as post-conflict—the former being drafted under conditions of occupation after the Second World War and the latter after the experience of independence and violent partition. However, the examples discussed in this chapter highlight distinctive challenges of state-building and resolution of violent conflict occurring alongside constitution-making.

[14] Mark Tushnet, 'Some Skepticism about Normative Constitutional Advice', *William and Mary Law Review* 49:4 (2008) 1473.

[15] Inclusive Security, *How Women Influence Constitution Making after Conflict and Unrest* (2018), 1.

[16] Jennifer Widner, 'Constitution Writing and Conflict Resolution', *Round Table* 94:381 (2005) 503.

[17] Balghis Badri and Aili Mari Tripp, eds, *Women's Activism in Africa: Struggles for Rights and Representation* (Zed Books 2017), 19.

[18] International IDEA, *Constitution Building after Conflict: External Support to a Sovereign Process* (2011).

The dynamics of post-conflict constitution-making

Numbers do not provide the full justification for a turn to studying unamendability in post-conflict settings, however. The second needed corrective has to do with the conditions under which drafting takes place in conflict-affected contexts and the import of these conditions on the content of the final product. One observation has to do with sequencing: there is a widespread assumption, whether implied or explicit, that constitution-making neatly follows the end of violence and the peace process. The reality, however, is far messier. It does not neatly adhere to a sequence of ceasefire/peace agreement followed by interim/temporary arrangements and culminating in a permanent constitution. Instead, constitution-building increasingly happens alongside, and can be both supported or undermined by, processes of political pacting between elites and (often) military forces involved in the conflict.[19]

Moreover, the rise of interim constitutional arrangements has brought both opportunities and challenges—the chance for more time to deliberate and reach an agreement and to experiment with constitutional solutions, but also the risks of missing out on the window to reach a settlement and the danger of temporary arrangements becoming permanent.[20] That some of these interim constitutions themselves may include unamendable provisions—as arguably the 1993 interim South African constitution did in the form of constitutional principles that would need to be adhered to in the permanent constitution[21]—makes them even more worthy of serious study.

These dynamics are not just crucial for an understanding of the political context within which constitutions emerge. They will also have a direct impact on how constitutional actors behave and interpret the fundamental law. Evidence suggests that constitutional courts in post-conflict settings take seriously the peace-building function of the constitutions they are the guardians of, engage in purposive interpretation in their jurisprudence, and prioritize peace over other constitutional concerns when conflicts arise.[22] As we will see, this insight also bears out in the adjudication of post-conflict unamendability.

[19] International IDEA, *Sequencing Peace Agreements and Constitutions in the Political Settlement Process* (2016).

[20] On the rise of interim constitutional arrangements, see Charmaine Rodrigues, 'Letting off Steam: Interim Constitutions as a Safety Valve to the Pressure-Cooker of Transitions in Conflict-Affected States?', *Global Constitutionalism* 6:1 (2017) 33; International IDEA, *Interim Constitutions: Peacekeeping and Democracy-Building Tools* (2015); Andrew Arato, 'Multi-Track Constitutionalism beyond Carl Schmitt', *Constellations* 18:3 (2011) 324; and, generally, Andrew Arato, *Post Sovereign Constitution Making: Learning and Legitimacy* (Oxford University Press 2016).

[21] See Schedule 4, Constitution of the Republic of South Africa 1993. See also Certification of the Constitution of the Republic of South Africa, [1996] ZACC 26 for the South African Constitutional Court's decision on the permanent draft's compliance with these principles.

[22] Jenna Sapiano, 'Courting Peace: Judicial Review and Peace Jurisprudence', *Global Constitutionalism* 6:1 (2017) 131.

The internationalization of post-conflict constitution-making

A further observation is that constitution-making processes in general, and those in the aftermath of conflict in particular, have become internationalized. The case of Bosnia and Herzegovina, whose constitution was annexed to the 1995 Dayton Peace Agreement, was drafted outside the country, in English, and agreed upon by wartime leaders under the aegis of foreign powers, may be seen as an extreme example. Iraq's Constitution being drafted under military occupation may also be seen as an extreme, though by no means unique, case.[23] However, it is the rare constitution-building process in the past three decades that will not have seen involvement by or at least influence from international actors and international norms. To take only one more recent example, Tunisia's much-praised constitution-making was both supported and influenced by international actors. The United Nations offered financial support but also lobbied for changes to constitutional provisions on human rights or judicial independence.[24] The Venice Commission of the Council of Europe, at the request of the Tunisian government, reviewed a late draft of the constitution for its compliance with international human rights standards.[25]

This internationalization may widen the gulf between the formal and material constitutions, between the text and its political hinterland, insofar as drafters may be far removed from local realities.[26] What this means for our understanding of unamendable provisions is that they must be understood in light of this internationalization, rather than be assumed as creatures of a purely endogenous process. Scholars have begun paying attention to this interplay between national and transnational norms in the content and enforcement of eternity clauses, but more work remains to be done. Chapter 5 goes into further depth on the influence of transnational forces on both the content and the adjudication of unamendable constitutional norms.

Post-conflict constitution-making as state-building

A fourth observation is that in conflict-affected settings, as well as more broadly in the case of states transitioning to democracy, constitution-making will often

[23] Andrew Arato, *Constitution Making Under Occupation: The Politics of Imposed Revolution in Iraq* (Columbia University Press 2009). On other constitution-making processes under occupation, see Albert et al. (2019).

[24] *The UN Constitutional: A Newsletter on United Nations Constitutional Support* 2:spring/summer (2014) 16–17. See also Salma Besbes, 'L'ONU—Acteur du Processus Transitionnel en Tunisie', Tunisia in Transition: German–Arab Research Group, Working Paper (December 2013), 6.

[25] 'Opinion on the Final Draft Constitution of the Republic of Tunisia Adopted by the Venice Commission at its 96th Plenary Session (Venice, 11–12 October 2013)', CDL-AD(2013)032, 17 October 2013.

[26] Denis J. Galligan and Mila Versteeg, eds., *Social and Political Foundations of Constitutions* (Cambridge University Press 2013), 32.

be part of a broader, often contested, contentious state-building project.[27] In such settings, state capacity tends to be weak, with new institutions often taking some time to be set up (if they ever are) and even longer to become fully functional. An infamous example is Cameroon's 1996 constitution, where until recently twenty-four of sixty-nine constitutional provisions—including on the creation of a Constitutional Council and Senate—had remained unimplemented.[28] Another is Somalia's, where political, social, and territorial fragmentation and decentralization raised doubts about the prospects not just of constitutionalism, but of statehood itself, at least in its western understanding.[29] Libya's constitution-making process, expected to play a unifying role, was similarly plagued by sociopolitical rifts that undermined both constitution- and state-building.[30] While constitutional scholars may warn that state-building must precede constitution-building if constitutions are to be effective, this often does not happen in conflict-affected contexts.[31] State weakness is also not black and white, as some states may display weakness in some areas but not in others.[32] Tunisia's much-lauded 2014 constitution envisioned the creation of a constitutional court to act as its guardian, but disagreement over judicial appointments has meant that, as of the time of writing, the court was still not operational.[33]

Constitution-making in such contexts therefore is not just a technical exercise, aimed at establishing and fine-tuning state institutions and power; it also plays a foundational role 'by defining the political bond between the people and embedding state institutions in society'.[34] Post-conflict constitutions also frequently struggle to perform a traditional power-structuring role alongside providing recognition of competing identities and playing the role of default peace

[27] Joanne Wallis, *Constitution Making during State Building* (Cambridge University Press 2014); Kristi Samuels, 'Post-Conflict Peace-Building and Constitution-Making', *Chicago Journal of International Law* 6:2 (2006) 663.

[28] Charles Manga Fombad, 'Problematising the Issue of Constitutional Implementation in Africa' in Charles Manga Fombad, ed., *The Implementation of Modern African Constitutions: Challenges and Prospects* (University of Pretoria Press 2016) 10, 13–4.

[29] Hatem Elliesie, 'Statehood and Constitution-Building in Somalia: Islamic Responses to a Failed State' in Rainer Grote and Tilmann Röder, eds., *Constitutionalism in Islamic Countries: Between Upheaval and Continuity* (Oxford University Press 2012) 553.

[30] Felix-Anselm van Lier, 'Constitution-Making as a Tool for State-Building? Insights from an Ethnographic Analysis of the Libyan Constitution-Making Process', Max Planck Institute for Social Anthropology Working Paper No. 192, 2018.

[31] Ernst-Wolfgang Böckenförde, *Constitutional and Political Theory: Selected Writings* (Mirjam Künkler and Tine Stein eds., Oxford University Press 2017), 148. Böckenförde argues that 'the constituent power of the people cannot be activated unless a people can be identified as a tangible political entity within an organized system of interactions, which means that a group of humans exists as a state people by virtue of definitive affiliation'. As Chapter 5 will further show, this understanding of constituent power is challenged by the reality of transnational constitution-making.

[32] Nimer Sultany, *Law and Revolution: Legitimacy and Constitutionalism After the Arab Spring* (Oxford University Press 2017), 79.

[33] This has meant that important legislation, including on reforming inheritance rules, transitional justice, and police use of force, could not be subject to constitutionality checks. See Daniel Brumberg and Maryam Ben Salem, 'Tunisia's Endless Transition?', *Journal of Democracy* 31:2 (2020) 110, 117.

[34] Wallis (2014), 2.

agreements.[35] This is complicated even further where the constitution is part of dual processes of state- and nation-building, as is not infrequent in post-conflict scenarios.[36] Thus, post-conflict constitutions will not infrequently be expected to 'reconstruct[] or even establish[] in the first place essential state functions'.[37]

This is doubly relevant for our study of eternity clauses. On the one hand, much of the literature on unamendability reads these provisions as insulating a purported original agreement surrounding core values of the constitution or features of the state, even going so far as to view them as repositories of constituent intent.[38] However, what we know about conflict-affected constitution-making processes reveals them to be messy, not always participatory, and often internationalized to the point of disempowering local actors. This has begun to shift in recent years, with the international community more aware of the need to engender national ownership over the new constitution and an emergent norm of popular participation in constitution-making.[39] Nevertheless, the fact remains that many eternity clauses we have on the books today have emerged from internationalized processes where the values enshrined therein were hardly negotiated locally. They may well acquire broad societal acceptance over time, but the conditions of their adoption should at least have us pause before ascribing such eternity clauses constituent intent in the sense of a unified, autochthonous will. More significantly still, these values may be deeply contested, in flux, or simply nascent. Expecting them to play an additional role as non-negotiable identifiers of a conflict-affected and often still deeply divided political community may backfire spectacularly.

On the other hand, the institutions directly responsible for enforcing eternity clauses are likely to be fragile and inexperienced in the first instance in performing this task (assuming they are set up to begin with). Samuel Issacharoff has cautioned that legislatures in new democracies may be distinctly weaker than their counterparts in consolidated democracies and as such less able to resolve fundamental contestations of power[40] and less inclined, or able, to push back against executive

[35] On constitutions needing to recognize and include a variety of voices and identities, see Vivien Hart, 'Constitution-Making and the Transformation of Conflict', *Peace & Change* 26:2 (2001) 153, 156. On the interplay between constitutions and peace agreements and constitutions *as* peace agreements, see Christine Bell, *On the Law of Peace: Peace Agreements and the Lex Pacificatoria* (Oxford University Press 2008), 19; Nathan Lace, 'The Real Deal? The Post-Conflict Constitution as a Peace Agreement', *Third World Quarterly* (2020) 1.

[36] Armin von Bogdandy, Stefan Häußler, Felix Hanschmann, and Raphael Utz, 'State-Building, Nation-Building, and Constitutional Politics in Post-Conflict Situations: Conceptual Clarifications and an Appraisal of Different Approaches', *Max Planck Yearbook of United Nations Law* 9 (2005) 579. See also contributions in the special issue entitled 'National Identity and Constitutionalism in Europe' in *Nations and Nationalism* 16:1 (2010).

[37] Von Bogdandy et al. (2005), 608.

[38] Roznai (2017) and Maria Cahill, 'Ever Closer Remoteness of the Peoples of Europe? Limits on the Power of Amendment and National Constituent Power', *Cambridge Law Journal* 75 (2016) 245.

[39] See discussion in Chapter 6 of this book.

[40] Samuel Issacharoff, 'Constitutional Courts and Democratic Hedging', *Georgetown Law Journal* 99 (2011) 961, 971.

encroachment.[41] The same is true for constitutional courts, 'created to be central actors in securing the democratic objectives of the transition in the long term', but also to enforce counter-majoritarianism.[42] How confrontational such courts will be will vary over time and space, but assuming that they would immediately upon creation be ready to step in and invalidate constitutional amendments may be to ignore the realities of new democracies.[43] Indeed, as Tunisia has shown, sometimes delays in setting up constitutional courts extend to years. These are among the reasons why some scholars have argued in favour of rethinking the push for courts with strong constitutional review powers in new democracies, viewing them as possibly resulting in 'unnecessary pressures and strains in an already difficult context'.[44]

Finally, we should not overstate the importance of unamendability during constitutional negotiations. Amendment rules in general are seen by some as the most important part of a constitution and its gatekeepers,[45] but this rarely reflects the priorities of constitutional drafters, certainly in conflict-affected settings. The magnitude of the task of rebuilding the state alongside crafting a new constitution will mean the focus of constitutional bargaining will more likely be on political institutional design, managing territorial divisions, distributing access to resources, etc., all while seeking to reconcile internal and external expectations. We should therefore not overestimate the attention paid to eternity clauses, even where their content is potentially hugely consequential. For example, the unamendable commitment to Islam in Afghanistan's constitution caused early condemnation and fears that the country was on its way to becoming a theocracy. However, accounts of the debates surrounding this drafting choice reveal that 'no one really focused on the juristic consequences of the proposed Islamic republic and what it might mean for the judiciary and the legal system'.[46] Instead, a constitutionalized Islamic republic was seen by its proponents as a political gesture meant to appeal to public sentiment.[47]

41 Samuel Issacharoff, *Fragile Democracies: Contested Power in the Era of Constitutional Courts* (Cambridge University Press 2015), 192.

42 Ibid., 138 and 276.

43 Thus, despite his careful analysis, Issacharoff remains favourably predisposed to the role courts may play in stabilizing new democracies. He has been faulted for case selection bias on this account, insofar as his case studies highlighted instances where constitutional review *did* make a difference, as opposed to others where it did not. See Aziz Z. Huq, Tom Ginsburg, and Mila Versteeg, 'The Coming Demise of Liberal Constitutionalism?', *University of Chicago Law Review* 85:2 (2018) 239, 254.

44 Stephen Gardbaum, 'Are Strong Constitutional Courts Always a Good Thing for New Democracies?', *Columbia Journal of Transnational Law* 53 (2015) 285, 289–90. Gardbaum instead argues in favour of consolidating judicial independence in such settings, together with 'weak' powers of judicial review (falling short of legislative strike-down powers). For a partially contrary view, see Wojciech Sadruski, *Poland's Constitutional Breakdown* (Oxford University Press 2019), 86–8.

45 Richard Albert, *Constitutional Amendments: Making, Breaking, and Changing Constitutions* (Oxford University Press 2019), 2.

46 Mohammad Hashim Kamali, 'References to Islam and Women in the Afghan Constitution', *Arab Law Quarterly* 22 (2008) 270, 283.

47 Ibid.

Post-conflict constitutional incoherence

A fifth observation has to do with the assumption that the resulting constitution represents a coherent document and serves the same purposes as in other settings—that is, primarily to create the power map of governance institutions and stipulate the fundamental rights and obligations of individuals. Within such constitutions, eternity clauses are assumed to play an important ordering function: they indicate a hierarchy of constitutional norms that can then structure and guide constitutional interpretation.[48] However, post-conflict constitutions are often patchworks, may be incoherent and their drafting and subsequent implementation are likely to suffer due to weak institutional capacity in the state.[49] The Bosnian constitution's unamendable commitments to international human rights and a discriminatory power-sharing institutional set-up that excludes rights of political participation to whole groups is an example of such incoherence. Crucially, these contradictions are *internal to* the constitution itself, and can only be explained on the basis of the difficult compromises at the time of constitution-making. While they are *also* tasked with designing a system of power and governance, the social and political context within which post-conflict constitutions are negotiated thus trump assumptions that constitution-making is an act of wholly rational design.[50] As will be seen, this should also temper our expectations of eternity clauses in conflict-affected settings.

Constitutions generally, and post-conflict ones even more severely, are not purist documents but the product of hard-fought political bargains that are reflected in their provisions. This does not just amount to the rather obvious observation that law and politics are mixed at the time of drafting. It carries real implications in post-conflict settings that would not normally be on the agenda otherwise. A good illustration of this is the rise of the constitutionalization of immunities and amnesties—a concern that would simply not be present in fundamental texts drafted under conditions of relative social peace and stability but which are key bargaining tools in conflict-affected situations.[51] But even beyond such provisions, the role eternity clauses play in post-conflict constitutions is distinctive. As I have argued elsewhere, post-conflict eternity clauses are themselves an instrument of political negotiation and conflict resolution and often embody the core of the political bargain that facilitated the adoption of the entire constitution.[52] In other words,

[48] Albert (2010), 683–4.

[49] Donald L. Horowitz, 'Conciliatory Institutions and Constitutional Processes in Post-Conflict States', *William and Mary Law Review* 49:4 (2008) 1213, 1227–30.

[50] Heinz Klug, 'Constitution Making and Social Transformation' in David Landau and Hanna Lerner, eds., *Comparative Constitution Making* (Edward Elgar 2019) 47.

[51] Roznai's classification of such provisions as 'reconciliatory' is somewhat simplistic. It misses the link to political insurance understandings of constitutions and to the specific role played by amnesties and immunities in post-conflict constitution-making (Roznai (2017) 35).

[52] Suteu (2017b).

drafters will often adopt an unamendable provision to seal the non-negotiables of a political deal without which the constitution would simply not have been adopted. In this sense, then, unamendability after conflict takes on a far more pragmatic, instrumental quality than the literature has ascribed it.

2.2 Unamendability after conflict: signalling compliance, political insurance, insulating elites

To argue that unamendability functions differently in post-conflict settings is not to say that the content of eternity clauses in such contexts is necessarily different to that of such provisions elsewhere. This may happen, as the amnesties/immunities example above has already alluded to. But it also happens that post-conflict unamendability looks very similar to eternity clauses in contexts unaffected by violent conflict and serves to signal, internally but crucially, also externally, that the drafters are committed to respecting key aspects of constitutionalism and rights protection. What are likely to be different, however, are the conditions under which such clauses have come about—of deep division overcome via the constitution as a fragile political settlement—and under which they are bound to be given effect—weak institutions, likely including weak, inexperienced and/or politicized constitutional courts. In instances where the balance of power during constitutional negotiations was skewed, such as where the conflict resulted in clear winners without incentives to compromise, it is also possible to find unamendable provisions that more overtly insulate the concerns of the winning side.

Signalling compliance: unamendable human rights commitments

Eternity clauses in new democratic constitutions, especially those forged in the aftermath of conflict, may perform a signalling role. They indicate to the international community as well as domestically that the new polity is committed to good behaviour in accordance with international norms. The foremost example of eternity clauses serving a signalling role are those protecting fundamental rights, whether in their entirety, a baseline of rights protection, or else specific individual rights. Such clauses are widespread in the constitutions of new democracies, and post-conflict constitutions are no exception.[53] The differences in their drafting

[53] For examples, see constitutions of Algeria (Article 212(5)), Angola (Article 236(e)), Brazil (Article 60(4)(IV)), the Central African Republic (Article 153), Chad (Article 227), the Democratic Republic of Congo (Article 220), Guatemala (Article 140 rendered unamendable by Article 281), Kosovo (Article 144(3)), Moldova (Article 142(2)), Morocco (Article 175), Mozambique (Article 292(1)(d)), Namibia (Article 131), Portugal (Article 288(d)), Qatar (Article 146), Romania (Article 152(2)), Russia (Article

are not accidental, however, and serve different purposes. For example, the constitution of Timor-Leste refers to an unamendable duty to 'respect' rights (Article 156(1)(b)), whereas the constitution of Kosovo seeks to prevent the diminishing of rights protection (Articles 113(9) and 144(3)) and Afghanistan's similarly allows only amendments that will improve fundamental rights (Article 149).

Religious supremacy clauses

The signalling role played by eternity clauses in the post-conflict constitutions must be understood contextually, however. In some instances, other constitutional provisions are at first glance in tension with these rights- and democracy-protecting clauses. Afghanistan's constitution is a case in point, insofar as its rights-protecting eternity clause coexists with equally unamendable commitments to Islam as the official religion and as the source of law. In fact, studies have shown that the incidence of Islamic supremacy clauses actually goes up during periods of democratization, alongside more expansive rights catalogues.[54] The result of uneasy compromises, such provisions are to be found elsewhere in constitutions resulting from hard-fought political bargains during transitions to democracy.[55] In other instances, a post-conflict eternity clause may go so far as to render the country's entire international human rights commitments unamendable. As the examples of Bosnia and Herzegovina and Kosovo below show, this type of clause adds a supranational dimension to the adjudication of unamendability that may itself cause contestation. Both of these scenarios merit more in-depth exploration.

Article 149 of the Afghan Constitution only allows amendments to fundamental rights 'in order to make them more effective'. Such 'non-regression' or 'standstill' clauses[56] are not uncommon and may be seen as aiming to entrench a minimum standard of rights protection rather than as rendering rights and freedoms untouchable. Germany's Article 79(3) may also be seen in this light, with the German Constitutional Court having interpreted it as prohibiting 'a fundamental abandonment of the principles mentioned therein' rather than their amendment *tout court*.[57]

What the Afghan example also illustrates, however, is the potential contradictions within a post-conflict constitution that sought to balance 'outside actors'

135(1)), Sao Tome and Principe (Article 154(d)), Somalia (Article 132(1)), Tunisia (Article 49), Turkey (Article 2 rendered unamendable by Article 4), and Ukraine (Article 157).

[54] Dawood I. Ahmed and Tom Ginsburg, 'Constitutional Islamization and Human Rights: The Surprising Origin and Spread of Islamic Supremacy in Constitutions', *Virginia Journal of International Law* 54:3 (2013) 615.

[55] See Suteu (2017b).

[56] Nina-Louisa Arold Lorenz, Xavier Groussot, and Gunnar Thor Petursson, *The European Human Rights Culture—A Paradox of Human Rights Protection in Europe?* (Martinus Nijhoff 2013), 209.

[57] The *Klass* case (30 BVerfGE 1, 24 (1970)), cited in 'Final Draft Report: On Constitutional Amendment Procedures', European Commission for Democracy through Law (Venice Commission), CDL(2009)168, 4 December 2009, fn. 161.

demands for the acceptance of international standards with the demands of domestic actors, notably Islamist politicians and the *ulama*, for a constitution that conforms to their understanding of Islam and empowers Islamic elites'.[58] This tension is made apparent when considering the coexistence of the unamendable commitment to a baseline of rights protection, as well as other constitutional provisions on compliance with Afghanistan's international human rights law commitments, with Article 149(1) of the fundamental law. The latter stipulates that 'the principles of adherence to the tenets of the Holy religion of Islam as well as Islamic Republicanism' are unamendable. It is to be read in conjunction with Article 2, which declares Islam the state religion (while also stipulating the rights of followers of other faiths) and with Article 3, which bans laws that contravene 'the tenets and provisions of the holy religion of Islam'. The text obscures the intense negotiations that led to the passing of these provisions. The international community's red lines were balanced against domestic actors seeking to inscribe their own understanding of the state onto the constitution; all of this within the context of a constitutional tradition that had long recognized not just Islam, but Hanafi jurisprudence specifically.[59] While the constitution retained a mention of Hanafi jurisprudence as stepping in to fill any gap in the text or other laws (Article 130), the more general wording of Article 2 together with mentions of Shia Muslims elsewhere have been read as an opening in the Afghan text towards a less restrictive understanding of sharia.[60]

Ran Hirschl has nominated Afghanistan, whose constitution he views as enshrining a 'mixed system of religious law and general legal principles', as a prominent example of what he has termed 'the theocratic challenge to constitution drafting in post-conflict states'.[61] Constitutional theocracy, according to Hirschl, challenges key components of constitutionalism, including the separation of powers and power-sharing agreements.[62] His account must be supplemented and, where relevant corrected, by more contextualized understandings of supremacy clauses that show them to be democratically popular, the result of political bargains, and in some instances a more liberal choice than the alternative repugnancy clauses.[63]

[58] Barnett R. Rubin, 'Crafting a Constitution for Afghanistan', *Journal of Democracy* 15:3 (2004) 5, 13–4.

[59] See Article 2 of the 1964 Afghan Constitution, which had stated: 'Islam is the sacred religion of Afghanistan. Religious rites performed by the State shall be according to the provisions of the Hanafi doctrine.'

[60] Rubin (2004), 14. See also Said Mahmoudi, 'The *Shari'a* in the New Afghan Constitution: Contradiction or Compliment?', *Zeitschrift für ausländisches öffentliches Recht und Völkerrecht* 64 (2004) 867.

[61] Ran Hirschl, 'The Theocratic Challenge to Constitution Drafting in Post-Conflict States', *William and Mary Law Review* 49:4 (2008) 1179, 1195.

[62] See generally Ran Hirschl, *Constitutional Theocracy* (Harvard University Press 2010).

[63] Whereas supremacy clauses declare Islam 'a' or even 'the' source of law, repugnancy clauses declare void any laws incompatible with Islam. See Ahmed and Ginsburg (2013), 621.

The added layer of rendering such commitments unamendable complicates the analysis. As the Afghan example demonstrates, it is not just that religion remains at the heart of the constitution—the tension between the unamendable commitment to Islam and other commitments, notably to individual rights and international legal obligations, unavoidably empowers the Supreme Court as final arbiter.[64] It has been argued that, given the dominance of *ulama* on the Afghan Supreme Court, this displacement of authority may have been a miscalculation on the part of secular forces. We may compare this to the unamendable recognition of Islam as the state religion in Tunisia, also a choice whose true consequences will only become apparent once the Tunisian Constitutional Court is operational and opines on the matter.[65] The stakes in balancing unamendable Islam and rights commitments therefore shift from the drafting of the eternity clause to the design of constitutional courts and other bodies tasked with constitutional interpretation.[66]

Non-regression clauses

What of unamendable rights guarantees elsewhere, however? Surely an eternity clause seeking to prevent rights regression or elimination would be less subject to contestation. And surely when those protections extend to international human rights norms, the scope of contestation would be even lesser.[67] The devil, as always, is in the details.

If we look at Kosovo's eternity clause, we find it is meant to prevent the diminishment of any of the rights and freedoms in Chapter II of the constitution—a section containing no fewer than thirty-five articles and covering a vast array of protections. This provision, in conjunction with the two-thirds majority rule and veto powers over amendments granted to ethnic communities, form structural elements meant to ensure a certain rigidity of Kosovo's consociational post-conflict constitution.[68] Moreover, Article 113(3)(4) adds a supranational layer insofar as it tasks the Constitutional Court to review the compatibility of proposed amendments with binding international agreements. This extends to a list of eight named international human rights instruments (Article 22) and incorporates a duty to interpret human rights guarantees consistently with decisions of the European Court of Human Rights (ECtHR) (Article 53).

64 See also Ramin S. Moschtaghi, 'Constitutionalism in an Islamic Republic: The Principles of the Afghan Constitution and the Conflicts between Them' in Rainer Grote and Tilmann Röder, eds., *Constitutionalism in Islamic Countries: Between Upheaval and Continuity* (Oxford University Press 2012) 683.

65 Suteu (2017b), 82.

66 Ahmed and Ginsburg (2013), 695.

67 On this, see Rosalind Dixon and David Landau, 'Transnational Constitutionalism and a Limited Doctrine of Unconstitutional Constitutional Amendment', *International Journal of Constitutional Law* 13:3 (2015) 606.

68 Fisnik Korenica and Dren Doli, 'The Politics of Constitutional Design in Divided Societies: The Case of Kosovo', *Croatian Yearbook of European Law and Policy* 6:6 (2010) 265.

It has been argued that the constitutionalization of these treaties was meant to mitigate the uncertain international status of Kosovo, the latter of which would mean it could not (at least initially) directly become party to these treaties.[69] When Kosovo's Constitutional Court was called upon to review a package of twenty-two amendments in 2012, whose aim was to ensure the country's transition from international supervised independence, the court also had to rule on their compatibility with the eternity clause.[70] The court found only one of the proposed amendments, which had sought to remove the guarantee of the freedom of movement and the right to property of refugees and internally displaced persons, to diminish the rights guarantees in Chapter II and as such to be invalid.[71]

Article X(2) of the Constitution of Bosnia and Herzegovina also protects rights via a transnational referent as defined by institutions beyond the state. Article II lists both individual rights and incorporates international human rights obligations directly into domestic law, granting them precedence. The constitution entrenches both individual and collective rights (the latter pertaining both to 'peoples' and to the federal 'entities'), without clarifying the hierarchy between them, and unhelpfully does not clearly delineate the limitations on or exhaustively list remedies for these rights either.[72] Article II(2) not only makes the European Convention on Human Rights and its Protocols directly applicable and the superior law of the land, but was adopted seven years before the country had even become a member of the Council of Europe.[73] Even more astonishing, the provision appears to have incorporated treaties which had not entered into force for any other country, such as the 1994 Framework Convention for the Protection of Minorities and the 1992 European Charter for Regional and Minority Languages.[74] Moreover, the Bosnian Constitution instituted a complex web of institutions tasked with human rights protection, among which: a constitutional court with mixed international and domestic membership; the Human Rights Commission staffed with a majority of international members; and the Office of the High Representative, tasked with overseeing the civilian implementation of the Dayton Agreement. Some of these

[69] Visar Morina, Fisnik Korenica and Dren Doli, 'The Relationship between International Law and National Law in the Case of Kosovo: A Constitutional Perspective', *International Journal of Constitutional Law* 9:1 (2011) 274, 295.

[70] Case K038/12 Assessment of the Government's Proposals for Amendments of the Constitution submitted by the President of the Assembly of the Republic on 12 April 2012, 15 May 2012.

[71] Ibid., paras. 80–93.

[72] David Feldman, 'The Nature and Effects of Constitutional Rights in Post-conflict Bosnia and Herzegovina' in Colin Harvey and Alex Schwartz, eds., *Rights in Divided Societies* (Hart 2012) 151.

[73] Donna Gomien, 'Human Rights in Bosnia and Herzegovina: European Practice, Fraught Federalism and the Future' in Wolfgang Benedek, ed., *Human Rights in Bosnia and Herzegovina after Dayton: From Theory to Practice* (Kluwer Law International 1999) 107, 109. One commentator has referred to this choice as 'smuggling' the Convention into the legal system. Zoran Pajic, 'A Critical Appraisal of Human Rights Provisions of the Dayton Constitution of Bosnia and Herzegovina', *Human Rights Quarterly* 20:1 (1998) 125, 131.

[74] See Gomien (1999), 107–8.

institutions found themselves with overlapping jurisdictions.[75] Added onto this would be the Council of Europe apparatus once Bosnia became a member.

Christine Bell has explained this structure as part of a state-building project driven by the international community. She describes human rights protections in the Bosnian Constitution as meant to 'take the sting out of the sovereignty issue' and institutions tasked with their implementation as 'aim[ing] not merely to police the division between law and politics found in the polity, as in the classic liberal-democratic state, but also *create* the polity by mediating communal divisions'.[76] The central Bosnian state was designed to be weak as compared to the federal entities, except in the realm of human rights protections. Bell referred to the multiple human rights institutions created as a way for the international community to try to 'claw back the unitary state from the separate Entities to which it devolves power', to 'revers[e] the ethnic cleansing which resulted in the Entity division' and to 'give the international community an ongoing role in implementation'.[77] This continuing role for international actors was downplayed before the general public.[78] How to balance the implementation of human rights protections against the entrenchment of territorial devolution along ethnic lines was not straightforward but was seen as an inevitable consequence of the 'compromise between opposing demands of separation and sharing' at the heart of Bosnia's constitution.[79]

These tensions in the constitution came to the fore in dramatic fashion in two 2006 cases contesting the very foundations of the polity. One, decided by the country's Constitutional Court, concerned an appeal by the Party for Bosnia and Herzegovina and Mr Ilijaz Pilav, the latter having been denied inclusion on the candidacy list for the presidency and the House of Peoples as a Bosniak living in the territory of Republica Srpksa.[80] The other, the now famous case of *Sejdić and Finci*, concerned a challenge brought before the ECtHR by two applicants, one a Bosnian Roma and one a Bosnian Jew, claiming that the constitutional provision restricting the office of the tripartite presidency only to members of ethnically Bosniak, Croat, and Serb communities was discriminatory.[81] While neither of these cases involve direct challenges to the constitution's Article X(2), they are nevertheless significant. They demonstrate the tension between the basic law's consociational regime and human rights principles which the constitution also enshrines, not least via the eternity clause. Moreover, these cases also illustrate the fraught relationship

[75] Examples are the Human Rights Commission and the Refugee Property Commission with competing jurisdictions over property restitution. Gomien (1999), 110.

[76] Christine Bell, *Peace Agreements and Human Rights* (Oxford University Press 2003), 199.

[77] Ibid., 196. See also Gomien (1999), 112, discussing how the federal structure allowed authorities to claim that responsibility for human rights violations was to be attributed to each federal unit rather than the state as a whole.

[78] Pajic (1998), 127.

[79] Bell (2003), 196.

[80] Constitutional Court of Bosnia and Herzegovina, Case No. AP-2678/06, 29 September 2006.

[81] *Sejdić and Finci v. Bosnia and Herzegovina*, Application Nos. 27996/06 and 34836/06, 22 December 2009.

between at least two custodians of this constitution: the Constitutional Court and the ECtHR. The cases indicate that the unamendable provision does not help resolve the question of ultimate authority over rights protection in the Bosnian Constitution and as such complicates rather than sheds light on constitutional hierarchy.

The national case involved a direct challenge to Article V of the constitution, which indicates that the tripartite presidency of the country includes 'one Bosniac and one Croat, each directly elected from the territory of the Federation, and one Serb directly elected from the territory of the Republika Srpska', together with Article 8(1) paragraph 2 of the Electoral Law of Bosnia and Herzegovina, which also stipulates that 'one Serb shall be elected by voters registered to vote in the Republika Srpska'. Mr Pilav's case had been dismissed on the grounds that it clearly contravened these provisions.[82] In his appeal, he contended that the decision had been exclusively based on ethnic/national origin and had amounted to a violation of Article 1 of Protocol No. 12 to the European Convention on European Rights. He further invoked Article II(2) as grounds to view the Protocol, as well as other international human rights instruments guaranteeing political rights of participation, as being at least equivalent to Article V.

The Constitutional Court reiterated the margin of appreciation left by the ECtHR in this area and acknowledged that the provisions in question in the case restricted Mr Pilav's rights. It nevertheless found these restrictions justifiable in the context of the country: 'Taking into account the current situation in Bosnia and Herzegovina, the restriction ... is justified at this moment since there is a reasonable justification for such treatment'.[83] Judge Feldman, concurring in the case, indicated the presence of special circumstances justifying otherwise impermissible discriminatory treatment and stated that 'the time has not yet arrived when the State will have completed its transition' away from them.[84] Judge Grewe, dissenting, disagreed on this point. She admitted that Bosnia's democratic transition was ongoing, but thought that 'the Dayton Agreement architecture is evolving and has to adapt to the different stages of evolution in BiH'.[85] She viewed the status quo as allowing an unfortunate combination of territorial and ethnic structures which de facto disenfranchised ethnic Bosniaks and Croats living in Republica Srpska and ethnic Serbs living elsewhere. This combination, she stated, was 'inconsistent with the Dayton Agreement's goal of a multi-ethnic State and with the principle of equality of constituent peoples in both entities'.[86] The only available means of remedy was to exclude the territorial criterion from presidential elections. Finally, she invoked Articles II(2), II(3), and X(2) to find that the international human

[82] Decision No. Iž-15/06 of 10 August 2006.
[83] Case No. AP-2678/06, para. 22.
[84] Separate concurring opinion of Judge Feldman, Case No. AP-2678/06, para. 3.
[85] Separate dissenting opinion of Judge Constance Grewe, Case No. AP-2678/06.
[86] Ibid.

rights provisions under scrutiny had at least the same rank as Article V of the constitution. As such, and contrary to the view of Judge Feldman, Judge Grewe had no qualms about finding compliance with human rights and the European Convention to have priority over any other law.

The case is significant in two respects. The first has to do with the conflicting interpretations of the state of Bosnia's transition and to the role of the constitution within it. As the dispute between Judges Feldman and Grewe illustrates, even while agreeing that there was still work to be done, there remained reasonable disagreement as to whether this should continue to permit deviation from human rights standards of non-discrimination. The same question was answered very differently in the following case. The second important observation here, however, is that the status of international human rights instruments as included in the constitution and the Dayton Agreement remained controversial. The Constitutional Court had in previous decisions taken the position that the European Convention on Human Rights could not have superior status vis-à-vis the constitution. Because it had entered into force by virtue of the constitution, the court had held, the Convention's authority derived from the constitution.[87] Judge Grewe had dissented in those cases and again invoked Article X(2) as evidence of a hierarchy of norms which allowed the court to engage in the judicial review of conformity with the European Convention.[88] This would be another point upon which the ECtHR would reach a different conclusion.[89]

The case of *Sejdić and Finci* represents a turning point in the constitutional development of Bosnia and Herzegovina. The applicants invoked violations of Article 14 of the European Convention on Human Rights, Article 3 of Protocol No. 1 and Article 1 of Protocol No. 12 to the Convention on the grounds of their Roma and Jewish origins. The ECtHR found in their favour. With regard to admissibility, the court indicated the government's responsibility was incurred: 'leaving aside the question whether the respondent State could be held responsible for putting in place the contested constitutional provisions ... the Court considers that it could nevertheless be held responsible for maintaining them'.[90] The judgment then proceeded to analyse the compatibility of the impugned constitutional provisions with the Convention. It left somewhat unresolved the question of whether they satisfied the legitimate aim requirement. The court found that the conditions of drafting might justify the exclusionary definition of 'constituent peoples' but argued that either way the provisions in question were not proportionate to this aim.[91]

[87] Constitutional Court of Bosnia and Herzegovina, Case No. U-5/04 (2006), 31 March 2006. See also Constitutional Court of Bosnia and Herzegovina, Case No. U-13/05 (2006), 26 May 2006, in which the court reiterated this view and refused to review a constitutional provision for conformity with the European Convention because the latter did not enjoy superior legal status.

[88] Separate Dissenting Opinion of Judge Constance Grewe, Case No. U-13/05 (2006).

[89] *Pilav* v. *Bosnia and Herzegovina*, Application No. 41939/07, 9 June 2016.

[90] *Sejdić and Finci*, para. 30.

[91] Ibid., para. 45.

The most controversial aspect was the court's assessment of whether the time was ripe to engage in constitutional reform so as to alleviate the discriminatory nature of institutional arrangements in the Bosnian Constitution. Contrary to the government's position that majoritarian rule remained dangerous in a country where mono-ethnic parties continued to dominate politics,[92] the court emphasized the positive developments in the country since Dayton.[93] It relied on the analysis of the Venice Commission to hold that there existed alternative power-sharing mechanisms which would not totally exclude members of other ethnic communities and which would reach the same ends.[94] The Venice Commission recommendations in question were quite detailed.[95] This coupled with the fact that the Bosnian Constitution had been successfully amended on one prior occasion apparently convinced the court that constitutional change was possible in Bosnia.

While the majority remained silent on whether reaching such a conclusion was within its remit at all, the dissenting judges in the case were more vocal. Judges Mijović and Hajyev, partly dissenting, wondered:

> Are the special constitutional arrangements in Bosnia and Herzegovina still deemed necessary and can the current situation still be justified, despite the passing of time? Is it up to the European Court of Human Rights to determine when the time for change has arrived?[96]

Judge Bonello, dissenting, was even more intransigent in his opinion. He found the majority judgment to have completely divorced the country 'from the realities of its own recent past' and to have disrupted the delicate Dayton Agreement.[97] He found the ECtHR to have behaved 'as the uninvited guest in peacekeeping multilateral exercises and treaties that have already been signed, ratified and executed'.[98] Moreover, Judge Bonello questioned whether the court's far-reaching powers also extended to

> undoing an international treaty, all the more so if that treaty was engineered by States and international bodies, some of which are neither signatories to the Convention nor defendants before the Court in this case? More specifically, does the Court have jurisdiction, by way of granting relief, to subvert the sovereign action of the European Union and of the United States of America, who together

[92] Ibid., para. 34.

[93] Ibid., para. 47.

[94] Ibid., para. 48.

[95] With respect to presidency reform, for instance, the Commission called for the concentration of all executive power in the Council of Ministers (a collegiate body already exercising some executive functions) and for the indirect election of a single president based on a wide majority and with rules for rotation of his/her ethnic affiliation. See *Sejdić and Finci*, para. 22

[96] Partly Concurring and Partly Dissenting Opinion of Judge Mijović, Joined by Judge Hajiyev, *Sejdić and Finci*, 49–50.

[97] Dissenting Opinion of Judge Bonello, *Sejdić and Finci*, 52.

[98] Ibid., 52–3.

> fathered the Dayton Peace Accords, of which the Bosnia and Herzegovina Constitution—impugned before the Court—is a mere annex?[99]

He admitted that 'the whole structure of the Convention is based on a primordial sovereignty of human rights' but found the values of equality and non-discrimination to be at least on equal footing with those of peace and reconciliation[100]. Instead, 'the Court has canonised the former and discounted the latter.'[101] Finally, Judge Bonello questioned the involvement of a court so remote from the situation in assessing whether to engage in constitutional overhaul or not. Instead, he argued, this would have been a case where judicial self-restraint should have ruled.[102]

The ECtHR's decision was surprising, even more so as it went against its own prior case law of restraint in reviewing consociational arrangements.[103] McCrudden and O'Leary explain the ECtHR's assertiveness as resulting from three factors: the growth of its anti-discrimination doctrine; the rise in criticism of consociational arrangements particularly by the Venice Commission; and the peculiarities of the Bosnian context, in particular its commitments to the Council of Europe and to the European Union.[104] They view the ECtHR as having seized the opportunity to trigger the transformation of Bosnia's consociational arrangements, seeing itself as 'supporting the emerging consensus that things had to change.'[105] Whether the court judgment is read restrictively in this sense, or more broadly as signifying the death knell of Bosnia's power-sharing agreement, it remains problematic. I agree with McCrudden and O'Leary that whichever of these interpretations one ascribes to, 'the key issues are when to make the changes, and how, and who has the legitimate authority to do so.'[106] In other words, the ECtHR saw its own assessment of whether and when the Bosnian Constitution was to be reformed as superior to that of the national government. It did so in disregard of the government's argument that the impact of such changes at the time would amount to the unravelling of the agreement upon which the constitution, and the state, were based.[107] Moreover, the court promoted as the alternative a civic model of constitutionalism,[108] as recommended by the Venice

[99] Ibid., 53.
[100] Ibid.
[101] Ibid.
[102] Ibid., 54.
[103] See *Cases relating to certain aspects of the laws on the use of languages in education in Belgium* [1968] ECHR 1474/62, 1 EHRR 252 (1968) and *Mathieu-Mohin* v. *Belgium* [1987] ECHR 9267/81, 10 EHRR (1988) 1. See also discussion in Christopher McCrudden and Brendan O'Leary, 'Courts and Consociations, or How Human Rights Courts May De-stabilize Power-Sharing Settlements', *European Journal of International Law* 24:2 (2013a) 477.
[104] Ibid., 490.
[105] Ibid.
[106] Ibid., 491.
[107] Ibid., 492.
[108] Begić and Delić refer to the court effectively calling upon Bosnian authorities to find a '"lucky" combination of civil and ethnic constitutional model' (Zlatan Begić and Zlatan Delić, 'Constituency of

Commission, which it presented as neutral by ignoring its practical consequences in Bosnia.[109]

Beyond such criticisms of individual decisions, however, the ineffectiveness of Bosnia's constitutional arrangements remains. Some have indeed argued that it has not been institutional arrangements as such which have stalled the country's democratic transition as much as its poor socio-economic situation.[110] In the words of Sumantra Bose, 'Bosnia is so fragile because of these factors, not because of some original sin visited on it in Dayton, Ohio in November 1995'.[111] Nevertheless, one cannot ignore the impact which the constitution has had in both ending the conflict and perpetuating instability in the country. If it is true that disagreement in Dayton was not so much over power-sharing as over whether the state should exist at all,[112] one wonders whether enough has changed in this respect in the decades since. Human rights provisions, including via an unamendable commitment to international human rights law, were adopted as core pillars of the delicate political settlement meant to sustain the state. There are echoes of Germany's constitutional beginnings when one reads arguments that Bosnia's settlement has never been seen as anything other than temporary.[113] However, unlike in Germany, the Bosnian polity remains embattled and 'visions of a post-power-sharing system among the parties are diametrically opposed and often reduce the incentives to render the existing institutional setup effective'.[114] Post-*Sejdić and Finci*, the need for constitutional reform remains stark but as elusive as ever.[115]

Political insurance: unamendable term limits

One of the clearest instances of eternity clauses adopted as political insurance are unamendable executive term limits. Such clauses are relatively frequently found in

Peoples in the Constitutional System of Bosnia and Herzegovina: Chasing fair Solutions', *International Journal of Constitutional Law* 11:2 (2013) 447, 465).

[109] To quote McCrudden and O'Leary again, one of those implications of the decision would be 'to move Bosnia decisively in the direction of the preferred Bosniak position, because a central element of most Bosniaks' politics is to move towards majoritarian democracy' (McCrudden and O'Leary (2013a), 494).

[110] Florian Bieber, 'The Balkans: The Promotion of Power-Sharing by Outsiders' in Joanne McEvoy and Brendan O'Leary, eds., *Power-Sharing in Deeply Divided Places* (University of Pennsylvania Press 2013) 312, 313.

[111] Sumantra Bose, 'The Bosnian State a Decade after Dayton', *International Peacekeeping* 12:3 (2005) 322, 330.

[112] Bieber (2013), 313.

[113] Ibid., 325.

[114] Ibid.

[115] See Valery Perry, 'Constitutional Reform Processes in Bosnia and Herzegovina' in Soeren Keil and Valery Perry, eds., *State-Building and Democratization in Bosnia and Herzegovina* (Routledge 2015) 15; Amra Bašić, '*Sejdić-Finci* and *Pilav*: Bosnia-Hercegovina's Road to Implementation of the European Convention on Human Rights', *Transnational Law & Contemporary Problems* 29:1 (2019) 569.

Latin American and African countries trying to overcome a history of executive overstay and coups.[116] The prevalence of term limits in these countries is no coincidence and can be explained on account of experience with coups and military rule. Some scholars have included these provisions among a wider category of eternity clauses which uphold the state's political structure by entrenching democracy, the sovereignty of the people, or the nature of elections.[117] While I do not dispute they are inherently linked to such general democratic commitments, I also believe there are aspects particular to the tool of executive term limits which make them worthy of a separate investigation. Unlike a general commitment to democracy, and similar to but still separate from commitments to *multiparty* democracy specifically, term limit unamendability is a direct response to past democratic failure by way of executive usurpation. Seeing it as an extreme version of bans on executive term extension therefore better explains why they have been adopted and the likelihood of their effectiveness.

Restrictions on executive terms of office are quite common in constitutions around the world, especially in presidential and semi-presidential systems.[118] The 22nd Amendment to the United States Constitution, Article 6 of the French Constitution, and Article 52 of the German Basic Law are examples of such clauses in three of the most influential fundamental laws. Limitations on the number and length of term limits have been found to be on the rise[119] and they have come to be called 'one of the defining features of democracy'.[120] These types of rules present obvious advantages, particularly in the long run: they ensure rotation of office, limit incumbent advantage in elections, and encourage political competition; conversely, they can be viewed as an illiberal constraint on citizens' choice, discouraging experienced governance, underestimating the potential disruptive role of ex-leaders, and are potentially abused.[121]

The literature on both unentrenched and entrenched term limits has also tackled the normative challenge they pose, as well as the question of their effectiveness. From a normative point of view, they have been said to create 'an unhappy dilemma' when a popular leader reaches the end of tenure but wishes to remain in power.[122] As Ginsburg et al. have put it, '[t]he resulting conflict is one between a

[116] Among these are: Algeria (Article 212), Burkina Faso (Article 165), the Central African Republic (Article 35), Egypt (Article 226), El Salvador (Article 248), Guatemala (Article 281), Honduras (Article 374), Mauritania (Article 99), Guinea (Article 154), Madagascar (Article 163), Niger (Article 175), Senegal (Article 103), and Tunisia (Article 48).

[117] Roznai (2017), 30–1.

[118] Gideon Maltz, 'The Case for Presidential Term Limits', *Journal of Democracy* 18:1 (2007) 128.

[119] Tom Ginsburg, James Melton, and Zachary Elkins, 'On the Evasion of Executive Term Limits', *William and Mary Law Review* 52 (2011) 1807, 1840.

[120] Maltz (2007), 129.

[121] Ginsburg et al. (2011), 1818–27.

[122] Tom Ginsburg, Zachary Elkins, and James Melton, 'Do Executive Term Limits Cause Constitutional Crises?' in Tom Ginsburg, ed., *Comparative Constitutional Design* (Cambridge University Press 2012) 350, 354. See also Ginsburg et al. (2011), 1830.

majority (or plurality) that yearns for "four [or five or six] more years" and a minority that demands the implementation of constitutional rules'.[123] The countermajoritarian rule, in other words, may end up being perceived as sacrificing short-term democratic choice for the system's long-term health.[124] Moreover, the constitutional crisis this unpopular trade-off may spark is especially damaging given the personalization of the conflict at its heart.[125] Executive term limits have also been criticized as an exceedingly blunt instrument which does not take into account external conditions.[126]

From the point of view of their effectiveness, term limits are also contested. They are suspected of inducing constitutional crisis, but also possibly increasing the likelihood of presidents overstaying in the future and degrading democracy as a whole.[127] However, empirical studies testing these assumptions have called term limits 'surprisingly effective in constraining executives from extending their terms, at least in democracies'.[128] Not entirely surprisingly, the same authors have found that, in democracies, the gap between constitutional rules on term limits and practice is narrower.[129] Moreover, the very bluntness of these rules may be linked to their successful enforcement.[130] To the counterargument that they may always be overcome via constitutional amendment, these authors put forth a theory of executive term restrictions as default rules—only effective as long as they are not amended out of the constitution (and thus not eternal after all).[131] These rules present an obstacle to executives extending their tenure, the argument goes, by raising its costs: 'Term limits . . . raise the degree of political support required for an executive to maintain office from the ordinary electoral majority baseline to the higher constitutional amendment threshold, which we may think of as a supermajority, although amendment provisions vary.'[132] In other words, they may be viewed as supermajoritarian rules rather than absolute prohibitions.

The same empirical studies, however, indicate that, while not 'associated with the death or disability of democracy', term limits may in some circumstances trigger early constitutional replacement.[133] This does not appear too bothersome to the authors, who see both term limits and their alternatives as imperfect instruments posing 'problems of calibration'.[134] As will be discussed below, however, the

[123] Ginsburg et al. (2011), 1830.
[124] Maltz (2007), 139, has termed this trade-off 'restricting the immediate power of the majority, but thereby preserving and facilitating genuine democracy'.
[125] Ginsburg et al. (2011), 1830.
[126] Ibid., 1829.
[127] See Ginsburg et al. (2012), 370.
[128] Ginsburg et al. (2011), 1814.
[129] Ibid., 1854.
[130] Ibid., 1868.
[131] Ibid., 1828.
[132] Ibid., 1828–9. See also Maltz (2007), 141.
[133] Ginsburg et al. (2011), 1814.
[134] Ibid., 1865.

consequences of constitutional crises involving (if not outright triggered by) executive term limits are potentially dire. When entrenched by way of an absolute prohibition, not to mention cases where the eternity clause itself is entrenched (and its trespass criminalized, as in Honduras), the 'raised costs' of attempts to extend executive tenure are higher.[135] The post-authoritarian context in which these eternity clauses almost invariably occur make these costs, up to and including constitutional replacement, not as easily written off as failures of calibration.

Two cases of constitutional crises surrounding attempts at overcoming executive term limits will be discussed. One of these, Honduras, is an especially pertinent case study as a country having an eternity clause entrenching the ban on executive term extension, but also having entrenched the eternity clause itself. Recent judicial developments in Honduras have yet again brought this issue to the fore. The other, Colombia, while not having a similarly unamendable provision in its constitution, saw its constitutional court come up with a judicial doctrine of constitutional replacement which prohibited the extension of the number of presidential terms to more than two. These are not the only cases of judicial enforcement of term limits,[136] but they serve to illustrate different aspects of this democratically problematic instrument.

Amending an unamendable term limit

In 2009, the Honduran President Manuel Zelaya sought to override an entrenched term limit despite waning support. His bid to organize a non-binding public consultation on holding a referendum on whether to set up a body tasked with changing the constitution was opposed by the judiciary, parliament, and the military. Despite his protestations to the contrary, many in the country saw this as Zelaya's attempt to override the one-term limit. This included the Constitutional Chamber of the Honduran Supreme Court, which held that the proposed referendum could not go ahead as it was in breach of the constitutional term limit. The constitutional crisis resulted in the president's forceful removal from office by the military and exile. A Supreme Court judge would justify this as nothing more than the military carrying out a lawful arrest warrant.[137] The prevailing view appears to be that,

[135] Although there are those who view the entrenchment of term limits, and the entrenchment of that entrenchment, as a positive step. See Maltz (2007), 141.

[136] Another example would be Niger, whose constitutional court invalidated a presidential attempt to hold a referendum on the extension of the maximum number of terms, finding that he could not do so in light of the country's eternity clause (Article 136). See AVIS No. 002/2009/CC of 25 May 2009. The president eventually went ahead with the referendum in spite of the decision and obtained an extension of his mandate by three years, as well as an increase in his powers which transformed the republic into a presidential system. Following a year-long constitutional crisis, the military staged a coup to remove him from power. See 'Military Coup Ousts Niger President Mamadou Tandja', *BBC News*, 19 February 2010, http://news.bbc.co.uk/1/hi/world/africa/8523196.stm.

[137] Joshua Goodman and Blake Schmidt, 'Honduras Supreme Court Judge Defends President Ouster (Update1)', *Bloomberg*, 1 July 2009, http://www.bloomberg.com/apps/news?pid=newsarchive&sid=axGENUiy9yKs.

while the methods employed were unfortunate, there was also a very real threat to democracy had plans to override the executive term ban gone ahead.[138] The role played by the eternity clause to this effect is more ambiguous.

Article 374 of Honduras's 1982 Constitution states:

> The foregoing article [the general amendment procedure], this article, the Articles of the Constitution relating to the form of government, national territory, the presidential term, the prohibition from reelection to the presidency of the republic, the citizen who has served as president under any title, and to persons who may not be president of the republic for the subsequent period may not be amended.

The extent of restrictions on the presidential office is noteworthy. The ban on presidential re-election after one term is compounded by additional constitutional provisions which attach severe penalties to its breach or attempted breach. Thus, Article 239 stipulates that a person who violates the ban on re-election or even advocates for its amendment will be disqualified from public office for ten years. Moreover, Article 42 mandates the loss of one's citizenship for 'inciting, promoting, or supporting the continuation or reelection' of the president. Honduras seems to have experimented with unamendable term limits from as early as its 1957 Constitution; although the rule had previously been derogated from, at the time of Zelaya's efforts an absolute ban on re-election and its proposed amendment had remained in force since 1982.[139]

Some commentators saw the term limit provision and its double entrenchment as the immediate cause for the 2009 Honduran crisis.[140] Others were careful to distinguish between the substantive prohibition on term limit extension and the 'second-order proscriptions on debate or proposal of amendments'.[141] The latter opined that, while some core issues may best be protected by taking them off the table, term limits 'do not seem so contentious as to prohibit all discussion of

[138] See Douglass Cassel, 'Honduras: Coup d'Etat in Constitutional Clothing?', *ASIL* 13:9 (2009); Mariana Llanos and Leiv Marsteintredet, 'Epilogue: The Breakdown of Zelaya's Presidency: Honduras in Comparative Perspective' in Mariana Llanos and Leiv Marsteintredet, eds., *Presidential Breakdowns in Latin America: Causes and Outcomes of Executive Instability in Developing Democracies* (Palgrave Macmillan 2010) 229; J. Mark Ruhl, 'Honduras Unravels', *Journal of Democracy* 21:2 (2010) 93; Frank M. Walsh, 'The Honduran Constitution Is Not a Suicide Pact: The Legality of Honduran President Manuel Zelaya's Removal', *Georgia Journal of International and Comparative Law*, 38 (2010) 339.

[139] Leiv Marsteintredet, 'The Honduran Supreme Court Renders Inapplicable Unamendable Constitutional Provisions', *I-CONnect Blog*, 2 May 2015, http://www.iconnectblog.com/2015/05/marsteintredet-on-honduras/.

[140] Albert (2010) 663, 692. He states: 'It was none other than this constitutional clause that pit the leading popular democratic institution in Honduras—the presidency—versus the other national democratic institutions, namely the legislature, courts, and leading independent bodies.'

[141] Tom Ginsburg, 'The Puzzle of Unamendable Provisions: Debate-Impairing Rules vs. Substantive Entrenchment', *I-CONnect Blog*, 13 August 2009, http://www.iconnectblog.com/2009/08/the-puzzle-of-unamendable-provisions-debate-impairing-rules-vs-substantive-entrenchment/.

them'.[142] Others still, placing Honduras in a wider Latin American context, saw Zelaya's bid as an effort at 'constitutional subterfuge': using the cover of legality to break down constitutional barriers to his re-election.[143] Few would have been able to predict the U-turn the Honduran court would make in a few short years.

In a decision on 22 April 2015, the Constitutional Chamber of the Honduran Supreme Court declared the ban on presidential re-election unconstitutional and effectively repealed Article 239.[144] It found the article to be in conflict with the freedoms of speech and thought; to unduly limit political participation and debates; to be contrary to international human rights obligations; and to have been relevant at an earlier time, but no longer because Honduras had stabilized its democracy. Moreover, the court relied on the recommendations of the truth commission set up by Zelaya's successor to clarify the events of 2009 and to make recommendations meant to prevent such crises.[145] The latter had found the actions of the military in ousting Zelaya to have been illegal and unjustifiable and called for comprehensive constitutional reform.

As David Landau has argued, the 2015 decision makes curious use of both the unconstitutional constitutional amendment doctrine and of arguments rooted in international human rights law.[146] The court had used the unconstitutional constitutional amendment doctrine to strike down not an amendment to the constitution, but a provision of the original text—amounting effectively to endorsing an 'unconstitutional constitution doctrine'.[147] Moreover, it had invoked international human rights, in particular freedom of expression, against their core purposes.[148] Finally, Landau posits, the court decision sealed the loss of an opportunity for wider constitutional reform in the aftermath of the 2009 coup by dealing with the term limit rule in isolation.[149] The court's interpretation of the supremacy of international law in Honduran law and of the content of relevant international human rights norms was, however shaky, and the consequences of its intervention—leaving the system

[142] Ibid.

[143] Forrest D. Colburn and Alberto Trejos, 'Democracy Undermined: Constitutional Subterfuge in Latin America', *Dissent* 57:3 (2010) 11.

[144] Supreme Court of Justice, Constitutional Chamber, Decision of 22 April 2015, http://www.poderjudicial.gob.hn/Documents/FalloSCONS23042015.pdf.

[145] Comisión de la Verdad y la Reconciliación (CVR), 'Hallazgos y recomendaciones Para que los hechos no se repitan', July 2011, https://www.oas.org/es/sap/docs/DSDME/2011/CVR/Honduras%20-%20Informe%20CVR%20-%20RECOMENDACIONES.pdf.

[146] David Landau, 'The Honduran Constitutional Chamber's Decision Erasing Presidential Term Limits: Abusive Constitutionalism by Judiciary?', *I-CONnect Blog*, 6 May 2015, http://www.iconnectblog.com/2015/05/the-honduran-constitutional-chambers-decision-erasing-presidential-term-limits-abusive-constitutionalism-by-judiciary/. See also David Landau, Rosalind Dixon, and Yaniv Roznai, 'From an Unconstitutional Constitutional Amendment to an Unconstitutional Constitution? Lessons from Honduras', *Global Constitutionalism* 8:1 (2019), 60–6.

[147] Landau et al. (2019). On the possibility of unconstitutional constitutions more generally, see Richard Albert, 'Four Unconstitutional Constitutions and their Democratic Foundations' 50:2 (2017) *Cornell International Law Journal* 169.

[148] Landau (2015).

[149] Ibid.

without any presidential term limit whatsoever, as well as invalidating a constitutional provision thirty years after its adoption—potentially dire.

Term limits and constitutional replacement

Colombia's Constitution does not contain an eternity clause; in fact, the text is comparatively easy to amend: a simple majority is required at first reading and an absolute majority at the second (Article 375). Article 197 does, however, limit the number of presidential terms in office. In 2005, the still-popular President Alvaro Uribe Velez steered the passing of a constitutional amendment allowing for his re-election—the constitution only mandating for a maximum of one term in office at that time. The Colombian Constitutional Court had been petitioned to find the amendment unconstitutional, both on procedural grounds and on substantive ones for violating the separation of powers, the principle of alternative exercise of political powers, and electoral equality.[150] The court rejected the arguments about the amendment's unconstitutionality.[151] It was to revisit the issue soon thereafter, when another amendment extending the executive term limit to three mandates was challenged before it.[152]

In both decisions, the court relied upon its previously expounded 'constitutional replacement' or 'substitution' doctrine.[153] The doctrine, first delineated in 2004, could initially be summarized thus: 'a constitutional amendment is a constitutional replacement if it replaces an element defining the identity of the constitution'.[154] (On the difficulties of distinguishing between such permissible amendment and impermissible replacement, see the corresponding discussion in Chapter 7.) The difficulties in operationalizing the 'identity element' to render it judicially useful, by defining the concept or providing criteria for its application, have been noted by the literature.[155] The court gave further contour to the doctrine by replacing the concept of an 'identity element' with that of an essential element and identifying seven steps in a constitutional replacement test.[156] Carlos Bernal has convincingly proven that several of these steps are problematic, either because they are ambiguous and create uncertainty, because they elide reasonable disagreement about constitutional fundamentals, or because they are simply circular.[157] Colombia's is

[150] See discussion in Carlos Bernal, 'Unconstitutional Constitutional Amendments in the Case Study of Colombia: An Analysis of the Justification and Meaning of the Constitutional Replacement Doctrine', *International Journal of Constitutional Law* 11:2 (2013) 339, 345.

[151] Sentencia C-1040/05, 19 October 2005.

[152] Sentencia C-141/10, 26 February 2010.

[153] For an analysis of the doctrine's history and elements, see Bernal (2013). See also Joel Colón-Ríos, 'Carl Schmitt and Constituent Power in Latin American Courts: The Cases of Venezuela and Colombia', *Constellations*, 18:3 (2011) 365, 372–6 and his *Weak Constitutionalism: Democratic Legitimacy and the Question of Constituent Power* (Routledge 2012), 134–8.

[154] Bernal (2013), 343. The judgment where the court first defined this doctrine was Sentencia C-970/04, 7 October 2004.

[155] Bernal (2013), 343.

[156] Ibid., 344.

[157] Ibid., 344–5.

thus yet another case where a court not originally empowered to do so developed a doctrine of substantive review of amendments.

In the second case, involving an extension from two to three executive terms, the Colombian Constitutional Court took great pains to explain that the circumstances of the case made such a change especially pernicious. The extended mandate would have allowed Uribe to appoint the leadership of virtually all institutions set up as a check on the presidency. Moreover, his incumbent advantage would only have grown over time. Thus, the court reasoned, the amendment in question would have amounted to a 'constitutional replacement' because Uribe's second re-election 'would create such a strong presidency as to weaken democratic institutions'.[158] In other words, the court did not analyse the constitutionality challenge before it in a vacuum, but took into account the impact on the constitutional system of the proposed amendment and deemed it too dangerous an affront to democracy. As such, David Landau has suggested, the court succeeded in preventing 'a serious erosion of democracy', even while this erosion may not have ended up amounting to a full slide to authoritarianism.[159] Colombia's hyper-presidential constitutional system, coupled with the ease of constitutional amendment, have also led Bernal to accept the 'constitutional replacement' doctrine in the specific context of the country.[160] This doctrine, he has argued, is but one of more innovative tools of control over the government which the court has had to devise in Colombia's distinct political landscape.[161]

From an empirical perspective, the story of term limit unamendability has recently been complicated by renewed efforts by presidents in both Latin America and Africa to change constitutional limits on their mandates.[162] What is perhaps surprising about these developments is that the constitutional term limits, even unamendable ones, did not make much difference in the face of determined executive actors. Nor did courts intervene to block these changes. As seen in several Latin American cases, courts have even argued that the term limits themselves are affronts to democracy.[163] Moreover, in three instances—Costa Rica, Nicaragua, and Honduras—the unconstitutional constitutional amendment doctrine was invoked by the incumbents themselves and deployed by the courts against term limits.[164]

[158] Landau (2013a), 203.
[159] Ibid.
[160] Bernal (2013), 352.
[161] Ibid.
[162] Micha Wiebush and Christina Murray, 'Presidential Term Limits and the African Union', *Journal of African Law* 63:1 (2019) 131; David Landau, 'Presidential Term Limits in Latin America: A Critical Analysis of the Migration of the Unconstitutional Constitutional Amendment Doctrine' *Law & Ethics of Human Rights* 12:2 (2018a) 225; Charles Manga Fombad and Enyinna Nwauche, 'Africa's Imperial Presidents: Immunity, Impunity and Accountability' *African Journal of Legal Studies* 5 (2012) 91; Cheryl Hendricks and Gabriel Ngah Kiven, 'Presidential Term Limits: Slippery Slope Back to Authoritarianism in Africa' *The Conversation*, 17 May 2018, https://theconversation.com/presidential-term-limits-slippery-slope-back-to-authoritarianism-in-africa-96796. See also discussion in Chapter 5.
[163] Landau (2018a).
[164] Ibid., 239.

Nor have these courts followed in the footsteps of the Colombian Constitutional Court to develop constitutional replacement doctrines that would act analogously to an unconstitutional constitutional amendment doctrine and block term limit suspension. In the case of Bolivia, for example, the Constitutional Court lifted the presidential term limit in spite of popular support for retaining it, expressed in a national referendum.[165] These examples challenge widespread expectations that courts, especially those in new democracies, will intervene to constrain political power.

Insulating elites: unamendable amnesties and immunities

The already mentioned unamendable immunities and amnesties are especially attractive in post-conflict settings. It is not just that they insulate past perpetrators of crimes from responsibility, but their constitutionalization—first seen in South Africa[166]—elevates the matter from the realm of ordinary to that of extraordinary politics. Once the cloak of unamendability is added, they become even more difficult to challenge.

Unamendable amnesties have been adopted in constitutions such as Niger's 2010 and Fiji's 2013 basic laws.[167] The former protected amnesties granted to 'the authors, co-authors and accomplices of the coup d'état of eighteen (18) February 2010'. The Fijian constitution contained extensive provisions on immunities and amnesties for conduct during the 2006 *coup d'état*; significantly, it further removed the 2010 decree having provided for these immunities and amnesties from the possibility of amendment (Chapter X). In some instances, the question is addressed in transitional provisions. Ghana's Constitution protects from any court or tribunal proceedings those involved in past government overthrows and constitutional suspensions in the First Schedule of its Transitional Provisions (Sections 34, 36, and 37). In Tunisia, the approach taken was precisely to stipulate that no amnesties would prevent transitional justice (Article 148(9)),

[165] Tribunal Constitucional Plurinacional Sentencia Constitucional Plurinacional No. 0084/2017. See Verdugo (2019).

[166] On the first instance of constitutionalisation of amnesties, in South Africa, see Daniel R. Mekonnen and Simon M. Weldehaimanot, 'Transitional Constitutionalism: Comparing the Eritrean and South African Experience', paper presented at ANCL-RADC annual conference, 'The Internationalisation of Constitutional Law', Rabat, Morocco, 2–5 February 2011, 10. Amnesties for human rights violations were made conditional upon the fulfilment of certain conditions such as public apology and voluntary confession.

[167] Richard Albert, 'The Unamendable Core of the United States Constitution' in András Koltay, ed., *Comparative Perspectives on the Fundamental Freedom of Expression* (Wolters Kluwer 2015a) 13, 19; Tom Ginsburg and Yuhniwo Ngenge, 'The Judiciary and Constitution Building in 2013' in Sumit Bisarya, ed., *Constitution Building: A Global Review (2013)*, International IDEA, 2014, 32; Albert (2010), 693–8.

although that article, part of Title Ten on Transitional Provisions, was not declared unamendable.[168]

Fiji's example is especially instructive, insofar as the battle over amnesties and immunities for repeated coups has been conducted on constitutional ground. The 2013 Constitution is an embattled document drafted by government legal officers in the attorney general's chambers, following the scrapping of a draft prepared by a committee headed by Yash Ghai.[169] That draft, produced under a military government, had attempted a compromise solution regarding immunities, seeking to guarantee them without legitimizing past coups. Office holders were thus granted immunity on condition of taking an 'oath of allegiance and reconciliation' to respect democracy, the rule of law, and the constitution.[170] The country's unstable constitutionalism had been marked by recurrent coups and constitutional replacement since independence, with power-sharing constitutional arrangements unable to ease ethnic competition and tensions.[171] Fijian courts had repeatedly intervened and attempted to restore the 1997 Constitution. The Court of Appeal did so following the 2000 coup,[172] which resulted in the return to democratic rule. The High Court, conversely, in a 2008 judgment legitimated the 2006 coup when it recognized presidential prerogative powers inherent in the 1997 Constitution that allowed him to protect the stability of the state in exceptional circumstances by ruling by decree.[173] In so doing, it also endorsed the dismissal of the democratically elected prime minister, the dissolution of parliament, and the unconditional grant of amnesties and immunities to the military and coup leaders. The Court of Appeal again intervened and invalidated the 2006 coup, finding no such exceptional prerogative powers that would allow the president to impose a revolutionary regime.[174] The government abrogated the 1997 Constitution the day after the judgment.

A new, participatory process of constitution-making was to be initiated following a 2012 presidential decree.[175] Except not only was popular participation

[168] Indeed, subsequent developments have shown how precarious the transitional justice system instituted in Tunisia's constitution was, with a law passed in 2017 to grant amnesties to former elites accused of corruption and other economic crimes. Tarek Amara, 'Tunisia Parliament Approves Controversial Amnesty for Ben Ali-era Corruption', *Reuters*, 13 September 2017, https://uk.reuters.com/article/uk-tunisia-politics-corruption/tunisia-parliament-approves-controversial-amnesty-for-ben-ali-era-corruption-idUKKCN1BO2KY.

[169] Coel Kirkby, 'A Cure for Coups: The South African Influence on Fijian Constitutionalism' in Rosalind Dixon and Theunis Roux, eds., *Constitutional Triumphs, Constitutional Disappointments: A Critical Assessment of the 1996 South African Constitution's Local and International Influence* (Cambridge University Press 2018) 312.

[170] Ibid., 328.

[171] Yash Ghai and Jill Cottrell, 'A Tale of Three Constitutions: Ethnicity and Politics in Fiji' in Sujit Choudhry, ed., *Constitutional Design for Divided Societies: Integration or Accommodation?* (Oxford University Press 2008) 287.

[172] *Republic of Fiji* v. *Prasad* [2001] 2 LRC 74.

[173] *Qarase* v. *Bainimarama* [2008] FJHC 241.

[174] *Qarase* v. *Bainimarama* [2009] FJCA 9.

[175] Constitutional Process (Constitutional Commission) Decree No. 57 of 2012, Official Gazette 13(98) (18 July 2012).

never meant to be more than symbolic, but a number of substantive non-negotiable principles were imposed on the constitution-making process.[176] Among these were democratic goals such as: a common and equal citizenry; a secular state; an independent judiciary; one person, one vote, one value; (especially relevant in the Fijian context) the elimination of ethnic voting; but also provisions that dealt with immunity. In this way, amnesty and immunity provisions that had existed in both the 1990 and the 1997 constitutions were retained in the 2013 one, but this time entrenched to the point of unamendability. Moreover, by retaining the military's role 'to ensure at all times the security, defence and well-being of Fiji and all Fijians' (Article 131(2)), the 2013 text ensured that 'the future of constitutional government in Fiji will depend on the military's tacit consent'.[177]

Amnesties may be viewed as the best example of how the normative aspirations of a constitution—to the consolidation of democracy, the rule of law, and human rights protections—come into tension with the elite deals necessary for political settlements in post-conflict settings. On the one hand, the intention behind the entrenchment of such amnesties seems clear: it provides guarantees to formerly warring parties that they will not face prosecution once the new constitution comes into force and as such ensures their buy-in for the broader political settlement. Some scholars agree and view these as a separate type of eternity clause they call 'reconciliatory', whose aim is:

> to avoid a contentious and potentially destabilizing criminal or civil prosecution of wrongdoers by putting prosecution off the table altogether. The goal is instead to allow opposing factions to start afresh, free from threat of legal action, and sometimes in tandem with a Truth and Reconciliation Commission to give victims the opportunity to air their views and to record their memories but without invoking the consequence of legal duty and violation.[178]

Other scholars, reflecting on the Fijian provisions, point to their origin in backlash against the Court of Appeal decision declaring the 2006 seizure of power as illegal; the 2013 Fijian Constitution thus sought to legitimate the regime but also to curtail the expansion of judicial power.[179] On this reading, unamendability is chosen as a response to prior judicial intervention on issues that the political branches seek to put beyond judicial reach.

On the other hand, the constitutionalization of amnesties will not extinguish the complexity involved in addressing past wrongdoings during post-conflict

[176] Abrak Saati, 'Participatory Constitution-Building in Fiji: A Comparison of the 1993–1997 and the 2012–2013 Processes', *International Journal of Constitutional Law* 18:1 (2020) 260.

[177] Coel Kirkby, 'Analysis: Constitution of Fiji', *IACL–AIDC Blog*, 14 September 2015, https://blog-iacl-aidc.org/new-blog/2018/5/27/analysis-constitution-of-fiji.

[178] Albert (2015), 19. See also Albert (2019), 143–4.

[179] Ginsburg and Ngenge (2014), 32.

transitions. The South African Constitutional Court acknowledged as much in a case involving a challenge to amnesties for criminal and civil liabilities granted to perpetrators having disclosed the truth about past atrocities.[180] The court upheld the granting of amnesties but limited its analysis to a review of constitutionality, while at the same time acknowledging that the case involved

> a difficult, sensitive, perhaps even agonising, balancing act between the need for justice to victims of past abuse and the need for reconciliation and rapid transition to a new future ... It is an act calling for a judgment falling substantially within the domain of those entrusted with law-making in the era preceding and during the transition period.[181]

In other words, the court deferred judgment on the appropriateness of amnesties as reconciliation devices to lawmakers and restrained its own intervention on the matter to a constitutionality check, but perhaps with inadequate consideration of international human rights law. Like the Bosnian Constitutional Court decisions discussed above, here was a national court acutely aware of treading the line between peace and justice that lawmakers and peacemakers the world over struggle to define optimally for their polities.

The fate of amnesty laws in Latin America is also instructive, insofar as it highlights the internal conflict between human rights and criminal justice norms, but also has a supranational dimension in the form of the conventionality control exercised by the Inter-American Court of Human Rights. Argentina's amnesty laws, for example, were adopted in 1987 in the aftermath of the country's military rule and a fledgling return to democratic rule.[182] The laws were subsequently repealed by Congress in 2003, but only with effect for the future. In 2005, the Argentinian Supreme Court struck down the laws and removed any doubt as to whether trials of the military could resume.[183] It argued that crimes against humanity were not subject to statutes of limitation and also that it was duty-bound to follow the Inter-American Court of Human Rights, which had previously struck down Peru's amnesty law.[184] Constitutional reforms enacted in 1994 had elevated the status of certain international treaties, including the American Convention on Human Rights, to the same level as the constitution and complementing its rights

[180] *Azanian People's Organization (AZAPO) and Others* v. *President of the Republic of South Africa and Others* 1996 (4) SA 672 (CC), 25 July 1996.

[181] Ibid., para 21.

[182] José Sebastián Elías, 'Constitutional Changes, Transitional Justice, and Legitimacy: The Life and Death of Argentina's "Amnesty" Laws', *Hastings International & Comparative Law Review* 31:2 (2008) 587.

[183] *Simón, Julio Héctor y otros s/privación ilegítima de la libertad*, Supreme Court, causa No. 17.768 (14 June 2005) S.1767.XXXVIII.

[184] *Barrios Altos* v. *Peru*, Inter-American Court of Human Rights, Judgment of 14 March 2011 (Merits).

protections (Article 75(22)). As I discuss in more detail in Chapter 5, this form of conventionality control—whereby domestic courts internalize and enforce international norms even when these conflict with constitutional ones—has been read as a supranational version of unamendability.

The constitutional unamendability of immunities and amnesties thus primarily serves to indicate the commitment of drafters to maintaining amnesties beyond the ratification of the new constitution. Such pledges are especially important to minority or weaker parties, who may otherwise fear that the majority would amend constitutional amnesties once the basic law is ratified. The granting of amnesties in general carries legitimacy problems which hark back to peace versus justice debates and to controversies over the rise of individual criminal responsibility in international law.[185] Alternatively, problems may arise if an eternity clause enshrining amnesties is one-sided, for instance where amnesties are granted to one party to the conflict but not to the other. The few examples of unamendable amnesties we have thus far suggest that the primary objective behind their adoption is reaching agreement around a political settlement and the legitimation of a new regime, all of which are sought before the adoption of the new constitution. How such unamendability would fare were it to be seriously contested post-ratification remains at the level of speculation for now. Without a doubt, however, any such contestation would expose the uneasy relationship between the political agreement having made the constitution possible and the latter's normative aspirations.

2.3 Conclusion

This chapter has not argued that post-conflict constitutions *should* incorporate eternity clauses. Instead, it has proceeded from the observation that they often do and that this choice must be understood on its own terms. To the extent that either the content of these provisions or else their intended function are different, as well as the nature of their enforcement by courts in fragile contexts, post-conflict eternity clauses have a qualitative distinctiveness that should be recognized.

On the one hand, this chapter has shown that the different dynamics of conflict-affected constitution-making will have an impact on the negotiation and substance of any unamendable clauses as well. These provisions will reflect the messy, incoherent, internationalized, and conflictual nature of constitution-making in post-conflict settings. They may be in tension with other constitutional provisions within a constitutional text that often struggles to strike the balance between competing interests domestically, international pressures, and, not infrequently,

[185] See discussions in Francesca Lessa and Leigh A. Payne, *Amnesty in the Age of Human Rights Accountability* (Cambridge University Press, 2012) and Mark Freeman, *Necessary Evils: Amnesties and the Search for Justice* (Cambridge University Press, 2009).

a fraught state-building project. And, in some instances, despite possible far-reaching consequences, unamendability in these constitution-making processes is an afterthought rather than the momentous choice we might assume it to be.

On the other hand, the chapter investigates three distinctive functions played by eternity clauses in post-conflict constitutions: signalling compliance with international norms, most typically through the protection of human rights; acting as political insurance mechanisms, such as when executive term limits are rendered unamendable; and insulating elite agreements, as when amnesties and immunity for past crimes are constitutionalized. In all three scenarios, the choice of unamendability is shown to be pragmatic and its subsequent enforcement deeply dependent on the robustness and good faith of other constitutional actors. An examination of these unamendable provisions over time reveals them to be vulnerable to the institutional weaknesses and power realignments that are likely to occur in post-conflict contexts. The story of unamendable term limits is particularly instructive in this regard. Any optimism about their ability to constrain political power and act as insurance against executive overstay now needs to be tempered in the face of empirical evidence. The ease with which term limits have been lifted in Latin America and Africa cautions us against expecting too much from either post-conflict unamendability or the courts enforcing it. It was precisely when they were under pressure that these constitutional restraints proved ineffective.

PART II

ETERNITY CLAUSES IN CONSTITUTIONAL ADJUDICATION

Constitutional Identities, Basic Structures, and Minimum Cores

3

Eternity and Expressive Values

Unamendability as the Embodiment of Constitutional Identity

This chapter engages with the literature on constitutional identity, which has made significant advances in addressing eternity clauses. Theories of constitutional identity have built sophisticated arguments around unamendable provisions, which they view as expressing core values of the polity. Given the centrality of the values they enshrine, eternity clauses are to be understood—and accepted—as an important expressive site within the constitution. In this vein, constitutional identity is a rhetorical device through which to grasp unamendability, one intrinsically linked to the project of liberal constitutional democracy. Increasingly, however, constitutional identity has also seeped into constitutional adjudication and has provided the foundation for judicial protectionism against supranational law.

The chapter proceeds in four steps. First, I am interested in sketching the contours of the concepts used in identity-based explanations of unamendability. I thus seek to delineate the main understandings of the concept of constitutional identity and explore its definition, amendment, and specificity as a legal concept. In so doing, I also expose gaps and inconsistencies in the literature on constituent identity, as well as the concealed assumptions underpinning this concept—notably its commitment to liberal constitutionalism as well as to a certain kind of pluralism. I show that expectations that a pacified constitutional identity is inherent in democratic constitutionalism mask the very real instances where exclusionary values are placed at the heart of democratic constitutions. Second, I map the main arguments surrounding unamendable provisions—as a subset of amendment rules—as expressive of constitutional identity and, relatedly, of a particular constitutional hierarchy. Third, I trace the rise of constitutional identity review in the context of European integration, in Germany and other European states. Identity-based arguments employed in tugs of war between national and supranational courts showcase the import of constitutional identity theories on constitutional adjudication. They also illustrate what the judicialization of a primarily sociological concept looks like in practice, with all its attendant problems. Finally, I discuss the potential for 'abusive' uses of constitutional identity arguments, as exemplified by a recent Hungarian decision.

This chapter concludes that constitutional identity is a concept that often obscures more than it illuminates, especially with regard to unamendable provisions.

Eternity Clauses in Democratic Constitutionalism. Silvia Suteu, Oxford University Press. © Silvia Suteu 2021.
DOI: 10.1093/oso/9780198858867.003.0004

The numerous theoretical and practical difficulties it raises should have us question its use beyond merely describing eternity clauses. The case studies discussed all raise important doubts as to unamendability's purported inherent link to uncontested values of liberal constitutionalism. They also show unamendability's potential as an anchor for sovereigntist and autocratic projects, whether resisting supranational forces or quashing internal contestation of the constitutional (un) settlement.

3.1 Constitutional law as expressive of constitutional identity

Defining constitutional identity

Accounts of constitutional identity have focused on actual features of the constitution (the system of government, territorial make-up, etc.); on 'the relation between the constitution and the culture in which it operates'; and on 'the relation between the identity of the constitution and other relevant identities' (national, religious, ideological).[1] Often, scholars invoking the notion of constitutional identity seem to presume we more or less know what we are talking when invoking it. At the heart of the concept they place a notion of core values, higher principles, perhaps even an essence of the constitution—'the language of eternity'.[2] Conversely, scholars who seek to retain only its legal meaning proceed to define constitutional identity indirectly: they identify the legal processes through which it is supposed to emerge but thereby ignore the distinctly sociological nature of the process of identification itself.[3] In my view, these gaps and formal moves in the literature reflect the difficulty of pinning down constitutional identity, especially given its interstitial nature between legal and sociological concept.

Two scholars writing on constitutional identity are an exception to this rule: Michel Rosenfeld and Gary Jacobsohn.[4] Rosenfeld conceives of constitutional identity 'as belonging to an imagined community that must carve out a distinct self-image'.[5] Rosenfeld centres his account on three questions: '*To whom* should the constitution be addressed? *What* should the constitution provide? And *how*

[1] Michel Rosenfeld, 'Constitutional Identity' in Michel Rosenfeld and András Sajó, eds., *The Oxford Handbook of Comparative Constitutional Law* (Oxford University Press 2012), 757.

[2] Denis Baranger, 'The Language of Eternity: Judicial Review of the Amending Power in France (or the Absence Thereof)', *Israeli Law Review* 44:3 (2011) 389.

[3] See Monika Polzin, 'Constitutional Identity as a Constructed Reality and a Restless Soul', *German Law Journal* 18:7 (2017) 1595.

[4] See, primarily, Michel Rosenfeld, *The Identity of the Constitutional Subject: Selfhood, Citizenship, Culture, and Community* (Routledge 2009) and Gary J. Jacobsohn, *Constitutional Identity* (Harvard University Press 2010).

[5] Rosenfeld (2012), 759.

can the constitution be justified?'[6] Rosenfeld's most ambitious contribution, in my view, is his attempt to provide an account of the birth of constitutional identity. He thus spells out the dialectical process through which constitutional identity comes into being via two general propositions:

> First, constitutions rest on a paradox inasmuch as they must at once be alienated from, and congruent with, the very identities that make them workable and coherent. And second, all constitutions depend on elaboration of a constitutional identity that is distinct from national identity and from all other relevant pre-constitutional and extra-constitutional identities. Moreover, these two propositions are related in that constitutional identity emerges from the confrontation of the very paradox on which its corresponding constitution rests.[7]

Rosenfeld acknowledges the ambiguity in answering the 'who' question, as the notion of constitutional subject could refer to 'the makers of the constitution, those subjected to it, or its subject-matter'.[8] Even if we were to settle on one of these three, he goes on to explain, the identity of the constitutional subject would not be clarified. We would still need to answer whether the makers of the constitution were those who actually drafted it or those in whose name it was drafted; who those legitimately subjected to the constitution are; as well as what the subject matter of the constitution is—that which the text states or its evolving interpretations?[9] The constitutional subject, Rosenfeld stresses, is pluralistic—both individualistically and communally so.[10] It is bound together by a common project for the polity: 'the elaboration of a commonly shared constitutional identity'.[11]

Summing up, for Rosenfeld, the process of constitutional identity creation is dynamic and dialectical, in the sense that it requires confronting contradictions which, once overcome, give rise to new contradictions.[12] It also remains forever unfinished, in that constitutional identity needs to be constantly adjusted.[13] Finally, it is a process which depends on the harmonization of the three different poles of identity of the constitutional subject: the subject as constitution-maker, as the collectivity bound by the constitution, and as interpreter, elaborator, and custodian of the constitution.[14] In more concrete terms, Rosenfeld argues that a polity will emerge following a break with the past in need of a new constitutional identity. Via the process of negation, it will distance itself from prior traditions and from those

[6] Rosenfeld (2009) 10.
[7] Ibid.
[8] Ibid., 18–19.
[9] Ibid., 19.
[10] Ibid., 22.
[11] Ibid., 26.
[12] Ibid.
[13] Ibid.
[14] Ibid.

prior identities which it sought to leave behind. However, it will need a positive identity and this will be achieved through a complex, dialectical, and ever incomplete process of incorporation, which will engage other types of identities and prior traditions but carve out a separate space for itself.

What constitutional identity is not, and what Rosenfeld also distinguishes it from, is national identity, as well as 'all other relevant pre-constitutional and extra-constitutional identities'.[15] Although a constitution will inevitably draw on national identity, to fold the two into one another would be to deny the constitution an identity of its own.[16] Constitutional identity should also not be confused with constitutional patriotism, although Rosenfeld acknowledges the latter as a potential tool towards forging constitutional identity. Understood as loyalty to constitutionalism, constitutional patriotism can play a negative role in countering nationalistic patriotism;[17] it may even play a positive role in constructing a positive constitutional identity at the transnational level, albeit the latter is a shakier proposition.[18] Presumably, constitutional identity is also different from constitutional culture, to which Rosenfeld makes occasional references.[19] The differentiation between the two concepts is tricky, however, and some authors distinctly conflate them.[20] A fuller account of this last distinction goes beyond the scope of my analysis here and, while acknowledging the similarities in the literatures dealing with these two concepts, I will refer to constitutional identity as the frame of reference for understanding eternity clauses throughout.[21]

Jacobsohn does not have a similarly well-developed account of the generative processes behind constitutional identity. He does not seem preoccupied with constructing such a theory at all, preferring instead to describe constitutional identity and its components in various polities. He emphasizes the dialogical nature of constitutional identity, its expressive nature and resistance to change:

> I will argue that a constitution acquires an identity through experience, that this identity exists neither as a discrete object of invention nor as a heavily encrusted

[15] Ibid., 10.

[16] Ibid., 29. See also Polzin (2017), 1603–4, arguing that constitutional identity is a formal, albeit constructed, concept to be found in the making, application, and interpretation of the constitution itself, whereas national identity can only be ascertained empirically.

[17] Rosenfeld (2009), 175 and 258.

[18] Ibid., 258–69.

[19] Ibid., 23, 132, 162, 181, and 230.

[20] See, for instance, Jan-Werner Müller, *Constitutional Patriotism* (Princeton University Press 2007), 56.

[21] Definitions of constitutional culture share similarities with notions of constitutional identity. For example, Ferejohn et al. state: 'constitutionalism rests on a complex and only partly visible collection of norms and practices of constitutional interpretation—what we are calling a constitutional culture' (John Ferejohn, Jack N. Rakove, and Jonathan Riley, eds., *Constitutional Culture and Democratic Rule* (Cambridge University Press 2001), 14). See also Jason Mazzone, 'The Creation of a Constitutional Culture', *Tulsa Law Review* 40 (2005a) 671, 672, emphasizing the people's understanding and acceptance of their constitution and its limits.

> essence embedded in a society's culture, requiring only to be discovered. Rather, identity emerges *dialogically* and represents a mix of political aspirations and commitments that are expressive of a nation's past, as well as the determination of those within the society who seek in some ways to transcend that past. It is changeable but resistant to its own destruction, and it may manifest itself differently in different settings.[22]

The emphasis on experience and on a delicate balance between political commitments past and present are congruent with Rosenfeld's account. They lead Jacobsohn to describe 'the fundamental dynamics of identity' as less a cultural or historical contingency and more 'the expression of a developmental process endemic to the phenomenon of constitutionalism'.[23] Jacobsohn's theory thus places great emphasis on dialogic engagement in several dimensions, including, interestingly, in the transnational.[24] It also links constitutional expressiveness with identity to the point of merging the two concepts. 'An expressive component is present in all constitutional identities', he writes, and where, as in Ireland, 'the principal marks of identity are largely a projection of the extant social or cultural condition rather than mainly or even partly a reproach to it, expressiveness might be viewed as a synonym for the concept of identity and not merely a component of it'.[25]

Complicating Jacobsohn's account is what he terms 'constitutional disharmony', which he links to the contestability of constitutional identity. Disharmony, he argues, refers to the dissonance (not incoherence) of constitutions, and 'the course of constitutional identity is impelled by the discord of ordinary politics within limits established by commitments from the past'.[26] Contestability is thus crucial in understanding constitutional identity,[27] as long as there exist 'identifiable continuities of meaning within which dissonance and contradiction play out'.[28] For Jacobsohn, therefore, constitutional identity is not to be equated to an essence ('some core essence that at its root is unchangeable'),[29] but is the outcome of a continuous, and continuously fraught, process. To this Rosenfeld could be seen as agreeing. However, Rosenfeld has also emphasized the need for constitutional identity to cohere, 'both at the level of the constitution as a whole and of particular constitutional provisions and most notably those most likely to provoke contestation'.[30] The conditions for this difficult equilibrium (or is it a back and forth?)

[22] Jacobsohn (2010), 7.
[23] Gary J. Jacobsohn, 'The Formation of Constitutional Identities' in Tom Ginsburg and Rosalind Dixon, eds., *Comparative Constitutional Law* (Edward Elgar 2011) 129, 130.
[24] Ibid., 136.
[25] Ibid., 31.
[26] Jacobsohn (2011), 135.
[27] Jacobsohn (2010), 15.
[28] Ibid., 4.
[29] Ibid.
[30] Rosenfeld (2012), 759.

between coherence and disharmony is something which the theorists of constitutional identity have not been able to pinpoint. An easy answer would be to say that it can only be evaluated in a particular context. A more honest answer would be that constitutional theory has not, and perhaps does not have the tools to, put forth a complete account of the inner mechanisms of constitutional identity.

Like Rosenfeld, Jacobsohn distinguishes between constitutional and national identity but acknowledges the distinction is sometimes difficult to sustain. He gives the example of Turkey's Kemalist conflation of national and constitutional identities as one of the 'situations where the express purpose of the constitution is to separate the future from the past in ways that will have transformative effects on social behavior'.[31] Moreover, Jacobsohn talks of a constitutional identity of the text versus of the people, which are not always aligned.[32] He gives the uneven developments in US constitutional law as an example and argues that '[u]ltimately, stability in the identity of the constitutional order depended on convergence of the two'.[33]

Accounts of constitutional identity were enriched as part of debates on whether the European integration project was compatible with the constitutional identity of member states and, indeed, whether there existed something called a 'European constitutional identity'.[34] They will re-emerge in section 3.3 in this chapter. For now, it suffices to note that the meta-constitutional concept of identity has reached beyond the state and found currency, and contestation, at the supranational level. However, the concept was not used uniformly in that context either, with commentators vacillating between notions of constitutional and national identity and between constitutional identity as a sole-standing concept or as an interpretive aid. In other words, we find similar conceptual confusion when invoking constitutional identity at the European level.

Amending constitutional identity

Given the complex task of defining constitutional identity, what can we say about its transformation over time, specifically via amendment? An important objection to constitutional identity theories is precisely that they do not provide a sound account of how constitutional identity is to change lawfully.[35] One aspect of this objection points to the static notions of identity thought to imbue expressivist

[31] Jacobsohn (2010), 10.

[32] Jacobsohn (2011), 141.

[33] Ibid.

[34] These debates, sparked by the eastward enlargement of the European Union and culminating during the ratification process of the Treaty of Lisbon, are too rich to cover here. See, inter alia, essays in 'Symposium on the Proposed European Constitution', *International Journal of Constitutional Law* 3: 2–3 (2005) and in 'Confronting Memories: Constitutionalization after Bitter Experiences', *German Law Journal* 6:2 (2005).

[35] See Rosalind Dixon, 'Amending Constitutional Identity', *Cardozo Law Review* 33:5 (2012) 1847.

theories of constitutional law more generally.[36] Furthermore, comparative work investigating the practicalities of amending constitutional identity has yielded mixed results and has not clarified the tension between amendments and constitutional identity.[37] Theoretical scholarship also seems to struggle with addressing changes in constitutional identity, seemingly stuck in the conundrum of distinguishing between constitutional amendment and constitution-making or re-making or else offering revolution as the only alternative. This is hardly surprising given the recurrence of debates on what constitutes a fundamental constitutional change in general.[38]

Rosenfeld, for instance, talks about constitutional amendment and its impact on constitutional identity and contrasts it with constitution-making. If '[a]mending the constitution involves changing it without threatening its overall unity or identity', he notes, constitution-making 'does require creating a new unity and identity which, in turn, depends on repudiation of preceding constitutional identities and of other pre-constitutional and extra-constitutional ones'.[39] Rosenfeld acknowledges, however, that the distinction between the two is clear at the level of the formal constitution, but blurrier at the level of the material (living) constitution. To him, amendment is a site which aptly embodies the tension between sameness and selfhood as the two facets of constitutional identity: sameness is textual and may be complemented or contradicted by selfhood, which is interpretive and corresponds to evolving understandings of otherwise unchanged text.[40] Admitting that some constitutions are more rigid than others, and some even explicitly restrict the scope of legitimate amendments, Rosenfeld asks: 'can there be any cogent way to determine at what point do constitutional amendments threaten to destroy constitutional identity?'.[41] He gives the example of an amendment lowering the voting age in the USA, which clearly does not; conversely, Hungary's use of amendments to completely overhaul its pre-1989 constitution clearly negated the latter's identity while preserving its formal shell.[42] Civil War amendments in the USA are a more ambiguous example. In contrast to amendment, which can go either way (either

[36] Rosalind Dixon, 'A Democratic Theory of Constitutional Comparison', *American Journal of Comparative Law* 56:4 (2008) 947; Vicki Jackson, 'Comparative Constitutional Law: Methodologies' in Michel Rosenfeld and András Sajó, eds., *The Oxford Handbook of Comparative Constitutional Law* (Oxford University Press 2012) 54, 67. See also Mark Tushnet, 'Some Reflections on Method in Comparative Constitutional Law' in Sujit Choudhry, ed., *The Migration of Constitutional Ideas* (Cambridge University Press 2007) 67, 81.

[37] Dixon (2012), 1858.

[38] One aspect of these debates was discussed in Chapter 1 of this book in the context of exercises of constituent power; another will be explored in Chapter 7, on attempts to repeal eternity clauses.

[39] Rosenfeld (2009), 30.

[40] Rosenfeld gives the example of the US Constitution: its text has remained the same since 1787, with the exception of the twenty-seven amendments; its interpretation, however, has evolved. To the extent that these interpretations can be organically understood as a process of adaptation and growth, they can be seen as constructing and preserving identity in the sense of selfhood (ibid., 27).

[41] Ibid.

[42] Ibid., 31.

bolster or erode constitutional identity), constitution-making would seem to necessarily 'negate[] past constitutional identities to launch new ones'.[43] This conclusion does not necessarily hold if we consider France's fifteen constitutions since 1789 (formally having distinct identities but materially, perhaps not) versus the USA's single constitution (formally having one identity but materially, several).[44] Thus, Rosenfeld concludes that it is best to rely on substantial rather than formal criteria for distinguishing between amending versus changing constitutional identity.[45]

Jacobsohn more directly acknowledges the problem. Writing on India, he admits that 'the jurisprudential record is slim in theorizing the changes in constitutional identity that extant circumstances may require'.[46] If contestation is already bounded within the confines of an eternity clause expressive of constitutional identity, as he argues, then the only recourse left when attempting to change those boundaries is revolution. Jacobsohn accepts this possibility and says that when a constitution's heritage is deplorable, 'its identity perhaps *should* be destroyed and reconstituted'.[47] On Sri Lanka's rejection of a basic structure doctrine in pursuit of ethnic republicanism, for example, Jacobsohn writes: 'that ... the immutability of an identity in tension with the precepts of liberal constitutionalism should be held sacrosanct by a judicial tribunal is by no means self-evident'.[48] He expresses similar concerns with regard to Turkey and its constitutionalization of secularism.[49]

I would argue that both of these accounts are unsatisfactory. Rosenfeld's move amounts to little more than displacing the problem. Invoking substantive criteria—identified, via mixed methods, in various provisions of the written constitution and cherry-picked aspects of constitutional practice—for determining a change in the material constitution and thus in constitutional identity leads us back to hoping we know it when we see it. Jacobsohn's call for major constitutional overhaul is limited to contexts where constitutional identity is illiberal and 'deplorable'. Moreover, this option is costly and amounts to a major disruption of the legal order. We are thus left with knowing that a constitutional identity may and should develop over time,[50] but unsure of how its contours may be shifted once in place.

The more legalistic understandings of constitutional identity seek to avoid this problem by limiting the scope of the concept to legal processes. They construe the scope of constitutional identity broadly and almost boundlessly in the written constitution, in authoritative interpretations of constitutional norms by courts, and in

[43] Ibid.
[44] Ibid., 31–2.
[45] Ibid., 207.
[46] Jacobsohn (2010), 18.
[47] Jacobsohn (2011), 132.
[48] Jacobsohn (2010), 69.
[49] Ibid.
[50] As Franz Mayer has said, 'Identity, be it European or national, is nothing that can simply be written into a constitutional text and then it is there. It has to develop over time, which also means that it *can* in fact develop over time' (Franz C. Mayer, 'Rashomon in Karlsruhe: A Reflection on Democracy and Identity in the European Union', *International Journal of Constitutional Law* 9:3–4 (2011) 757, 785).

other, non-constitutional sources of law.[51] Within such accounts, then, constitutional identity evolves continuously and remains contested. The problem, I would argue, is in trying to move from such amorphous, evolutive understandings of constitutional identity to operationalizing it as a normative concept whose boundaries are to be policed through adjudication at a given point in time. In other words, these accounts do not manage to circumvent the problem of determining unlawful amendments of constitutional identity *as such*, distinctive from generic breaches of constitutional norms.

The specificity of constitutional identity

For a new concept to be useful, it should be clear what its distinctive explanatory value is. This not only aids conceptual clarity, but also ensures we do not engage in unnecessary proliferation of constitutional concepts. To help test the specificity of constitutional identity, we should investigate whether it can avoid collapsing into other concepts, in other words, whether it captures something about the world that these other concepts do not.

A first question is whether when we invoke constitutional identity we are not in fact discussing constitutionalism itself. One way to ask this question is to wonder whether an account such as Rosenfeld's should not, in the first instance, explain what constitutionalism itself has to offer to explain its pull, particularly given its invocation at the transnational level. In the words of Gianluigi Palombella, 'it is uncertain where the pull toward constitutionalism, as a drive to reconciliation, comes from unless one presupposes a further normative identity ethos of inherent constitutionalist substance'.[52] This is also a worthwhile reminder to those writing on eternity clauses without differentiating much between arguments in favour of unamendability and those in favour of the role of constitutions generally.[53]

A possible solution is proposed by Bosko Tripkovic, who differentiates between general and particular constitutional identity. By the former, he means the 'evaluative commitments that are generally applicable in any constitutional system of government', whereas by the latter, the 'specific values discernible from the layers of moral judgments that have been made in local constitutional practices'.[54] This tension between the universal and the local is present in all constitutions.[55] However,

[51] See Polzin (2017), 1604–7.

[52] Gianluigi Palombella, 'Structures and Process in the Constitutional Self: Coping with the Future?', *International Journal of Constitutional Law* 8:3 (2010) 656, 660.

[53] See Beau Breslin, *From Words to Worlds: Exploring Constitutional Functionality* (John Hopkins University Press 2009).

[54] Bosko Tripkovic, *The Metaethics of Constitutional Adjudication* (Oxford University Press 2018) 14.

[55] Śledzińska-Simon, for example, views the particularist and universalist dimensions of constitutional identity as coexisting rather than mutually exclusive, and the multiple dimensions of constitutional identity as 'a reflection of a multicentric, or polycontextual, character of the legal environment'

neither the purported universality of constitutional values, nor their claimed local specificity, are sufficient—on their own—to justify what Tripkovic calls 'the argument from constitutional identity'. Drawing on case law from the USA, South Africa, and Germany, Tripkovic shows that not only is the content of constitutional identity 'fluid and imprecise', but it is unclear 'which conception of value is in the background of the argument from constitutional identity'.[56] General constitutional identity risks collapsing into an argument from universal reason, such as when courts appeal to foreign law to find support for moral judgments, whereas particular constitutional identity 'expands into the argument from common sentiment' (referring to prevailing sentiments in society).[57] Thus, insofar as constitutional identity is to form the basis for adjudication, it thus cannot be treated as a self-standing source of value.[58]

A second objection relates to the lack of clarity as to the explanatory value of constitutional identity as a concept. As Neil Walker has observed with regard to Rosenfeld's theory, it is unclear whether we need the constitutional variables ascribed to constitutional identity are 'discrete causal forces rather than as one of many deeply sedimented and closely intertwined factors that make up the community's political way of life'.[59] In other words, if we can easily tell the story of constitutional evolution in various national settings without recourse to the concept of constitutional identity, why invoke it in the first place? Both Rosenfeld and Jacobsohn assume the existence of the notion of constitutional identity and set about defining its contours. They largely ignore the question of its explanatory necessity. Jacobsohn does engage with some critics of the concept and addresses Laurence Tribe's scepticism of constitutional identity.[60] However, Walker's concern here is not the same as Tribe's objection that there is a lack of unity in constitutional vision. It is a more clearly methodological one: we need a more concrete notion of the explanatory power of constitutional identity as distinct from other variables. Neither of the two main theories of constitutional identity provides this.

Exclusionary constitutional identity

Finally, we need to clarify the normative assumptions underpinning the concept of constitutional identity. Do theories built around it presuppose a particular

(Anna Śledzińska-Simon, 'A Model of Individual, Relational, and Collective Self and Its Application in Poland', *International Journal of Constitutional Law* 13:1 (2015) 124, 128).

[56] Tripkovic (2018), 58.

[57] Ibid.,

[58] Ibid., 50.

[59] Neil Walker, 'Rosenfeld's Plural Constitutionalism', *International Journal of Constitutional Law* 8:3 (2010) 677, 680–1.

[60] See Jacobsohn (2010), 3–4.

understanding of constitutionalism and its objectives? In other words, is this an agnostic concept, or is it laden with normative baggage? As the examples discussed later in this chapter show, constitutional identity proponents presuppose a liberal constitutionalist ethos behind the concept. Moreover, the propensity for a constitutional identity to be defined by exclusionary values within certain democratic constitutions finds no answer within these theories.

Scholars have expressed similar fears about the normative foundations of constitutional identity.[61] Melissa Schwartzberg has written of the possible non-inclusive entrenchment of values, giving the example of entrenching official language rights in places like Romania and Azerbaijan to illustrate the point.[62]

Helen Irving has called gender 'the missing referent' in theories of constitutional identity. What she means by this is that by treating gender as an irrelevant difference, Rosenfeld's theory in particular rests on a tendentious definition of pluralism centred on ethno-cultural (extending to religious) difference, with a shared constitutional identity advanced as the corrective for disruptive identities. The emphasis on reconciliation and peaceful coexistence is, to Irving, an elision of the claims of non-disruptive groups, including women. His is a constitutional identity theory that rests on excluding women's specific form of difference (co-majoritarian, permanent, and universal) and that relies on a notion of pluralism principally concerned with accommodating and neutralizing difference. As will be seen below when discussing Germany's eternity clause and adjudication surrounding abortion, the absence of gender as a referent in conceptions of constitutional identity—in that case, an identity with human dignity at its pinnacle—has dire consequences for women and their equality claims.

Ayelet Shachar is less specific and more speculative in her fears but does wonder, also reacting to Rosenfeld's theory, whether 'the threat of extreme nationalism, religiosity, and identity politics of all kinds is far more influential than is acknowledged in [his] text'.[63] Taking this insight further in the realm of religious protection, Shachar posits that Rosenfeld's pluralist commitment only allows religion to thrive if

> pacified and tempered so as never to challenge the lexical superiority of the society's *constitutional* identity. In the process, religions and other comprehensive ways of life are 'disarmed' so as to remove their potentially disruptive power

[61] Melissa Schwartzberg, *Democracy and Legal Change* (Cambridge University Press 2009); Helen Irving, 'Constitutional Identity Theory and Gender: The Missing Referent', Sydney Law School Research Paper No. 17/56 (2017); Ayelet Shachar, 'The Return of the Repressed: Constitutionalism, Religion, and Political Pluralism', *International Journal of Constitutional Law* 8:3 (2010) 665.

[62] Schwartzberg (2009), 24. See also Chapter 1 in this book for a more in-depth discussion of unamendable language provisions.

[63] Shachar (2010), 667.

> to challenge the semisacred, high modernist stance of constitutionalism as a 'civil religion' that generates the *highest* law of the land.[64]

She thus ascribes to Rosenfeld a bounded pluralism, tolerant of difference only insofar as it poses no threat: 'Pluralism is permitted only within a bounded set of margins that are not incompatible with basic constitutional or human rights standards.'[65] Shachar is not the only one to question the nature of Rosenfeld's pluralism,[66] and her critique reaches beyond Rosenfeld's work. The contestation and divisiveness which characterize identity politics do not magically disappear when moving to the constitutional realm. Nor are they only to be found when constitutional identity veers into ethnic politics and illiberalism, as Jacobsohn suggested. Contestation can vary from reasonable disagreement about fundamental values to outright incompatibilities between different ways of life and constitutional forms and it is unclear whether constitutional identity theories solve or conceal the problem.

These observations can be supplemented by constitutional theoretical investigations into the origins of the concept of constitutional identity in specific national contexts. Monika Polzin has analysed the genealogy of this concept in Germany.[67] She has found it to be linked to Schmittian thinking and to a static and exclusionary notion of the constitution, acting as the basis for theories of implicit limits on amendment to the Weimar constitution. Rooted in his theory of constituent power, Schmitt viewed constitutional identity as not to be altered by constituted powers, even while he maintained that its unamendable elements could not be listed, nor that a procedure for the people to exercise their constituent power could be regulated.[68] Polzin has shown, in fact, that the concept of constitutional identity did *not* inform the drafting of the German *Grundgesetz* and was only reintroduced later, in the context of European Union law. I will delve deeper into this rise of constitutional identity review in the context of European integration below. Polzin's account is invaluable at this more general level of the analysis as well, insofar as it reveals the exclusionary roots as well as relative novelty of constitutional identity thinking in German constitutional law. Together with other deeply contextual analyses, such accounts suggest that democratic constitutions may develop constitutional identities that are incoherent, majoritarian, or even exclusionary.[69]

[64] Ibid., 667–8.

[65] Ibid., 669.

[66] Neil Walker calls Rosenfeld a plural constitutionalist rather than constitutional pluralist ((2010), 678).

[67] Monika Polzin, 'Constitutional Identity, Unconstitutional Amendments and the Idea of Constituent Power: The Development of the Doctrine of Constitutional Identity in German Constitutional Law', *International Journal of Constitutional Law* 14:2 (2016) 411.

[68] Ibid., 420.

[69] Examples of such contextual work include: on Malaysia, Jaclyn L. Neo, 'A Contextual Approach to Unconstitutional Constitutional Amendments: Judicial Power and the Basic Structure Doctrine in Malaysia', *Asian Journal of Comparative Law* 15 (2020) 69; on Poland, Śledzińska-Simon (2015); and on

3.2 Eternity clauses as sites of constitutional expression

There are two ways in which to think of eternity clauses as repositories of constitutional identity.[70] One is purely expressive or symbolic, meant to capture eternity clauses' descriptive nature. The emphasis is thus on the values and principles they enshrine, assumed to define the polity. The other is functional, emphasizing the particular nature of the entrenchment operated by eternity clauses. The emphasis here is not so much on their content, as on the ordering role they play within the constitution, ultimately sitting atop a relatively clear hierarchy of constitutional values. I discuss both in turn, ultimately finding the two roles to be interrelated.

Amendment rules as repositories of constitutional identity

A now common reading of amendment rules views them as expressive of constitutional values, with eternity clauses a subtype meant to act as repository of constitutional identity.[71] This expressiveness has been said to be both internal, addressing those who will be bound by the constitution, and external, speaking to the larger world.[72] In other words, alongside other functions they may perform—such as distinguishing constitutional from ordinary law and regulating the process of constitutional change—amendment rules 'should also be understood as one of several sites where constitutional designers may entrench and thereby express constitutional values'.[73] In the case of Germany, its *Ewigkeitsklausel* would hence not only serve to delineate the material limits of constitutional amendment, but also to 'define the essential elements of the foundation myth' and 'keep the memory and the appreciation of the constituent power alive'.[74] The tiered design of amendment rules—stipulating different thresholds for amending different parts of the

Romania, Silvia Suteu, 'The Multinational State That Wasn't: The Constitutional Definition of Romania as a National State', *Vienna Journal on International Constitutional Law* 11:3 (2017a) 413.

[70] Roznai similarly speaks of unamendability's expressive and functional roles, which overlap and build on each other. Yaniv Roznai, *Unconstitutional Constitutional Amendments: The Limits of Amendment Powers* (Oxford University Press 2017), 26.

[71] Richard Albert, *Constitutional Amendments: Making, Breaking, and Changing Constitutions* (Oxford University Press 2019), 85–6. This view is not unanimous, however. See Polzin (2017) 1607–8, arguing that eternity clauses should be viewed as, at most, an indicator of the elements of constitutional identity, but that they should not be conflated with repositories of it.

[72] Richard Albert, 'The Expressive Function of Constitutional Amendment Rules', *McGill Law Journal* 59:2 (2013) 225, 229.

[73] Ibid., 230.

[74] Ulrich K. Preuss, 'The Implications of "Eternity Clauses": The German Experience', *Israel Law Review* 44 (2011) 429, 445.

constitution—is similarly meant to be expressive of a hierarchy of values.[75] Richard Albert views the expressivity of amendment rules as more or less authentic, where authenticity is given by the distance between aspirations in the constitution and the implementation of these political commitments into reality.[76] Thus, in Albert's understanding, amendment rules may be expressive of inauthentic values as well and are thus 'susceptible to authoritarian commandeering'.[77] Rules for constitutional change may become sites where authoritarian regimes express values they have no intention of pursuing in order to 'secur[e] for themselves the goodwill that may come from their public, even if dishonest, association with democratic ideals'.[78]

Expressive understandings of unamendability are difficult to refute insofar as they make a modest claim: that the rules framers of a constitution adopt regarding the change of that text express their more or less 'authentic' values. Within such readings, eternity clauses find their merit precisely in their expressive function: 'by identifying a constitutional feature of statehood as unamendable, entrenchment signals to citizens just as it does to observers what matters most to the state by fixing the palette of non-negotiable colors in its self-portrait'.[79] For Albert, therefore, unamendable provisions go beyond the expressive function performed by constitutionalism or constitutional law generally—because 'there is nothing unarticulated about entrenchment', he says, they leave no doubt as to the values binding citizens.[80] Perhaps because it is difficult to deny that provisions which explicitly articulate constitutional values have some expressive role—indeed, one may even view it as tautological if expressivity is used as synonym for 'value talk'—a great proportion of the literature on eternity clauses has focused on their link to constitutional identity.[81]

To say eternity clauses are expressive is not necessarily to view them as unique or even specific to their political community. Just like any other provisions, eternity clauses can also make their way into a constitutional text by way of accident, negotiation give-and-take, and as a result of biases towards neighbours and historical experience.[82] How else to explain the word-for-word eternity clause present in eleven of the constitutions of the Dominican Republic but as a case of constitutional copy/paste? Similarly, one need not look farther than Portugal's lengthy

[75] Rosalind Dixon and David Landau, 'Tiered Constitutional Design', *George Washington Law Review* 86:2 (2018): 438.

[76] Albert (2013), 257.

[77] Ibid., 260. See also Albert (2019), 50–1.

[78] Albert (2013), 260. This is an argument reminiscent of Jacobsohn's on illiberal constitutional identity.

[79] Richard Albert, 'Constitutional Handcuffs', *Arizona State Law Journal* 42:3 (2010) 663, 699–700.

[80] Ibid., 700.

[81] See also Roznai (2017), 148–50 and Yaniv Roznai, 'Unamendability and the Genetic Code of the Constitution', 27:2 *European Review of Public Law* (2015) 775.

[82] Donald L. Horowitz, 'Conciliatory Institutions and Constitutional Processes in Post-Conflict States', *William and Mary Law Review* 49:4 (2008) 1213, 1227–30. See also Chapter 2 in this book.

Article 288 as the model for eternity clauses in the constitutions of former colonies Angola (Article 236), Cape Verde (Article 313), Mozambique (Article 292), Sao Tome and Principe (Article 154), and East Timor (Article 156). This objection does not, of course, negate the possibility that even an exogenous eternity clause may grow roots in its adoptive constitutional setting and come to be accepted as expressing its constitutional identity. To determine whether this is the case, however, requires in depth contextual analysis. On the one hand, this is a problem inherent to understandings of the migration of constitutional ideas in general. On the other hand, given the nature of the values incorporated in eternity clauses and the consequences deriving from their adoption, their unreflective migration raises more important problems than that of other constitutional provisions. We need to keep this in mind given that eternity clauses adoption might be on the rise, either due to a 'demonstration effect' between countries or due to the growing internationalization of constitution-making.[83]

Returning to Rosenfeld and Jacobsohn as the main theorists of constitutional identity, their accounts make more or less direct reference to unamendability. As noted above, Rosenfeld deals with it only implicitly, when pointing to substantive limitations on constitutional change as markers of the preservation or destruction of constitutional identity.[84] Jacobsohn's account of constitutional identity more directly makes room for arguments about eternity clauses. For him, identity is a fluid concept but not one without boundaries, 'and textual commitments such as are embodied in preambles often set the topography upon which the mapping of constitutional identity occurs'.[85] Thus, a constitutive political commitment such as Turkey's to secularism—insulated from amendment by its constitution's Article 4—will in Jacobsohn's view not preclude evolution: 'its specific content would vary over time, tethered to the text, but only loosely, so as to accommodate the dialogical interactions between codified foundational aspirations and the evolving mores of the Turkish people'.[86] It is slightly paradoxical that Jacobsohn relies on this example to advocate his dialogic argument given that the Turkish eternity clause does not allow even the proposal of an amendment to secularism and other basic characteristics of the state. Similarly, in the case of India, he argues, while the commitment to secularism may be fundamental to the country's constitutional identity, the meanings people ascribe to it will differ.[87]

The problem here, again, is that if the concept of constitutional identity is to do its intended work, there needs to be more we can say about when its boundaries are

[83] On the latter, see Chapter 5 in this book.

[84] Rosenfeld (2009), 207.

[85] Jacobsohn (2010), 12.

[86] Ibid., 14.

[87] Jacobsohn (2011), 139. Richard Albert and Yaniv Roznai, 'Religion, Secularism and Limitations on Constitutional Amendment' in Rex Ahdar, ed., *Research Handbook on Law and Religion* (Edward Elgar 2018), 154.

unlawfully transgressed. Jacobsohn seems content to describe elements constitutive of the constitutional identity of one country or another and looks to eternity clauses as prime sites of its expression. Implicit in his reliance on constitutional court decisions is also the assumption that it is these bodies, above others, which are to be entrusted with policing the frontiers of and changes in constitutional identity. As the example discussed later in this chapter show, constitutional identity is an especially fluid concept in the judiciary arsenal.

One site among many: preambles as expressive of constitutional identity

As noted above, it is generally accepted that some provisions in the constitutional edifice are more likely to indicate core normative commitments than others. Amendment rules, with eternity clauses as a subset, however, have only more recently come to be seen as performing this function. Prior 'usual suspects' were constitutional preambles, although other sites are also possible—for example, explicit declarations of principles such as are found in the South African and Spanish constitutions.[88] In fact, conventional views on preambles have been extended by analogy to eternity clauses: just as the former are (largely non-justiciable) symbolic statements so too are the latter. In the words of Jon Elster, unamendable provisions are to be seen as 'mainly symbolic'.[89] The problem with this line of argument is that it does not always hold true for preambles and it is even less true of eternity clauses.

Preambles have been described as 'particularly useful for an expressivist'.[90] They have been viewed, alternatively, as: a combination of pabulum with 'some effort to capture a sense of national identity;'[91] as 'typically the portion of a traditional constitutional draft where the polity articulates its most important aims and objectives;'[92] and as encapsulating 'the ostensible "essence" of the people or nation in whose name the constitution has been drafted, whether defined in terms of religion, language, ethnicity, shared history of oppression, or even commitment to some scheme of universal values'.[93] In short, preambles are viewed as perhaps the most prominent site for expressing constitutional identity.[94]

[88] Albert (2013), 244. See generally, Wim Voermans, Maarten Stremler, and Paul Cliteur, *Constitutional Preambles: A Comparative Analysis* (Edward Elgar 2017).

[89] Jon Elster, 'Constitutionalism in Eastern Europe: An Introduction', *University of Chicago Law Review* 58:2 (1991) 447, 471.

[90] Tushnet (2007), 79.

[91] Mark Tushnet, 'Constitution-Making: An Introduction', *Texas Law Review* 91 (2013) 1983, 2001.

[92] Breslin (2009), 50.

[93] Sanford Levinson, 'Do Constitutions Have a Point? Reflections on "Parchment Barriers" and Preambles' in Ellen Frankel Paul, Fred D. Miller, Jr, and Jeffrey Paul, eds., *What Should Constitutions Do?* (Cambridge University Press 2011) 150, 177.

[94] Jacobsohn (2011), 132. See also Vicki Jackson, *Constitutional Engagement in a Transnational Era* (Oxford University Press 2010), 18.

Preambles go beyond this, however. As Levinson has aptly observed, they are not meant merely to provide 'an additional patch of text for use in the standard arsenal of legal arguments'.[95] According to Tushnet, they veer from 'largely precatory' to occasionally having legal force.[96] He associates the latter with the presence of constitutional review, with preambles at the core of structural constitutional interpretation in several jurisdictions.[97] A recent study has in fact found that preambles have been increasingly used in constitutional interpretation, with an identifiable trend towards giving them greater binding force.[98] Perhaps the most famous example here is that of the French Constitutional Council elevating the preamble of the 1958 Constitution to full constitutional status in 1971, as part of a *bloc de constitutionalité* with the 1789 Declaration of the Rights of Man and of the Citizen and the preamble of the 1946 Constitution.[99] Comparative work has shown that constitutional preambles in other jurisdictions have shifted from mere hortatory language to legal effect.[100] The lesson here is that no statement in the constitutional text may be safely assumed to remain symbolic, irrespective of how far from justiciable its drafters intended it to be. In contexts which allow for expansive constitutional review, moreover, the likelihood that such statements are used as basis for interpretation increases.

Comparative empirical studies have also exposed just how unoriginal and unreflective preamble language often is.[101] Ginsburg et al. have argued that despite the widespread understanding of preambles 'as the local part' of the constitution, 'they frequently seem to speak in an international idiom'.[102] By the latter they mean that preambles 'often adopt terms or memes from other constitutions, they frequently invoke international treaties, and they sometimes contain language that amounts to foreign policy statements'.[103] Even innovations, when they do occur, do so in temporal and regional clusters: they come in global waves and are influenced by neighbours' innovations.[104] These findings lead the authors to suggest that

> The broad pattern we observe is one of stasis, followed by periods of change. These periods are determined globally, and not simply by domestic developments.

[95] Levinson (2011), 166.

[96] Tushnet (2013), 2001–2.

[97] Ibid., 2003–4.

[98] Liav Orgad, 'The Preamble in Constitutional Interpretation', *International Journal of Constitutional Law* 8:4 (2010) 714.

[99] Conseil Constitutionnel, Décision No. 71–44 DC of 16 July 1971.

[100] Justin O. Frosini, 'Constitutional Preambles: More than Just a Narration of History', *University of Illinois Law Review* (2017) 603.

[101] Tom Ginsburg, Nick Foti, and Daniel Rockmore, '"We the Peoples": The Global Origins of Constitutional Preambles', *George Washington International Law Review* 46:2 (2014) 305. See also David S. Law, 'Constitutional Archetypes', *Texas Law Review* 95:2 (2016) 153, arguing that there are three broad archetypes identifiable across the preambles of world constitutions.

[102] Ginsburg et al. (2014), 337.

[103] Ibid.

[104] Ibid., 311.

> Preambles, then, are internationally embedded texts, whose production is related to their peers in time and place.[105]

While a similarly comprehensive empirical study of the migration of the language of unamendability has not been performed, the available evidence points to the likelihood of similar findings in the case of eternity clauses.[106]

There is an additional question raised by proponents of preamble-like understandings of eternity clauses, however: if merely symbolic, why would there need to be an additional site of expressing the polity's core values within its constitution? Why not relegate such symbolism to the preamble alone? Levinson observed about preambles that they 'presumably ... have a point, but it really cannot be the same kind of point that would be attributed to the main body of a written constitution'.[107] One could reverse this and say eternity clauses really cannot serve the same aim as the preamble of the constitution. To assume otherwise amounts to assuming redundant drafting and ignoring the reality of unamendability's justiciability.

Eternity clauses atop a constitutional hierarchy

A variation on arguments about eternity clauses as expressive of core values is that unamendable provisions also serve an ordering function by establishing a hierarchy of constitutional values. Richard Albert's work is again relevant here. He has written about the variation in difficulty of amendment rules as motivated, at least sometimes, by a considered judgment about their importance.[108] He has concluded that the entrenchment of a formal constitutional hierarchy can reflect a multitude of motivations, including political bargaining during drafting, self-interest, the expression of values, or 'some combination of these three'.[109] In other words, it is not merely that drafters express constitutional values in eternity clauses as one type of amendment rule; they also seek to signal the precedence of those values over others in the constitution. The unavoidable consequence is the reliance on these apex values, to the exclusion of others, in resolving constitutional conflicts. A familiar example here might be the protection of human dignity in Germany via Article 1 of the Basic Law, in turn rendered unamendable by Article 79(3), which permeates and orders the entire value structure of the constitution.[110] The lawyerly

[105] Ibid., 337.

[106] See Yaniv Roznai, 'Unconstitutional Constitutional Amendments—The Migration and Success of a Constitutional Idea', *American Journal of Comparative Law* 61 (2013) 657 and Roznai (2017), Appendix, 236–74.

[107] Levinson (2011), 157.

[108] Other reasons are political compromise and distrusting future generations as self-interested. Albert (2013), 245–7 and Albert (2019), 43.

[109] Albert (2013), 247.

[110] See Edward J. Eberle, 'Human Dignity, Privacy, and Personality in German and American Constitutional Law', *Utah Law Review* (1997) 963.

discomfort with disorder thus translates into a desire for a gradation even within higher law, with eternity clauses signalling the 'authoritative predetermined hierarchy of values, whether formally or informally entrenched'[111] which Albert deems necessary to mediate between competing and contested values.[112]

The problem with such arguments is that it is unclear whether establishing a hierarchy of norms internal to the constitution is either wise or practical. In previous work, Albert had himself deemed it imprudent to establish a hierarchy of constitutional norms via eternity clauses, on the basis that:

> [t]o regard the constitution as a mere compilation of individual provisions, each subject to a sliding scale of worth, is to devalue the constitutional text as a document whose constituent parts must be read together to give the larger whole its full meaning.[113]

Moreover, he claimed, 'the reasons or principles according to which some constitutional provisions are elevated above others may be neither apparent nor even logically sound to those bound by its terms'.[114] While I do not agree with the more extreme stance—viewing such a constitutional hierarchy of norms as threatening 'to deplete the text of its intrinsic value' as an institution of authority[115]—I do think more thought should be expended considering the logical ordering of constitutional values of which eternity clauses might be part. To establish a kind of constitution-within-a-constitution, as unamendable provisions are in this narrative, raises questions about the sliding authority of different parts of the constitution and about how to mediate conflicts between them. It also ignores the possible use of higher norms for private political agendas.[116]

Defenders of constitutional hierarchies view these conflicts internal to the constitutional text as articulations of 'alternative visions or aspirations that may embody different strands within a common historical tradition'[117] which generate healthy 'disharmony' in constitutional identity. I am more sceptical. I see such a 'quest for a compelling unity'[118] as ignorant of the potentially large number of incongruities and inner contradictions in the constitutional text. It assumes consensus surrounding the hierarchy of values, including about unamendable values—even though these are typically entrenched in very general language and will require extensive interpretation to be enforced. In some instances, a consistent

[111] Albert (2013), 240.
[112] This view is not unavoidable. For a discussion of the rejection of a doctrine of supraconstitutional norms, see Baranger (2011), 402–3.
[113] Albert (2010), 683.
[114] Ibid.
[115] Ibid., 684.
[116] Baranger (2011), 403.
[117] Jacobsohn (2010), 133
[118] This is the title of the third chapter in Jacobsohn (2010), 84–135.

application of the eternity clause as an ordering mechanism might require an extensive and unpredictable reshuffling of constitutional commitments. In short, it might create more problems than it solves. This, of course, assuming the ordering norms themselves are coherent and easily identifiable—a precondition more easily met by Germany's Article 79(3) than by India's shifting basic structure doctrine, or indeed by Bosnia's vast apparatus of international human rights commitments.

Even where the eternity clause was intended to entrench the values atop the constitutional hierarchy, there may be unintended or questionable outcomes to this choice. The German unamendable commitment to human dignity, for example, has been at the root of a rich constitutional jurisprudence ranging from lifetime imprisonment to counter-terrorism measures.[119] It was also, however, at the heart of constitutional conflicts surrounding access to abortion. In a 1975 case where it was asked to review the constitutionality of new legislative measures designed to liberalize access to abortion for West German women, the German Constitutional Court framed the issue as one of balancing: the woman's right to self-determination pitted against the right to life of the foetus.[120] While both were linked to human dignity, the threat to the right to life would always trump an interest in self-determination and as such, the court mandated the retention of abortion criminalization. The court only backtracked after reunification, when it retained its understanding of abortion as a dignity question but accepted parliament's choice of means to give effect to the interests of the foetus.[121] Though in practice available thanks to legal loopholes, abortion remains illegal under German law as of the time of writing. Constitutionally, the primacy of human dignity, enshrined in Article 1(1) of the German Basic Law and bolstered by its unamendable status, thus served as a trump, in conjunction with the right to life of the foetus, against other interests. It also framed how the abortion question would be adjudicated. Absent this constitutional primacy of dignity, it may be that equality-based arguments would have had more weight.

It is also interesting to note that access to abortion in East Germany was much more liberal than in its western counterpart, and that reunification meant the two disparate abortion regimes had to be reconciled. There is an interesting question of constitutional legitimacy to be raised here. German reunification was originally meant to occur in line with the original Articles 23 and 146 of the Basic Law. The former delineated the territorial applicability of the Basic Law to a list of Western *Länder*, the rest to come under its jurisdiction upon accession, while the latter indicated the temporary nature of the Basic Law, to be replaced by a new constitution adopted freely by the German people. This provisional nature of the Basic Law in

[119] 45 BVerfGE 187 ('*Life Imprisonment*') and 115 BVerfGE 118 ('*Aerial Security Law*'). For a brief discussion, see Albert (2019), 52–8.

[120] 39 BVerfGE 1 ('*Abortion I*').

[121] 88 BVerfGE 203 ('*Abortion II*').

fact had served to alleviate the democratic shortcomings in the adoption of the fundamental law.[122] However, reunification was achieved not via a new constitution-making exercise, but instead took the form of an accession of eastern *Länder* to West Germany on the basis of former Article 23. The provisional Basic Law was thus enshrined as the permanent constitution of unified Germany, complete not just with its eternity clause but also with the jurisprudence of the Constitutional Court surrounding it.

I therefore agree with the view that because of the conditions in which it takes place, the constitution-making process 'is much more conducive to partial or even conflicting innovations than it is to the adoption of coherent designs whose elements reinforce each other'.[123] As such, 'even a search for a consistent body of principles within a single constitutional document presents formidable problems'.[124] Constraints on time and resources, biases, accidents, pre-existing institutional capacity,[125] and above all the nature of negotiation and bargaining—'often involving an exchange of incommensurables'[126]—are not immediately conducive to a 'considered judgment' about constitutional hierarchy and coherence. There is no reason to assume that a constitution's eternity clause benefited from more virtuous drafting than the rest of the text and as such it is at least open to similar scrutiny, not veneration. Nor should we automatically assume drafters' intention for the unamendable provision to function as an ordering device, particularly in constitutions which do not explicitly grant courts review powers over it.

One might argue that constitutions are messy documents and it is the task of judicial interpretation to make sense of them. Walter Murphy identified two missions of constitutional interpretation: 'the first mission involves imposing a high but not rigid degree of order on what is typically unordered and often badly disordered'; the second is to apply values and principles to particular problems with 'political prudence'.[127] As will become apparent below, however, relying on notions of constitutional identity renders this double mission more difficult for courts and risks departing from the flexibility and prudential approach Murphy championed.

[122] Christoph Möllers, '"We Are (Afraid of) the People": Constituent Power in German Constitutionalism' in Martin Loughlin and Neil Walker, eds., *The Paradox of Constitutionalism: Constituent Power and Constitutional Form* (Oxford University Press 2008) 87, 96–7. The presence of an eternity clause, however, created some ambiguity about the provisional nature of the Basic Law. See Werner Heun, *The Constitution of Germany: A Contextual Analysis* (Hart 2011), 10 and Vicki Jackson, 'What's in a Name? Reflections on Timing, Naming, and Constitution-making', *William and Mary Law Review* 49:4 (2008) 1249, 1300.

[123] Horowitz (2008), 1226–7. This is especially true in post-conflict contexts, on which see Chapter 2 in this book.

[124] Walter F. Murphy, 'An Ordering of Constitutional Values', *South California Law Review* 53 (1980) 703, 704.

[125] Horowitz (2008), 1227–30.

[126] Ibid., 1230.

[127] Murphy (1980), 706.

Eternity clauses as expressive of exclusionary constitutional identity

As we have seen above, constitutional identity as a concept has been developed on the basis of a number of assumptions, including its purported affinity with liberal constitutionalism and a pacified notion of pluralism. We have also seen, however, that such theories risk excluding constitutional subjects from the ambit of constitutional identity, as well as being overly optimistic about the unifying potential of constitutions. I believe eternity clauses are also at risk of this original sin. While they are most often read as coextensive with the goods of liberal constitutionalism, we have already seen in Part I of this book that the content of eternity clauses may be liberal democratic in name but operate quite differently in practice. What I want to suggest here is that eternity clauses can also enshrine exclusionary values and thereby ground an exclusionary constitutional identity. I do not mean instances where these provisions have been subverted, commandeered, or abused. Nor do I mean eternity clauses in authoritarian or theocratic contexts, where they help prop up undemocratic constitutions. Instead, I am referring to exclusionary unamendability at the heart of democratic constitutionalism. Two examples will illustrate this possibility: unamendability in Romania and Israel.

The Romanian Constitution defines Romania as 'a national state, sovereign and independent, unitary and indivisible' (Article 1(1)). This definition is rendered unamendable via Article 152(1), which contains the constitutional eternity clause. I have shown elsewhere that interpreting this constitutional definition as civic as opposed to ethnic nationalist ignores its roots in early-twentieth-century nation-building efforts, the negotiations surrounding it in the 1990–1 constituent assembly, as well as the constitutional jurisprudence of the Romanian Constitutional Court.[128] Importantly, this exclusionary constitutional understanding of the state coexists, on the level of authority, with liberal democratic commitments to the independence of the judicial system, political pluralism, and fundamental rights, all of which are also part of the eternity clause. Chapter 1 in this book has already discussed how a seemingly benign unamendable official language provision can be interpreted and enforced in exclusionary ways.

The point here is slightly different: if we were to try and define the constitutional identity of Romania, this ethnic-based understanding of the political community would be difficult to avoid. The protection of minority rights and prohibition of discrimination guaranteed elsewhere in the constitution, and even the unamendable commitment to fundamental rights in Article 152(2), might have counterbalanced it.[129] In practice, however, this has not

[128] Suteu (2017a).

[129] Article 152(2) states that 'no amendment shall be adopted if it would result in the elimination of the fundamental rights and freedoms of citizens or of the guarantees of these rights and freedoms.'

happened.[130] While the Romanian Constitutional Court has not thus far relied on the concept of constitutional identity, its track record in enforcing unamendability is no reason for optimism. For example, a 2014 decision struck down attempts to revise the constitution, including to provide a basis for administrative territorial reorganization, on the grounds, inter alia, of breaching Article 1(1).[131] The Court did not disambiguate the national and unitary state principles, though it was clearly concerned with the proposed changes' purported effects on national unity:

> The unity of the nation, including from the perspective of traditions, is not compatible with the recognition of a different status, in the sense of administrative autonomy, for a portion of the country's population, based on the criterion of an identity of 'traditions'.[132]

The unacknowledged bogeyman was the threat of granting regional autonomy to the country's Hungarian minority. Also telling is a 2016 decision reviewing the constitutionality of a citizen initiative to amend the constitutional definition of the family as between a man and a woman.[133] In its review of whether the initiative breached the eternity clause, the Romanian court managed to entirely avoid raising the question of discrimination. Instead, the court determined that, given that the initiative did not eliminate the constitutional right to marry but merely specified its scope, it did not 'eliminate' this right and as such did not breach Article 152(2).[134] The court also invoked the heterosexual understanding of marriage at the time of the constitution's adoption in 1991, despite the fact that the language of the constitution—referring neutrally to 'spouses'—would have been sufficiently capacious to accommodate a more inclusive interpretation. It is not that the Romanian court should have forced the legal recognition of same-sex marriage in an abstract review of a popular initiative. However, its highly formalistic (and partially originalist) approach to determining the scope of the eternity clause illustrates the limits of unamendability as a normative benchmark. In constitutional identity terms, there is a tension between the democratic, rights-protecting, and pluralist elements of the Romanian constitution and its exclusionary ones.

As Mazen Masri has shown, despite not having a full or formal constitution, Israel does exhibit two forms of unamendability.[135] These include a form of

[130] For a more optimistic view of the prospects of constitutional identity in Romanian constitutionalism, see Simina Tănăsescu, 'Despre Identitatea Constituţională şi Rolul Integrator al Constituţiei', *Curierul Judiciar* 5 (2017) 243.

[131] Decizia nr. 80/2014, 16 February 2014.

[132] Ibid., para. 33. See also discussion in Suteu (2017a), 429.

[133] Decision No. 580/2016, 20 July 2016.

[134] Ibid., paras. 40–3.

[135] Mazen Masri, 'Unamendability in Israel: A Critical Perspective' in Richard Albert and Bertil Emrah Oder, eds., *An Unamendable Constitution? Unamendability in Constitutional Democracies* (Springer 2018) 169. See also Mazen Masri, *The Dynamics of Exclusionary Constitutionalism: Israel as a Jewish and Democratic State* (Hart 2017).

concealed unamendability, which prevents certain kinds of amendments through controlling the composition of the *Knesset*, and judicially introduced unwritten unamendability. Masri shows how both forms serve expressive *and* preservative functions, resulting in entrenching the Jewish definition of the state and creating a hierarchy among the citizenry and the entrenchment of favourable status for certain groups. In this context, then, unamendability becomes 'one manifestation of the significance of this [state] definition and the tensions and contradictions that inhere in it'.[136]

The story of unamendability in Israel is an unconventional one. In the first instance, the Supreme Court confirmed the constitutional status of Basic Laws and declared them a partial constitution, thereby introducing the requirement that only another Basic Law could amend them.[137] Given that no special entrenchment rules exist for the passing of such laws, this would appear not to be a significant hurdle to amendment. However, Masri argues that restrictions on the right to participate in parliamentary elections, found in Section 7A of Basic Law: the Knesset and other instruments regarding the registration of parties and the internal procedures of the *Knesset*, make certain constitutional amendments impossible.[138] This provision prohibits the express or implied negation of the existence of Israel as a Jewish and democratic state and incitement to racism. It gives legislative footing to ideas first developed in the 1965 *Yerdor* case, which had proclaimed restrictions on the electoral participation of parties that did not respect the 'fact' of Israel's founding as an eternal Jewish state, fulfilling the right to self-determination of the Jewish people.[139] The Supreme Court has taken a narrow approach to enforcing this provision and adopted a high evidentiary threshold. However, it has been argued that the screening in advance of the *ideas* that can enter the *Knesset* amounts to an implicit eternity clause.[140] Moreover, revolutionary amendments are neutralized 'not at the end of the road, in order to strike them down following their ratification, but at the gates of the constituent assembly, thereby neutralizing their potential initiators'.[141] This choice, reminiscent of the criminalization of even attempting to amend executive term limits in Honduras, seeks to stifle even the possibility of a legislative debate surrounding the definition of the state.[142]

This definition of the Israeli state is inescapable even by appeal to constituent power. The *Knesset* is recognized as authorized to exercise constituent power,

[136] Masri (2018), 170.

[137] CA 6821/93 *Bank Mizrahi HaMe'ouha* v. *Migdal Kfar Shitofui* (1995), IsrSC 49 (2) 221.

[138] Masri (2018), 175.

[139] Ibid., 176, citing EA 1/65 *Yerdor* v. *Chairman of the Central Elections Committee for the Sixth Knesset* (1965), IsrSC 19(3) 365.

[140] Masri (2018), 178.

[141] Sharon Weintal, 'The Challenge of Reconciling Constitutional Eternity Clauses with Popular Sovereignty: Toward Three-track Democracy in Israel as a Universal Holistic Constitutional System and Theory', *Israel Law Review* 44 (2011) 449, 468.

[142] On Honduras's term limit, see Chapter 2 in this book.

but subject to certain constitutional values.[143] These limits have been clarified by the Israeli Supreme Court as being the fundamental values of the state as Jewish and democratic.[144] Earlier optimism that only a narrow, restrained, and rights-affirming doctrine of unconstitutional constitutional amendment would emerge in Israel—in particular given its as yet incomplete constitution-making—missed the broader implications of unamendability.[145] As Masri has shown, unamendability in Israel 'is not merely descriptive: it plays an important role in defining the polity, the public culture, immigration rights, state policies and the scope of protection of constitutional rights. It also mandates that Israel must have a Jewish majority.'[146] It permeates the entire legal system and legal interpretation and is enforceable even while it remains deeply contested. Moreover, the trend has been towards further entrenchment of this exclusionary ethos, not least through the passing of the 2018 Basic Law: Israel as the Nation State of the Jewish People.[147]

In both these cases, the constitutions themselves retain an exclusionary core—they are, in fact, founded upon it. The fact that both constitutions otherwise enshrine liberal democratic values, including minority and fundamental rights, does not eliminate this problem. Universal and particular values are entrenched alongside each other: democracy and a commitment to fundamental rights on the one hand, and an ethnic-national (in Romania) and ethnic/religious (in Israel) definition of the state on the other.[148] Romanian and Israeli constitutional identities are therefore foundationally exclusionary in a way that is not simply reflective of constitutional 'disharmony'. They have had real consequences in the interpretation of both constitutions, and unamendability has served to bolster this exclusion.

3.3 Constitutional identity as a limit to European integration

Constitutional identity has been embraced in adjudication by a number of constitutional courts, nowhere more actively than in the area of European integration. Different national courts have invoked constitutional identity in order to limit the application of European law or else the transfer of sovereign powers to the European Union. In some instances, constitutional eternity clauses have been

143 *Bank Mizrahi*, 394.

144 HCJ 6427/02 *The Movement for the Quality of Governance in Israel* v. *The Knesset* (2006) and HCJ 4908/10 *Bar-On* v. *The Knesset* (2010).

145 Aharon Barak, 'Unconstitutional Constitutional Amendments', *Israel Law Review* 44 (2011) 321.

146 Masri (2018), 177.

147 Tamar Hostovsky Brandes, 'Basic Law: Israel as the Nation State of the Jewish People: Implications for Equality, Self-Determination and Social Solidarity', *Minnesota Journal of International Law* 29:1 (2020) 65.

148 See also discussion in Masri (2018), 185, 188–90.

interpreted as the repositories of the values making up this constitutional identity—in other words, they have become limits not just on constitutional amendment at the domestic level, but also on a process of supranational pooling of sovereignty and lawmaking.

Matters are further complicated by the fact that a concept of national identity is recognized within European Union law itself. Article 4(2) of the Treaty on European Union (TEU) guarantees respect for member states' 'national identities, inherent in their fundamental structures, political and constitutional'. How far this respect for domestic variance is meant to go remains unclear, including the ever-frequent question of whether Article 2(4) can be relied upon to justify breaches of European law.[149] There is great variation across European courts' reliance on the concept of constitutional identity, both in terms of its relationship to Article 4(2) and in terms of the very nature of the review they are engaging in. We know from the literature on expressive amendment rules that '[t]he task of interpreting entrenched values need not commit us to a particular technique of interpretation, be it originalism, living constitutionalism, or another method'.[150] The growing constitutional identity jurisprudence of European courts, and in particular that of the German Constitutional Court, showcases the rise of constitutional identity review as one such method.

Constitutional identity review in Germany

As noted above, the German *Ewigkeitsklausel* (Article 79(3)) was drafted without reference to the concept of constitutional identity.[151] The concept was only later reintroduced in German constitutional thinking and only explicitly embraced by the Constitutional Court in its *Lisbon* decision in 2009.[152] That decision came on the heels of a series of judgments around European integration in which the German court sought to establish limits on the supremacy of European law[153] and to 'surrender[ing] by way of ceding sovereign rights to international institutions the identity of the prevailing constitutional order of the Federal Republic by breaking into its basic framework, that is, into the structure which makes it up'.[154] Those initial decisions did not rely on Article 79(3) to identify these limits, but on a holistic interpretation of Article 24(1) of the *Grundgesetz* which formed the basis for sovereignty transfers to international organizations at the time. In 1992, a new

[149] Polzin (2017), 1597. See also Elke Cloots, *National Identity in EU Law* (Oxford University Press 2015) 127, refuting the position that Article 4(2) qualifies the principle of primacy of EU law.
[150] Albert (2013), 264.
[151] Polzin (2016).
[152] 2 BvE 2/08, 30 June 2009.
[153] 37 BVerfGE 271, 29 May 1974 ('*Solange I*').
[154] 73 BVerfGE 339, 22 October 1986 ('*Solange II*').

Article 23(1) was adopted which clarified the legal basis for European integration and its limits in Article 79(2) and (3).[155]

The 1993 *Maastricht* decision further developed the German jurisprudence on limits to European integration by firmly establishing the democracy principle as part of these limitations, as well as the more contested principle of loss of German statehood.[156] The *Maastricht* decision did rely on Article 79(3) in conjunction with Article 20(1) to ground this principle of democracy, as well as to provide the contours within which any transfer of sovereignty under Article 23(1) was to take place. Interestingly, the court also considered the limits of the eternity clause itself, finding that it could only be overcome by a revolutionary act of novel constitution-making; the court also explicitly rejected the possibility of legislative amendment of Article 79(3) endorsed by a popular referendum.[157]

The *Lisbon* case originated in four complaints brought by members of the extreme right and the extreme left of the political spectrum. The complaints questioned the constitutionality of three acts: the Act Approving the Treaty of Lisbon, the Act Amending the Basic Law (Articles 23, 45, and 93), and the Act Extending and Strengthening the Rights of the German Federal Parliament (*Bundestag*) and the German Federal Council of States (*Bundesrat*) in European Union Matters. The claimants could not point to a specific injury so much as they wanted a review of the Treaty of Lisbon itself. This amounted to an abstract review which the court decided to engage in. The court held the first two acts compatible with the Basic Law but found the third to insufficiently empower the German Parliament vis-à-vis European policymaking and EU treaty amending procedures. This resulted in the German parliament rushing through a new law strengthening parliamentary oversight of European integration.

The court's analysis which is relevant here, however, came mostly in comments made *obiter dicta*, as part of the examination of whether the applicants' Article 38(1) rights had been violated by way of infringements of provisions in Articles 20(1), 20(2), 23(1), and 79(3).[158] The judges referred to an 'inalienable constitutional identity'[159] which the court alone was entrusted to protect against transgression, including by way of European integration. The *Bundesverfassungsgericht*

155 Article 23(1) declares Germany's participation in the European project, establishes the principle of subsidiarity, and links European integration to Article 79(2) and (3) ('The establishment of the European Union, as well as changes in its treaty foundations and comparable regulations that amend or supplement this Basic Law, or make such amendments or supplements possible, shall be subject to paragraphs (2) and (3) of Article 79').

156 89 BVerfGE 155, 12 October 1993 ('*Maastricht*'). On the debates surrounding whether statehood is an implicit part of the German eternity clause, as well as whether loss of German statehood is to be a limit on European integration, see Polzin (2016), 428.

157 *Maastricht* decision, para. 180.

158 Article 38(1) reads: 'Members of the German Bundestag shall be elected in general, direct, free, equal and secret elections. They shall be representatives of the whole people, not bound by orders or instructions, and responsible only to their conscience.'

159 *Lisbon* decision, para. 219.

even went so far as to find a separate type of judicial review, termed 'identity review', which it could employ alongside ultra vires review of EU law to determine the latter's compatibility with Germany's inalienable Article 79(3) values.[160] The court thus explained that it could in the future declare European law inapplicable in Germany.[161] EU law's primacy had limits, and in Germany those limits were reinforced by the eternity clause. Despite the court's discussion of the legislature possibly creating 'an additional type of proceedings before the Federal Constitutional Court that is especially tailored to ultra vires review and identity review',[162] commentators have rightly noted that the judgment reads as though such identity control was already in the court's power.[163]

Much ink has been spilled in unpacking the decision's arguments and the literature abounds in analyses of its implications and contradictions.[164] I discuss two aspects of the judgment here that illustrate why constitutional identity is such a thorny concept in constitutional jurisprudence: the practical difficulties of judicial identity review and the problematic link the court establishes between constitutional identity and constituent power.[165]

First, there are serious qualms over the consequences of the Constitutional Court engaging in identity control of constitutionality, particularly in the European context. Some have worried about the destabilizing effects of such identity review, seeing it as tilting the delicate balance created via the German court's past *Solange* jurisprudence and endangering 'the stability of the relationship between German constitutional law and European law in the realm of fundamental rights; fundamental rights problems are simply going to be declared identity problems'.[166] Not only is there a risk of recasting *constitutional* issues as matters of constitutional identity, but there is the danger of European member states recasting all sorts of issues in the language of identity. 'Allowing the concept to have a substantial function in legal terms', it has been argued, 'may turn out to be a Pandora's box',[167] and, in rendering the concept of identity meaningless: 'If anything is national identity, nothing will be'.[168]

[160] Ibid., para. 240.
[161] Ibid. para. 241.
[162] Ibid.
[163] See Mayer (2011), 783.
[164] See articles in *German Law Journal* Dieter Grimm 10:8 (2009); Dieter Grimm, 'Defending Sovereign Statehood Against Transforming the Union Into a State', *European Constitutional Law Review* 5:3 (2009) 353; Mayer (2011); Kalypso Nicolaïdis, 'Germany as Europe: How the Constitutional Court Unwittingly Embraced EU Demoi-cracy', *International Journal of Constitutional Law* 9:3–4 (2011) 786; Jo Murkens, *From Empire to Union: Conceptions of German Constitutional Law since 1871* (Oxford University Press 2013), 178–212.
[165] A third aspect of the *Lisbon* case, regarding the court's interpretation of the principle of open statehood in the German constitution, will be discussed in Chapter 5 of this book, in the context of debates surrounding unamendability and supranational law.
[166] Mayer (2011), 762.
[167] Ibid., 784.
[168] Ibid.

While these fears may have initially been exaggerated, the core concern—that the court is relying on a concept which creates more problems than it solves—remains. Indeed, it is boosted by the admission that not only is it difficult to operationalize, but constitutional identity (and other concepts the court relies on in its judgment, such as sovereignty) does not appear to have a sound constitutional foundation in the Basic Law.[169] To its harshest critics, the court 'respond[ed] to questions that the case does not raise with answers the Constitution does not provide',[170] and, in so doing, undermined its own standing and exceeded its competence.[171] Moreover, the court's unacknowledged reliance on 'constitutional ideology' (including with regard to the concepts of state, sovereignty, identity, and *Volk*) arguably rendered its claims to a power to review constitutional identity infringements by European law dubious.[172] Others saw in the *Lisbon* decision a judicial strike back against the European Union's ever-expanding democratic deficit, defensible insofar as it sought to reinforce parliamentary democracy and democratic control of the European integration process.[173] Many found themselves somewhere in the middle, critiquing the court's messy reasoning but applauding its democratic emphasis.[174] From the point of view of my analysis of constitutional unamendability, what *Lisbon* did was state, in no uncertain terms, that the development of European law was subject to the German eternity clause.

Second, the *Lisbon* decision drew a connection between constitutional identity and limits on constituent power. That Article 79(3) 'prevents a constitution-amending legislature from disposing of the identity of the free constitutional order'[175] is congruent with the aims behind the *Ewigkeitsklausel*. The court went further, however, and left open the question of whether these substantive limitations also apply to the constituent power:

> It may remain open whether, due to the universal nature of dignity, freedom and equality alone, this commitment even applies to the constituent power, i.e. to the

[169] Murkens (2013), 207 and Polzin (2016).

[170] Christoph Schönberger, 'Lisbon in Karlsruhe: Maastricht's Epigones At Sea', *German Law Journal* 10:8 (2009) 1201, 1214.

[171] Murkens (2013), 208.

[172] Ibid.

[173] Philipp Kiiver, 'The Lisbon Judgment of the German Constitutional Court: A Court-Ordered Strengthening of the National Legislature in the EU', *European Law Journal* 16:5 (2010) 578 and Erik Oddvar Eriksen and John Erik Fossum, 'Bringing European Democracy Back In—Or How to Read the German Constitutional Court's Lisbon Treaty Ruling', *European Law Journal* 17:2 (2011) 153. *Cf* Lars Vinx, 'The Incoherence of Strong Popular Sovereignty', *International Journal of Constitutional Law* 11:1 (2013) 101.

[174] Mayer (2011); Nicolaïdis (2011).

[175] *Lisbon* decision, para. 216. See also para. 218, where the court states that 'the constituent power has not granted the representatives and bodies of the people a mandate to dispose of the identity of the constitution. No constitutional body has been granted the power to amend the constitutional principles which are essential pursuant to Article 79.3 of the Basic Law. The Federal Constitutional Court monitors this.'

> case that the German people, in free self-determination, but in a continuity of legality to the rule of the Basic Law, gives itself a new constitution.[176]

One reading of this statement may be that, given the universality of the principles in question, they also apply to the drafting of a new constitution, not just to legislative amendments. Such an interpretation may be in line with one strand of constitutional scholarship in Germany which has read Article 79(3) as an implied limitation on Article 146, the Basic Law's provision on the adoption of a new constitution.[177] This strand is not without its critics, however, who are reluctant to expand the reach of the *Ewigkeitsklausel* beyond its text and original aims.[178] The court's *obiter* statements on this matter have also been interpreted as reflecting the positive predisposition of German constitutional law and theory towards natural law principles, the operation of which is to serve as an additional, supraconstitutional safeguard against a return to fascism.[179] Whether there are substantive limitations on constitution-making and how to identify them is a thorny, as yet underdeveloped, question in constitutional theory.

Another reading of this statement, however, is potentially more worrisome. In a judgment wherein the court asserts its power as protector of Germany's constitutional identity internally and externally, one could read here a judicial warning that even wholly new exercises of constituent power could come under the court's Article 79(3) scrutiny. In the European context, this would mean that even were the German people to express their desire for a new constitution, possibly even one which allowed integration within a federal European Union, this new act of constitution-making would still be reviewed by the court. Thus, the court left open the possibility of Article 79(3)—or at least some of its principles—to reach beyond its original understanding within the confines of legislative amendments and to regulate constitutional revolution itself.[180]

The German Constitutional Court has continued to negotiate the relationship with European law via identity review.[181] In its 2014 *OMT* decision, for example, the court ruled on the legality of the Outright Monetary Transaction Programme of the European Central Bank.[182] It stated in no uncertain terms that the constitutional identity of the Basic Law is 'laid down' in Article 79(3) and proceeded to

[176] Ibid., para. 217.

[177] See Murkens (2013), 174.

[178] Ibid., 174–5.

[179] Polzin (2016), 431.

[180] The idea that constituent power is subject to material limits derived from natural law is not new in constitutional theory, even while remaining contested. See Joel Colón-Ríos, *Constituent Power and the Law* (Oxford University Press 2020), 158.

[181] For an overview of these developments, see Christian Calliess, 'Constitutional Identity in Germany: One for Three or Three in One?' in Christian Calliess and Gerhard van der Schyff, eds., *Constitutional Identity in a Europe of Multilevel Constitutionalism* (Cambridge University Press 2019) 153.

[182] 142 BVerfGE 123 ('*OMT*'), 14 January 2014.

identify a principle of budgetary parliamentary responsibility in the constitution's unamendable principle of democracy.[183] In its 2015 *Arrest Warrant II* decision, the German court found the principle of individual guilt to be founded on the unamendable guarantee of human dignity in the Basic Law and as such also protected from supranational interference.[184] In 2020, the *PSPP* judgment reiterated that European integration found its limits in Article 79(3) and that the inalienable principle of democracy included the budgetary powers of the *Bundestag*.[185] Should the German authorities wish to retroactively amend European law to allow more expansive competences to European institutions, this could only be done within the confines of the German eternity clause.[186]

Constitutional identity review beyond Germany

Subsequent developments in other European states have seen their constitutional courts similarly declare limits on European integration stemming from national constitutional law, with or without reference to eternity clauses.[187] For example, in 2018, Italy's Constitutional Court embraced constitutional identity review as part of a more defensive attitude towards European integration than in previous years.[188] The judgment was rendered in reaction to the European Court of Justice's *Taricco* decision, which had determined that Italian tax judges could set aside statutes of limitation in investigations and prosecutions of tax fraud against the financial interests of the European Union. Italian constitutional judges saw this as a breach of the constitutional principle of legality, especially the prohibition of retroactivity in criminal law. The 2018 judgment has been seen as shifting Italian law from a more pluralist, dialogic stance vis-à-vis European law that had emphasized common constitutional traditions, towards a more statist, protective one grounded in the notion of constitutional identity.[189] The Czech Constitutional Court was an early adopter of identity review, building on its jurisprudence in defence of a

[183] Ibid., para. 120.

[184] 2 BvR 2735/14 ('*European Arrest Warrant II*'), 15 December 2015.

[185] 2 BvR 859/15 ('*PSPP*'), 5 May 2020.

[186] Ibid., para. 109.

[187] For a comparative discussion of these developments, see Alejandro Saiz Arnaiz and Carina Alcoberro Llivina, eds., *National Constitutional Identity and European Integration* (Intersentia 2013); Stefan Theil, 'What Red Lines, If Any, Do the Lisbon Judgments of European Constitutional Courts Draw for Future EU Integration?', *German Law Journal* 15:4 (2014) 599; Federico Fabbrini and András Sajó, 'The Dangers of Constitutional Identity', *European Law Journal* 25 (2019) 457, 459–61.

[188] Ordinanza n. 24/2017 and Sentenza n. 115/2018.

[189] See discussion in Federico Fabbrini and Oreste Pollicino, 'Constitutional Identity in Italy' in Christian Calliess and Gerhard van der Schyff, eds., *Constitutional Identity in a Europe of Multilevel Constitutionalism* (Cambridge University Press 2019) 201.

substantive constitutional core rooted in its eternity clause.[190] In 2012, the Czech court went further and actually disapplied European law when it declared ultra vires the European Court of Justice's ruling in *Landtova*.[191] In 2016 the Danish Supreme Court set aside a European Court of Justice judgment claiming that it breached entrenched labour law principles.[192] Courts in Belgium and France have also evoked the concept.[193]

The significance of the *Lisbon* decision and its other European counterparts cannot be understated. From the point of view of the European project, they seem to represent 'a symptom for unresolved issues of European integration that remain unresolved even with the new legal order that the Lisbon Treaty establishes'.[194] They also echo earlier calls to caution against a damaging competition between national courts and their supranational counterpart rooted in sociological and cultural resistance to integration.[195] From the perspective of democratic constitutionalism, we might be tempted to see in this 'narrative diversity' a plus, 'the spirit of European demoi-cracy' in action.[196] European courts invoking principles of democracy and national ownership over the integration process would at first glance be a win for democracy.

However, the rise of constitutional identity review in Europe is cause for democratic anxiety as well. On the one hand, it is a judicial creation, seeing national courts attempt to claw back control over legal interpretation.[197] They may do this in the name of democracy, but the move is grounded in an appeal to an amorphous, malleable, and unpredictable concept of constitutional identity. The German court's anchoring of identity review in Article 79(3) did not solve the 'incurable lack of determinacy' of the concept of constitutional identity.[198]

[190] Decisions Pl. ÚS 19/08: Treaty of Lisbon I, 26 November 2008 and Pl. ÚS 29/09: Treaty of Lisbon II, 3 November 2009. See discussion in David Kosař and Ladislav Vyhnánek, 'Constitutional Identity in the Czech Republic: A New Twist on an Old Fashioned Idea' in Christian Calliess and Gerhard van der Schyff, eds., *Constitutional Identity in a Europe of Multilevel Constitutionalism* (Cambridge University Press 2019), 85. See also Chapter 1 in this book.

[191] Pl. ÚS 5/12: Slovak Pension XVII, 31 January 2012.

[192] Case 441/14 *Dansk Industri* v. *Rasmussen*, 19 April 2016.

[193] Fabbrini and Sajó (2019), 461.

[194] Mayer (2011), 785.

[195] Julio Baquero Cruz, 'The Legacy of the Maastricht-Urteil and the Pluralist Movement', *European Law Journal* 14:4 (2008) 389.

[196] Nicolaïdis (2011), 786.

[197] Writing before the recent rise of constitutional identity review in Europe, Joseph Weiler was sceptical about constitutional courts claiming to defend core national constitutional values. He viewed their attempts to place limits on the power of political branches as 'accompanied by a huge dose of judicial self-empowerment and no small measure of sanctimonious moralizing'. For Weiler, then, '[d]efending the constitutional identity of the state and its core values turns out in many cases to be a defence of some hermeneutic foible adopted by five judges against four' (Joseph H. H. Weiler, 'Federalism without Constitutionalism: Europe's Sonderweg' in Kalypso Nicolaïdis and Robert Howse, eds., *The Federal Vision: Legitimacy and Levels of Governance in the United States and the European Union* (Oxford University Press 2001) 54, 64–5).

[198] Fabbrini and Sajó (2019), 458. For a critique of the radical indeterminacy of constitutional identity, see Pietro Faraguna, 'Constitutional Identity in the EU—A Shield or a Sword?', *German Law Journal* 18:7 (2017) 1617.

Questions remain as to whether the eternity clause is the exclusive limit on transfer of sovereignty to Europe, as well as about how narrowly or flexibly to interpret Article 79(3) and the *Lisbon* judgment's hint that it may even place limits on constituent power.[199] On the other hand, national constitutional identity increasingly appears as a synonym for national sovereignty. European constitutional courts seem to be shifting in their attitude towards European integration, from proactive and dialogic to defensive in the form of a 'them and us' perspective.[200] In other words, such efforts to guard the national legal space and correct a supranational democratic deficit risk slipping into parochialism. No doubt there is much soul-searching, and reform, that the European Union should engage in. That should not blind us to the dangers of national courts embracing constitutional identity review, however.

3.4 Abusive constitutional identity review

Another instance of a court embracing constitutional identity review is cause for concern for different reasons. In 2016, the Hungarian Constitutional Court issued a judgment in an abstract review of the compatibility between the country's constitution and the European Council's temporary relocation mechanism for asylum seekers.[201] The decision was the culmination of the Orbán government's anti-refugee policies pursued first by a failed referendum on whether the country should reject the European Union's relocation plan, and later via a failed attempt to pass the Seventh Amendment to defend Hungarian constitutional identity.[202] The amendment, which narrowly failed to reach the required two-thirds majority to pass, would have created a state duty to defend constitutional self-identity, rooted in the 'historical constitution', to the National Avowal; added explicit limits to the Europe clause; and altered the prohibition against expulsion of foreign citizens. The court, by then packed by the Orbán government, sought to clarify whether state authorities were required to implement European law if this was in conflict with fundamental rights under the Hungarian Fundamental Law; whether they had to implement European law when this was ultra vires; and whether the relocation of foreign citizens (in this case, from one European member state to another) was permissible under the Hungarian Constitution.[203] The latter issue, framed as potentially in conflict with the prohibition of collective expulsion under Hungarian

[199] Calliess (2019), 167–9.
[200] Mayer (2011), 785; Fabbrini and Pollicino (2019).
[201] Decision 22/2016. (XII. 5.) AB.
[202] For an overview of the saga, see Gábor Halmai, 'Abuse of Constitutional Identity: The Hungarian Constitutional Court on Interpretation of Article E) (2) of the Fundamental Law', *Review of Central and East European Law* 43 (2018a) 23.
[203] Ibid., 30.

constitutional law, was not resolved by the court on grounds that it exceeded its competence.

The Hungarian court, citing the German *Lisbon* decision, found that it too had the competence to determine limits to the primacy of European law. It considered itself duty-bound to examine whether the application of European law 'results in a violation of human dignity, the essential content of any other fundamental right or the sovereignty (including the extent of the competences transferred by the State) and the constitutional self-identity of Hungary'.[204] Citing the German *Solange* and *European Arrest Warrant II* reasoning, the Hungarian court also found that constitutional fundamental rights, including the protection of human dignity, limited all exercises of public authority. Relying on Article B) (1) of the Fundamental Law, the court reiterated the principle that public power derives from the people and found that 'the maintenance of Hungary's sovereignty should be presumed when reviewing the joint exercise of competences' that have already been conferred on the European Union.[205] The court also explained that Article 4(2) TEU empowered it to engage in constitutional identity review, together with the Fundamental Law itself. It determined that Hungarian constitutional identity was not a static or closed list of values, its content being determined on the basis of the entire Fundamental Law, the National Avowal, as well as Hungary's 'historical constitution'. As this identity was not created, only acknowledged, by the 2011 Fundamental Law, it could not be waived by way of an international treaty.[206] As such, the Hungarian Constitutional Court itself remained the ultimate guardian of both sovereignty and constitutional identity.

The judgment has been the subject of much criticism, even while the Hungarian court had been careful to indicate it was not reviewing the European Council decision itself (and thereby possibly engaging in an ultra vires act), but merely indicating the limits to such decisions on the basis of constitutional identity review.[207] It is not just that the court was seen as exceeding its constitutional competences of review or that the issue of asylum-seeker relocation was shoehorned into a constitutional identity question.[208] The court's reference to constitutional identity as rooted in Hungary's 'historical constitution' rightly gave legal commentators pause. This is an amorphous idea, whose contours were never defined and which, given its thousand-year span, would include a longer tradition of authoritarian rule than of democracy.[209] The judgment has also been criticized for casting

[204] Decision 22/2016. (XII. 5.) AB, para. 46.
[205] Ibid., paras. 59–60.
[206] Ibid., para. 67.
[207] Halmai (2018), 39.
[208] Ibid.
[209] Ibid., 40–1; Pál Sonnevend, András Jakab, and Lóránt Csink, 'The Constitution as an Instrument of Everyday Party Politics: The Basic Law of Hungary' in Armin von Bogdandy and Pál Sonnevend, eds., *Constitutional Crisis in the European Constitutional Area: Theory, Law and Politics in Hungary and Romania* (Hart 2015) 33, 36.

European institutions in the role of 'Other' and developing an exclusionary notion of constitutional identity.[210] It has also been viewed in regional perspective, as one piece of a wider Central and East European puzzle that has seen courts in the region developing 'ethnocultural' notions of constitutional identity in order to eschew their European obligations.[211] The defence of constitutional identity, rooted in Hungary's historical constitution, has since been formally entrenched in the Fundamental Law. Following a renewed supermajority in parliament, the Orbán government passed a constitutional amendment in 2018 providing a textual basis for constitutional self-defence.[212]

The Hungarian Constitutional Court judgment and the 2018 amendment allow us to investigate the normative underpinnings of constitutional identity theory more clearly. In what way can we speak, with its critics, of 'abusive' constitutional identity? As we have seen in section 3.3, constitutional identity review is no longer just an instrument facilitating dialogue between national and European courts—it has become instead the vehicle for limiting European integration. Thus, the turn inward of the Hungarian judgment cannot constitute the sole grounds for critique. The judgment's conflation of a cultural identity (understood in ethnic terms), rooted in a nebulous historical constitution, with constitutional identity is indeed worrying. It not only showcases the dangers of a radically indeterminate concept.[213] To my mind, it also illustrates the malleability of a concept whose contours were never purely legal. Despite the growing juridification of constitutional identity, therefore, it seems poised always to retain its extralegal—and therefore possibly exclusionary and undemocratic—elements.[214]

3.5 Conclusion

This chapter has sought to clarify the concept of constitutional identity and its potential import for theories of unamendability. The investigation put forth has shown this concept to be problematic in several senses. First, it has found it to be indeterminate and to carry dubious explanatory value as an autonomous notion. Second, the same indeterminacy of the concept makes it difficult to clarify when and how it will be unlawfully trespassed. Third, the normative underpinnings of

[210] Zsolt Koertvelyesi and Balazs Majtenyi, 'Game of Values: The Threat of Exclusive Constitutional Identity, the EU and Hungary', *German Law Journal* 18:7 (2017) 1721.

[211] Kirszta Kovacs, 'The Rise of an Ethnocultural Constitutional Identity in the Jurisprudence of the East Central European Courts', *German Law Journal* 18:7 (2017) 703.

[212] Bill number T/332, Seventh amendment of the Basic Law of Hungary.

[213] Faraguna (2017); Fabbrini and Sajó (2019).

[214] See also discussion in R. Daniel Kelemen and Laurent Pech, 'The Uses and Abuses of Constitutional Pluralism: Undermining the Rule of Law in the Name of Constitutional Identity in Hungary and Poland', *Cambridge Yearbook of European Legal Studies* 21 (2019) 59, who draw a link between the evolution of constitutional identity review and the unresolved tensions within understandings of constitutional pluralism.

the idea of constitutional identity must be made visible, in particular its liberal and pluralist assumptions and possible exclusions. Fourth, unamendable provisions inevitably lead to the identification of a normative superstructure within the constitution, which is then jealously guarded by constitutional courts. They are meant to sit atop this hierarchy as ordering mechanism. This ignores the often incoherent priorities entrenched in the constitution and may oversimplify deep-seated constitutional conflicts. When non-inclusive values are built into this hierarchy, including via eternity clauses, constitutional identity reveals its lack of neutrality and potentially exclusionary implications.

The link between eternity clauses and an independent hierarchy of norms in the constitution is also at the centre of conflicts between constitutional courts and their supranational counterparts. In the European Union context, national courts have pushed back against European integration by resorting to constitutional identity claims. Where available, they have grounded these claims in national eternity clauses, seeing them as the repositories of constitutional identity. This is a very different application of unamendability from what has been envisioned by scholars of eternity clauses, but it was inevitable. The rise of constitutional identity review in Europe illustrates that unamendability's expressive and preservative functions are unavoidably fused. Indeed, it would make little sense to eternalize fundamental values if they were to remain merely symbolic.

In my view, the developments discussed in this chapter should caution against employing the concept of constitutional identity in a legal sense. Constitutional identity has had a remarkable arc, going from a more sociological notion used to capture constitutional specificity, to a normative concept meant to express constitutional fundamentals, to a method of constitutional review vis-à-vis supranational law. It has been said that eternity clauses are there to define and preserve the constitutive elements of the foundation myth.[215] We can accept this proposition more easily if it is meant as a descriptor or guide for identifying a polity's constitutional identity in the sociological sense, as a constantly changing, ever restless 'process of becoming'. Once constitutional identity claims enter the courtroom, however, we find ourselves in the slippery situation of having courts attempt to police the boundaries of this exercise in myth creation. Suddenly, a complex, constructed, disharmonious, ever-changing constitutional identity is subjected to the vagaries of constitutional adjudication and, in the European context, to a vertical tug of war between national and supranational authorities. The Hungarian example has shown just how easily constitutional identity arguments can be subverted to prop up an increasingly autocratic regime. It should have us wonder whether the dangers of speaking the language of identity are indeed ever worth it.

[215] Preuss (2011), 445.

4

Eternity as Judicially Created Doctrine

Implicit Unamendability as the Embodiment of the Constitution's Basic Structure or Minimum Core

The previous chapter dealt primarily with unconstitutional constitutional amendment doctrines developed to enforce a formal eternity clause, including the recent rise of constitutional identity review. Chapter 4 looks at judicially created doctrines in the absence of or supplementing any formal unamendability in the constitution. India's basic structure doctrine is the prime example of this, although similar doctrines have now been adopted in a number of jurisdictions. Understanding how such doctrines operate and under what conditions they bolster democratic constitutionalism has therefore never been more timely.

The chapter proceeds in four steps. I first delineate arguments in favour of implicit unamendability, which posit that all constitutions rest on certain inalienable principles that should not be open to change through ordinary amendment. These could be in addition to a formal eternity clause or be entirely judicially discovered, whether on the basis of constitutional preambles, tiered amendment rules or otherwise. Moreover, they should be enforced by courts via material amendment review. I then analyse the most widespread category of implicit unamendability doctrines: basic structure doctrines. Starting in India, the chapter offers a comparative overview of the global rise of the basic structure doctrine as a judicial tool to review amendments. Already here, a mixed picture appears, wherein the danger of judicial overreach justified on the basis of violations of the constitutional basic structure becomes clear. Third, I discuss in detail doctrinal and scholarly attempts to reign in doctrines of implicit unamendability, all relying on judicial self-restraint. Through case law in which the unamendable principle of judicial independence was relied on to block reasonable attempts at constitutional reform, I show the difficulty in trying to institute a limited doctrine of implicit unamendability. Finally, I discuss why unamendability doctrines might not be of much help in preventing democratic backsliding.

The chapter concludes that implicit unamendability is an especially powerful tool of judicial self-empowerment that is open to the dangers of both over- and under-reach. It is not just that it rests on democratically shaky ground given that it

Eternity Clauses in Democratic Constitutionalism. Silvia Suteu, Oxford University Press. © Silvia Suteu 2021.
DOI: 10.1093/oso/9780198858867.003.0005

is a purely judicial creature. The even greater risk comes from the unclear scope of the implicitly unamendable principles and the impossibility of delineating a workable standard of material amendment review.

4.1 The contours of implicit unamendability

Defining implicit unamendability

Arguments in favour of courts embracing unconstitutional constitutional amendment doctrines do not always hinge on whether the constitutional text formally includes an eternity clause upon which to ground such doctrines. Typically illustrated by the most famous instance of such a judicially created doctrine, the Indian basic structure doctrine, such thinking does not take the absence of a textual hook as determinative. Quite on the contrary, there is an underlying assumption that all democratic constitutions, insofar as they were not meant to be suicide pacts, should be seen as empowering their guardians—taken to be constitutional courts—with the power to strike down constitutional amendments on substantive grounds. Indeed, this is the same thinking at the root of constitutional courts interpreting formal eternity clauses as presupposing the power to enforce them in practice, even where the constitution is silent on the matter of substantive amendment review or, as in the case of the original Turkish 1982 Constitution, explicitly limits courts to procedural amendment review. In some instances, such as in Italy, implicit unamendability has been recognized alongside formal eternity clauses.[1] In others, as in the Bangladeshi case discussed below, a judicially created doctrine of unamendability may end up formalized via constitutional amendment. One of the very first instances of a formal eternity clause, Article 112 in Norway's 1814 Constitution, sought to protect 'the spirit of the constitution' as a whole, thereby blurring the distinction between explicit and implicit unamendability.[2]

There are clear overlaps between such arguments and those discussed in Chapter 1, regarding the militant democracy justifications for unamendability. The difference is that formal eternity clauses are envisioned by the constitutional drafters themselves as defences against abuses, whereas implicit unamendability is judicially developed. There are also similarities between unconstitutional

[1] Sentenza n. 1146/1988.

[2] Eivind Smith, 'Old and Protected? On the "Supra-Constitutional" Clause in the Constitution of Norway', *Israel Law Review* 44 (2011) 369. See also Juliano Zaiden Benvindo, 'Brazil in the Context of the Debate Over Unamendability in Latin America' in Richard Albert and Bertil Emrah Oder, eds., *An Unamendable Constitution? Unamendability in Constitutional Democracies* (Springer 2018) 345, arguing that, while formal eternity clauses may be thought of as narrower than judicially created doctrines of unamendability, this is not always the case, particularly when eternity clauses enshrine open-ended values. He gives the example of the open-ended unamendability of rights protections under the Brazilian Constitution.

constitutional amendment doctrines and constitutional identity review. Indeed, the concept of constitutional identity has been developed in scholarship reflecting on experiences with unconstitutional constitutional amendment doctrines, with the Indian case prominent among them.[3] While the rise of constitutional identity review is currently seen primarily through a European lens, as the battleground between national constitutionalism and supranational integration, its conceptual limits are not defined by this European milieu.[4] Equally, we can observe that basic structure and minimum core doctrines of unamendability also often invoke—implicitly or explicitly—the expressive nature of the values and principles they seek to protect. The example of the Czech Republic discussed in Chapter 1 illustrates precisely this blurry distinction: a formal eternity clause, written in quite a general language, formed the basis for a material core doctrine of unamendability that morphed from an initial democracy-protecting aim to applications in the context of determining the limits of European integration. Last but not least, there are interplays here with theories of constitutional replacement discussed in Chapter 2, insofar as in their starkest incarnation, violations of implicit unamendable principles may amount to constitutional replacement.

Some terminological clarifications are in order. The first has to do with the way we refer to this type of unamendability. It has been termed 'implicit',[5] which implies that it underpins the constitution regardless of judicial discovery, or alternatively 'interpretive',[6] which carries a closer connection to the judicial process that constructs this form of unamendability. I employ the first terminology not because I subscribe to this view of unamendability as inherent in all constitutions, but because I believe it best captures judicial arguments. As we will see, judicial self-legitimation usually invokes immanent constitutional principles rather than progressive judicial interpretation.

A second set of distinctions is necessary when comparing 'basic structure' doctrines with 'minimum core' ones. The idea behind the former is identitarian and preservative, without a clear limit. It is identitarian insofar as the basic structure of a constitution is taken to include those principles, values, and institutions which are 'basic', i.e. foundational, essential, etc. It is preservative insofar as basic structure doctrines will seek to defend these defining elements on the ground that were they to be amended this would amount to a constitutional replacement. One advantage of basic structure doctrines is that the emphasis is on the bigger picture, on the propensity

[3] Gary J. Jacobsohn, *Constitutional Identity* (Harvard University Press 2010).

[4] It shares attributes with the idea of 'invisible constitution', the notion that all constitutions have invisible features that play a role in the interpretation, legitimacy, and stability of the constitutional system. See Rosalind Dixon and Adrienne Stone, *The Invisible Constitution in Comparative Perspective* (Cambridge University Press 2018).

[5] Yaniv Roznai, *Unconstitutional Constitutional Amendments: The Limits of Amendment Powers* (Oxford University Press 2017), 39.

[6] Richard Albert, *Constitutional Amendments: Making, Breaking, and Changing Constitutions* (Oxford University Press 2019), 149.

of amendments to undermine the whole constitutional architecture or transversal constitutional principles. This could be especially helpful in the face of attempts to undermine democratic constitutionalism, which are often difficult to capture as violations of discrete constitutional provisions. The Indian basic structure doctrine has been understood along these lines. It is said to be about values or principles that must exist in order for constitutionalism itself to exist.[7] It rests on the idea that a constitution is more than a mere bundle of provisions, but is instead an architectural framework with a particular identity.[8] While it may rely on textual anchors, the basic structure doctrine necessarily goes beyond the constitutional text in order to be able to capture the distinction between legitimate and illegitimate constitutional change.[9]

Minimum core doctrines, conversely, aim to capture a constitutional essence. As the name suggests, they are minimalist, in the sense of purporting to identify a floor of protection for certain values, principles, or institutions without which the constitutional order would no longer be the same. Elements of the minimum core will form part of the basic structure of a constitution, whereas the latter will likely include other elements as well.[10] One understanding of the minimum core has linked it to a thin conception of democracy, justified as a means to protect the constitutional order against attacks on competitive democracy.[11] The value in such doctrines would therefore rest in their democracy-protecting abilities.

The basic structure doctrines I will discuss below can also be distinguished from broader implicit limits on constitutional change. One such category includes political limits on amendment, such as in constitutions of the United Kingdom and the Netherlands.[12] Insofar as these constitutions are politically enforced and as the final word remains with legislatures, this form of informal or political unamendability is fundamentally different from judicial doctrines that have blocked constitutional amendment. Another category includes what might be termed sociological limits on amendment, referring to those instances where a constitutional text may appear flexible but societal understandings of particular values mean that they will not be changed in practice. This form of de facto unamendability has been discussed with reference to certain features of the United States and Canadian constitutions, for example.[13] As with political unamendability, however, the different source and

[7] Madhav Khosla, 'Constitutional Amendment' in Sujit Choudhry, Madhav Khosla, and Pratap Bhanu Mehta, eds., *The Oxford Handbook of the Indian Constitution* (Oxford University Press 2016) 232, 248.

[8] Ibid., 234.

[9] Ibid., 241.

[10] Rosalind Dixon and David Landau, 'Competitive Democracy and the Constitutional Minimum Core' in Tom Ginsburg and Aziz Huq, eds., *Assessing Constitutional Performance* (Cambridge University Press 2016) 268.

[11] Ibid.

[12] Gert Jan Geertjes and Jerfi Uzman, 'Conventions of Unamendability: Covert Constitutional Unamendability in (Two) Politically Enforced Constitutions' in Richard Albert and Bertil Emrah Oder, eds., *An Unamendable Constitution? Unamendability in Constitutional Democracies* (Springer 2018) 89.

[13] Albert (2019), 158 refers to this as 'constructive unamendability'.

consequences of this type of unamendability render it qualitatively different from judicially created unamendability.[14] Finally, the possible existence of supranational limits on constitutional change is discussed in Chapter 5.

Locating implicit unamendability

Believing certain constitutional principles to be implicitly unamendable is one thing. Finding a workable methodology for identifying them is a more complex task indeed. As in the case of constitutional identity (see Chapter 3), proponents of the notion that all democratic constitutions contain a set of foundational or structural elements that are implicitly unamendable are confident these elements will also be easily identifiable. The starting point will be the written constitutional text, supplemented by constitutional jurisprudence and other sources. Like with constitutional identity theories, we find less of a general criterion for locating implicit constitutional unamendability and more of a self-assured 'know it when you see it' attitude.

The courts engaged in developing unconstitutional constitutional amendment doctrines have themselves relied on imprecise methodologies for detecting these implicitly unamendable constitutional elements. As will be seen below, the Indian Supreme Court has repeatedly declined invitations to provide an exhaustive list of elements it deems part of the constitutional basic structure, alternatively grounding them in the constitutional preamble, certain substantive clauses of the Indian constitution, as well as Article 368, the amendment clause itself.

This lack of precision has led some authors to refer to doctrines of implicit unamendability as instances of 'judicial discovery' or, more critically, 'judicial constitution-making'.[15] Others have seen this lack of methodological precision as unavoidable and analogous to the judicial self-empowerment seen in other jurisdictions with strong versions of judicial review, whereby courts interpret themselves as the final authority on legislation amending the constitution.[16] Yaniv Roznai has argued that courts will need to develop their own theories of unamendable principles, on the basis of which to identify them in their respective constitution.[17] These principles will unavoidably display 'semantic openness', which carries the advantages of being able to accommodate evolutive interpretation and dialogue between constitutional actors, while having the disadvantages of being prone to

[14] Vicki C. Jackson, 'The (Myth of Un)amendability of the US Constitution and the Democratic Component of Constitutionalism', *International Journal of Constitutional Law* 13:3 (2015) 575.

[15] Richard Albert and Bertil Emrah Oder, 'The Forms of Unamendability' in Richard Albert and Bertil Emrah Oder, eds., *An Unamendable Constitution? Unamendability in Constitutional Democracies* (Springer 2018) 1, 22.

[16] Joel Colón-Ríos, 'A New Typology of Judicial Review of Legislation', *Global Constitutionalism* 3:2 (2014) 143, 153–4.

[17] Roznai (2017), 213.

manipulation and expansive discretion in interpretation.[18] For him, vagueness is not a disadvantage as such because it is inherently flexible.[19]

As we will see when discussing comparative case law, we should ask ourselves who this semantic openness and vagueness actually benefit in practice. As will be seen, comparative practice cautions against unbridled optimism about implicit entrenchment. For example, accepting preambles as repositories of constitutional essentials that will then be enforced against attempted constitutional amendments risks overstating the intended role of preambles, as well as their nature. As Nimer Sultany reminds us about Egypt's constitutional preamble, preambles lie and do so on purpose; they are useful legitimation exercises and tools of myth-making during and after constitution-making.[20] We already saw in the previous chapter that preambles yearn for homogeneity and more often than not mask deep contestation and even constitutional exclusion. We have also seen that captured courts may themselves develop notions of constitutional identity rooted in authoritarian constitutions, such as the Hungarian Constitutional Court has recently done. Such courts often follow a similar methodology to the one discussed here and are similarly fond of constitutional preambles. Finally, semantic openness may also leave room for unexpected and arguably incongruous elements being declared part of the constitution's unamendable core or identity. Examples include Colombia's Constitutional Court expanding its constitutional replacement doctrine to include a supposed constitutional requirement to criminalize drug possession or the Croatian Constitutional Court reading freedom of entrepreneurship into its constitutional identity doctrine.[21]

Like in the case of constitutional identity then, even when we accept the existence of an implicitly unamendable constitutional structure or core, it is fraught by radical indeterminacy. Arguments that this can be kept in check at the level of adjudication—whether through developing clear standards of review or else by anchoring doctrines of unconstitutional constitutional amendment in a transnational referent—will be explored below. I now turn to an in-depth examination of how such doctrines have been developed in practice. This will show that, rather than it fostering discomfort, courts appreciate and seek to retain this methodological fuzziness when it comes to locating implicit constitutional unamendability.

[18] Ibid., 214.

[19] Ibid., 216.

[20] Nimer Sultany, *Law and Revolution: Legitimacy and Constitutionalism after the Arab Spring* (Oxford University Press 2017), 119.

[21] Rosalind Dixon and David Landau, 'Transnational Constitutionalism and a Limited Doctrine of Unconstitutional Constitutional Amendment', *International Journal of Constitutional Law* 13:3 (2015) 606, 620 and Jurij Toplak and Đorđe Gardašević, 'Concepts of National and Constitutional Identity in Croatian Constitutional Law', *Review of Central and East European Law* 42 (2017) 263, 286.

4.2 Basic structure doctrines: India and beyond

India's basic structure doctrine

The Indian Constitution was drafted by a Constituent Assembly set up by the British in 1946, before independence and partition. The Assembly was made up of members elected indirectly by the provincial assemblies and, once the delegations of areas incorporated into Pakistan withdrew, was dominated by the Indian National Congress. Drafting and deliberations took more than three years and the new constitution was adopted in late 1949 and came into force on 26 January 1950. It set up a parliamentary system of government and established India as a federation with some unitary elements. The Indian Constitution had to fit but also unify a diverse society rife with religious, social, ethnic, linguistic, and regional tensions, a mission accomplished through what one scholar has termed 'constructive ambiguity': embracing such conflicts and importing them into the constitution via the deliberate ambiguous formulation of constitutional provisions.[22] This was a strategy to accommodate diversity and allow room for the uncertainties at the time of founding (such as the fate of Muslims in newly independent India) and led to the development of a distinctive type of legal pluralism.[23] Drafters thus had to pursue the objectives of nation-building and the cultivation of a common identity and loyalty alongside minority protection at a time of lawlessness and violence.[24] With these grim beginnings and with India not meeting any of the social and economic prerequisites which democracy theorists at the time associated with democratic survival, predictions about its transition to democracy were pessimistic.[25] However, the subsequent consolidation of Indian democracy proved these early estimates wrong and has called into question arguments that democracy is more likely in culturally homogeneous societies.[26] The constitution and the Supreme Court have played a central role in this story of unexpected success.

Granville Austin provides a rich account of the debates in the Constituent Assembly surrounding the provisions in the constitution which established the Supreme Court and its review powers, as well as the amendment rules.[27] Different views were expressed in the Assembly as to the best architecture and role for the

[22] Hanna Lerner, *Making Constitutions in Deeply Divided Societies* (Cambridge University Press 2011), 149 and generally, 109–51.

[23] Ibid., 149.

[24] Yash Ghai, 'Ethnicity and Competing Nations of Rights' in Colin Harvey and Alexander Schwartz, eds., *Rights in Divided Societies* (Hart 2012), 62.

[25] See Ashutosh Varshney, 'Why Democracy Survives', *Journal of Democracy* 9:3 (1998) 36; Sumit Ganguly, 'Six Decades of Independence', *Journal of Democracy* 18:2 (2007) 30.

[26] See discussion in Sankaran Krishna, 'Constitutionalism, Democracy and Political Culture in India' in Daniel P. Franklin and Michael J. Braun, eds., *Political Culture and Constitutionalism: A Comparative Approach* (M.E. Sharpe 1995) 161, 175–7.

[27] Granville Austin, *The Indian Constitution: Cornerstone of a Nation* (Clarendon Press 1966), 164–85 and 255–64.

court, as well as the different models to emulate. While the British tradition was inescapable insofar as the country's inherited judicial system, drafters looked at the American Supreme Court as the model for their own apex court.[28] Unlike the US body, however, they chose to make the Indian Supreme Court's review powers explicit in the text so as to reinforce its role as guardian of the constitution (Article 124). Moreover, various statements on the desirability of a unified court system (as opposed to separate federal and state systems), as well as of a unified federal law interpreted uniformly by the courts point to the drafters' understanding of the legal and judicial system as elements of state-building.[29] These aspirations for a strong, independent judiciary resulted, among others, in the Supreme Court being given wide jurisdiction: original, appellate, and advisory (Articles 131–5).[30] Furthermore, judicial review was entrenched as a right to constitutional remedies and was made part of the Fundamental Rights section in the constitution (Article 32).[31]

As far as the formal amendment formulas adopted in the constitution, we can count three distinct paths. One, regulated by Article 368, requires a special majority and, in some cases, ratification from at least half of the states; a second involves provisions which expressly allow for their change by ordinary laws of parliament; while a third is similar to the second method but specifies further requirements such as presidential recommendation, consultation, or request from the states.[32] Austin traces these back to disagreements over the optimal balance to be struck between flexibility and rigidity in the new constitution.[33] Those in favour of a flexible constitution had advocated a simple majority amendment formula, believing that the new constitution would be unavoidably flawed and as such should be easily amended, at least in its early years.[34] Those opting for a more rigid procedure were concerned with the survival of the federation and as such wanted state rights to be reflected in the method for changing the constitution. At a more fundamental level, the latter also perceived a real risk of the entire constitution unravelling if

[28] See also P. K. Tripathi, 'Perspectives on the American Influence on the Constitution of India', in Lawrence Ward Beer, ed., *Constitutionalism in Asia: Views of the American Influence* (University of California Press 1979) 59.

[29] Austin (1966), 167 and 184. For a view that a European concept of 'state' was borrowed by Indian framers and inadequately grasped by Indian jurists, including by the Supreme Court in its basic structure jurisprudence, see R. Sudarshan, '"Stateness" and Democracy in India's Constitution' in Zoya Hasan, E. Sridharan, and R. Sudarshan, eds., *India's Living Constitution: Ideas, Practices, Controversies* (Permanent Black 2002) 159.

[30] See, generally, Burt Neuborne, 'Constitutional Court Profile: The Supreme Court of India', *International Journal of Constitutional Law* 1:3 (2003) 476, 478–9 and Venkat Iyer, 'The Supreme Court of India' in Brice Dickson ed., *Judicial Activism in Common Law Supreme Courts* (Oxford University Press 2007) 121, 123–5.

[31] See discussion in Iyer (2007), 124.

[32] See discussion in Mahendra Pal Singh, 'India' in Dawn Oliver and Carlo Fusaro, eds., *How Constitutions Change: A Comparative Study* (Hart 2011) 169, 172–85.

[33] Austin (1966), 255–64.

[34] See also discussion in P. B. Gajendragadkar, *The Constitution of India: Its Philosophy and Basic Postulates* (Oxford University Press 1969), 84–8.

amendment was to be too easy. The solution chosen in the end—after surprisingly little debate in the constituent assembly—was the compromise outlined above. The Indian Constitution has proven easy to amend, with 104 amendments having been adopted between 1950 and 2020.

The context of the development of the basic structure doctrine is key to a proper understanding of its status in Indian constitutional law. The period following independence was marked by numerous amendments to the constitutional text. As a consequence, some scholars have evaluated the Supreme Court's subsequent activism as an immediate response to this time, when it was '[f]aced with an executive branch of government which was prepared to sacrifice hard-won freedoms and rights on the altar of populist and increasingly authoritarian policies, and a legislature which was captive to the ruling party of the day'.[35] Against this background, the court decided the *Golaknath* case. In it, it had to rule on whether constitutional amendments enacted by the parliament in accordance with Article 368 of the constitution were to be subjected to Article 13 rights review.[36] In what was a deeply controversial decision, the court found that amendments did constitute 'law' within the meaning of Article 13, that the Supreme Court could judicially review them, that this approach was also inherent in the nature of the fundamental rights as enshrined in the constitution, and that a doctrine of implied limitations on the sovereignty of parliament was applicable.[37] There were serious conceptual problems with this reasoning, which was also not coherent with other references to 'law' in the constitution. The decision has been described as providing an answer that was 'simple, but . . . not convincing'.[38]

The basic structure doctrine was announced in the *Kesavananda* case six years later, which also overturned the *Golaknath* decision.[39] While seemingly refuting the notion of implied limitations on parliament's power to amend the constitution, the *Kesavananda* court nevertheless took the view, albeit by a narrow majority, that

> though the power to amend cannot be narrowly construed and extends to all the Articles it is not unlimited so as to include the power to abrogate or change the identity of the Constitution or its basic features.[40]

[35] Iyer (2007), 131.

[36] *Golaknath* v. *State of Punjab*, AIR 1967 SC 1643. Article 13(2) of the Indian Constitution provides that 'The State shall not make any law which takes away or abridges the rights conferred by this Part and any law made in contravention of this clause shall, to the extent of the contravention, be void.' Article 13(3) provided a non-exhaustive list of the types of legislative acts to be considered 'law'—not explicitly including amendments.

[37] See discussion in Sudhir Krishnaswamy, *Democracy and Constitutionalism in India* (Oxford University Press 2009), 11–23 on the court's development of these four lines of argument. For an account of the wider political context of the decision, see Granville Austin, *Working a Democratic Constitution: A History of the Indian Experience* (Oxford University Press 2003), 173–233.

[38] Khosla (2016), 239.

[39] *Kesavananda* v. *State of Kerala* (1973) 4 SCC 225. See also discussion of the political context of the decision in Austin (2003), 234–77.

[40] *Kesavananda*, para. 639.

The plurality of opinions and interpretive techniques deployed to identify the constitutional basis for the doctrine makes it difficult to paint a coherent picture of its genesis.[41] Some have even argued this to be irrelevant, claiming the doctrine 'was really advanced on a common sense basis'.[42] What nobody could deny, however, was that the decision's 'effects were little less than seismic'.[43] It was prophetically termed 'the constitution of the future'[44] and has come to be seen 'as the high-water mark of judicial activism in the entire history of independent India'.[45]

The *Kesavananda* decision initially 'appeared revolting to the basic tenets of democracy'[46] and triggered a swift reaction from the government.[47] What followed was the suppression of judges on the Supreme Court in an attempt to undermine the institution, including via a series of constitutional amendments which, unlike previous ones, now sought to secure executive power against the judiciary.[48] After the emergency period (1975–7), the Supreme Court became more assertive, perhaps in a bid to undo the damage to its reputation during the emergency.[49] The basic structure doctrine has since been relied upon in a variety of cases, with the result that a growing list of principles have been identified as part of the basic structure. The original five announced in the *Kesavananda* decision included the supremacy of the constitution, the republican and democratic form of government, secularism, the separation of powers, and federalism.[50] They have since been said to consist of secularism,[51] democracy,[52] the rule of law,[53] federalism,[54] and the independence of the judiciary.[55] Not all of these were cases wherein the

[41] For a detailed account of the disparate arguments put forth in support of the basic structure doctrine in the *Kesavananda* case, see Krishnaswamy (2009), 1–42.

[42] Ibid., 39.

[43] Iyer (2007), 130.

[44] Upendra Baxi, 'The Constitutional Quicksands of Kesavananda Bharati and the Twenty-Fifth Amendment', *Supreme Court Cases* 1 (1974) 45.

[45] Iyer (2007), 130.

[46] S. P. Sathe, *Judicial Activism in India: Transgressing Borders and Enforcing Limits* (Oxford University Press 2002), 8.

[47] Austin (2003), 278–92; O. Chinnappa Reddy, *The Court and the Constitution of India: Summit and Shallows*, (Oxford University Press 2010), 65–72.

[48] Chinnappa Reddy (2010), 65–6.

[49] Pratap Bhanu Mehta, 'India's Unlikely Democracy: The Rise of Judicial Sovereignty', *Journal of Democracy* 18:2 (2007) 70, 79.

[50] *Kesavananda*, para. 315.

[51] *S.R. Bommai* v. *Union of India*, AIR 1975 1994 SC 1918, *R.C. Poudyal* v. *Union of India*, AIR 11993 SC 1804 and *Pravin Bhai Toghadia* v. *State of Karnataka*, AIR 2004 SC 2081. I discuss the protection of Indian secularism in greater detail in Chapter 1.

[52] *Indira Gandhi* v. *Raj Narain*, AIR 1975 SC 2299, *Kihoto Hollohan* v. *Zachilhu*, 1992 (Supp) 2 SCC 651 and *Union of India* v. *Association of Democratic Reforms*, AIR 2002 SC 2113.

[53] *Indira Gandhi* v. *Raj Narain* and *Rameshwar Prasad* v. *Union of India* (2006) 2 SCC 1.

[54] *S.R. Bommai* v. *Union of India* and *Rameshwar Prasad* v. *Union of India*.

[55] *Sambamurthy* v. *State of AP, Minerva Mills*, AIR 1987 SC 663, *Kihoto Hollohan* v. *Zachilhu*, *Chandra Kumar* v. *Union of India*, AIR 1997 SC 1125 and *Sampath Kumar* v. *Union of India*, AIR 1987 SC 386. These five elements were also identified as the nearly unanimously accepted features of the doctrine. See Soli Sorabjee, 'The Ideal Remedy: A Valediction' in Pran Chopra, ed., *The Supreme Court versus the Constitution* (Sage 2006) 199, 204.

court intervened to reinforce democracy—some resulted in democracy's dilution instead.[56] Moreover, the doctrine has been tested in cases extending beyond the review of constitutional amendments—notably including national and regional emergency power, legislative power, and executive power—again, with mixed results.[57]

The rich history and increasing appreciation of the doctrine has not spared it from criticism. It has been called 'a stability device that throws sand into the gears of the constitutional amendment process'[58] and 'a counter-majoritarian check on temporary legislative majority in order to prevent it from throwing away the basic principles of constitutionalism'[59] by supporters. Detractors view it as 'a form of originalism that embalms the normative commitments made by "we, the people of India" in 1950'.[60] The Supreme Court has been criticized for having failed to provide sound democratic[61] and theoretical[62] foundations for the doctrine. Its fluctuating formulation has been criticized as imprecise and open to abuse even by well-intentioned judges.[63] Some have predicted its demise, anticipating that 'while the horizon of the basic structure doctrine may expand to include legislative as well as executive actions, its use for considering the validity of a constitutional amendment may become rare'.[64] In terms of its implementation, the doctrine has been said to act 'much like a suspensory veto to ensure that the people of India really want the constitutional changes enacted by their leaders,'[65] in other words, to ensure that revision of certain core constitutional principles only takes place via a new constitutional moment. I explore this latter point in greater detail in Chapter 7, where I also discuss the doctrine's place in recent constitutional reform initiatives in India.

A comprehensive analysis of the basic structure doctrine case law as developed over more than four decades of Indian jurisprudence is beyond my scope here. I will instead focus on its theoretical foundations and the continued criticism that the doctrine is inherently undemocratic and therefore unjustifiable. I will seek to reconstruct the notion of constituent power upon which the Indian constitution may be said to rest and identify its implications for understandings of the basic structure doctrine. My conclusion is that while the doctrine has become widely

[56] Mehta (2007), 79.

[57] For an in-depth discussion, see Krishnaswamy (2009), 43–69.

[58] Vivek Krishnamurthy, 'Colonial Cousins: Explaining India and Canada's Unwritten Constitutional Principles', *Yale Journal of International Law* 34:1 (2009) 207, 237.

[59] Sathe (2002), 11.

[60] Krishnamurthy (2009), 237.

[61] Pratap Bhanu Mehta, 'The Inner Conflict of Constitutionalism: Judicial Review and the "Basic Structure"' in Zoya Hasan, E. Sridharan and R. Sudarshan, eds., *India's Living Constitution: Ideas, Practices, Controversies* (Permanent Black 2002) 179.

[62] Sathe (2002), 10.

[63] Ashok Desai, 'Constitutional Amendments and the "Basic Structure" Doctrine' in Venkat Iyer, ed., *Democracy, Human Rights and the Rule of Law* (Butterworths India 2000), 90.

[64] Sathe (2002), 98.

[65] Krishnamurthy (2009), 238.

accepted, an assessment of its legitimacy in the Indian context yields a complicated picture. The body of case law and doctrinal evidence around it provides evidence for several competing narratives, including one which reconciles the basic structure doctrine with Indian democratic commitments. However, the delicate balance which needs to be struck in order for such a doctrine to be democratically legitimate has proven difficult for the Supreme Court to strike in certain cases.

Perhaps due to the strong British and American influences on its foundations, Indian constitutional discourse seems to eschew notions of constituent power.[66] It relies instead on the language of popular sovereignty. The constitution's preamble invokes it when it declares the Indian state a 'sovereign socialist secular democratic republic'[67] in the name of 'we, the people of India' who 'in our constituent assembly . . . do hereby adopt, enact and give to ourselves this constitution'. Scholars have attempted to reconstruct 'the people' behind this declaration, either as an 'imagined community',[68] or as a multivocal, multivalent reflection of imaginations and expectations attributed to people within and behind the Constituent Assembly.[69] I follow the latter in reconstructing the foundational narratives underpinning Indian democracy and linking these to the theoretical roots of the basic structure doctrine.

Competing narratives have been put forth to make sense of India's constitutional foundations.[70] One set of explanations places emphasis on continuity and British-style incrementalism in constitutional development. According to this view, India's independence was elite-driven and influenced by British notions of constitutionalism; as such, it was not meant to amount to a rejection of tradition and complete break with the past. A second reading of the Indian constitution is purely normative, seeing it as 'an ahistorical grundnorm that generated its own validity'.[71] The entire constitutional order thus draws its validity from this norm, which also provides the normative justification for judicial review of legislation. A third set of interpretations focuses on the shortcomings of the Indian constitution when it comes to society's socio-economic transformation. Influenced by Marxist understandings of revolution, this scholarship sees India's constitution as 'an attempt to preserve the status quo by political and professional elites through arguments and justifications reminiscent of those advanced by the operators of the

[66] An exception is Upendra Baxi, 'Some Reflections on the Nature of Constituent Power' in Rajeev Dhavan and Alice Jacob, eds., *Indian Constitution: Trends and Issues* (N.M. Tripathi 1978) 122.

[67] The terms 'socialist' and 'secular' were added during the 1975–7 emergency via The Constitution (Forty-second amendment) Act, 1976.

[68] David Gilmartin, 'Election Law and the "People" in Colonial and Postcolonial India' in Dipesh Chakrabarty, Rochona Majumdar, and Andrew Sartori, eds., *From the Colonial to the Postcolonial: India and Pakistan in Transition* (Oxford University Press 2007) 55.

[69] Kalyani Ramnath, '"We the People": Seamless Webs and Social Revolution in India's Constituent Assembly Debates', *South Asia Research* 32:1 (2012) 57.

[70] See overview of these competing narratives in Sarbani Sen, *The Constitution of India: Popular Sovereignty and Democratic Transformations* (Oxford University Press 2007), 30–40.

[71] Ibid., 35.

colonial administrative system'.[72] Finally, there are also interpretations which emphasize the distinctiveness of India's historical experience and its indigenous revolutionary constitutional politics.[73] According to this last view, not only was there broad popular consent for a break with the past, mobilized via a distinctive model of leader-citizen engagement, but this type of interaction has reoccurred in cyclical patterns of popular mobilization for change.

This brief foray shows just how contested the foundational narrative has been in India. Moreover, one can establish clear links between these narratives and interpretations of the basic structure doctrine—by the judiciary and scholarship alike. With regard to the former, commentators appear in agreement that the Supreme Court has gone from a 'narrowly positivist' to a 'broad purposive approach to the enunciation and enforcement of fundamental constitutional rights that verges on natural law'.[74] Scholars' views are similarly divided. Those subscribing to notions of parliamentary sovereignty in the British tradition would view the idea of material limits on constitutional change as an aberration. To them, popular sovereignty is exclusively expressed by representatives in parliament, and judicial interference with constitutional amendment is a sign of a judiciary overstepping its mandate.[75] Scholars who focus on the transformative ambition of the Indian text will be prone to evaluate the basic structure doctrine according to its implementation in concrete cases, looking to establish whether it is an instrument which merely reinforces the status quo or a tool for socio-economic progress.[76] Finally, much of the scholarship emphasizing popular sovereignty as the basis for legitimacy of the Indian constitution at the same time accepts a distinction between acts of the people themselves versus their representatives. According to this view, the former requires entrenchment, including via the basic structure doctrine, so as to prevent subsequent temporary majorities from undoing the work of revolutionary popular mobilization.[77] In this reading, the basic structure doctrine protects the supremacy of the people against the ruling elite, rather than of the judiciary.[78] As we will see shortly, however, the Supreme Court has more recently veered toward using the basic structure doctrine precisely to protect judicial supremacy.

[72] Ibid., 37.

[73] Ibid., 32–5.

[74] Neuborne (2003), 479–80. See also Sathe (2002), 6. Venkat Iyer has identified three distinct periods of activity of the court: a first period (1950–73) of 'fairly principled and doctrinally sustainable approach', during which the basic structure doctrine was also enunciated; a second period (1974–7) of subservience to the executive; and a third (1978–present) wherein the court has been activist, albeit in a 'somewhat undisciplined and theoretically questionable' manner (Iyer (2007), 121).

[75] See below similar attitudes within the judiciary of other former British colonies entertaining the adoption of basic structure doctrines.

[76] Baxi has described the Supreme Court's turn to judicial populism in developing its social action litigation (what has since been termed 'public interest litigation') as proof of it finally becoming 'the Supreme Court for Indians' (Upendra Baxi, 'Taking Suffering Seriously: Social Action Litigation in the Supreme Court of India', *Third World Legal Studies* 4 (1985) 107).

[77] Sen (2007), 33.

[78] Sathe (2002), 85.

My aim here has been to establish this correlation between particular foundationalist narratives and notions of democracy, popular sovereignty, and judicial review entertained by both the Indian judiciary and scholarship. Reconstructing this wider theoretical framework is necessary in order to understand outcomes in individual cases, as well as jurisprudential shifts in basic structure interpretations. Some will be more convincing than others, but any assessment of the legitimacy of the doctrine inevitably rests on an assessment of this broader set of theoretical commitments of Indian democracy. Based on this analysis, I will explore the feasibility of calls for the doctrine to be formalized, whether in the constitutional text itself or in an authoritative judicial enumeration of its elements, in Chapter 7.

The basic structure doctrine beyond India

The transnational influence of the basic structure doctrine has been significant. It has 'migrated' to a number of jurisdictions and, even where expressly rejected, as in Sri Lanka, the Indian basic structure jurisprudence has been seriously engaged with. Alternatively, national courts such as South Africa's have indicated they might, in the future, be ready to engage in the material review of constitutional amendments, and did so by reference to Indian jurisprudence.[79] The basic structure doctrine also shares important similarities with the Czech 'substantive core' doctrine discussed in Chapter 1.

Bangladesh

The doctrine was embraced early on by the Bangladeshi Supreme Court, first in 1989 to strike down the Eighth Amendment which had sought to divide the High Court Division into seven permanent benches.[80] The court viewed the legislature's amendment power as subject to material limitations and not to be used to dismantle the basic structure or 'fabric' of the constitution. The court would employ a holistic interpretation of the constitution to make its determinations of a breach. The judges could not agree on a definitive list of elements of that basic structure, alternatively including among them the rule of law, popular sovereignty, supremacy of the constitution, democracy, the unitary state, the separation of powers, fundamental rights, and judicial independence.[81]

[79] This was the case in South Africa. See discussion in Avinash Govindjee and Rosaan Kruger 'The Basic Structure Doctrine Debate: South African Explorations' in Sanjay S. Jain and Sathya Narayan, eds., *Basic Structure Constitutionalism: Revisiting Kesavananda Bharti* (Eastern Book Company 2011) 209. See also Heinz Klug, *Constituting Democracy: Law, Globalism and South Africa's Political Reconstruction* (Cambridge University Press 2000), 155.

[80] *Anwar Hossain Chowdhury* v. *Bangladesh*, 1989, 18 CLC (AD).

[81] Ridwanul Hoque, 'Constitutionalism and the Judiciary in Bangladesh' in Sunil Khilnani, Vikram Raghavan, and Arun K. Thiruvengadam, eds., *Comparative Constitutionalism in South Asia* (Oxford University Press 2014) 303, 316; Roznai (2017), 48.

This judgment, issued in the final year of Bangladesh's military rule, has been seen as an attempt by the Supreme Court to protect not just the rule of law, but the identity of the state itself.[82] The doctrine was later deployed in a number of cases[83] until being formally constitutionalized via the Fifteenth Amendment Act in 2011. Since then, the Bangladeshi constitution's Article 7B lists 'the basic provisions of the constitution' that 'shall not be amendable by way of insertion, modification, substitution, repeal or by any other means'. There remains some controversy over whether the eternity clause displaces the basic structure doctrine as developed judicially or whether the two remain coextant. Controversy also remains over whether the eternity clause introduces contradictory unamendable values, seeing as it entrenches both Islam and secularism.[84] The active role of the Bangladeshi Supreme Court has been attributed to its special position within the constitutional system against the background of the country's tumultuous recent past, a past that includes lengthy experiences with autocratic rule and martial law.[85] As will be seen below, however, not all findings of a breach of the basic structure have remained uncontested. When the Sixteenth Amendment, on judicial impeachment, was struck down by the Supreme Court on the grounds that it breached judicial independence and the separation of powers principle, the court came under fire for judicial overreach. Moreover, the court has never specified a time limit for its amendment review, thereby leaving the door open to amendment strike-down many years after an amendment was passed—as indeed has happened in the case of the Fifth, Seventh, and Thirteenth Amendments.[86]

Pakistan

In Pakistan, the Supreme Court vacillated between embracing a basic structure, or 'salient features', constitutional doctrine for many years. The court did not fully embrace material review of constitutional amendments even though it adopted a structural method of interpretation taking into account the constitution's 'basic structure',[87] finding that its existence did not imply the judicial power to review its breach by the legislator.[88] In other words, the court for many years declined to make the step from recognizing a basic structure to a judicial doctrine of implicit unamendability that could result in strike-down of constitutional amendments. It

[82] Hoque (2014), 315.

[83] Ibid., 313–18; Roznai (2017), 48–9.

[84] Hoque (2018), 224.

[85] Hoque (2014). See in particular the case of *Bangladesh Italian Marble Works Ltd* v. *Bangladesh* (2006) BLT (Special) (HCD) 1, 29 August 2005, in which the Supreme Court struck down the Fifth Amendment originally passed in 1979. This amendment had declared the validity of the first martial law imposed in the country during 1975–9.

[86] For a critique of this aspect of Bangladeshi basic structure doctrine, see Rokeya Chowdhury, 'The Doctrine of Basic Structure in Bangladesh: From "Calfpath" to *Matryoshka* Dolls', *Bangladesh Journal of Law* 14:1–2 (2014) 43.

[87] *Al-Jehad Trust* v. *Federation of Pakistan* PLD 1996 SC 324.

[88] *Wukala Mahaz Barai Tahafaz Dastoor* v. *Federation of Pakistan* PLD 1998 SC 1263.

viewed this issue through the lens of a political question doctrine, with a legislative rather than judicial remedy: 'A constitutional amendment posed a political question, which could be resolved only through the normal mechanisms of parliamentary democracy and free elections.'[89] Thus, while recognizing features such as federalism and the parliamentary form of government blended with Islamic provisions,[90] the Pakistani Supreme Court established in three decades' worth of jurisprudence that it would not step in to review amendments substantively.[91]

This would change after Pervez Musharraf left office and once the previously removed Chief Justice Chaudhry was reinstated in 2009. In 2015, the Pakistani Supreme Court was called on to review the constitutionality of the Eighteenth and Twenty-first Amendments, the former meant to roll back Musharraf-era changes, the latter instituting the referral of cases of suspected terrorists to trial by military courts.[92] While it upheld both amendments, the court clarified that it embraced the notion of an enforceable basic structure of the constitution. It did so in spite of the seemingly clear language of Articles 239(5) and (6) in the constitution, which sought precisely to oust its jurisdiction over constitutional amendments. Tied to a structural method of interpretation—'the inherent integrity and scheme to the Constitution'—this basic structure was said to consist of a number of salient features (different across the eight different judges who sought to clarify this point but in general linked to the constitutional preamble), inter alia: 'democracy, federalism, parliamentary form of government blended with the Islamic provisions, independence of judiciary, fundamental rights, equality, justice and fair play'.[93] These features were tied to 'the ideological basis for the creation of the State, the core values which define the people', as well as to 'a bitter and tragic past of oppression, dictatorship, fascism, civil war or ethnic cleansing' and contexts 'where core values or substantive provisions pertaining to the rights of the people or internal architecture of the Constitution are vulnerable'.[94] It is this past vulnerability that justified the safeguarding of these features against other branches, including against parliament. And while these features were not meant to be seen as 'forbidden fruit', the legislature was not to 'repeal or abrogate' them, 'or substantively alter i.e. to significantly [a]ffect [their] essential nature'.[95]

The judgment has been the subject of critique, including for designating an overly narrow feature as salient: the parliamentary form of government. But

[89] *Pakistan Lawyers Forum* v. *Federation of Pakistan* PLD 2005 SC 719, para. 57.

[90] *Mahmood Khan Achakzai* v. *Federation of Pakistan* PLD 1997 SC 426.

[91] The Supreme Court was acutely aware of the dangers were it to take this step, having been cautioned that sitting in judgment over constitutional amendment would amount to 'judging democracy' itself. See Osama Siddique, 'The Judicialization of Politics in Pakistan: The Supreme Court after the Lawyers' Movement' in Mark Tushnet and Madhav Khosla, eds., *Unstable Constitutionalism: Law and Politics in South Asia* (Cambridge University Press 2015) 159, 186.

[92] *District Bar Association, Rawalpindi and Others* v. *Federation of Pakistan* PLD 2015 SC 401.

[93] Ibid., 233–4.

[94] Ibid., 264–5.

[95] Ibid., 267.

whereas some have decried the impossibility of reform that might move the system in a more presidential direction,[96] others have drawn out a more problematic consequence of the judgment. Unlike in India where the basic structure includes the principle of secularism, the Pakistani Supreme Court's embrace of Islamic limits to the parliamentary form of government might result in changes to the constitutional role of the Supreme Court vis-à-vis religion within Pakistani constitutionalism.[97] The 2017 judgment disqualifying Prime Minister Sharif from parliament illustrates the logic behind these fears.[98] His disqualification was the result of the Supreme Court assessing him to have violated his constitutional duty (contained in Article 62(1)(f)) as a parliamentarian to show Islamic honesty (to be *ameen*) following revelations in the Panama Papers. Subsequent proposals to amend this provision raise the prospect of the Supreme Court invalidating such an amendment on the basis of its violating the parliamentary form of government blended with Islamic provisions as a salient feature of the constitution.[99] In other words, given the constitutional status of Islam in Pakistani constitutionalism, the fate of Pakistan's basic structure doctrine may diverge quite significantly from India's. The doctrine plays a role not just in the tug of war between parliamentary and judicial power, but may yet empower the Supreme Court as final arbiter regarding parliamentary engagement with Islam.[100]

Taiwan

The basic structure doctrine travelled beyond India's immediate neighbours as well. Taiwan's Constitutional Court, for example, first relied on implicit unamendability during the transition to democratic rule to strike down amendments to the National Assembly election and term duration.[101] It declared that '[s]ome constitutional provisions are integral to the essential nature of the Constitution and underpin the constitutional normative order' so that their amendment 'would bring down the constitutional normative order in its entirety'.[102] Among these implicitly unamendable provisions were the principle of a democratic republic

[96] See discussion in Isaam Bin Haris, 'Judicial Review of Constitutional Amendments—Pakistan's Uneasy Subscription to the Basic Structure Doctrine', *UK Constitutional Law Blog* (24 September 2015), https://ukconstitutionallaw.org/2015/09/24/isaam-bin-haris-judicial-review-of-constitutional-amendments-pakistans-uneasy-subscription-to-the-basic-structure-doctrine/.

[97] Matthew J. Nelson, 'Indian Basic Structure Jurisprudence in the Islamic Republic of Pakistan: Reconfiguring the Constitutional Politics of Religion', *Asian Journal of Comparative Law* 13:2 (2018) 333.

[98] *Imran Ahmed Khan* v. *Mian Muhammad Nawaz Sharif*, 2017 PLD 692 SC.

[99] Nelson (2018), 354.

[100] Ibid., 355. See also Moeen H Cheema, 'Beyond Beliefs: Deconstructing the Dominant Narratives of the Islamization of Pakistan's Law', *American Journal of Comparative Law* 60:4 (2012) 875.

[101] Judicial Yuan Interpretation No. 499, 24 March 2000. The National Assembly had been the authoritative legislative body under the 1947 Constitution but its powers were gradually reduced during the democratization reforms and especially after the presidential elections in 2000, until it was entirely abolished in 2005.

[102] Ibid., para. 2.

(Article 1), popular sovereignty (Article 2), the protection of constitutional rights (Chapter II) and principles providing for the separation of powers and checks and balances. Its intervention has been read as part of a more activist stance taken by the court during the democratization period, when it established itself as both facilitator and guardian of democracy.[103] Implicit unamendability has reappeared in the court's jurisprudence since, such as when certifying electoral reform in 2014.[104] The reform, which reduced the number of parliamentary seats and introduced proportional representation with a 5 per cent threshold, was challenged before the Constitutional Court by smaller parties disadvantaged by the changes. The court did not find that the amendment breached the constitutional democratic order and upheld its validity. The Taiwanese Constitutional Court has been praised for calibrating its interventions, especially into the electoral arena, a balancing act made possible by Taiwan's relatively stable democratization process.[105]

Malaysia

Courts in Malaysia and Singapore have been more reluctant to embrace a basic structure doctrine and resisted doing so for decades.[106] The Malaysian Federal Court, for example, declared the notion of implicit unamendability a fallacy in a 1977 case, as 'it concedes to the court a more potent power of constitutional amendment through judicial legislation than the organ formally and clearly chosen by the Constitution for the exercise of the amending power'.[107] However, the court later moved away from its view that only manner and form limits could constrain amendments, finding that the doctrine of parliamentary supremacy did not apply in Malaysia.[108] The Malaysian Federal Court invoked the basic structure doctrine in 2017, when it asserted that the power of judicial review rested exclusively in the judiciary and that basic features such as the separation of powers and judicial independence could not be removed legislatively.[109] This move appeared to negate the controversial 1988 amendments that had subordinated judicial review powers to the parliament, although it was not entirely clear whether the court grounded its reasoning on the basic structure doctrine or on the principle of legality as other common law courts had done.[110] The Federal Court's

[103] Ming-Sung Kuo, 'Moving Towards a Nominal Constitutional Court? Critical Reflections on the Shift from Judicial Activism to Constitutional Irrelevance in Taiwan's Constitutional Politics', *Washington International Law Journal* 25:3 (2016) 597, 598.

[104] Judicial Yuan Interpretation No. 721, 6 June 2014.

[105] Po Jen Yap, *Courts and Democracies in Asia* (Cambridge University Press 2017), 108.

[106] Yvonne Tew, *Constitutional Statecraft in Asian Courts* (Oxford University Press 2020), 53–7; Jaclyn L. Neo, 'A Contextual Approach to Unconstitutional Constitutional Amendments: Judicial Power and the Basic Structure Doctrine in Malaysia', *Asian Journal of Comparative Law* 15 (2020) 69.

[107] *Loh Kooi Choon* v. *Government of Malaysia* [*1977*] *2* MLJ 187, 189, cited in Tew (2020), 53.

[108] *Sivarasa Rasiah* v. *Badan Peguam Malaysia* [2010] 2 MLJ 333.

[109] *Semenyih Jaya* v. *Pentadbir Tanah Daerah Hulu Langat* [2017] 3 MLJ 561. See discussion in Tew (2020), 98–104.

[110] Neo (2020), 89. On the 1988 amendments and their impact on judicial power, see Tew (2020), 92–106.

'clearest affirmation' of the basic structure doctrine came in 2018, in a case involving freedom of religion of minors and a jurisdictional tussle between civil and Shyariah courts.[111] That case solidified the court's assertion of judicial power against the political branches, though the restoration of judicial independence and democratic constitutionalism in Malaysia remains a work in progress.[112]

Singapore

The trajectory of the basic structure doctrine in Singapore has been similar. The Singaporean High Court rejected implicit unamendability in 1989, finding that '[i]f the framers of the Singaporean Constitution had intended limitations on the power of amendment, they would have expressly provided for such limitations'.[113] The Court of Appeal inched towards embracing the doctrine, such as by referring to the separation of powers and the right to vote as elements of the constitutional basic structure, even while avoiding giving a clear statement on whether the doctrine applied in Singapore.[114] In 2017, the High Court again revisited the issue, finding that the doctrine had not yet received explicit judicial recognition in Singapore.[115] In any case, the court found, only a thin or minimalist version of the basic structure doctrine had been discussed in extrajudicial and *obiter* statements, one that 'appeared to be no more than a broad restatement of the truism that the Constitution rests on an overarching principled framework embracing the precepts of the rule of law and the separation of powers'.[116] As in Malaysia, we thus see Singaporean courts still wrestling with delineating the contours of their own judicial review powers in a context long conceived of as resembling de facto parliamentary supremacy.[117]

Sri Lanka

The basic structure doctrine's transnational influence has also been felt where it has been explicitly rejected. In Sri Lanka, for example, the Supreme Court expressly invoked Indian case law but ultimately rejected calls to review the constitutionality of amendments on substantive grounds.[118] It did so in the context of certifying the Thirteenth Amendment to the 1978 Constitution, which introduced a measure of devolution in the country. The amendment was contested on the grounds that it undermined the unitary state principle (Article 2) and the inalienable principle of popular sovereignty (Article 3). The amendment was the result of the Indo-Sri Lanka Accord

[111] *Indira Gandhi a/p Mutho* v. *Pengarah Jabatan Agama Islam Perak & Ors and other appeals* [2018] 1 MLJ 545. See also Neo (2020), 91–3.
[112] Neo (2020), 94.
[113] *Teo Soh Lung* v. *Minister of Home Affairs* [1989] 1 SLR(R) 461.
[114] *Yong Vui Kong* v. *Public Prosecutor* [2015] SGCA 11.
[115] *Ravi s/o Madasamy* v. *Attorney-General* [2017] SGHC 163.
[116] Ibid., paras. 65–6.
[117] Kenny Chng, 'The Theoretical Foundations of Judicial Review in Singapore', *Singapore Journal of Legal* Studies [2019] 294, 300.
[118] *In Re the Thirteenth Amendment to the Constitution and the Provincial Councils Bill* (1987) 2 SLR 312.

signed in 1987 and meant to end the civil war; it created provincial councils and recognized Tamil as an official language alongside Sinhalese while retaining English as the 'link language'. While upholding the amendment, the court was also intent on reassuring the Sinhalese Buddhist majority that the pre-eminence of Sinhala Buddhism and the unitary nature of the state were not undermined.[119] The minority judges, who would have embraced the basic structure doctrine, would have struck down the amendment. They sought to formulate the nature of the threat in the abstract structural terms of the basic structure doctrine.[120] Even while some aspects of the Sri Lankan Constitution are harder to amend and subject to referendum locks, including the freedom of religion and worship, the pre-eminence of Sinhalese Buddhism, and the unitary nature of the state, this entrenchment does not preclude their repeal.[121] These features are interconnected and form part of a more general rejection of efforts to pluralize the state and a retrenchment of centralized state power.[122]

Viewed in this comparative lens, basic structure doctrines appear to be growing in popularity. While the cases discussed here have focused on the Asian context, the influence of Indian jurisprudence on implicit unamendability has been felt beyond it as well.[123] Their spread has not been linear though, with some national courts still reluctant to enforce a constitutional basic structure when reviewing constitutional amendments. Even where they might accept that the constitution does rest on certain core pillars, courts may not be ready to deduce from there the power to strike down amendments that violate these pillars. In the case of formal eternity clauses, resistance to their enforcement has been attributed to a certain formalism in constitutional interpretation.[124] Resistance to the basic structure doctrine may have less to do with formalism and more to do with stronger traditions of parliamentary supremacy in many of the countries discussed. As we have seen, battles over the basic structure in many of these countries were also battles about the proper scope of judicial review and whether courts would be substituting themselves for the legislative power if engaging in substantive amendment review.

[119] Gary J. Jacobsohn and Shylashri Shankar, 'Constitutional Borrowing in South Asia: India, Sri Lanka, and Secular Constitutional Identity' in Sunil Khilnani, Vikram Raghavan, and Arun K. Thiruvengadam, eds., *Comparative Constitutionalism in South Asia* (Oxford University Press 2014) 180, 194–5.

[120] Ibid., 201.

[121] Ibid., 195.

[122] Asanga Welikala, 'Southphalia or Southfailure? National Pluralism and the State in South Asia' in Stephen Tierney, ed., *Nationalism and Globalisation* (Hart 2015) 93. See also Benjamin Schonthal, *Buddhism, Politics and the Limits of Law: The Pyrrhic Constitutionalism of Sri Lanka* (Cambridge University Press 2016).

[123] For an overview of cases beyond those covered here, including African and Latin American ones, see Roznai (2017), 52–69. Most recently, a petition was filed on 16 September 2020 with the High Court of Kenya asking it to embrace a basic structure doctrine that would protect the constitution against unconstitutional amendments. See Jeremiah Wakaya, 'Kenya: Petitioners Seek Court's Interpretation on Constitutional Amendment Limitations', *CapitalFM*, 16 September 2020, https://allafrica.com/stories/202009160840.html.

[124] Richard Albert, Malkhaz Nakashidze, and Tarik Olcay, 'The Formalist Resistance to Unconstitutional Constitutional Amendments', *Hastings Law Journal* 70 (2019) 639.

4.3 Restraining doctrines of implicit unamendability

As we have seen in the preceding section, there is now rich comparative practice surrounding both developing a theory of implicit unamendability and enforcing it. While India's is the most well-known example, it is certainly not singular. This rich experience provides ample material for a serious investigation of the operation of implicit unamendability in practice. The question to answer is: assuming we accept that implicit material limits on constitutional amendment exist, and that they can be identified with sufficient certainty, how should these limits be adjudicated? When should courts step in to enforce them and on the basis of what standard of review? If we agree that unconstitutional constitutional amendment doctrines should be deployed as a last resort in the face of potential abusive amendments, can we define the threshold for court intervention? I discuss two sets of answers to these questions, both predicated on judicial restraint. I then test these in the context of courts adjudicating the unamendable principle of judicial independence.

Positing judicial self-restraint as a limit on unamendability

Limiting the potentially massive judicial power that comes with enforcing implicit unamendability has been a preoccupation for both doctrine and scholarship. Courts embracing a basic structure doctrine have themselves attempted to limit its scope. The Indian Supreme Court, for example, has stated that features of the basic structure cannot be 'damaged or destroyed', 'abrogated or emasculated', 'changed' or 'altered'—all standards employed in just the *Kesavananda* decision alone. Pakistan's Supreme Court explained that its basic structure doctrine was not meant to prevent all amendment, but only for parliament 'to repeal or abrogate the Salient Features of the Constitution or substantively alter i.e. to significantly [a]ffect its essential nature'.[125] The Malaysian Supreme Court, when endorsing its own basic structure doctrine, spoke of underlying constitutional principles that 'cannot be abrogated or removed'.[126] These efforts to self-limit are also meant to signal that the doctrine is a means of last resort against extreme legislative action. However, there remains some ambiguity as to the precise standard of review the courts will apply in concrete cases. This is where academic scholarship has attempted clarification.

[125] *District Bar Association, Rawalpindi and Others* v. *Federation of Pakistan*, 267–8.

[126] *Indira Gandhi a/p Mutho* v. *Pengarah Jabatan Agama Islam Perak & Ors and other appeals*, para. 90.

Structural interpretation and a sliding scale of amendment review intensity

One scholarly attempt to resolve the problem of an over-expansive application of unconstitutional constitutional amendment doctrines is proposed by Yaniv Roznai.[127] First, he suggests that the adjudication of unamendability should rest on structural or holistic interpretation.[128] In other words, when assessing whether an amendment is materially unconstitutional, the court should look to the entire constitutional edifice in making its determination. This proposition is congruent with the approaches developed in many constitutional systems, whether on the basis of constitutional provisions explicitly mandating structural interpretation or through judicial doctrine. Examples of the latter include the practice of constitutionally conforming interpretation in Germany and structural interpretation as embraced in American and Indian jurisprudences.[129] Several of the post-Arab Spring constitutions adopted explicit provisions mandating holistic or coherent interpretation of the text: Article 146 of Tunisia's Constitution speaks of harmonious interpretation of the constitution 'as an indissoluble whole'; Article 227 of Egypt's 2014 Constitution clarifies that the constitutional text and the preamble are 'non-divisible' and the constitution 'one coherent unity; and Libya's draft 2016 Constitution, under Article 215, similarly integrates the preamble and declares the constitution 'a coherent organic unit'. Other constitutions mandate such holistic interpretation specifically for the bill of rights (see Article 39(2) of the South African Constitution). The general presumption of constitutionality should be even stronger in the case of constitutional amendments, so that they are only invalidated as a last resort.[130]

Roznai further suggests a sliding scale of intensity of review of constitutional amendments. This proposition hinges on his broader theory of amendment power as a limited secondary power, distinguished from the primary constituent power manifesting during constitution-making.[131] For Roznai, limits on amendment are more or less legitimate depending on the characteristics of the amendment process, specifically how inclusive, participatory, multi-procedural, or deliberative it is.[132] Tying this into the judicial review of amendments, he proposes to modulate the latter's intensity depending on the same qualities of the amendment process. Thus, what he terms government amendment powers—those resembling ordinary legislative procedures—are the most prone to manipulation and as such should

[127] Roznai (2017), 213–25.

[128] Ibid., 215.

[129] Donald P. Kommers, 'Germany: Balancing Rights and Duties' in Jeffrey Goldsworthy, ed., *Interpreting Constitutions: A Comparative Study* (Oxford University Press 2007) 161, 204; Vicki C. Jackson, 'Holistic Interpretation: Fitzpatrick v. Bitzer and Our Bifurcated Constitution', *Stanford Law Review* 53:5 (2001) 1259; and Manoj Mate, 'Judicial Supremacy in Comparative Constitutional Law', *Tulane Law Review* 92:2 (2017) 393, 418.

[130] Roznai (2017), 217–18.

[131] Ibid., 158–75.

[132] Ibid., 158, 219–20.

be subjected to more intense scrutiny: a 'disproportionate violation standard'.[133] He proposes to import proportionality review into the review of constitutional amendments, resulting in courts assessing whether the core of an unamendable principle was disproportionately violated in the same way they assess rights violations.[134] Roznai does not envision technical obstacles to adapting proportionality to amendment review, as it would allow the balancing of the core of the unamendable principle in question and the interests and means pursued by the amendment power.[135]

In the case of what he terms 'popular amendment'—those employing inclusive, participatory, and deliberative mechanisms aimed to approximate an original constituent process—Roznai proposes a 'fundamental abandonment standard'.[136] By this he means to balance the democratic credentials of the process with preventing constitutional replacement. This second test is 'one of degree and extent', by which Roznai intends to capture modifications of unamendable principles' essence.[137] The inspiration is clearly the constitutional replacement doctrine developed by the Colombian Constitutional Court (discussed in greater detail in Chapter 2 of this book). Roznai cites with approval the 1970 *Klass* case in German jurisprudence, where the German Constitutional Court employed the language of 'fundamental abandonment' to clarify the scope of Article 79(3).[138]

As we can see, Roznai is intent on showing that clear, predictable, and—importantly—*restrained* standards of review of unamendability can be developed. He encourages us to move beyond positivism not just in determining implicit unamendability, but also in setting the contours of its adjudication. He is also, rightly, critical of what he terms a 'minimal effect standard' that would see courts striking down any amendment that so much as touches an unamendable principle.[139] Not only would such a standard be too severe, but it might lead to absurd results such as ossifying any attempt to develop aspects of the constitution that relate to unamendable principles.

Looking at these propositions in the abstract, we can already identify potential problems. The neat distinction between governmental and popular amendment powers, one led by the political branches in a manner open to abuse and the other more participatory and therefore democratically legitimate, does not capture the reality of constitutional amendment rules. These are complex, often contain tiered thresholds, and involve different constitutional actors at different stages of the process. How would we classify an amendment process involving a popular initiative,

[133] Ibid., 220.
[134] Ibid., 221.
[135] Ibid., 220.
[136] Ibid., 221.
[137] Ibid., 223.
[138] 30 BVerfGE 1 (1970) ('*Klass*').
[139] Roznai (2017), 218.

certified by the constitutional court, having passed through two chambers of parliament, re-certified by the court, and then submitted to a popular referendum?[140] What about a process initiated by the government, deliberated on by a citizen assembly, subjected to a popular referendum, and completed by legislative action?[141] The problem is not just one of classification, however. Roznai links judicial review to the quality of the amendment process in a valiant effort to address democratic concerns about unamendability. However, as we have seen above, this ignores the justifications in favour of unamendability—especially its implicit version—that rely on a normative reading of the constitution. Insofar as material limits on amendment are defended as necessary to protect the very essence of liberal constitutionalism, the democratic credentials of the amendment process are presumably irrelevant.

The proposition to import proportionality analysis in amendment review is similarly doubtful. First, unamendability review often comes about as a form of abstract review, possibly triggered *ex officio* as part of the amendment process. This means any assessment of necessity, rationality, or balancing required by the proportionality test would be made without the benefit of a concrete case before the court. Roznai explicitly states that judicial review of amendments should not be used in judicial strike-down of policy choices.[142] Sceptics of proportionality review have long pointed out that it inches too close to doing just that, especially when moving away from the rights review context, so importing it into amendment review would seem especially problematic.[143]

Second, we should acknowledge the heated scholarly debates on whether proportionality is the best interpretive technique even in rights review.[144] Its critics have pointed out that we risk engaging in the balancing of incommensurables, viewing rights and interests as easily quantifiable and comparable even when they are not.[145] Two cases discussed in prior chapters in this book illustrate this problem when applied to unamendable principles. In the Turkish headscarf case, both the Turkish Constitutional Court and the European Court of Human Rights endorsed the ban on the basis of the importance of the state's unamendable commitment to secularism.[146] However, Judge Tulkens, dissenting in the *Şahin* case, disagreed

[140] This was the process followed by same-sex marriage popular initiative in Romania, ultimately rejected at referendum in 2018.

[141] This was the process leading to Ireland's successful constitutional amendment on abortion in 2018.

[142] Roznai (2017), 225.

[143] Jeff King, 'Proportionality: A Halfway House', *New Zealand Law Review* (2010) 327; Tom Hickman, 'Problems for Proportionality', *New Zealand Law Review* (2010) 303.

[144] See, inter alia, Stavros Tsakyrakis, 'Proportionality: An Assault on Human Rights?', *International Journal of Constitutional Law* 7:3 (2009) 468 and the various replies in that journal; Hickman (2010); Francisco J. Urbina, *A Critique of Proportionality and Balancing* (Cambridge University Press 2017).

[145] Urbina (2017), 39–74.

[146] *Leyla Şahin* v. *Turkey*, Application no. 44774/98, Grand Chamber Judgment, 10 November 2005. See further discussion in Chapter 1.

with the manner in which the majority applied the principles of secularism and equality, including via proportionality analysis. She saw it as 'necessary to seek to harmonise the principles of secularism, equality and liberty, not to weigh one against the other'.[147] In other words, by framing these as competing interests, the assumption that they could not be reconciled was already built into the analysis, with the outcome of depriving a young woman of the freedom to manifest her religion, express herself, and pursue her education. We also saw this framing problem in the 1975 *Abortion I* case.[148] The German Constitutional Court found both the woman's right to self-determination and the foetus's right to life to be grounded in the unamendable principle of human dignity, ultimately finding the latter could not be sacrificed even in the name of women's freedom to dispose of their own bodies.

Anchoring amendment review in a transnational referent

A further attempt to ensure unconstitutional constitutional amendment doctrines do not overreach comes from Rosalind Dixon and David Landau.[149] The two authors state clearly that they are less concerned with whether such a doctrine should be adopted as they are with *how* it is used, as well as with making it as useful as possible in practice.[150] They place their proposal squarely in the democratic hedging literature, within which judicial review plays the role of political insurance to political actors unsure of their electoral fortunes and can facilitate transitions.[151] A virtue of their proposal is that it grapples seriously with the reality of abusive constitutionalism, which has seen authoritarians working within the legal framework to entrench their hold on power and the rise of hybrid constitutional regimes.[152] Another is that they consider amendment review in a broader context, as only one of the constitutional mechanisms that could be deployed against democratic erosion (others they discuss include tiered amendment rules and political disincentives such as amnesties).[153] Given this threat, Dixon and Landau argue, a doctrine of unconstitutional constitutional amendment has the advantage of allowing judges to respond *ex post* once an abusive amendment has been adopted.[154]They propose to identify the content of implicit unamendability via a transnational democratic referent (more on which in Chapter 5).

[147] Dissenting Opinion of Judge Tulkens, para. 4. She also disagreed with how the majority balanced the competing interests in the case (see para. 17).

[148] 39 BVerfGE 1 ('*Abortion I*'). See further discussion in Chapter 3.

[149] Dixon and Landau (2015).

[150] Ibid., 612; Rosalind Dixon and David Landau, 'Transnational Constitutionalism and a Limited Doctrine of Unconstitutional Constitutional Amendment: A Rejoinder to Sujit Choudhry', *International Journal of Constitutional Law* 15:3 (2017) 833, 836.

[151] See, inter alia, Tom Ginsburg, *Judicial Review in New Democracies: Constitutional Courts in Asian Cases* (Cambridge University Press 2003); Samuel Issacharoff, *Fragile Democracies: Contested Power in the Era of Constitutional Courts* (Cambridge University Press 2015). See also Chapter 2 in this book.

[152] David Landau, 'Abusive Constitutionalism', *UC Davis Law Review* 47 (2013a) 189.

[153] Dixon and Landau (2015), 614; Dixon and Landau (2016), 280.

[154] Dixon and Landau (2015), 614. More on abusive constitutionalism below.

Dixon and Landau propose a broad but weak doctrine of unconstitutional constitutional amendment, premised on minimal substantive commitments, on the one hand, and judicial restraint and deference, on the other.[155] They dismiss a narrow doctrine that would only protect against the destruction of a small, core set of principles or institutions, such as those formalized in an eternity clause, as potentially inefficient in addressing abusive amendment, especially aggregative or incremental abuse. They similarly reject the adoption of a standard that would require strike-down of all potentially anti-democratic amendments as too broad. Instead, they recommend adopting a transnational referent to determine both the content of unamendable principles and when there is an actual threat, i.e. when courts are to deploy their power to invalidate amendments. The concrete models guiding them are India's basic structure doctrine and Colombia's constitutional replacement doctrine. These are said to have the advantage of not resting on exhaustive lists of elements determined *ex ante*, while at the same time being deployed on a case-by-case basis.[156]

Dixon and Landau suggest a sophisticated approach to limiting the risk of overuse or misuse of unconstitutional constitutional amendment doctrines both in terms of their scope and in terms of their effects. They do this by stipulating a minimum core, anchored in a thin notion of competitive democracy and in transnational elements, that is to be deemed unamendable, coupled with weak constitutional review.[157] A similar endorsement of unamendability doctrines has also come from other authors otherwise sceptical of strong court intervention. Mark Tushnet, for example, accepts a restrained version of an unconstitutional constitutional amendment doctrine, by which he means one that is used rarely: 'Its mere existence ... may serve as a political check on the amendment process, as a "sword of Damocles" that, because it occasionally drops, cautions political actors against devoting too many resources to attempting to alter the existing specification of some component of the basic structure.'[158]

Such attempts to reign in unconstitutional constitutional amendment doctrines as applied by courts can only be evaluated in practice. These authors' emphasis on judicial restraint as a safeguard against excessive judicial self-empowerment is persuasive only insofar as it captures how such doctrines have operated in practice. To their credit, Dixon and Landau admit that measuring changes to the minimum core of unamendability they have stipulated will be hard to predict.[159] They also envision the danger of courts misusing unamendability in order to protect their own

[155] Dixon and Landau (2015), 627.

[156] Ibid., 628.

[157] Rosalind Dixon and Felix Uhlman, 'The Swiss Constitution and a Weak-Form Unconstitutional Amendment Doctrine?', *International Journal of Constitutional Law* 16:1 (2018) 54. See also Colón-Ríos (2014), 157–62 on weak basic structure review.

[158] Mark Tushnet, 'Amendment Theory and Constituent Power' in Gary J. Jacobsohn and Miguel Schor, eds., *Comparative Constitutional Theory* (Edward Elgar 2018) 317, 332.

[159] Dixon and Landau (2016), 285.

jurisprudential lines.[160] The fact remains, however, that these authors see promise in unconstitutional constitutional amendment doctrines being limited and operating as a measure of last resort against democratic erosion in a way that can counterbalance any democratic deficit.

In my view, we should more clearly tailor our expectations of how judicially created doctrines of unamendability will operate in practice to the realities of the political and constitutional contexts in which they are most likely to be invoked. For one, much will depend on the nature and self-understanding of the court expected to protect unamendable principles, on its positioning within the constitutional system and on the internal and external pressures it faces. This concern has already been raised when discussing courts in new democracies.[161] Courts in these contexts may themselves be under threat by the same democratic backsliding forces and as such unable to intervene, or else they risk such political backlash if they intervene too forcefully, that they may think twice before doing it for reasons of self-preservation. As we have seen in Chapter 2, unamendability is sometimes less about lofty ideals of democratic constitutionalism and more about pragmatism and deal-making. The same can be true for constitutional adjudication of that unamendability, whether formal or implicit: the constitutional courts we envision as guardians of the constitution are themselves actors in need of legitimation, which they may well seek to build by strategically avoiding conflict with the other branches, at least in the early years of the institution. This has been the case with the much-lauded South African Constitutional Court as much as with courts elsewhere in new democracies.[162] The Indian Supreme Court has been described as competing with other branches of government for public legitimacy and seeking to play the role of a conflict manager, often more concerned with public opinion than 'legal niceties'.[163] In some cases, such as Turkey's, courts will seek to serve political elites in power by reducing electoral competition, such as via party bans in the name of eternal principles.[164]

[160] Dixon and Landau (2015), 615.

[161] Sujit Choudhry, 'Transnational Constitutionalism and a Limited Doctrine of Unconstitutional Constitutional Amendment: A Reply to Rosalind Dixon and David Landau', *International Journal of Constitutional Law* 15:3 (2017) 826, 830. Dixon and Issacharoff have identified different strategies of judicial deferral, by which constitutional courts in new democracies delay the practical effect of their decisions in order to avoid direct political confrontations and to build institutional legitimacy over time (Rosalind Dixon and Samuel Issacharoff, 'Living to Fight Another Day: Judicial Deferral in Defense of Democracy', *Wisconsin Law Review* (2016) 683).

[162] Choudhry (2017), 831. For another example, see Bianca Selejan-Guţan, 'The Constitutional Court and Others in Romanian Constitutionalism—25 Years After', *Vienna Journal of International Constitutional Law* 11:4 (2017) 565. In general, see David Landau, 'Institutional Failure and Intertemporal Theories of Judicial Role in the Global South' in David Bilchitz and David Landau, eds., *The Evolution of the Separation of Powers: Between the Global North and the Global South* (Edward Elgar 2018b) 31.

[163] Pratap Bhanu Mehta, 'The Indian Supreme Court and the Art of Democratic Positioning' in Mark Tushnet and Madhav Khosla, eds., *Unstable Constitutionalism: Law and Politics in South Asia* (Cambridge University Press 2015) 233, 234.

[164] Gözde Böcü and Felix Petersen, 'Debating State Organization Principles in the Constitutional Conciliation Commission' in Felix Petersen and Zeynep Yanaşmayan, eds., *The Failure of Popular Constitution Making in Turkey: Regressing Towards Autocracy* (Cambridge University Press 2019) 145, 150. See also discussion of party bans in Chapter 1 of this book.

To these institutional concerns, I would add another. The accounts above seem to assume a very particular type of court: discursive and interested in engaging in reasoned judging that deals reflectively with fundamental questions about democracy. Practice shows that this often overestimates what courts actually do. In many contexts, constitutional adjudication is characterized by formalism, which then seeps into their enforcement of unamendability. For example, constitutional courts in Romania and Serbia have developed their constitutional amendment jurisprudence in this way.[165] Both the Indian Supreme Court and the Turkish Constitutional Court have also been criticized for developing only formal, procedural conceptions of democracy, and not necessarily coherent ones either.[166] When imagining standards of review of unamendability, therefore, we cannot do so in a vacuum. Specifically, we cannot ignore the legal cultural milieu in which courts adjudicate and the specific interpretive techniques they are likely to resort to. As we know, such formalism has at times resulted in formal eternity clauses not being enforced by courts at all.[167]

Arguments that courts enforcing unamendable limits, especially implicit ones, can strike the right balance between interventionism and self-restraint still accept that courts *are* the right forum for these types of battles. In some instances, they will not be, simply by virtue of the attacks on democratic constitutionalism being non-constitutional in nature. The strongest case for constitutional adjudication, however, seems to take the form of a separation of powers argument: as guardians of the constitution, surely there is no stronger justification for courts to intervene than in order to protect the basic structure or minimum core of the constitution. To do otherwise is for courts to abandon their *raison d'être*.

Unamendable judicial independence and the limits of judicial self-restraint

I propose to look at the adjudication of unamendable judicial independence in order to test this last argument. This will help illuminate the matter on several fronts. First, it allows us to sidestep much of the controversy over delineating the content of implicit unamendability. There is consensus, even among political insurance and democratic hedging constitutional theorists and among proponents of minimalist versions of the unconstitutional constitutional amendment doctrine,

[165] Resorting to what Roznai had called and dismissed as 'minimal effect standard'. See Silvia Suteu, 'The Multinational State That Wasn't: The Constitutional Definition of Romania as a National State', *Vienna Journal on International Constitutional Law* 11:3 (2017a) 413 and Darko Simović, 'Constitutional Rigidity and Aporias of the Amendment Procedure in the Republic of Serbia', Fondacija Centar za javno pravo (2017).

[166] Choudhry (2017), 831; Böcü and Petersen (2019), 153.

[167] Albert et al. (2019).

that judicial independence is a pillar of democratic constitutionalism. Second, there are plenty of international and regional standards on judicial independence, allowing for the determination of a minimum core anchored transnationally.[168] Third, constitutional judges should be uniquely well placed to adjudicate attacks on judicial independence, insofar as it is their bread and butter. Finally, attacks on judicial independence have been at the heart of democratic backsliding in a number of contexts, from India and Pakistan to Hungary and Poland. So, is comparative practice in the area of unamendable judicial independence adjudication cause for optimism?

Unamendable judicial supremacy in judicial appointments

Let us look at several settings in which unamendable judicial independence was reviewed by apex courts. India's 2016 *National Judicial Appointments Commission (NJAC)* decision is perhaps the most famous.[169] As we have seen, the basic structure doctrine of the Indian Supreme Court has evolved into a rich and varied judicial tool, now used not just in substantially reviewing amendments, but also as a method of judicial interpretation and to review states' legislation and executive decisions. The *NJAC* case concerned the Ninety-Ninth Amendment to the Indian Constitution, which sought to create a National Judicial Appointments Commission. The new method of judicial appointments changed the previous collegium system which had been dominated by Supreme Court justices when it came to high court appointments. The NJAC would retain as members the Chief Justice of India and two other senior justices, but would also include the union minister of law and justice, and two 'eminent persons'.[170] Two members could veto an appointment. The reform was meant to increase transparency and accountability in judicial appointments, including by creating a system that incorporated political and civil society representatives.[171]

The Supreme Court, however, struck down the amendment as contravening the basic structure doctrine. It found that by removing judicial supremacy in the judicial appointments process—i.e. the justices' determinative role—the amendment affected judicial independence and was as such unconstitutional. The court interpreted the constitutional duty of the president to consult with senior justices in the judicial appointment process (Article 124(2) of the constitution) to amount to a mandatory duty to follow that advice. It even spoke of preventing *any* political involvement in judicial appointments, ignoring the fact that the president's cabinet

[168] For an overview, see International Commission of Jurists, *International Standards on the Independence and Accountability of Judges, Lawyers and Prosecutors*, https://www.icj.org/themes/centre-for-the-independence-of-judges-and-lawyers/international-standards/.

[169] *Supreme Court Advocates-on-Record Association* v. *Union of India* (2016) 4 SCC 1.

[170] The two eminent persons would be selected from a panel consisting of the Chief Justice, the prime minister, and the leader of the opposition in the Lok Sabha (the lower house of the Indian parliament).

[171] Rehan Abeyratne, 'Upholding Judicial Supremacy in India: The NJAC Judgment in Comparative Perspective', *George Washington International Law Review* 49 (2017) 569.

had actually had the final say in the matter until this was changed via the Supreme Court's case law in 1993.[172] While judicial independence was recognized as part of the basic structure doctrine as early as the *Kesavananda* case, the *NJAC* judgment did not clarify why judicial primacy was integral to it. A comparative analysis has found, moreover, that India is unique in affording such primacy in the appointments process to its senior justices, a feature of its system that evolved for historical reasons.[173] A more charitable reading of the *NJAC* case would see it as an attempt to preserve the principle that parliament's powers are never sovereign and that parliamentary action remains subject to justification.[174] However, it is difficult to avoid the conclusion that the Indian Supreme Court sought to guard the status quo for institutional rather than principled reasons.

The Indian Supreme Court has certainly not been alone in relying on the basic structure doctrine in cases seeking to reform judicial appointments procedures. As we saw above, the Bangladeshi Supreme Court adopted its own basic structure doctrine in a case involving judicial restructuring—used with the intention of subordinating judicial review politically—and declared judicial independence an essential feature of the constitution.[175] In 2016, the court invalidated the Sixteenth Amendment, which had restored verbatim an original constitutional provision regarding the removal of the Supreme Court judges.[176] The original system empowered the president to remove judges based only on proven misbehaviour or incapacity, following a two-thirds vote in parliament, and was removed via constitutional amendment in 1975. During the military rule that followed, a peer system of judicial appointments, centred on a Supreme Judicial Council, was introduced. The Supreme Court struck down the Sixteenth Amendment on the ground that it violated judicial independence by granting parliament too much influence in the judicial removal process. It did this despite the fact that legislation to determine the process for judicial impeachment had still to be passed. Furthermore, the court reasoned that because the original constitutional provision was being *re*introduced, this was an act of *derivative* constituent power and as such reviewable judicially. It has been noted, rightly I think, that this decision constituted the Supreme Court itself violating the separation of powers and 'led to the marginalization—indeed

[172] Ibid., 611.

[173] Ibid., 570.

[174] Khosla (2016), 245.

[175] *Anwar Hossain Chowdhury* v. *Bangladesh*, 1989, 18 CLC (AD). For a discussion of the case as a justified intervention in the face of attempted political capture of judicial review, see Ridwanul Hoque, 'The Judicialization of Politics in Bangladesh: Pragmatism, Legitimacy, and Consequences' in Mark Tushnet and Madhav Khosla, eds., *Unstable Constitutionalism: Law and Politics in South Asia* (Cambridge University Press 2015) 261, 278–9.

[176] *Advocate Asaduzzaman Siddiqui* v. *Bangladesh*, Writ Petition No. 9989 of 2014, 5 May 2016. See discussion in Ridwanul Hoque, 'Developments in Bangladeshi Constitutional Law: The Year 2016 in Review', *ICONnect Blog* (12 October 2017), http://www.iconnectblog.com/2017/10/developments-in-bangladeshi-constitutional-law-the-year-2016-in-review/.

defiance—of the constituent power of the founding people of Bangladesh who chose the parliamentary model of judicial removal'.[177]

An interesting comparison may also be drawn with Pakistan. When called on to review the Eighteenth Amendment, the Pakistani Supreme Court took issue with the changes instituted to the judicial appointment process.[178] Whereas the final word previously rested with the chief justices of superior courts, the amendment sought to create a hybrid system comprised of a judicial commission and a parliamentary committee. It should be noted that the previous system was itself the result of judicial interpretation of the president's constitutional duty to 'consult' the chief justices in judicial appointments.[179] The Supreme Court did not immediately strike down the amendment on this basis however. After all, this was a far-reaching amendment seeking to roll back legal changes adopted under Musharraf's regime and widely perceived as bolstering democracy in Pakistan. Instead, the court issued an interim order, indicating its views to parliament.[180] The latter accepted most of the court's recommendations and passed the Nineteenth Amendment; the only exception was to retain the final word in judicial appointments to the parliamentary committee. This approach has been termed 'dialogic' and the Supreme Court praised for its restraint when assessing whether the reform violated the constitution's basic structure, relying as it did on the threat to invalidate a constitutional amendment rather than immediately doing so.[181] However, the court later reasserted its final authority in the matter by declaring the decisions of this parliamentary committee to be justiciable. This has led even defenders of the Pakistani Supreme Court to label its interventions in the area of judicial appointments as 'push[ing] doctrinal boundaries'[182] and a 'patently self-serving' assertion of judicial power.[183]

Similar interventions in the name of protecting judicial independence have occurred not just under the umbrella of basic structure doctrines, but also under that of constitutional replacement doctrines such as that of the Colombian Constitutional Court. In two decisions in 2016, the Colombian court struck down attempts at constitutional revision that it deemed to have contravened the constitutional replacement doctrine originally developed in the area of executive

[177] Hoque (2017).

[178] *District Bar Association, Rawalpindi and Others* v. *Federation of Pakistan* PLD 2015 SC 401.

[179] *Al-Jehad Trust* v. *Federation of Pakistan* PLD 1996 SC 324, also known as the 'Judges' case'. See Moeen H. Cheema, 'The "Chaudhry Court": Deconstructing the "Judicial-ization of Politics" in Pakistan', *Washington International Law Journal* 25:3 (2016) 447, fn. 45.

[180] *Nadeem Ahmad and Others* v. *Federation of Pakistan*, PLD 2010 SC 1165. The Supreme Court identified the reduced role of the chief justice, the equal say given to the executive in judicial nominations, and the virtual veto power given to the parliamentary committee over the recommendations of the judicial commission as problematic aspects.

[181] Cheema (2016), 458.

[182] Ibid., 476.

[183] Moeen H. Cheema, 'Two Steps Forward One Step Back: The Non-linear Expansion of Judicial Power in Pakistan', *International Journal of Constitutional Law* 16:2 (2018) 503, 520.

term limits.[184] It thereby struck down the newly created Judicial Governance Council, with competences in the governance and administration of the judiciary, and the Commission of *Aforados*, tasked with prosecuting criminal and disciplinary offences by justices of the Supreme Court, the Constitutional Court, the Council of State, the Judicial Governance Council, and also the Attorney General of the Nation. The Judicial Governance Council was deemed not to respect the principle of self-government of the judiciary and both institutions were seen as undermining judicial independence and the separation of powers. Politically, the decisions received immediate backlash from both the governmental majority and the opposition.[185] Doctrinally, the application of the constitutional replacement doctrine was also dubious as both institutions in question retained a diverse and mainly judicial membership and would have at least been plausible replacements for their predecessors.[186] The court's intervention appeared to ignore the fact that the impetus behind the reform was to enhance judicial accountability and efficiency.

The most recent addition to this list is Slovakia, whose Constitutional Court in 2019 struck down a constitutional amendment introducing a new vetting procedure for judicial appointments.[187] The court invoked for itself a new power to review constitutional amendments in order to protect the 'material core' of the constitution.[188] It ultimately found, four years after the proceedings had been initiated, that the amendment in question was unconstitutional on the basis of breaching the principles of democracy and rule of law on which the Slovak Constitution is based and which are enshrined in its Article 1(1). Like its counterparts elsewhere, the Slovak court read the changes to the judicial appointments process as contravening the related principles of separation of powers and judicial independence.

These judgments showcase the dangers of expansive interpretation of an unconstitutional constitutional amendment doctrine in the name of protecting judicial independence. The decisions revolved around changes to judicial self-governance structures, equating reforms of the latter with attacks on judicial independence. As recent comparative work on judicial accountability has shown, however, we should not be too quick to assume that maximizing judicial self-government is the

[184] Decision C-285 of June 1, 2016 and Decision C-373 of July 13, 2016. See discussion in Mario Alberto Cajas-Sarria, 'Judicial Review of Constitutional Amendments in Colombia: A Political and Historical Perspective, 1955–2016', *Theory and Practice of Legislation* 5:3 (2017) 245.

[185] Cajas-Sarria (2017), 267.

[186] Ibid., 267–8.

[187] PL. ÚS 21/2014.

[188] Marek Domin, 'A Part of the Constitution Is Unconstitutional, the Slovak Constitutional Court Has Ruled', *Verfassungsblog*, 8 February 2019, https://verfassungsblog.de/a-part-of-the-constitution-is-unconstitutional-the-slovak-constitutional-court-has-ruled/; Simon Drugda, 'Slovak Constitutional Court Strikes Down a Constitutional Amendment—But the Amendment Remains Valid', *ICONnect Blog*, 25 April 2019, http://www.iconnectblog.com/2019/04/slovak-constitutional-court-strikes-down-a-constitutional-amendment-but-the-amendment-remains-valid/

optimum way to guarantee judicial independence.[189] Not only are judicial councils themselves vulnerable to politicization, but depending on their design they may also have broader negative systemic consequences, such as increased bureaucratization, judicial self-empowerment, and selective accountability.[190] At the very least, a variety of institutional designs are possible while retaining respect for judicial independence and the separation of powers.

Resisting limits on constitutional review powers

The above examples are illustrations of judicial independence as an implicit unamendable principle, or else as embedded in a constitutional replacement doctrine. Judicial independence can also be formally entrenched as unamendable however. Romania's eternity clause, for example, lists it alongside unamendable state characteristics and fundamental rights protection (Article 152(1) and (2)). In its decision on the 2014 constitutional revision, the Romanian Constitutional Court found some of the proposed reforms to its competences to have run afoul of the eternity clause. Specifically, lawmakers had attempted to remove Article 146(l), which empowers the Constitutional Court 'to carry out also other duties stipulated by the organic law of the Court'. The court found this problematic as it would remove two additional competences that had been granted it via the organic law: the power to review, *ex officio*, the constitutional revision law, and the power to review the constitutionality of parliamentary resolutions. In other words, the court tried to block the removal of additional competences it had only gained via legislation and which had never been constitutionalized directly. It did so not in the name of judicial independence as such, but of access to constitutional justice as an unamendable fundamental right.[191]

It should be noted that these two competences were included neither in the 1991 original text of the Romanian Constitution, nor in the 2003 revisions. In fact, the Constitutional Court was originally envisioned as a Kelsenian negative legislator and only later, through legislative and jurisprudential changes, did it transform itself into a positive legislator.[192] The only *ex officio* power of abstract review of constitutionality included in the Romanian Constitution allows the court to review the constitutional revision *initiative*, whether legislative[193] or popular.[194] Via changes to the organic law on the functioning of the court, it now exercises a double control of constitutionality, abstract and *ex officio*: at the start of the amendment process, when it certifies that

[189] David Kosař, *Perils of Judicial Self-Government in Transitional Societies* (Cambridge University Press 2016) and Aida Torres Pérez, 'Judicial Self-Government and Judicial Independence: The Political Capture of the General Council of the Judiciary in Spain', *German Law Journal* 19:7 (2018) 1769.

[190] Kosař (2016), 16.

[191] Decizia nr. 80/2014, para. 442.

[192] Selejan-Guţan (2017).

[193] Decizia nr. 148/2003, 12 May 2003 and Decizia nr. 799/2011, 23 June 2011.

[194] As was the case in 2016, when the court certified the constitutionality of the popular initiative on the constitutional definition of the family. Decizia nr. 580/2016, 20 July 2016.

the revision *initiative* is within the procedural and material limits of the constitution; and again once the legislative amendment process has concluded but before a ratification referendum has been held, when the court checks whether the revision *law* still complies with these limits. So, in 2014, the Constitutional Court was objecting to the removal of this second prong of its abstract constitutionality control powers, on the grounds that it affected access to constitutional justice as an unamendable principle. Incidentally, the second objection, to the removal of its powers to review parliamentary resolutions, is no less controversial, as these were always objected to as an interference by the court into parliamentary affairs.[195] Like the Indian Supreme Court, the Romanian Constitutional Court could only accept the constitutionality of supplementing, not limiting, its review powers.

These examples are not meant to argue that judicial independence is not an important constitutional principle, nor indeed—where a basic structure doctrine is developed by courts—that it should not be a recognized element of that structure. However, the cases discussed above illustrate just how difficult it might be to reign in courts that have developed the power to materially review constitutional amendments. We might view these as instances involving the self-interest of the courts themselves: the judiciary's role in judicial appointments processes in India, Bangladesh, Pakistan, and Colombia, and the scope of constitutional review powers in Romania. However, in neither case did these apex courts display the self-restraint advocated by proponents of limits on unamendable constitutional amendment doctrines. Neither did they show much interest in identifying a transnational referent that would have helped temper their fears of judicial independence being undermined. One could even argue that a court engaging in review of implicit unamendability would have some comparative backing for a position that only judicial self-governance with judicial supremacy respects the principle of judicial independence. Instead, these courts sought to protect their jurisprudential or institutional turfs, even where the link between the reforms proposed and undermining unamendable principles was tenuous.

4.4 Implicit unamendability as protection against democratic backsliding?

The appeal of unconstitutional constitutional amendment doctrines has grown in no small measure due to expectations that they could help stave off abusive constitutionalism.[196] More concretely, it has been argued that the substantive constitutional review of abusive constitutional amendments could form part of the arsenal against autocrats trying to undermine democratic constitutionalism through legal means.[197]

[195] Selejan-Guţan (2017), 574.

[196] Landau (2013a).

[197] Gábor Halmai, 'Unconstitutional Constitutional Amendments: Constitutional Courts as Guardians of the Constitution?', *Constellations* 19:2 (2012) 182; Fruzsina Gárdos-Orosz,

Attacks on democratic institutions today often take on a legal guise, and constitutional amendments are used as means to legitimize otherwise anti-democratic measures. The removal of executive term limits in Latin American and African countries discussed in Chapter 2 is one such example. As we have seen, India's basic structure doctrine was born in part as a reaction to emergency-era attempts to remove electoral accountability mechanisms (its earlier roots in property cases often ignored). In the face of such changes, the argument goes, courts carefully embracing and refining doctrines of unconstitutional constitutional amendment could at least act as a roadblock, or speedbump, against abuse.[198]

Whether in the form of a basic structure doctrine, which protects the overall constitutional edifice, or of a minimum core one, which seeks to maintain a baseline of protection to ensure electoral competition or rule of law guarantees, unamendability would be able to address the specificity of democratic backsliding in its new guise. Modern autocrats have been called 'legalistic autocrats' for deploying the law to undermine the constitutional system bit by bit and in ways whose overall effect may be difficult to see until it is too late.[199] What is novel, then, is that 'the new autocrats come to power not with bullets but with laws. They attack the institutions of liberal constitutionalism with constitutional amendments. They carefully preserve the shell of the prior liberal state—the same institutions, the same ceremonies, an overall appearance of rights protection—but in the meantime they hollow out its moral core.'[200] The outcome has been termed a 'Frankenstate': a state composed of perfectly reasonable components when taken individually, but monstrous when looked at as a whole.[201] Only a holistic evaluation of these attacks' impact on the constitutional order would be able to capture what, precisely, is undemocratic and illiberal about it, and—it has been hypothesized—that evaluation could be part of an unconstitutional constitutional amendment doctrine. Such a doctrine could also identify when stealth constitutional replacement was underway, disguised as mere constitutional amendment.

Calls to resist democratic backsliding through implicit unamendability in Hungary

Hungary is one case where such arguments initially carried much sway. As soon as he came to power with a parliamentary supermajority in 2010, Hungarian Prime Minister Viktor Orbán engaged in concerted and incremental constitutional

'Unamendability as a Judicial Discovery? Inductive Learning Lessons from Hungary' in Richard Albert and Bertil Emrah Oder, eds., *An Unamendable Constitution? Unamendability in Constitutional Democracies* (Springer 2018) 231; Dixon and Landau (2015).

[198] Dixon and Landau (2015), 613.

[199] Kim Lane Scheppele, 'Autocratic Legalism', *University of Chicago Law Review* 85 (2018) 545.

[200] Ibid., 582.

[201] Kim Lane Scheppele, 'The Rule of Law and the Frankenstate: Why Governance Checklists Do Not Work', *Governance* 26:4 (2013) 559, 560.

change to alter the foundations of Hungarian constitutional democracy.[202] Initially, he did so by passing ten constitutional amendments within thirteen months.[203] A new Fundamental Law was then adopted in 2011, followed by a number of constitutional amendments—easily passed given the government's initial two-thirds majority in parliament—that chipped away at rule of law and democratic protections. Even before the new constitution was enacted, judicial independence was in the firing line via changes to the retirement age for justices resulting in unprecedented turnover. Coupled with the packing of the Constitutional Court, there was soon little that could be done constitutionally to oppose the Orbán government's moves. Changes to the electoral system and to media laws would also make electoral competition more difficult and further entrench his hold on power.

The constitutional nature of the changes in Hungary might have made it a perfect candidate for the country's Constitutional Court to step in via an unconstitutional constitutional amendment doctrine. Contrary to Poland, where attacks on judicial independence and the undermining of the Constitutional Court were done at the sub-constitutional level through ordinary legislation, in Hungary there would have been opportunities for constitutional amendments to be reviewed on substantive grounds.[204] As these changes were unfolding and before the packing of the Constitutional Court, hopes remained that it would embrace an implicit unamendability doctrine in order to strike down the proposed changes.

In 2010, a new law that imposed a 98 per cent tax on severances paid to state employees leaving public service (which the government argued had been used by its predecessor as a reward system for loyalists) was struck down by the Hungarian Constitutional Court.[205] The government responded by passing an amendment that allowed for retroactive legislation in certain cases and precluded the Constitutional Court's jurisdiction over budgetary and tax policy legislation.[206] In its decision reviewing the amendment, however, the Constitutional Court refused to endorse implicit unamendability.[207] The judgment has been criticized for employing a selective comparative method and for misunderstanding the jurisdictional question the court was tasked with answering in terms of its power to review amendments.[208] Its substantive analysis was also contradictory, for while it found

[202] Miklós Bánkuti, Gábor Halmai, and Kim Lane Scheppele, 'Hungary's Illiberal Turn: Disabling the Constitution', *Journal of Democracy* 23:3 (2012) 138; Renáta Uitz, 'Can You Tell When an Illiberal Democracy Is in the Making? An Appeal to Comparative Constitutional Scholarship from Hungary', *International Journal of Constitutional Law* 13:1 (2015) 279; Andrew Arato, Post Sovereign Constitutional Making: Learning and Legitimacy (Oxford University Press 2016), 161; András L. Pap, *Democratic Decline in Hungary: Law and Society in an Illiberal Democracy* (Routledge 2018).

[203] Halmai (2012), 194.

[204] For an overview of backsliding in Poland, see Wojciech Sadurski, *Poland's Constitutional Breakdown* (Oxford University Press 2019).

[205] Decision 184/2010. (X. 28.).

[206] Halmai (2012), 192.

[207] Decision 61/2011. (VII. 13.).

[208] Halmai (2012), 192–3.

serious procedural problems with the passing of the amendment, as well as *jus cogens* norms that were breached, the court did not from there derive a power to intervene and strike down the amendment.[209] The court has been blamed for 'voluntarily signing the death sentence of judicial review' and thereby having 'given up on the ideal of constitutionalism'.[210]

It should be noted that such arguments had a foundation in the Hungarian Constitutional Court's own transitional jurisprudence. Immediately after the fall of communism, Hungary did not adopt a new constitution but chose instead to drastically amend its existing, 1949 Constitution. In its first decade, the Hungarian Constitutional Court emerged as quite an activist court and developed an 'invisible constitution' concept on which it relied to fill in gaps in the country's transitional constitutionalism.[211] The brainchild of its first chief justice, the 'invisible constitution' was meant to operate as a theoretical framework both supplementing the constitution and superseding it when it might be amended in a way that violated certain core values.[212] It was both a device meant to institute coherence within the constitutional system and a system of higher values. The 'invisible constitution', part of which were commitments to human dignity and the freedom of expression that the Constitutional Court developed via its case law, was thus meant to establish a 'liberal democratic constitutional identity'.[213] It was subject to criticism from its first enunciation, on the grounds that relying on unwritten new rights to declare laws unconstitutional was problematic.[214] While different from implicit unamendability—indeed, the possibility of adopting an eternity clause was considered but rejected when amending the 1949 Constitution,[215] and the Constitutional Court had also previously considered and rejected amendment review[216]—the concept of the 'invisible constitution' might have helped ground a doctrine of unconstitutional constitutional amendment in Hungarian law.

The matter was definitively put to rest in 2013, when in reviewing the Fourth Amendment to the Fundamental Law, the Constitutional Court upheld the amendment and also refused to endorse the substantive review of amendments in general; the Fundamental Law now also specifically disallows substantive review.[217]

209 Ibid., 194–7.
210 Ibid., 199.
211 Gábor Halmai, 'Silence of Transitional Constitutions: The "Invisible Constitution" Concept of the Hungarian Constitutional Court', *International Journal of Constitutional Law* 16:3 (2018b) 969 and Gábor Attila Tóth, 'Lost in Transition: Invisible Constitutionalism in Hungary' in Rosalind Dixon and Adrienne Stone, eds., *The Invisible Constitution in Comparative Perspective* (Cambridge University Press 2018) 541.
212 Halmai (2018), 972.
213 Ibid., 981.
214 Ibid., 977.
215 Gábor Halmai, 'Transitional Constitutional Unamendability?', *European Journal of Law Reform* 21:3 (2019) 259, 269–70.
216 Halmai (2012), 193–4.
217 Decision on. 12/2013 (V. 24.). Halmai (2019), 273.

In light of these developments, optimism about an unconstitutional constitutional doctrine's prospects against majoritarian abuses were tempered.[218] Its proponents in Hungary returned instead to an appreciation of the effectiveness of 'well-functioning constitutional conventions' and 'a developed constitutional culture' as vehicles against unbridled state power.[219]

The limited role of unamendability in cases of democratic backsliding

It is not that unamendability proponents are unreservedly optimistic about its prospects as a bulwark against democratic backsliding. Dixon and Landau, for example, admit that the evidence for how unamendability fares in practice is so far mixed. On the one hand, we have the Colombian Constitutional Court initially devising a balanced constitutional replacement doctrine and successfully preventing the removal of executive term limits. On the other, however, we have courts in Honduras, Costa Rica, and Nicaragua relying on the unconstitutional constitutional doctrine possibly to benefit rather than prevent abuse.[220] Even where a court previously deployed such a doctrine to protect democracy, it may not always do so and may overstep—the decisions discussed above are just such examples. Dixon and Landau's thesis is therefore narrower: that under the right conditions, and with their proposed limits in place, an unconstitutional constitutional amendment doctrine may be useful in combatting democratic threats. Indeed, they are careful to explain that they are less concerned with arguing *for* the adoption of such a doctrine as much as for explaining *how* it could be shaped and constrained so as to make it both effective against autocratic constitutional change and not itself prone to abuse.[221] Their search shifts then to identifying the right political conditions under which judicial intervention can work to enforce unamendability.

The case of Hungary highlights several problems with even this more cautious approach. At its most basic level, it should have been the ideal context within which a doctrine of unconstitutional constitutional amendment might have been relied on to prevent or at least delay backsliding. Many of the changes to the constitutional order were done via constitutional amendments, thereby raising at least the prospect of their constitutional review. There was even a window, before it was packed, when the country's Constitutional Court—a court with strong powers of constitutional review and an activist past—might have embraced substantive amendment review. And while incremental and insidious, several of the Orbán government's reforms might have made good candidates for implicit unamendable principles, such as judicial independence, competitive democracy, or even the rule

[218] Halmai (2019), 277.
[219] Gárdos-Orosz (2018), 236.
[220] Dixon and Landau (2017), 835. A lengthier discussion of these cases is found in Chapter 2 of this book.
[221] Dixon and Landau (2017), 836.

of law. In many ways, there could hardly be a better contender for unconstitutional constitutional amendment doctrines.

We could conclude, rather cynically, that Hungary's was an instance in which law just could not stave off politics. I believe, however, that there are important lessons to be learned from this experience, including about our expectations from constitutions and constitutional adjudication. First, there is a lesson about courts. The expectation that the Hungarian Constitutional Court should and would be able to intervene was premised on a certain view of that and other courts with strong powers of constitutional review. Such courts have long been promoted as the guardians of, indeed as *sine qua nons*, of democratic constitutionalism.[222] It is only more recently that comparative constitutional scholarship has begun to reckon with the fact that how courts position themselves vis-à-vis attacks on democratic constitutionalism varies. It is not just whether they have been packed or otherwise captured politically that matters, but also their institutional self-understanding as democratic actors. Increasingly, empirical evidence suggests that the correlation between strong judicial review powers and political competition, i.e. between courts with far-reaching review powers and their using such powers to protect and enhance democratic pluralism, is mixed.[223] In fact, this insight is not entirely new when considering the adjudication of eternity clauses, even those formally meant to protect democracy. As was seen in previous chapters of this book, even where formal eternity clauses entrench plural democracy and alternation in power, they have been interpreted as grounds for courts reducing electoral competition, including by removing from it competitive parties (Turkey), or as obstacles to democratic voting in the case of overstaying presidents (Honduras). Sometimes, it was precisely by appealing to courts with strong judicial review that political actors could circumvent entrenchment, including unamendability: 'Strong forms of judicial review can provide would-be authoritarians with the means of achieving their objectives without being bound by the constraints of a federal division of power, the separation of legislative and executive powers, or even formal limits on constitutional amendment.'[224]

A second lesson is about our expectations of what would-be authoritarians do once in power.[225] Gone are past assumptions that extremist or populist parties

[222] Ginsburg (2003), 26. See also Paul Blokker, 'Dilemmas of Democratisation from Legal Revolutions to Democratic Constitutionalism?', *Nordic Journal of International Law* 81 (2012) 437.

[223] Maria Popova has shown how in new democracies, intense political competition magnifies the benefits of subservient courts to incumbents, thus reducing rather than increasing judicial independence (Maria Popova, *Politicized Justice in Emerging Democracies: A Study of Courts in Russia and Ukraine* (Cambridge University Press 2012), 38). Alexei Trochev has cautioned against focusing only on judicial review success stories in comparative scholarship (Alexei Trochev, *Judging Russia: The Role of the Constitutional Court in Russian Politics 1990–2006* (Cambridge University Press 2008), 11).

[224] Rosalind Dixon and David Landau, 'Abusive Judicial Review: Courts against Democracy', 53 *UC Davis Law Review* (2020) 1313, 1350.

[225] For a reassessment on this topic, see contributions to the special issue 'Dealing with Populists in Government', *Democratization* 23:2 (2016).

would naturally moderate once in power, through coalition-building and the need to enlarge their electorates. Gone are also any assumptions that such parties are anti-institutionalist in the sense of trying to outright dismantle institutions that can check their power. Instead, when able, they deactivate checks and balances, weaken political opposition and skew electoral competition, and empower majoritarian institutions they control. Given such constitutional quicksand, the prospects of unamendability doctrines saving the democratic constitutional order are overstated. They may even backfire in cases where, as in Hungary, politically subservient courts entrench illiberal principles.

Third, and relatedly, we should note among the novelty of current democratic backsliding its sequencing. It was not coincidental that in both Hungary and Poland, the early attacks on rule of law institutions centred on the judiciary, undermining its independence, and reducing its powers to hold political actors to account. Or, in the words of one commentator, sometimes the focus behind backsliding may be the court itself, especially if it had previously been confrontational.[226] This is relevant with regard to unamendability too. In order for doctrines of unconstitutional constitutional amendment to work as they are intended to, there are institutional preconditions that must be met. Among these is a working, independent court with strong powers of constitutional review and a willingness to step into the political fray. If new evidence suggests that such a court is among would-be authoritarians' first targets, this suggests we should seriously temper our enthusiasm for unamendability to save us when the constitutional order is under attack.

Fourth, we should remember that the risks of courts over- and under-reaching when enforcing unamendability—courts intervening too actively or else failing to intervene at all—can coexist. Hungary's example is again a good illustration. As we have seen in this section, the Hungarian Constitutional Court might be viewed as an instance of under-reach insofar as the court missed its opportunity to develop an unconstitutional constitutional amendment doctrine at a crucial moment. However, if we remember the discussion of the same (by then packed) court developing a doctrine of 'abusive' constitutional identity in Chapter 3, we may also view it as an exponent of overreach. By then, the Hungarian court seemed ready to embrace constitutional non-negotiables in order to resist European law.

Where does all this leave us, finally? I believe we will not be able to respond to widespread democratic backsliding before we reckon with its underlying causes and the constitutional shortcomings that might have facilitated it. I have argued elsewhere that I view the so-called populist turn in countries in Central and Eastern Europe specifically as fuelled by a crisis of democratic representation and backlash against technocratic politics—aided in no small part by the particular

[226] Choudhry (2017), 832. For this reason, Choudhry suggests a better focus of the search for defences against backsliding would be traditional judicial review rather than constitutional review.

brand of hyper-legal constitutionalism entrenched in the region.[227] I argued there that seeking to further judicialize politics, including via unamendability doctrines, is a misguided attempt to offer 'more of the same' to what is not (or not just) a crisis of constitutionalism. What is certain, however, is that the 'counter-playbook' to resist backsliding will need to operate on multiple fronts, most likely involving major structural elements of constitutional, institutional, and democratic design.[228] The newfound sophistication of the attacks on democratic constitutionalism requires nothing less.

4.5 Conclusion

Unconstitutional constitutional amendment doctrines, at their most basic level, aim to prevent bad faith amendments. Amendments should not be used to undermine the basic structure or minimum core of the constitutional edifice nor, in their most extreme form, to achieve constitutional replacement by subterfuge. Faced with the threat of democratic backsliding affecting democracies old and new, hopes that such doctrines will be able to safeguard democratic constitutionalism run high.

This chapter has sought to highlight the problems with such expectations. In a sense, unconstitutional constitutional amendment doctrines attempt the impossible: they seek to juridify good faith in amendment practice. They start from theories of implicit unamendable principles (alongside or absent formal eternity clauses) and end with complex judicial doctrines of basic structures and constitutional replacement. Proponents of such doctrines trust that the law will still provide protection when constitutional and political processes break down. However, as the examples in this chapter have shown—and as the continued rise of autocratic legalism shows more broadly—sometimes law is itself part of the problem. Moreover, constitutional practice will always be broader than constitutional form can encompass. One thing we have learned from the rise to power of would-be autocrats in democracies around the world is just how reliant these democratic systems have always been on constitutional conventions, traditions, and informal practices. Seeking to juridify these, including via judicially enforcing implicit unamendable principles, risks constraining democratic avenues of constitutional change without the guarantee that judicially enforced rigidity will protect the democratic constitutional order. We now know that, rather than the last institution standing against a descent into authoritarianism, courts have become first targets

[227] Silvia Suteu, 'The Populist Turn in Central and Eastern Europe: Is Deliberative Democracy Part of the Solution?', *European Constitutional Law Review* 15:3 (2019) 488.

[228] Stephen Gardbaum, 'The Counter-playbook: Resisting the Populist Assault on Separation of Powers', *Columbia Journal of Transnational Law* 59:1 (2020 forthcoming).

in processes of democratic erosion. In such scenarios, the risk of judicial underreach in amendment review—indeed, in constitutional review more generally—is rife.

Studies of countries which have developed unconstitutional constitutional amendment doctrines have concluded that courts have proven assertive about defending their power of judicial review and jurisdiction but less emphatic 'when critical issues for the parliament and the executive are at stake'.[229] This decreased confidence was due to moderation and deference to other branches only in some cases and not in others. Such findings reinforce criticism of basic structure doctrines, and eternity clauses more generally, as unpredictable instruments in the hands of judges. As the case of India has shown, even in the birth country of the doctrine, laying a coherent doctrinal foundation for it has proven difficult. Nor has the Supreme Court of India, for all its often welcome activism, been fully able to avoid overreach and arbitrary interventions. Thus, while the basic structure doctrine may be defended on democratic constitutionalist grounds in certain cases, 'the court itself has obscured its own intimations of a principled defence by an indiscriminate use' of the doctrine in the years since *Kesavananda*.[230] The more recent turn towards using doctrines of implicit unamendability, in India and elsewhere, to protect judicial turf, is even more problematic. Legitimate attempts at legislative reform, such as of judicial appointments processes, have repeatedly been struck down in the name of unamendable judicial independence. The risk of overreach thus remains, including in jurisdictions with now decades-long experience adjudicating implicit unamendability.

[229] Michael Freitas Mohallem, 'Immutable Clauses and Judicial Review in India, Brazil and South Africa: Expanding Constitutional Courts' Authority', *International Journal of Human Rights* 15:5 (2010) 765, 781–2.

[230] Mehta (2002), 181.

PART III

ETERNITY CLAUSES IN CONTEMPORARY CONSTITUTIONAL REFORM PROCESSES

Transnational Forces, Popular Participation, and Constitutional Renewal

5

Eternity in a Global Context

Unamendability, Internationalized Constitution-Making, and Transnational Values

Eternity clauses can no longer be studied without acknowledging the global forces influencing both their content and their interpretation. Comparative constitutional scholars have also been grappling with the globalization of contemporary constitutionalism, seeking to disentangle, critique, and foresee their likely impact.[1] However, while some valuable interventions focused on unamendability do exist,[2] we are only just beginning to understand the impact of the transnational in this area.

This chapter proposes to further our understanding of eternity clauses and doctrines of unconstitutional constitutional amendment in global perspective along two fronts. The first concerns the content of unamendable provisions, which are shown increasingly to converge in terms of the principles and institutions they insulate. This is explained both by comparative learning across jurisdictions and by the widespread internationalization of constitution-making processes themselves. Be it supranational, state, or non-governmental actors, transnational actors influence and even drive processes of constitution-building worldwide, especially but not exclusively in post-conflict and post-authoritarian contexts. There are significant differences between the drafting of the constitutions of Bosnia and Herzegovina, Kosovo, and Tunisia, but the trend towards internationalization is clear and it recurrently results in the adoption of eternity clauses. This raises distinctive practical and theoretical problems to do with the democratic legitimacy

[1] Vicky C. Jackson, *Constitutional Engagement in a Transnational Era* (Oxford University Press 2010); Christine Bell, 'What We Talk about When We Talk about International Constitutional Law', *Transnational Legal Theory* 5:2 (2014) 241; Cheryl Saunders, 'Designing and Operating Constitutions in Global Context' in Mark Elliott and David Feldman, eds., *The Cambridge Companion to Public Law* (Cambridge University Press 2015) 256; Dennis Davis et al., eds, *An Inquiry into the Existence of Global Values: Through the Lens of Comparative Constitutional Law* (Hart 2015); Dieter Grimm, *Constitutionalism: Past, Present, and Future* (OUP, 2016) 315; Geoffrey Shaffer, Tom Ginsburg, and Terence C. Halliday eds., *Constitution-Making and Transnational Legal Order* (Cambridge University Press 2019).

[2] Lech Garlicki and Zofia A. Garlicka, 'External Review of Constitutional Amendments? International Law as a Norm of Reference', *Israel Law Review* 44 (2011) 343; Rosalind Dixon and David Landau, 'Transnational Constitutionalism and a Limited Doctrine of Unconstitutional Constitutional Amendment', *International Journal of Constitutional Law* 13:3 (2015) 606; Yaniv Roznai, *Unconstitutional Constitutional Amendments: The Limits of Amendment Powers* (Oxford University Press 2017), 71–102.

Eternity Clauses in Democratic Constitutionalism. Silvia Suteu, Oxford University Press. © Silvia Suteu 2021.
DOI: 10.1093/oso/9780198858867.003.0006

of an unamendable fundamental law resulting from a heavily internationalized process—whether amounting to constitutional imposition[3] or forcing us to rethink old concepts such as that of constituent power.[4] Beyond looking at the international dimension of constitutional authorship today, this chapter also explores the standard-setting, norm diffusion, and monitoring role of several international organizations that have now ventured into the constitutional domain. Whether by norm conditionality, promoting best practices, or opining on draft constitutional changes, these international organizations have come to influence—sometimes quite extensively—processes of constitutional change.

The second line of inquiry looks specifically at adjudication, where courts developing doctrines of unamendability also do so with reference to the transnational, be it to interpret constitutional provisions in line with international or transnational values or else learning of the tool comparatively and crafting it locally. India's basic structure doctrine discussed in Chapter 4 is a case in point, because of both the comparative learning at its origins and the transnational influence it has had since. The present chapter disentangles the impact of transnational law in unamendability adjudication along two scenarios. The first scenario involves national courts themselves appealing to international norms, often in the area of human rights, in order to resist or justify changes to unamendable commitments. The second scenario sees supranational courts considering the constitutionality of constitutional amendments directly. In other words, international courts considering developing a form of supranational or conventional unconstitutional amendment doctrine themselves. This rather radical move has become especially appealing to those who seek supranational solutions to recent erosions of democratic constitutional guarantees.

The chapter goes beyond merely noting the successful migration of the constitutional idea of unamendability.[5] It seeks to elucidate the forces and processes responsible for this migration—the *who* and the *how*—and places them in the context of constitution-making and adjudication today. The chapter also demonstrates that, contrary to widespread assumptions, it is not only the universalistic values of the rule of law and human rights that we find in migration, but also particularistic values and mechanisms meant to resist transnational encroachment. Paradoxically perhaps, mechanisms of transnational learning and dialogue are shown sometimes to result in the rejection of the global, including via developing doctrines of unamendability.

[3] Richard Albert, Xenophon Contiades, and Alkmene Fotiadou, eds., *The Law and Legitimacy of Imposed Constitutions* (Routledge 2019).

[4] Philipp Dann and Zaid Al-Ali, 'The Internationalized Pouvoir Constituant—Constitution-Making under External Influence in Iraq, Sudan and East Timor', *Max Plank Yearbook of UN Law* 10 (2006) 423; Hans Agne, 'Democratic Founding: We the People and the Others', *International Journal of Constitutional Law* 10:3 (2012) 836.

[5] Yaniv Roznai, 'Unconstitutional Constitutional Amendments—The Migration and Success of a Constitutional Idea', *American Journal of Comparative Law* 61 (2013) 657.

5.1 Internationalized constitution-making and unamendability

Internationalized constituent power

The most influential study of unamendability to date justifies the legitimacy of substantive amendment review by courts on the basis of a distinction between original, or primary, constituent power and derivative, or secondary, constituent power.[6] As the amending power exercised by constituted bodies is a form of the latter, the argument goes, courts are justified to intervene and enforce material limits on amendments. The amendment power is only ever a delegated power, held in trust by the amendment authority and constrained within certain bounds. As guardians of the constitution, national courts are also guardians of the original, or primary, constituent power and its intended constitutional dispensation. As we saw in Chapter 1, this reading of eternity clauses is also congruent with theories of precommitment in liberal constitutionalism and with militant democratic aims.

However, this neat reading of unamendability has been called into question, not least because of the conceptual assumptions about constituent power it rests on. In Vicki Jackson's terms, such readings presuppose the constituent power to be an 'it' instead of a 'they', in the sense that a univocal people is presupposed where instead there is plurality.[7] She resists the temptation to reify the fiction of an original or primary constituent power, in whose name constitutional legitimacy is automatically presupposed. Rather, Jackson insists, we should investigate 'the legitimacy bases of the existing constitution' and have them 'weigh in the calculus of whether a subsequent amendment should be understood as unconstitutional'.[8] Popular consent is a necessary but not sufficient condition to establish constitutional legitimacy, which can only be ascertained through a holistic evaluation over time of both the democratic basis and the substantive commitments within a constitution.[9] This view is consistent with Stephen Tierney's reminder that whereas much constituent power literature assumes a singular *demos*, there are instead a multitude of *demoi* present in plurinational states, occasionally contesting the very foundations of the unitary state.[10] The risk is there to derive legitimacy from identity, ascribing it solely to the *who* of constitution-making without taking into account the *when*, *what*, and *how*

[6] Roznai (2017), 105–34.

[7] Vicki C. Jackson, '"Constituent Power" or Degrees of Legitimacy?', *Vienna Journal of International Constitutional Law* 12:3 (2018) 319.

[8] Ibid., 327–8.

[9] Ibid., 338. For another view that a constitution-making without any popular input is bound to fail, see Ulrich K. Preuss, 'Perspectives on Post-Conflict Constitutionalism: Reflections on Regime Change through External Constitutionalization', *New York Law School Law Review* 51 (2006) 467, 479.

[10] Stephen Tierney, '"We the Peoples": Constituent Power and Constitutionalism in Plurinational States' in Martin Loughlin and Neil Walker, eds., *The Paradox of Constitutionalism: Constituent Power and Constitutional Form* (Oxford University Press 2008) 229.

of the process.[11] Constituent power ascribed to a people as a monolith also risks eliding the contestation not just of the meaning but of the very existence of a unified will.[12]

It is not just internal pluralism that constituent power theories have tended to underestimate. Attempts to reconcile the concept with the increasingly internationalized nature of constitution-making reveals another reality: that constituent power itself is no longer circumscribed by national borders or held solely by national actors. Post-constituent constitutionalism has been discussed in reference to the European Union and the challenges it presents to constitutional authority.[13] There have also been explorations of equivalents to 'the people' in international law in the context of the latter's constitutionalization.[14] We may thus indeed be witnessing the first steps towards a 'systematic theory of constituent power beyond the state'.[15] Scholars still concerned with constituent power as it legitimizes domestic constitutional orders have also called for serious revision of our understanding of the concept in order to reflect the transnational web within which constitution-making takes place. As we will see, this conceptual reframing has a significant impact on how we understand constitutional unamendability.

Christine Bell finds a growing concern at the international level with regulating domestic exercises of constituent power. She identifies 'instances where international law appears to attempt to regulate constituent power by trying to constrain when and how polities legitimately constitute themselves as such' including by way of international standard-setting, emerging supranational adjudication, and an international technology of governance of constitution-making seeking to regulate constitutional transitions.[16] Unlike conversations on the constitutionalization

[11] Andrew Arato, *The Adventures of the Constituent Power: Beyond Revolutions?* (Cambridge University Press 2017), 31. See also Chapter 6 in this book for an attempt to evaluate unamendability as the outcome of participatory processes of constitution-making.

[12] Zoran Oklopcic, 'Constitutional Theory and Cognitive Estrangement: Beyond Revolutions, Amendments and Constitutional Moments' in Richard Albert, Xenophon Contiades, and Alkmene Fotiadou, eds., *The Foundations and Traditions of Constitutional Amendment* (Hart 2017) 51, 60.

[13] Neil Walker, 'Post-Constituent Constitutionalism? The Case of the European Union' in Martin Loughlin and Neil Walker, eds., *The Paradox of Constitutionalism: Constituent Power and Constitutional Form* (Oxford University Press 2008) 247.

[14] Peter Niesen, 'Constituent Power in Global Constitutionalism' in Anthony F. Lang and Antje Wiener, eds., *Handbook on Global Constitutionalism* (Edward Elgar 2017) 222; Aoife O'Donoghue, *Constitutionalism in Global Constitutionalisation* (Cambridge University Press 2014), 54–86; Bardo Fassbender, 'We the Peoples of the United Nations: Constituent Power and Constitutional Form in International Law' in Martin Loughlin and Neil Walker, eds., *The Paradox of Constitutionalism: Constituent Power and Constitutional Form* (Oxford University Press 2008) 269. For more sceptical views of the relevance of the concept in a transnational context, see Alexander Somek, 'The Constituent Power in a Transnational Context', *Transnational Legal Theory* 3:1 (2012) 31; Nico Krisch, '*Pouvoir Constituant* and *Pouvoir Irritant* in the Postnational Order', *International Journal of Constitutional Law* 14:3 (2016) 657.

[15] Markus Patberg, 'Constituent Power beyond the State: An Emerging Debate in International Political Theory', *Millennium Journal of International Studies* 42:1 (2013) 224.

[16] Bell (2014), 242.

of international law or the internationalization of constitutional law, therefore, Bell is focusing on an emergent 'international law of constituting polities'.[17] She looks at standards and practices produced and promoted by international and regional bodies such as the United Nations, the African Union, the Organization of American States, the European Union, and the Council of Europe expressly aimed at regulating and constraining constitution-making.[18] Moreover, she argues, international bodies have increasingly engaged in adjudicating such international standards, including in cases involving first order political questions in the domestic polity.[19] An example of this is provided by Bosnia and Herzegovina, whose case is detailed below.

From the point of view of constituent power and its relationship to eternity clauses, Bell's observations are significant in two respects. On the one hand and as I will show below, international bodies are increasingly involved in assessing the legitimacy of constitutional change processes. On the other hand, Bell's worry at these bodies' involvement in requiring constitutional reform which 'in essence challenge[s] and demand[s] a re-working of domestic constitution-framing efforts'[20] is also warranted. The result is the development of an unconstitutional constitutional amendment doctrine at the supranational level, which suffers from even more acute legitimacy problems than its domestic counterparts when we consider the precarious position of international judges as guardians of domestic constitutional orders. New constitutions can only stake a legitimacy claim in the name of universal values of constitutionalism such as democracy, the rule of law, separation of powers, human rights, and respect for and protection of minorities.[21] Constitutionalism is thus to be protected as a good in itself. The overlap with unamendable provisions which insulate similar principles is obvious. What Bell identifies, however, is the emergence of international guardians of these same principles that can and have clashed with their domestic counterparts. Examples discussed below provide evidence of first order political questions of the sort protected by eternity clauses increasingly becoming the battleground between the supranational and the domestic levels. Whether constitutional change is a legitimate act of the constituent power is no longer a domestic question but may be scrutinized from beyond the state.

Other scholars have also pointed out the incompleteness of solely inward-looking accounts of democratic state founding. Instead, they have proposed to incorporate an external view into our foundational narratives, which requires not just

[17] Ibid., 266.

[18] Ibid., 270. See also discussion of these international standards applicable to constitution-making later in this chapter.

[19] Ibid., 273.

[20] Ibid.

[21] Christine Bell, 'Litigating Constituent Power: The International Law of Constitutional Transitions', paper presented at the International Society of Public Law (ICON-S) Annual Conference, New York, 1–3 July 2015(on file with author). See also Jackson (2018).

self-constitution by a people but also recognition and agreement by actors beyond state borders.[22] These external constituents may even play a positive role insofar as they may help reduce oppression and enhance internal freedom. Zoran Oklopcic is similarly bold in his call for constitutional theory 'to "update" its foundational imaginary'.[23] He calls for it to accept the plurality of constituent powers involved in the creation of a constitutional order as well as to enlarge its perception of the geopolitical theatre in which these powers operate so as to include external constituent powers. Oklopcic relies on the examples of Bosnia and Herzegovina and Kosovo to argue that there, the very identity of the people or peoples was determined by external powers engaged in an act of map-drawing.[24] The normative requirements of restraint on the part of international actors involved in constitution-making were ignored in the Balkans, Oklopcic argues, so that:

> external constitutive powers determined who is the people (in Kosovo, Bosnia and Herzegovina, Montenegro), what counts as the exercise of its will (Montenegro), and the range of constitutional options available to it after the constitutional order has been put in place (Bosnia and Herzegovina and Kosovo).[25]

Indeed, we would be hard-pressed to find a constitution-making process in the past three decades in which international actors did not become involved, if not outright leading the process. In Bosnia and Herzegovina, the constitution was drafted by international actors as part of the 1995 peace process and annexed to the Dayton Peace Agreement.[26] The peace conference was led by representatives of the United States, European Union, and Russia and attended by the warring parties' presidents. The text was drafted in English, which remains the sole authoritative version, and came into force by virtue of Security Council Resolution 1031 (1995). This course of events produced the type of 'heavily negotiated outcome' with potentially conflicting provisions which often results in post-conflict constitution-making.[27] Rather than being a first step in this peace process, however, the Dayton Agreement and by implication the constitution, was presented as 'complete and final'.[28]

22 Agne (2012).

23 Zoran Oklopcic, 'Constitutional (Re)Vision: Sovereign Peoples, New Constituent Powers, and the Formation of Constitutional Orders in the Balkans', *Constellations* 19:1 (2012) 81; see, more generally, Zoran Oklopcic, *Beyond the People: Social Imaginary and Constituent Imagination* (Oxford University Press 2018).

24 Oklopcic (2012), 83.

25 Ibid., 85.

26 General Framework Agreement for Peace in Bosnia and Herzegovina ('the Dayton Peace Agreement'), 21 November 1995.

27 Donald L. Horowitz, 'Conciliatory Institutions and Constitutional Processes in Post-Conflict States', *William and Mary Law Review* 49:4 (2008) 1213, 1230; see also discussion in Chapter 2 in this book.

28 Christine Bell, *Peace Agreements and Human Rights* (Oxford University Press 2003), 228.

There was never any doubt about many of the substantive elements the constitution would contain, first and foremost strong human rights guarantees.[29] It instituted a comprehensive rights protection system alongside a consociational (power-sharing) system of government drawn along ethnic lines, including a tripartite Presidency and a House of Peoples wherein only members of the three constituent peoples could seek representation.[30] The constituent peoples were defined in the preamble, which declared the constitution in the name of 'Bosniacs, Croats, and Serbs, as constituent peoples (along with Others), and citizens of Bosnia and Herzegovina'. It is as part of this human rights arrangement that we must read the Bosnian constitution's eternity clause, contained in Article X(2), which proclaims: 'No amendment to this Constitution may eliminate or diminish any of the rights and freedoms referred to in Article II of this Constitution or alter the present paragraph.' Article II(2) thereby referenced, entitled 'International Standards', stipulates the supremacy and direct applicability of the European Convention of Human Rights and its Protocols.

Kosovo's Constitution was similarly forged in an internationalized process, one begun before the country's status as an independent state had even been settled. Resolution 1244 (1999) of the United Nations Security Council placed the country under the provisional administration of UNMIK (the United Nations Interim Administration in Kosovo). A Constitutional Framework for Provisional Self-Government of Kosovo followed in May 2001, followed by the Ahtisaari Comprehensive Settlement Proposal in March 2007, the Unilateral Declaration of Independence in 2008, and a final constitution in June 2008.[31] The influence of the Special Representative of the Secretary-General was significant throughout, as he retained far-reaching executive, legislative, and judicial powers under Resolution 1244 and was not subject to review.

Early on, the Special Representative announced a 'standards before status' policy whereby the ultimate recognition of Kosovo would be dependent on its respect for standards of human rights, democracy, and the rule of law.[32] The 2007 Comprehensive Settlement Proposal was to have been agreed jointly by Serbian

[29] See Paul C. Szasz, 'The Protection of Human Rights through the Dayton/Paris Peace Agreement on Bosnia', *American Journal of International Law*, 90:2 (1996) 301–16.

[30] It has been argued that by entrenching power-sharing institutions along ethnic lines, the Bosnian Constitution made it impossible for the country to meet its international human rights commitments, among which are anti-discrimination norms. See Zaid Al-Ali, 'Constitutional Drafting and External Influence' in Tom Ginsburg and Rosalind Dixon, eds., *Comparative Constitutional Law* (Edward Elgar 2011) 77, 83. For an overview of Bosnia's consociational arrangements, see Christopher McCrudden and Brendan O'Leary, *Courts and Consociations: Human Rights Versus Power-Sharing* (Oxford University Press 2013b), 21–34.

[31] For a deeper discussion, see Michael Riegner, 'The Two Faces of the Internationalized *Pouvoir Constituant*: Independence and Constitution-Making under External Influence in Kosovo', *Goettingen Journal of International Law* 2:3 (2010) 1035.

[32] Henry H. Perritt, Jr., *The Road to Independence for Kosovo: A Chronicle of the Ahtisaari Plan* (Cambridge University Press 2010), 75.

and Kosovar delegations but, when agreement failed, UN Special Envoy Martti Ahtisaari unilaterally submitted a final version to the UN Secretary-General.[33] The plan recommended independence supervised by the international community for Kosovo, on democratic constitutional foundations including a parliamentary system with strong minority protections and direct effect of international human rights instruments.[34] Thus, when constitution-making finally followed the unilateral declaration of independence in 2008, like in Bosnia's case, there was little doubt as to the substantive commitments the constitution would enshrine. The eternity clauses in Kosovo's Constitution, which seek to prevent the diminishment of rights commitments (Articles 113(9) and 144(3)), are also to be read in this key then—as part of a rigid constitutional structure predetermined by the international community and rendered a prerequisite for the country's very independence.

These are but two examples of just how internationalized constitution-making processes can become. I have discussed the examples of Afghanistan, Fiji, and Iraq in Chapter 2, and discuss Tunisia's in Chapter 6. These are all further examples of internationalized constitution-making, wherein constitutional negotiations are embedded in internationalized peace negotiations, happen under external occupation or under UN administration, or else receive far-reaching international assistance (sometimes tied to access to international aid or even state recognition). They illustrate not just the presence and serious influence of international actors, but also the far-reaching impact of these actors' constitutional agendas. As we will see in the next section, the body of international and regional norms governing constitution-making is ever expanding.

The argument here is not that these constitutions are necessarily illegitimate by virtue of being the result of internationalized constitution-making. Whether their embattled origins prove fatal to their acquiring legitimacy over time can only be ascertained retroactively and with the benefit of time. Nevertheless, the 'national myth' persists in constitutional imagination, including in scholarship on unamendability.[35] Presuming 'a distinct fit between a constitution and a particular national community', it also suggests a certain recursivity or feedback between constitutional norms and the identity of the people.[36] Accepting that constitution-making is a more dynamic process that has always been embedded transnationally will challenge such received notions of constitutional foundations.[37] Whether in the case of formal eternity clauses or the unwritten principles purported to underpin the constitutional order, their origins are revealed to be much more

[33] Ibid., 161–70.

[34] *Report of the Special Envoy of the Secretary-General on Kosovo's Future Status*, S/2007/168, 27 March 2001.

[35] Tom Ginsburg, Terence C. Halliday and Gregory Shaffer, 'Constitution-Making as Transnational Legal Ordering' in Geoffrey Shaffer, Tom Ginsburg, and Terence C. Halliday eds., *Constitution-Making and Transnational Legal Order* (Cambridge University Press 2019), 3.

[36] Ibid.

[37] Ibid., 9.

complex than simple attributions to a unified, internal constituent power suggests. This challenges the legitimation of constitutional unamendability by recourse to an imagined autochthonous constitutional authorship. As we will see in the next section, claims that unamendability is the expression of local constitutional norms are equally problematic when viewed in transnational perspective.

Transnational norm diffusion and the globalization of constitution-making

We have seen in previous chapters, notably Chapters 1, 3, and 4, that constitutional unamendability is often viewed through the lens of the particular. It is said that formal eternity clauses or unamendable unwritten principles reflect those core commitments the polity has made that define its identity. As such, their deep entrenchment is warranted and even required. Alternatively, such commitments are viewed as universal, as constituting the core not just of a given constitution, but of constitutionalism itself. Whether it be a robust bill of rights, the separation of powers, judicial independence, or constitutional review, it is precisely because the legitimacy of these norms transcends the national constitution that they are to be seen as unamendable. Were they to be open to amendment, the argument goes, we would end up with 'non-constitutional constitutions' instead.[38] The two strands of the argument are of course interlinked: the universal and the particular aspects of constitutional identity are said to reinforce each other, resulting in a constitution that both abides by universal standards and has local roots.[39]

I have shown in previous chapters how this view is incomplete and even problematic when we assess constitutional commitments more contextually. I argued in Chapters 3 and 4 that the particular and the universal find themselves in deep tension with each other more often than previously thought, with unamendability often serving to bolster exclusion in the name of the former. Here, I wish to challenge particularistic claims in constitution-making—including unamendability seen as the pinnacle of autochthonous constitutionalism—that underpin so much of the literature on eternity clauses and basic structure doctrines.

Transnational norm diffusion

Comparative constitutional scholarship has amassed significant evidence that norm diffusion is widespread in constitution-making worldwide. There is ample evidence that constitutional bills of rights are increasingly similar in content. Empirical scholars have found both that constitutions tend to contain more and

[38] Arato (2017).

[39] For a discussion of general and particular constitutional identity, see Bosko Tripkovic, *The Metaethics of Constitutional Adjudication* (Oxford University Press 2018) 13.

more rights provisions (the phenomenon of 'rights creep') and that the content of these rights tends to overlap more and more ('generic rights constitutionalism').[40] This has been attributed at least in part to international treaty ratification, notably the Universal Declaration of Human Rights and the International Covenant on Civil and Political Rights, as having provided constitutional drafters with a rights 'menu' influencing their drafting choices.[41] Rights talk is said to have become a 'global lingua franca', spoken equally by national and international legal orders and helping to blur the distinctions between the two.[42] There is also strong evidence that rights diffusion and globalization forces have gone hand in hand, with rights protections (especially property and contract rights) following global investment and migration patterns.[43] At least part of what drives this diffusion is that rights are 'cheap talk' or relatively inexpensive commitments to constitutionalize in order for a state to signal international compliance.[44]

This norm diffusion has been shown to have occurred even in the case of those presumed uncontested repositories of constitutional identity: preambles.[45] Commonalities and patterns in the language of constitutional preambles shows not only that they follow a limited number of archetypes, but also that they change under the influences of global forces. In other words, preambles are no less internationally embedded than constitutional language more generally has become.[46]

Of course, these empirical studies are suitable to show broad patters and changes over time and space. They still need to be complemented by in-depth contextual evidence to determine the precise contours of constitutional ideas' diffusion. For example, the eastern expansion of the European Union post-1989 was underpinned by norm conditionality that resulted in legislative and constitutional changes amounting to, it has been argued, an exercise in state-building.[47] Nor is

[40] David S. Law and Mila Versteeg, 'The Evolution and Ideology of Global Constitutionalism', *California Law Review* 99 (2011) 1163.

[41] Zachary Elkins, Tom Ginsburg, and Beth Simmons, 'Getting to Rights: Treaty Ratification, Constitutional Convergence and International Law', *Harvard International Law Journal* 54:1 (2013) 61.

[42] David S. Law, 'The Global Language of Human Rights: A Computational Linguistic Analysis', *Law & Ethics of Human Rights* 12:1 (2018) 111.

[43] David S. Law, 'Globalization and the Future of Constitutional Rights', *Northwestern University Law Review* 102 (2008) 1277.

[44] David S. Law and Mila Versteeg, 'Sham Constitutions', *California Law Review* 101 (2013) 863. Ginsburg et al. (2013), 82 show that directly incorporating references to international human rights treaties may lower the 'cost' of rights commitments even further.

[45] Tom Ginsburg, Daniel Rockmore, and Nick Foti, '"We the Peoples": The Global Origins of Constitutional Preamble', *George Washington International Law Review* 46 (2014) 305; David S. Law, 'Constitutional Archetypes', *Texas Law Review* 95:2 (2016) 153.

[46] Ginsburg et al. (2014), 337; see also David S. Law, 'Constitutional Dialects: The Language of Transnational Legal Orders' in Geoffrey Shaffer et al., eds., *Constitution-Making and Transnational Legal Order* (Cambridge University Press 2019) 110.

[47] Dimitry Kochenov, 'Overestimating Conditionality' in Inge Govaere, Erwan Lannon, Peter van Elsuwege, and Stanislas Adam, eds., *The European Union in the World Essays in Honour of Marc Maresceau* (Brill Nijhoff 2014) 541.

this diffusion free of ideology. It has in fact been argued that an international consensus has emerged on the content of domestic constitutional law favouring a thin version of democracy, some form of judicialized constitutional review, and a 'fundamentally neo-liberal' rights component favouring strong 'core' civil and political rights but unenforceable social and economic rights.[48] As Mark Tushnet has argued, '[d]epartures from this consensus are described as departures, not from "neo-liberal" or even "liberal" constitutionalism, but as departures from constitutionalism as such'.[49] Similarly, Vijayashri Sripati has shown how the United Nations' Constitutional Assistance projects in over forty countries have been premised on promoting four 'Civilized Standards': the rule of law, free markets, good governance, and civilized social practices.[50] Especially in the post-1989 era, both conflict-torn and stable states were encouraged to adopt a particular version of liberal constitutionalism as a means of securing peace and promoting development ('understood as market-oriented poverty reduction'), good governance, and so democracy.[51]

These findings have implications for our understandings of unamendability as well. Unamendability is no less transnationally embedded than other constitutional principles have become. When it comes to the interpretation of formal eternity clauses, courts can and often do have recourse to international and comparative legal sources in order to determine the content of abstract commitments such as to democracy, fundamental rights, or the separation of powers. The impact of the transnational is even greater when it comes to judicially created unamendability doctrines, which rely on identifying unwritten constitutional principles deemed so fundamental as to be unamendable. As we saw in Chapter 4, courts will not issue exhaustive lists of such principles but will nevertheless ground them in various constitutional provisions, such as in preambles, provisions on fundamental rights, judicial review, and the separation of powers. The underlying assumption is either a particularistic one—that these provisions inculcate the defining identitarian features of the polity—or else a universalistic one—that without these (typically liberal constitutionalist) commitments, the whole 'basic structure' of a given constitution would fall apart. In a sense then, there is a double entrenchment at play: one internally justified, based on claims that the original constituent has spoken and its decisions cannot be amended out of the constitution except by

[48] Mark Tushnet, 'The Globalisation of Constitutional Law as a Weakly Neo-liberal Project', *Global Constitutionalism* 8:1 (2019) 29. For stronger critiques of neoliberal constitutionalism in its Latin American and European incarnations, see, respectively, Helena Alviar García, 'Neoliberalism as a Form of Authoritarian Constitutionalism' and Michael A. Wilkinson, 'Authoritarian Liberalism as Authoritarian Constitutionalism', both in Helena Alviar García and Günter Frankenberg, eds., *Authoritarian Constitutionalism: Comparative Analysis and Critique* (Edward Elgar 2019).

[49] Ibid.

[50] Vijayashri Sripati, *Constitution-Making under UN Auspices: Fostering Dependency in Sovereign Lands* (Oxford University Press 2020).

[51] Ibid., 6.

revolutionary means; and a second, externally justified one, centred on the need to remain a player in good standing in line with global standards.

One might still argue, however, that the fact of global diffusion of a constitutional idea does not automatically render it a bad candidate for unamendability. After all, rights protection or constitutional review can just as well be core international *and* national commitments. Indeed, that is not what I wish to argue. However, I believe a critical appraisal of unamendability from the point of view of democratic constitutionalism must take seriously the transnational embeddedness of the values and principles purported to be beyond domestic amendment. That need is even greater when the diffusion itself is at least in part due to external pressure, whether in the form of accession conditionality to certain supranational organizations or when international and regional bodies develop norms governing constitution-making itself. I propose to turn to these two scenarios and provide examples of their interplay with constitutional unamendability.

Conditionality

The impact of supranational conditionality on internal legal norm change has been amply studied in the context of European Union enlargement. European norms have had an impact on legislative and constitutional change in aspiring member states in a number of areas. One example includes the promotion of minority rights protection as part of the package of European standards that states in Central and Eastern Europe had to meet to gain accession to the European Union. These were promoted as a condition for accession despite having uncertain normative grounds as part of the *acquis communautaire* and an ambiguous content in international law.[52] For example, they influenced not just the drafting of the 1997 Polish Constitution and the country's law on national minorities, but also the precise choice of legal framework to ensure that protection. Despite initial calls for a more communitarian, group rights-based approach during the constitutional and legislative negotiations, the choice was ultimately in favour of guaranteeing individual rights for minorities on the ground that this was a better fit with European standards.[53] European and NATO norms also played a primary role in Romania's constitutional revision in 2003, such as in adopting amendments in the area of equality and non-discrimination. These were more geared towards ensuring gender-neutral military recruitment and access to public, civil, and military

[52] Judith G. Kelley, *Ethnic Politics in Europe: The Power of Norms and Incentives* (Princeton University Press 2004); Gwendolyn Sasse, 'The Politics of EU Conditionality: The Norm of Minority Protection During and beyond EU Accession', *Journal of European Public Policy* 15:6 (2008) 842.

[53] Guido Scwellnus, 'The Adoption of Nondiscrimination and Minority Protection Rules in Romania, Hungary, and Poland' in Frank Schimmelfennig and Ulrich Sedelmeier, eds., *The Europeanization of Central and Eastern Europe* (Cornell University Press 2005) 51, 66–7.

positions and permitting European citizens to vote in local elections than towards more far-reaching equality guarantees.[54]

The impact of European conditionality is not straightforward, and resistance and negotiation of these norms can and did occur. Nor should formal adherence to norms be confused with their socialization. However, what is undeniable is that the EU has acted as a normative actor, even while promoting and monitoring norms inconsistently.[55] Its normative influence is not limited to its member states either. Through its European Neighbourhood Policy, it has opined on legislative and constitutional changes in countries from Ukraine and Moldova to those of the Western Balkans.[56] Its influence extends farther as well, through its international trade and aid activities. For example, the European Union condemned the 2000 and 2006 coups in Fiji (discussed in greater detail in Chapter 2), citing concern over the erosion of democracy and the rule of law and demanding a return to democratic elections.[57] It joined other external actors in imposing sanctions on Fiji following the overthrow of the democratically elected government in 2006 and demanded a return to democratic rule.

The cracks in the EU's normative armour have been exposed by the democratic backsliding in Hungary and Poland. Not only was the Union slow to react, but the infringement proceedings it has initiated against the two countries have demonstrated the shaky foundations of its commitment to democracy and the rule of law. The Union's normative framework surrounding democracy, the rule of law, and human rights has always been vague, defined only in general terms, developed ad hoc, and outside the scope of the Union's institutional competences until recently.[58] Thus, it should not have been surprising that even when it began infringement proceedings against backsliding member states, the Union was still more comfortable enforcing only thin conceptions of democracy and sanctioning transgressions against technocratic goals such as central bank independence, rather than measures eliminating democratic pluralism, media freedom, and basic human rights.[59]

[54] Elena Brodeala and Silvia Suteu, 'Women and Constitution-Making in Post-Communist Romania' in Ruth Rubio-Marin and Helen Irving, eds., *Women as Constitution-Makers: Case Studies from the New Democratic Era* (Cambridge University Press 2019) 81, 116–17.

[55] Sasse (2008); see also Eline de Ridder and Dimitry Kochenov, 'Democratic Conditionality in the Eastern Enlargement: Ambitious Window Dressing', *European Foreign Affairs Review* 16 (2011) 589.

[56] Gwendolyn Sasse, 'The European Neighbourhood Policy: Conditionality Revisited for the EU's Eastern Neighbours', *Europe-Asia Studies* 60:2 (2008) 295; Tatjana Sekulić, *The European Union and the Paradox of Enlargement: The Complex Accession of the Western Balkans* (Palgrave Macmillan 2020).

[57] Elena Fierro, *European Union's Approach to Human Rights Conditionality in Practice* (Martinus Nijhoff 2003), 338. The Union's relationship with Fiji is governed by the Cotonou Agreement, the partnership agreement between developing countries and the EU, whose Article 9 ties cooperation to 'essential elements regarding human rights, democratic principles and the rule of law, and fundamental element regarding good governance'.

[58] de Ridder and Kochenov (2011).

[59] Michael A. Wilkinson, 'Authoritarian Liberalism in the European Constitutional Imagination: Second Time as Farce?', *European Law Journal* 21:3 (2015) 313, 333; Sverker Gustavsson, 'The Need for Legitimate Opposition and Protectionism' in Olaf Cramme and Sara B. Hobolt, eds., *Democratic Politics in a European Union Under Stress* (Oxford University Press 2014) 236, 246–7.

Nor is the EU the sole actor using conditionality in ways that trigger legal change, including of constitutional fundamentals. Since the late 1980s, international loan conditionality resulted in several Latin American countries adopting constitutional provisions and practices meant to protect free trade. This was achieved 'through the enshrinement of constitutional provisions; by cloaking neoliberal policy as technical and apolitical; in shifting the ideological configuration of the Constitutional Court; and through regulatory or institutional transformation'.[60] Many simultaneously included generous social and economic rights and popular participation guarantees, reflecting political compromise but also resulting in inconsistencies.[61] The 'new constitutionalism' in Latin America thus comprised several different clusters of constitutional reforms, alternatively geared towards supporting neoliberal reforms, decentralizing the state, reforming judicial power and creating new institutions of horizontal accountability, and promoting new channels for popular participation.[62] Constitutional entrenchment of policy choices was also on the agenda, in some instances including in eternity clauses.[63] The result in those cases has been a permanent process of constitutional amendment insofar as new governments needed to seek constitutional reform to achieve their policy aims: 'if a constitution constitutionalizes a governmental agenda, subsequent governments are compelled—regardless of their ideology or public policy programmes—to make changes to the constitutional framework'.[64] Brazil's detailed constitution is a prime example. As we will see below, new governments continue to pass constitutional amendments in order to implement their governing agenda and have been accused of breaching the constitutional eternity clause as recently as 2016, when a new, decades-long tax regime was constitutionalized.

Norms governing constitution-making

Increasingly, international and regional organizations have developed norms specifically governing constitution-making.[65] In Europe, the European Commission for Democracy through Law (Venice Commission) of the Council of Europe has grown into the repository of constitutional norms not just of the Council of Europe but, as

[60] Alviar García (2019), 56.

[61] Ibid., 38, 55.

[62] Detlef Nolte and Almut Schilling-Vacaflor, eds., *New Constitutionalism in Latin America: Promises and Practices* (Routledge 2012), 15.

[63] On the role of constitutional law in the formation of the rules and structures associated with economic globalization, see David Schneiderman, *Constitutionalizing Economic Globalization Investment Rules and Democracy's Promise* (Cambridge University Press 2008).

[64] Rogério B. Arantes and Cláudio G. Couto, 'Constitutionalizing Policy: The Brazilian Constitution of 1988 and Its Impact on Governance' in Detlef Nolte and Almut Schilling-Vacaflor, eds., *New Constitutionalism in Latin America: Promises and Practices* (Routledge 2012) 203, 208.

[65] See Micha Wiebusch, 'The Role of Regional Organizations in the Protection of Constitutionalism', International IDEA Discussion Paper 17/2016, 24 August 2016; Markus Böckenförde and Daniel Sabsay, 'Supranational Organizations and Their Impact on National Constitutions' in Mark Tushnet et al., eds., *Routledge Handbook of Constitutional Law* (Routledge 2013), 469.

the European Union increasingly relies on standards the Commission has developed in the areas of democracy, human rights, and the rule of law, of the EU as well.[66] It is an advisory body of legal experts who offer constitutional advice to member states as well as a growing number of non-European partner states. The Venice Commission defines its mission as helping 'to ensure the dissemination and consolidation of a common constitutional heritage, playing a unique role in conflict management, and provid[ing] "emergency constitutional aid" to states in transition'. It has compiled standards, best practices, and comparative studies in a number of areas of constitutional concern, including regarding constitutional amendment.[67]

With regard to the judicial review of constitutional amendments, the Venice Commission took a balanced view in 2010.[68] It differentiated between formal and substantive review and considered that the presence of unamendable provisions in constitutional texts did not automatically, nor by logical implication entail that they were judicially enforceable—they could remain declarative only and still have a deterring effect.[69] The Commission painted a picture of unamendability in European states as the exception rather than the norm, as rarely judicially enforced, and seldom resulting in the setting aside of amendments even where substantive review existed. It also indicated the Turkish example as a negative case study, insofar as the unamendable principles in the Turkish constitution had been interpreted too widely by national courts.[70] On this basis, the Commission concluded that 'substantive judicial review of constitutional amendments is a problematic instrument, which should only be exercised in those countries where it already follows from clear and established doctrine, and even there with care, allowing a margin of appreciation for the constitutional legislator'.[71] It concluded that as long as the formal amendment routes prescribed in European constitutions were duly followed, 'these are and should be a sufficient guarantee against abuse'.[72]

The Venice Commission's work also extends to providing opinions on draft legislation and even draft constitutions, on the request of its members. With regard to unamendability, it appears to have retained its cautious approach. In its

[66] Bogdan Iancu, '*Quod licet Jovi non licet bovi?*: The Venice Commission as Norm Entrepreneur', *Hague Journal on the Rule of Law* 11 (2019) 189; Maartje de Visser, 'A Critical Assessment of the Role of the Venice Commission in Processes of Domestic Constitutional Reform', *American Journal of Comparative Law* 63 (2015) 963; Paul Craig, 'Transnational Constitution-Making: The Contribution of the Venice Commission on Law and Democracy', *UC Irvine Journal of International, Transnational and Comparative Law* 2 (2017) 57. On the Council of Europe generally, see Gwendolyn Sasse, 'The Council of Europe as a Norm Entrepreneur: The Political Strengths of a Weak International Institution' in Neil Walker, Jo Shaw, and Stephen Tierney, eds., *Europe's Constitutional Mosaic* (Hart 2011) 171.

[67] Venice Commission, *Report on Constitutional Amendment*, CDL-AD(2010)001, 19 January 2010 and *Compilation of Venice Commission Opinions Concerning Constitutional Provisions for Amending the Constitution*, CDL-PI(2015)023*, 22 December 2015.

[68] Venice Commission (2010), paras. 225–37.

[69] Ibid., para. 226.

[70] Ibid., paras. 233–4.

[71] Ibid., para. 235.

[72] Ibid., para. 236.

2020 opinion on a package of amendments to the Armenian Constitution, for example, the Commission reiterated that the constitutional unamendability was to be interpreted narrowly.[73] To suggestions that the Armenian Constitutional Court might rely on the constitutional eternity clause (Article 203, double entrenched) to extend the scope of review to the entire constitution, the Venice Commission reacted negatively, finding that 'it would be problematic if the Constitutional Court invalidated constitutional amendments based on vague principles loosely connected with or based on a broad interpretation of the unamendable provisions in the Constitution'.[74] It also cautioned the court to 'use extensive self-restraint and avoid any impression of favouring the personal interest of the judges when reviewing amendments concerning the Court itself'.[75] As will be discussed further below, not all interventions by the Venice Commission in the area of constitutional change have themselves abided by this call to self-restraint. In some areas, it has itself departed from merely checking compliance with general norms of democratic constitutionalism and human rights and veered into promoting narrower policy choices.

The Venice Commission has been praised as a potential model for regional bodies elsewhere, including in Africa.[76] African regional institutions, in particular the African Union (AU), have paid attention to developing, monitoring, and sometimes also enforcing democratic constitutional standards, including in processes of constitutional change.[77] Article 23(5) of the 2007 African Charter on Democracy, Elections and Governance in particular is relevant to the topic of amendments, insofar as it declares '[a]ny amendment or revision of the constitution or legal instruments, which is an infringement on the principles of democratic change of government' to be illegal and to trigger sanctions by the AU. This reflects the AU's concern with preventing constitutional power grabs, including its zero tolerance to military coups. Article 23(5) has not yet been invoked directly, however, and the AU has been said to have a poorer track record when it came to sanctioning 'constitutional coups'.[78] Such formally constitutionally compliant amendments have been used to remove or seriously weaken executive term limits on the continent, with

[73] Venice Commission, *Armenia: Opinion on Three Legal Questions in the Context of Draft Constitutional Amendments Concerning the Mandate of the Judges of the Constitutional Court*, CDL-AD(2020)016, 22 June 2020, para. 69.

[74] Ibid.

[75] Ibid., para. 80.

[76] Micha Wiebush and Christina Murray, 'Presidential Term Limits and the African Union', *Journal of African Law* 63:1 (2019) 131, 160.

[77] These mainly revolve around the 2000 Lomé Declaration on the Framework for an Organisation of African Unity Response to Unconstitutional Changes of Government (Lomé Declaration) and the 2007 African Charter on Democracy, Elections and Governance (ACDEG), supported by institutions including the Peace and Security Council, the African Commission on Human and Peoples' Rights, the African Court on Human and Peoples' Rights, and the African Peer Review Mechanism. See overview in Wiebusch (2016), 18–27.

[78] Wiebusch and Murray (2019), 150–1.

twenty-four cases (affecting eighteen countries) counted between 2000 and 2018.[79] The ineffectiveness of the AU in reacting to these moves has been attributed to the legal uncertainties regarding the scope of Article 23(5), to the inadequacy of the AU's monitoring mechanisms, but also to the limits on accessing the African Court of Human and Peoples' Rights, to which only nine member states allow petition rights to individuals and non-governmental organizations.[80]

Other regional organizations have developed standards applicable to constitutional governance. The Protocol on Democracy and Good Governance of the Economic Community of West African States (ECOWAS) enshrines democratic norms and tasks member states with upholding them when under attack. ECOWAS had debated adopting a region-wide ban on a third presidential term in office but eventually dropped it in 2015.[81]

At least two African cases involved the de facto or formal removal of unamendable term limits. In the Democratic Republic of Congo, the constitution bans amendments to, inter alia, 'the number and the duration of the mandates of the President of the Republic' (Article 220). In 2016, however, the Constitutional Court agreed to postpone presidential elections which in practice resulted in an extension of the president's second mandate, eventually by two years. The Republic of Congo's unamendable presidential term limit (Article 185 of the 2002 Constitution) was removed via referendum in 2015, despite the opposition's call for a boycott and protests in the run-up to the vote. The country's Constitutional Court gave the go-ahead for the referendum despite the clear constitutional eternity clause. In both instances, regional bodies were slow to react and ultimately could not prevent the subversion of term limits.

Finally, the Organization of American States has similarly developed standards of democratic governance with an impact on constitutional affairs.[82] Its Charter indicates the fundamental values member states are to respect (Article 3) and stipulates an incremental role for the Organization in case of an unconstitutional overthrow of the democratically constituted government of a member state, up to suspension from the Organization (Article 9). The Organization's role is supplemented by the Inter-American Commission on Human Rights and the Inter-American Court of Human Rights. Their work is grounded in the American Convention on Human Rights and has provided more detail regarding standards that member states are to follow, such as in the area of judicial independence.[83] As

[79] Ibid., 136.

[80] Ibid., 151 and 156. For an overview of Commission and Court case law regarding democratic standards, see Alain Didier Olinga, 'La promotion de la démocratie et d'un ordre constitutionnel de qualité par le système africain des droits fondamentaux: entre acquis et défis', *Annuaire Africain des Droits de l'Homme* 1 (2017) 239.

[81] 'West African Leaders Shelve Third-term Ban Proposal', *BBC News*, 20 May 2015, https://www.bbc.co.uk/news/world-africa-32808685.

[82] Weibusch (2016), 34–9.

[83] Inter-American Commission of Human Rights, *Guarantees for the Independence of Justice Operators*, OEA/Ser.L/V/II.Doc. 44, 5 December 2013.

will be discussed further below, the development of conventionality control within the inter-American system has had a direct impact on the constitutional review of amendments passed by states in the region. Insofar as it empowers domestic judges to review the constitutionality of all national laws against the American Convention on Human Rights, conventionality control has created the prospects of a truly supranational unconstitutional constitutional amendment doctrine.

5.2 Constitutional adjudication of unamendability in a transnational context

Supranational illegality of constitutional amendments: unamendability review against a transnational referent

As we have seen in Part II, constitutional courts have developed constitutional identity review and basic structure doctrines in an effort to ground the material review of constitutional amendments. Both are premised on the notion of there being substantive norms against which such amendments can be evaluated, whether these comprise the integrity of the constitution or else norms inherent or even superior to the constitutional text itself. Not unrelated to these ideas have been propositions that these evaluative norms can be found, at least in part, transnationally. Whether in international or comparative law, it is worth investigating whether and how constitutional amendment review could be legitimized and performed against a supranational referent.

The question of constitutional law's supranational illegality is not new from the point of view of international law. As the Vienna Convention on the Law of Treaties has long established, 'A party may not invoke the provisions of its internal law as justification for its failure to perform a treaty' (Article 27). Coupled with Articles 3 and 32 of the Draft Articles on State Responsibility, these rules are meant to ensure states undertake international legal obligations in good faith. Expanded to constitutional law, this would mean that, *from the perspective of international law*, a state cannot invoke its constitutional arrangements to evade its international obligations.

The same is true in the area of international human rights adjudication. For example, the African Commission on Human and People's Rights has ruled on constitutional amendments to presidential eligibility rules[84] and outlawing political parties and removing judicial remedies.[85] The European Court of Human Rights

[84] *Legal Resources Foundation* v. *Zambia* ACHPR 211/98, 7 May 2001 and *Mouvement Ivoirien des Droits Humains (MIDH)* v. *Côte d'Ivoire* Comm. No. 246/02 ACHPR 88, 29 July 2008.
[85] *Lawyers for Human Rights* v. *Swaziland* ACHPR 251/02, 11 May 2005.

has also on several occasions found member states in violation of their Convention obligations on account of constitutional provisions or interpretations found to violate European human rights standards.[86] In the dramatic case of *Sejdić and Finci*, the Strasbourg court found discriminatory the very power-sharing constitutional arrangements in Bosnia and Herzegovina that form the foundation of the country's post-conflict edifice. Because of its far-reaching jurisprudence, its techniques and methodologies, and the incorporation of the European Convention into its member states' constitutions, the Strasbourg court has been referred to as de facto a constitutional court.[87]

International law

There have been doctrinal arguments that such supranational illegality should also play a role at the constitutional level, and inform if not predetermine substantive review of constitutional amendments.[88] According to this view, at least in the European context with its density and clarity of supranational legal rules, we can speak of 'unconventional constitutional amendments'.[89] The concern here is, again, with abusive or 'disruptive' amendments and arming the national constitutional judge with an external norm of reference against which to evaluate such amendments (or, indeed, new constitutions).[90] Such arguments build on the German principle of the *Rechtstaat* and posit the need for all legal norms to have a superior legal referent; when it comes to constitutional amendments (or constitution-making), those 'unwritten (superior) principles floating above constitutional texts' are to be found in international standards, especially international human rights law.[91]

Insofar as the argument is read modestly, it is not revolutionary. International law has been used as a guide to constitutional interpretation the world over, from systems where there is an explicit constitutional basis for this[92] to dualist states where non-incorporated international law norms have been invoked to resolve

[86] E.g. *Klass* v. *Germany*, Application No. 5029/71, 6 September 1978; *United Communist Party of Turkey and Others* v. *Turkey*, Application No. 19392/92, 30 January 1998; *Sejdić and Finci* v. *Bosnia*, Applications Nos. 27996/06 and 34836/06, 22 December 2009; *Alajos Kiss* v. *Hungary*, Application No. 38832/06, 20 May 2010; *Anchugov and Gladkov* v. *Russia*, Application No. 11157/04, 4 July 2013.

[87] Alec Stone Sweet, 'On the Constitutionalisation of the Convention: The European Court of Human Rights as a Constitutional Court', *Revue Trimestrielle des Droits de l'Homme* 80 (2009) 923. Wojciech Sadurski has argued that this constitutionalization of the Strasbourg court (albeit incomplete) was in large part due to the eastern enlargement of the Council of Europe, which required the court to adopt a more activist stance when reviewing the national laws of the newly admitted countries. See Wojciech Sadurski, *Constitutionalism and the Enlargement of Europe* (Oxford University Press 2012), 1–51.

[88] Garlicki and Garlicka (2011); Lech Garlicki and Zofia A. Garlicka-Sowers, 'Unconstitutional Constitutional Amendments', *Vienna Journal of International Constitutional Law* 12:3 (2018) 307. See also discussion in Roznai (2017), 82–100.

[89] Garlicki and Garlicka (2011), 367.

[90] Ibid., 354.

[91] Ibid., 344 and 356.

[92] Article 39(1)(b) of the South African Constitution, for example, states that when interpreting the Bill of Rights, a court, tribunal, or forum 'must consider international law and may consider foreign law'.

interpretive ambiguity.[93] Constitutional courts exercising amendment review powers have their full interpretive arsenal at their disposal, and as cases discussed in previous chapters have shown, they have made full use of them, engaging in textualist, originalist, purposive, structural, and other types of constitutional interpretation. Where the constitution itself grants international law supremacy in the internal legal order, national courts may find it to have the final word in case of conflict with domestic norms.[94]

However, there is a stronger version of the argument regarding the supranational illegality of constitutional amendments. Its original proponents argue that, at the very least, it should result in the impugned amendment's illegitimacy, even in cases where domestic constitutional courts are reluctant to intervene in the material review of amendments.[95] They view it as a problem when national constitutional courts are not 'ready to submit to the perspective of international law'.[96] This is a perspective that views national constitutions as always subordinated to international law—they 'must always yield to international norms'[97]—and at least certain international norms—termed 'constitutional *ius cogens* or constitutional customary law'[98]—as applicable to the drafters of all constitutions. As they must also be effective, these supranational norms naturally form the basis for a third level of judicial review, of constitutional amendments against such supranational standards.[99]

Transnational norms

We have encountered an alternative but closely related appeal to the transnational in previous chapters, when discussing the work of Rosalind Dixon and David Landau. Theirs is an approach that directly recognizes the danger of judicial overreach in the name of unconstitutional constitutional amendment doctrines and seeks to mitigate this risk by grounding judicial interventions in a transnational referent.[100] As their main aim is preventing democratic backsliding, their emphasis

[93] See, e.g., the *R (SG)* v. *Secretary of State for Work and Pensions* [2015] UKSC 16 case, in which the UK Supreme Court relied on the non-incorporated United Nations Convention on the Rights of the Child to interpret domestic legislation.

[94] For a discussion, see Anne Peters, 'Supremacy Lost: International Law Meets Domestic Constitutional Law', *Vienna Journal on International Constitutional Law* 3:3 (2009) 170.

[95] Garlicki and Garlicka-Sowers (2018), 315–16.

[96] Ibid., 313.

[97] Ibid., 314.

[98] Garlicki and Garlicka (2011), 355.

[99] There are echoes here of arguments that there exist natural law limits on constitution-making, and as such also on constitutional amendments. As we saw in Chapter 3, such arguments occasionally resurface in constitutional adjudication of unamendability, such as in the case law of the German Constitutional Court. However, the arguments discussed here refer explicitly to supranational norms found either in international law or transnational legal practice, not natural law. See also discussion in Roznai (2017), 72–82 for why natural law cannot be operationalized as an anchor for unamendability doctrines.

[100] Dixon and Landau (2015).

is primarily on comparative state practice rather than international law, although some international and regional elements may be included. Thus, Dixon and Landau believe 'an international democratic "minimum core"' can be identified in the overlapping consensus among countries as to the minimum content of any 'basic structure' of a democratic constitution.[101] The comparative method should allow for greater variation in standards, whereas international or regional standards such as those developed by the Venice Commission can help identify provisions relevant to this minimum democratic core (among which they list 'those defining the form of government, the method of election and term of the chief executive, and the method of selection and jurisdiction of the high court').[102]

Given the increasing complexity of the transnational entanglements of constitutional orders everywhere, it was unavoidable that constitutional amendment review should go supranational as well. In what follows, I propose to evaluate these propositions critically. I do so not to dispute the role that international and transnational referents may play in the constitutional adjudication of amendments. Indeed, under the right conditions, it may well be that an appeal to international law in constitutional adjudication will result in a democracy- or rights-enhancing decision against problematic amendments. For example, in its judgments preventing the removal or extension of presidential term limits, the Colombian Constitutional Court invoked both international legal norms and comparative practice.[103] My intention, however, is to draw attention to potential risks and unintended consequences in proposing such supranational anchors in the constitutional adjudication of amendments. I do so by identifying four assumptions underpinning the appeal to the supranational in amendment review, some normative and others practical.

Contested transnational norms

A first observation is that international and regional norms are themselves often contested, even in the area of human rights or democratic governance. This has long been argued by proponents of third world approaches to international law and critical feminists, who view in international legal norms not (or not just) the prospects of emancipation but (also) renewed forms of subordination to a Eurocentric world view.[104] To this general observation, however, we can add a narrower one, more relevant to our discussion around what may make a constitutional

[101] Rosalind Dixon and David Landau, 'Competitive Democracy and the Constitutional Minimum Core' in Tom Ginsburg and Aziz Huq, eds., *Assessing Constitutional Performance* (Cambridge University Press 2016) 268, 278.

[102] Ibid., 286.

[103] Sentencia C-1040/05, 19 October 2005 and Sentencia C-141/10, 26 February 2010.

[104] See Makau Mutua, *Human Rights: A Political and Cultural Critique* (University of Pennsylvania Press 2002); Anne Orford, 'Feminism, Imperialism and the Mission of International Law', *Nordic Journal of International Law* 71:2 (2002) 275.

amendment unconstitutional. We can take two examples mentioned above, the European Court of Human Rights and the Venice Commission.

In its *Sejdić and Finci* decision, the European Court of Human Rights relied on its growing non-discrimination jurisprudence to find the constitutional arrangements around presidential elections in Bosnia and Herzegovina in breach of the European Convention. In fact, this is a decision cited positively by proponents of international law as a referent in constitutional amendment review.[105] The Strasbourg court has been criticized, however, for failing to give adequate weight in its assessment to the very peculiar Bosnian situation, wherein the impugned constitutional provision had been adopted as a pillar of the country's difficult post-conflict transition. In fact, the Constitutional Court of Bosnia and Herzegovina had carefully considered the case and reached a different conclusion, noting that the country was not ready to transition away from the delicate—and, yes, discriminatory to presidential candidates outside of the three recognized constituent peoples—power-sharing constitutional arrangements in place. At the very least, there is an argument that in this instance, domestic authorities were in a better position to determine whether the provision in question was still justified, despite its discriminatory nature. On balance, and taking full account of the constitutional eternity clause incorporating European human rights into the domestic legal space, the constitutional judges had determined that peace still trumped justice. It is therefore at least plausible to argue that the Strasbourg court's intervention was insufficiently attuned to local realities. Proponents of supranational amendment review described the case law of the European Court of Human Right as 'a logically organized whole in which individual precedents are simply tools for the implementation of general values'.[106] However, this risks concealing just how contested this case law may be, including when Strasbourg has ventured into reviewing constitutional arrangements.

When it comes to the Venice Commission, it would seem to be a perfect repository of regional human rights and democracy-related standards to be relied on in amendment review. In fact, as we saw above, the Commission has itself issued guidance to its member states regarding constitutional amendments. However, we increasingly have comparative studies that highlight some of the problems with the Commission's working methods and conclusions.[107] These studies show that while the Commission's role has transformed in recent years, making it an important player in advising and assisting during processes of constitutional reform, it has not necessarily adapted its approach to reflect these new responsibilities. Insofar as it is tasked with safeguarding and realizing the 'common heritage' of the Council of Europe member states, the Commission has been set up to protect three broad

[105] Garlicki and Garlicki (2011), 362; Roznai (2017).
[106] Garlicki and Garlicki (2011), 360.
[107] Iancu (2019) and de Visser (2015).

principles: respect for fundamental rights, democracy, and the rule of law.[108] As its role has expanded, however, the Commission has exhibited a 'creeping inclination to describe the facets of the common heritage in ever-greater detail'.[109] Put differently, it has confused general normative with specific policy imperatives.[110]

For example, in its opinion on Iceland's 2011 draft constitution, the Venice Commission did not merely insist on respect for judicial independence, but recommended the creation of a judicial council for judicial appointments despite variation in European practice in this area.[111] It also indicated that constitutional review by courts may be preferable to control by non-judicial bodies, again ignoring that several European countries also refrain from empowering their courts in this manner.[112] We have seen in Chapter 4 that national courts have made similar extrapolations—from the general principles of judicial independence and separation of powers—when applying basic structure doctrines. They did so to block legislative reform that tried to remove the primacy of the judiciary in processes of judicial appointments or to limit constitutional review powers.

Elsewhere, as well, the Commission has acted as a norm entrepreneur, and quite a militant one when dealing with its Eastern and Central European member states.[113] It has not only engaged in reviewing anti-corruption mechanisms in several countries in the region, but it has also promoted a particular, highly judicialized set of institutional arrangements—the so-called Romanian model—to Ukraine.[114] It has been argued—rightly, in my view—that this approach risks not only misrepresenting the degree of convergence across European legal systems, but may also undermine the Commission's legitimacy.[115]

These examples illustrate just how contested supranational norms themselves can be, including in the areas of democracy protection. This is not a flaw that can be overcome by more active norm entrepreneurship by these supranational institutions. Rather, it reflects the persistent diversity of institutional and policy approaches even within a regional legal space that otherwise shows great degrees of convergence. Thus, it may be that the transnational referent used to anchor a finding of unconstitutionality against a constitutional amendment would merely shift the locus of reasonable disagreement from national to supranational contestation.

108 de Visser (2015), 972.

109 Ibid., 999.

110 Iancu (2019), 192.

111 de Visser (2015), 1002–3; Venice Commission, *Opinion 702/2013 on the Draft New Constitution of Iceland*, 139.

112 de Visser (2015): 1001; Opinion 702/2013, paras. 114, 154–5.

113 Iancu (2019).

114 Ibid., 213. In reviewing Ukraine's legal reforms to combat corruption, the Commission even went so far as to state that nothing short of a specialized separate anti-corruption court would suffice to meet Ukraine's international obligations. See Venice Commission, *Ukraine Opinion on the Draft Law on Anti-Corruption Courts*, CDL-AD(2017)020, 9 October 2017, para. 75.

115 de Visser (2015) and Iancu (2019).

The methodology of transnational comparisons

A second observation has to do with the methodology national courts would employ when seeking to invoke transnational standards in amendment review. The use of comparative law material in constitutional adjudication certainly has the potential to enrich the latter's quality and persuasiveness.[116] It can also enhance one's understanding of one's own constitutional system, one's capacity for self-reflection, and knowledge of normatively preferable best practices in a given area.[117] However, we also know that courts may cherry-pick their comparators, that they often cite only a handful of other jurisdictions to which they may be culturally, linguistically, or geographically closer, and in general, that inclusive constitutional comparison is quite a demanding endeavour.[118] This is not to say that comparative law citations cannot be helpful in amendment review. It is, instead, to acknowledge that there is no guarantee that courts relying on such comparison will not cast their net too narrowly, resulting in 'an even less democratically sensitive version of the doctrine [of unconstitutional constitutional amendment]—because of an ability to generate apparent additional support for the doctrine's application in (highly selected) comparative sources'.[119] It has also been argued that packaged or sequenced amendments, whose anti-democratic effect is cumulative, may be especially tricky to address through constitutional comparison.[120]

To these concerns, I would add another. As we have seen in past chapters, there is growing comparative practice in the area of unconstitutional constitutional amendment doctrines that is itself problematic. This ranges from instances where unamendability has been relied on for exclusionary purposes to curtail minority rights, such as in Romania and Israel, to judicial reforms struck down in an effort to preserve judicial primacy such as in India, Bangladesh, Pakistan, Colombia, and Slovakia. Courts in these countries did not develop their interpretations of unamendable principles in isolation from supranational norms, quite on the contrary. For example, several Indian justices writing opinions in the controversial *National Judicial Appointments Commission* judgment invoked international and comparative law to underpin their finding of judicial supremacy in judicial appointments as a prerequisite for judicial independence or else to differentiate the Indian case from jurisdictions with different judicial appointment systems.[121] One

[116] For a comparative study, see Tania Groppi and Marie-Claire Ponthoreau, eds., *The Use of Foreign Precedents by Constitutional Judges* (Hart 2013).

[117] Vicki C. Jackson, 'Comparative Constitutional Law: Methodologies' in Michel Rosenfeld and András Sajó, eds., *The Oxford Handbook of Comparative Constitutional Law* (Oxford University Press 2012) 54.

[118] Madhav Khosla, 'Inclusive Constitutional Comparison: Reflections on India's Sodomy Decision', *American Journal of Comparative Law* 59:4 (2011) 909. On the comparative method in constitutional law generally, see Ran Hirschl, *Comparative Matters: The Renaissance of Comparative Constitutional Law* (Oxford University Press 2014).

[119] Dixon and Landau (2015), 633.

[120] Ibid., 634.

[121] *Supreme Court Advocates-on-Record Association* v. *Union of India* (2016) 4 SCC 1, Justice Chelameswar at para. 341 and Justice Joseph Kurian at para. 21, respectively.

could envision comparative methodology being deployed by a national court to reach similarly questionable outcomes—for example, to invalidate an otherwise legitimate attempt to reform the judicial appointments process in the name of unamendable judicial independence. Again, this is not to deny that transnational comparisons can provide valuable cues to national judges and even help them identify blind spots in their articulation of the abstract values and principles enshrined in eternity clauses or presumed part of a constitutional basic structure. However, we should remain aware of the fact that the comparative method is not a full-proof guarantee of good faith in constitutional adjudication, nor of outcomes that necessarily reinforce democratic constitutionalism.

Resistance to the transnational

A related observation here has to do with the assumption, inherent in much of the writing on supranational review of constitutional amendments, that there is normative convergence between the domestic and supranational levels. This reminds us of Vicki Jackson's work on the different stances exhibited by domestic courts towards the transnational, which range from resistance to convergence and engagement.[122] Resistance, manifested as explicitly articulated rejection or else simply as silence or indifference to foreign and international citations, typically seeks to protect the expressive function of the constitution as a distinctively autochthonous project.[123] Convergence, based either on a universalist view of rights or on a positivist commitment to international law enshrined in domestic law, is 'a posture that might view domestic constitutional law as a site for the implementation of international legal norms, or, alternatively, as a participant in a decentralized but normatively progressive process of transnational norm convergence'.[124] The posture of engagement aims to capture everything in between the prior two and allows for both harmony and dissonance between national and transnational norms.[125] The different postures overlap and can be exhibited by the same court at different times. The expanding body of comparative unamendability jurisprudence allows us to add several layers of complexity to Jackson's observations.

There are overlaps between arguments assuming convergence between the domestic and international levels and the development of a doctrine of conventionality control in the inter-American system of human rights protection. The Inter-American Court of Human Rights has found there to be a duty on national authorities to interpret domestic norms compatibly with the American Convention on Human Rights.[126] This duty is incumbent on authorities at all

[122] Jackson (2010).
[123] Ibid., 17–38.
[124] Ibid., 8.
[125] Ibid., 9.
[126] *Almonacid Arellano et al.* v. *Chile*, Preliminary Objections, Merits, Reparations, and Costs, Judgment, Inter-Am. Ct. H. R. (ser. C) No. 154, 26 September 2006, para. 124.

levels.[127] National judges are to engage in conventionality control *ex officio*.[128] The Inter-American Court has even gone so far as to order a national court, the Supreme Court of Argentina, to revoke in its entirety a previous judgment found to be in violation of the American Convention.[129] Embracing such a far-reaching doctrine has unsurprisingly garnered the court the moniker of 'Inter-American Constitutional Court', exercising a 'supranational judicial review' power.[130] Through an 'absolutist interpretation' of the American Convention, not only is it transformed into a norm hierarchically superior to domestic law, but the Inter-American Court is also 'placed as the final and sole proper interpreter of the Convention'.[131] Conventionality control would seem to be the fulfilment of proponents of supranational limits on constitutional amendments, insofar as it does not just legitimize, but *requires* national judges to resort to regional human rights standards as enshrined in the Convention and developed in Inter-American Court jurisprudence in their evaluation of domestic law. If a conflict between the two arises, domestic law is to yield to supranational norms.

The Inter-American Court's conventionality control doctrine has come under closer scrutiny recently, not least because of backlash it has sustained from domestic courts and national governments.[132] In 2017, the Argentine Supreme Court pushed back against the judgment requiring it to revoke one of its past decisions, impugning the Inter-American Court for acting as a fourth branch in the Argentine legal system.[133] The number of states denouncing the American Convention has also increased, from Trinidad and Tobago in 1998 to Venezuela in 2013 and the Dominican Republic in 2014. Scholars have also argued that the Inter-American Court overreached unnecessarily, expanding its doctrine at the expense of its own international legal authority.[134] Jorge Contesse has shown, for example, that Peruvian and Argentine courts had developed their own, bottom-up doctrines of conventionality control in the context of reviewing amnesty laws, finding that

[127] *Cabrera García and Montiel Flores* v. *Mexico*, Merits, Reparations, and Costs, Judgment, Inter-Am. Ct. H. R. (ser. C) No. 220, 26 November 2010, para. 225.

[128] *Dismissed Congressional Employees (Aguado Alfaro et al.)* v. *Peru*, Preliminary Objections, Merits, Reparations, and Costs, Judgment, Inter-Am. Ct. H. R. (ser. C) No. 158, 24 November 2006, para. 128.

[129] *Fontevecchia and D'Amico* v. *Argentina*, Merits, Reparations and Costs, Judgment, Inter-Am. Ct. H. R. (ser. C) No. 238, 29 November 2011.

[130] Ariel E. Dulitzky, 'An Inter-American Constitutional Court? The Invention of the Conventionality Control by the Inter-American Court of Human Rights', *Texas International Law Journal* 50:1 (2015) 45 and Marcelo Torelly, 'Transnational Legal Process and Fundamental Rights in Latin America: How Does the Inter-American Human Rights System Reshape Domestic Constitutional Rights?' in Rubim Borges Fortes et al., eds., *Law and Policy in Latin America: Transforming Courts, Institutions, and Rights* (Springer 2016) 21.

[131] Dulitzky (2015), 52.

[132] See discussion in Jorge Contesse, 'The International Authority of the Inter-American Court of Human Rights: A Critique of the Conventionality Control Doctrine', *International Journal of Human Rights* 22:9 (2018) 1168.

[133] *Ministerio de Relaciones Exteriores y Culto s/informe sentencia dictada en el caso 'Fontevecchia y D'Amico vs. Argentina' por la Corte Interamericana de Derechos Humanos*, Sentencia, 14 February 2017.

[134] Contesse (2018).

international human rights obligations demanded anti-impunity doctrines.[135] It was in a case regarding amnesties that the Inter-American Court itself had first articulated the doctrine of conventionality control. According to Contesse, however, it did not need thereafter to stretch the text of international treaties to ensure that states incorporate international legal norms: 'the doctrine, simply put, was already there'.[136]

Conventionality control at the domestic level has been proposed as an alternative route to amendment review, with 'domesticated' international human rights standards acting as benchmarks for an amendment's unconstitutionality. Amendment 95/2016 to the Brazilian Constitution, for example, brought about a new fiscal regime that imposed a twenty-year ceiling on public spending in the country, with especially dire effects on the education and healthcare sectors. The amendment has been castigated as contrary not just to the constitutional eternity clause—insofar as it leads to a reduction in social rights—but also to the country's regional human rights obligations.[137] As we saw above, the constitutionalization of policy choices in Brazil's detailed constitution made 'government by constitutional amendment' a recurrent feature. This detail in some areas of Brazil's Constitution contrasts with the general elements of its formal eternity clause. The absolute protection against abolishing 'individual rights and guarantees' in Article 60(4) has been interpreted as extending at least to the entirety of Article 5, with all its seventy-eight clauses, and possibly even to the full catalogue of social rights of the Brazilian Constitution.[138] Conventionality control would thus act as an alternative route to amendment invalidation in a context where the domestic interpretation of unamendability is already far-reaching.

The interplay between conventionality control and the review of constitutional amendments has been unpredictable, however. The Bolivian Constitutional Court, for example, relied on a strong interpretation of conventionality control to find that the executive term limit preventing Evo Morales from standing for re-election were contrary to international human rights standards.[139] The court argued that

[135] Ibid., 1169.

[136] Ibid. See also discussion in Chapter 2 on the constitutional entrenchment of amnesties, including via eternity clauses.

[137] Bárbara Mendonça Bertotti, '(Un)Constitutional Amendment No. 95/2016 and the Limit for Public Expenses in Brazil: Amendment or Dismemberment?', *ICONnect Blog*, 24 August 2018, http://www.iconnectblog.com/2018/08/unconstitutional-amendment-no-95-2016-and-the-limit-for-public-expenses-in-brazil-amendment-or-dismemberment/; Yaniv Roznai and Letícia R. Camargo Kreuz, 'Conventionality Control and Amendment 95/2016—A Brazilian Case of Unconstitutional Constitutional Amendment' 5:2 *Revista de Investigações Constitucionais* (2018) 35. Insofar as it undermined the social core of Brazil's Constitution, the amendment has also been deemed to amount to 'constitutional dismemberment'. Richard Albert, *Constitutional Amendments: Making, Breaking, and Changing Constitutions* (Oxford University Press 2019), 78.

[138] Juliano Zaiden Benvindo, 'Brazil in the Context of the Debate over Unamendability in Latin America' in Richard Albert and Bertil Emrah Oder, eds., *An Unamendable Constitution? Unamendability in Constitutional Democracies* (Springer 2018) 345, 349, 355, and 360.

[139] Tribunal Constitucional Plurinacional, Sentencia Constitucional Plurinacional No. 0084/2017, 28 November 2017. See also discussion in Verdugo (2019), 1120.

the limit contravened Article 23 of the American Convention on Human Rights on the right to participate in government, and that a strong, rights-maximizing decision required that the limit be ignored. As we saw in Chapter 2, other Latin American courts have read down executive term limits in this way, conventionality control notwithstanding.[140] However, the Bolivian example is striking insofar as the case hinged almost exclusively on conventionality control and relied on it to legitimize the outcome.[141] The Honduran Supreme Court has also interpreted international human rights law as superior to domestic law, finding that it could even declare inapplicable original constitutional provisions if found to be incompatible with international principles.[142] In striking down the previously unamendable executive term limit in the Honduran Constitution, the Honduran court thus purported to be affirming international human rights law, notably rights to political participation.

The former examples may be resisted as illustrating bad faith reliance on international legal norms in the adjudication of unamendability. Alternatively, they may be read as part of the growing pushback against international human rights law.[143] However, this pushback is not limited to the human rights context. As we saw in Chapter 3, the rise of constitutional identity review in Europe shows a growing unease with and even outright rejection of supranational law often grounded in unamendable constitutional principles. Germany's *Lisbon* decision provides a complex challenge to easy assumptions about the role of the supranational in adjudication of unamendability.[144] This 2009 decision was the first time the German Federal Constitutional Court explicitly embraced a constitutional identity doctrine in order to limit the reach of European law within the German legal order, the primacy and direct effect of European law notwithstanding. In so doing, the German court also relied on Article 79(3), the Basic Law's eternity clause, to determine the scope of the limits on European integration. These limits, the court found, were rooted in the principle of democracy the clause eternalizes.

It is important to note, however, that the Basic Law also contains explicit commitments to European integration in the form of the so-called 'open statehood' (*offene Staatlichkeit*) principle. This fundamental commitment to the accommodation of international law, which permeates several constitutional provisions, 'was meant to create a cosmopolitan constitutional order linking Germany's interests with the interests of the international community and integrating Germany into

[140] See also David Landau, 'Presidential Term Limits in Latin America: A Critical Analysis of the Migration of the Unconstitutional Constitutional Amendment Doctrine', *Law & Ethics of Human Rights* 12:2 (2018a) 225.

[141] Alexandra Huneeus, 'When Illiberals Embrace Human Rights', *AJIL Unbound* 113 (2019) 380, 382.

[142] Supreme Court of Justice, Constitutional Chamber, Decision of 22 April 2015.

[143] Colm O'Cinneide, 'Rights under Pressure', *European Human Rights Law Review* 1 (2017) 43.

[144] 2 BvE 2/08, 30 June 2009 ('*Lisbon*').

international law'.[145] In its *Lisbon* decision, the court paid lip service to the principle but relied on notions of sovereignty to (re)claim the supremacy of the domestic legal order over the international. It argued that sovereignty had not been waived and rested ultimately in the national constitution:

> There is therefore no contradiction to the aim of openness to international law if the legislature, exceptionally, does not comply with international treaty law—accepting, however, corresponding consequences in international relations—provided this is the only way in which a violation of fundamental principles of the constitution can be averted.[146]

Critics of this introspective stance taken by the German Constitutional Court have contested its isolationist bent in contradiction with the Basic Law's spirit and have accused the court of misunderstanding 'the core of open and transformed statehood which the Basic Law propounds'.[147] In other words, they have seen the court's decision as going against the pro-integration letter of the German Basic Law as encapsulated by its preamble and Article 23(1). Others have even chastised 'the truly provincial, parochial and inward perspective underlying many aspects of the reasoning'.[148] One can also observe the irony of a provision adopted with a view to preventing Germany's sliding back into authoritarianism being relied on to halt European integration. In the words of Franz Mayer:

> The [court's] reasoning is that what is precluded from alteration by constitutional amendment is also 'integration proof'. Yet wasn't Article 79 paragraph 3 GG, shielding the guarantee of human dignity and the fundamental principles of democracy, rule of law etc. from any amendment, primarily designed to protect the Germans from themselves, from a relapse into inhuman dictatorship, bondage and tyranny? Using this provision against Europe, where almost nothing else—at least from the point of view of our neighbors—has prevented more effectively the relapse of Germany into dictatorship, bondage, and tyranny than our participation in European integration, is—to say the least—remarkable.[149]

[145] Donald P. Kommers and Russell A. Miller, *The Constitutional Jurisprudence of the Federal Republic of Germany* (Duke University Press 2012), 302. For more on Germany's 'open state' jurisprudence, see ibid., 302–52.

[146] *Lisbon* decision, para. 340.

[147] Ingolf Pernice, 'Artikel 23: Europäische Union' in Horst Dreier ed., *Grundgesetz: Kommentar (Band II)* (Mohr Siebeck 1998), para. 35, cited in Jo Murkens, *From Empire to Union: Conceptions of German Constitutional Law since 1871* (Oxford University Press 2013), 206.

[148] Joseph Weiler, 'The "Lisbon Urteil" ICE and the Fast Food Culture', *European Journal of International Law* 20:3 (2009) 505, 506.

[149] Franz C. Mayer, 'Rashomon in Karlsruhe: A Reflection on Democracy and Identity in the European Union', *International Journal of Constitutional Law* 9:3–4 (2011) 757, 763.

Mayer is not the only one to have questioned the subjection of European integration to the same substantive scrutiny as fascism. Michael Wilkinson similarly decries the inward turn of the German court, in which he reads consequences for the entire European project:

> Although cast as its saviour, the German Constitutional Court defends 'militant democracy in one country' rather than the constitutional order as such; it also obstructs its upscaling into a supranational political democracy on the basis of a constitution that was engineered to encourage a 'European Germany' but is now, ironically, preventing anything but a 'German Europe'.[150]

The court in *Lisbon* departed from prior case law on open statehood, notably its *Maastricht* decision.[151] It even recast the 'open state' principle in different language, referring instead to the principle of 'openness to European law' (*Europarechtsfre undlichkeit*).[152] Subsequent case law seemed to suggest the German court would relax its interpretation of Article 79(3) with regard to EU mechanisms, notably the Economic and Monetary Union, by stating that it would not 'from the outset' find changes to the mechanism incompatible with the eternity clause.[153] This seemed to signal a 'return to openness' and a welcome exercise in judicial restraint.[154] However, more recent decisions such as *OMT* in 2014 and the *PSPP* judgment in 2020 have seen the German Constitutional Court reiterate the role of Article 79(3) as the 'ultimate limit' on European integration.[155]

To recapitulate: there is growing scholarly work arguing that a transnational or supranational referent in the adjudication of eternity clauses or basic structure doctrines can both empower domestic courts to respond to abusive amendments and help guard against judicial overreach. These accounts tend to rest on an assumption that domestic courts' stance towards the transnational will be one of openness with regard to unamendability adjudication, resulting in 'substantive convergence' in Vicki Jackson's terms (i.e. convergence not just in the methodologies used, such as proportionality analysis, but also in the substantive outcomes reached).[156] There is now enough comparative case law surrounding unconstitutional constitutional amendment doctrines to question whether this will always be the case. It is not just that national courts may reject supranational norms in the name of autochthonous constitutionalism, as European courts are increasingly

[150] Wilkinson (2015), 316.
[151] 89 BVerfGE 155, 12 October 1993 ('*Maastricht*').
[152] *Lisbon* decision, paras. 219–25; see also Murkens (2013), 179.
[153] 2 BvR 1390/12, 12 September 2012 ('*ESM*'), para. 221.
[154] Mattias Wendel, 'Judicial Restraint and the Return to Openness: The Decision of the German Federal Constitutional Court on the ESM and the Fiscal Treaty of 12 September 2012', *German Law Journal* 14:1 (2013) 21.
[155] 2 BvR 2728/13, 14 January 2014 ('*OMT*'), para. 29. 2 BvR 859/15 ('*PSPP*'), 5 May 2020.
[156] Jackson (2010), 42–3.

doing through constitutional identity review. It is also that we see domestic courts also relying on supranational norms in order to weaken democratic protections, such as the Honduran Supreme Court did in its unamendability jurisprudence. It was precisely the appeal to supranational norms, albeit misconstrued, that allowed it to uphold the removal of unamendable executive term limits and even to declare unconstitutional an original constitutional provision. Moreover, we have seen national courts strike down legal reforms that curtailed the judiciary's supremacy in judicial appointments processes in the name of international legal norms protecting purportedly unamendable judicial independence.[157]

Insofar as a transnational referent in constitutional adjudication is meant as a corrective for potential misuse of unamendability doctrines, its success will depend on a myriad of contextual factors. Given the variety of stances that domestic courts have exhibited vis-à-vis the transnational, it is reasonable to expect different postures in their propensity to go supranational when interpreting unamendable provisions as well.

Unamendability in international adjudication: a supranational unconstitutional constitutional amendment doctrine?

The previous section dealt with the role that supranational norms may play in the interpretation and even legitimation of domestic amendment review. In an age of democratic backsliding, the reverse question has increasingly come to the fore: can international courts themselves play a role in adjudicating the constitutionality of constitutional amendments at the national level, or even of entire national constitutions? As we will see, those who answer this question in the affirmative go beyond merely reinforcing international law's dismissal of internal law as a valid ground for state non-compliance. Instead, they envision the development of a full-blown unconstitutional constitutional amendment doctrine at the supranational level.

A recent case of the European Court of Human Rights is instructive in terms of the possible supranational future of unconstitutional constitutional amendment doctrines. In *Baka* v. *Hungary*, the Strasbourg court found the premature termination of the mandate of the former president of the Hungarian Constitutional Court, enacted via transitional provisions in the new Fundamental Law adopted in 2011, to amount to a breach of the European Convention on Human Rights.[158] Specifically, the applicant's inability to challenge his mandate's termination before a court and the link to views critical of the government he had expressed in his professional capacity were found to amount to violations of Articles 6 and 10 of the Convention, respectively.

[157] See discussion in Chapter 4.

[158] *Baka* v. *Hungary* (Application No. 20261/12), Grand Chamber Judgment, 23 June 2016.

The case was complicated by the fact that the former court president had not been explicitly denied access to a court. Instead, his mandate was de facto terminated when the Supreme Court was replaced by a new institution named *Kúria*, with new appointment requirements which he no longer met. The Hungarian government had argued that there was no individual right, under the Convention, to be a judge, an argument the Strasbourg court dismissed on the grounds that by not meeting requirements of generality of law, the legal changes undermined the principle of the rule of law.[159] While there is little doubt that the changes were intended precisely to result in the removal of sitting judges who were not loyal to the government,[160] the fact remains that the Strasbourg decision effectively reviewed a constitutional reform for convention compatibility. The judgment has been criticized precisely for applying a human rights lens to what was actually a separation of powers question over which the European Court did not have jurisdiction.[161] According to the critics:

> By doing this, not only the Strasbourg court *de facto* exercised an abstract review of supraconstitutionality, but recreated the legal conditions which would have been applied had the Transitional Provisions not existed, i.e. *de facto* struck down the Transitional Provisions with *ex nunc* effect.[162]

However, Hungarian scholars have seen it as inevitable that, given the transformation of the country's constitutional space, 'European institutions have become the fora of processing dissent expelled systematically from the domestic public debate.'[163] They have praised the willingness of the Strasbourg court to look at the broader Hungarian and European constitutional and political context when evaluating the application before it.[164]

The full effects of the Strasbourg court's intervention in this case are identified in the joint concurring opinions of Judges Pinto de Albuquerque and Dedov.

[159] Ibid., para. 117.

[160] For how this case fits in the broader story of the Hungarian government using changes in the retirement age of judges to remove sitting judges and replace them with loyalists, see Gábor Halmai, 'The Early Retirement Age of the Hungarian Judges' in Fernanda Nicola and Bill Davies, eds., *EU Law Stories: Contextual and Critical Histories of European Jurisprudence* (Cambridge University Press 2017) 471.

[161] David Kosař and Katarína Šipulová, 'The Strasbourg Court Meets Abusive Constitutionalism: Baka v. Hungary and the Rule of Law', *Hague Journal on the Rule of Law* 10 (2017) 83.

[162] Ibid., 95. The authors believe the Convention system to be ill-equipped to handle such structural problems (see ibid., 100–1).

[163] Renáta Uitz, 'Expelling Dissent: On Account of the ECtHR Judgment in Baka v Hungary', *Verfassungsblog* (3 June 2014) https://verfassungsblog.de/expelling-dissent-account-ecthr-judgment-baka-v-hungary-2/.

[164] Renáta Uitz, 'National Constitutional Identity in the European Constitutional Project: A Recipe for Exposing Cover Ups and Masquerades', *Verfassungsblog* (11 November 2016), https://verfassungsblog.de/national-constitutional-identity-in-the-european-constitutional-project-a-recipe-for-exposing-cover-ups-and-masquerades/.

They found 'perennial principles' in the Hungarian constitutional order in order to ground the constitutional continuity of principles of judicial independence and irremovability of judges between the 1949 and 2011 constitutions and, accordingly, principles regarding the retrospectivity of law and the rule of law.[165] Given their breach of such infra-constitutional principles, the transitional constitutional provision leading to the removal of judge Baka as court president was in effect an 'unconstitutional constitutional provision'.[166] While they praised the majority judgment for ignoring Hungary's dualism vis-à-vis international law, the concurring judges believed it 'imperative to assert, as a matter of principle, the judicial review of domestic legislation, including constitutional legislation, for the sake of effective and non-illusory protection of human rights in Europe'.[167] This constitutional review exercised by Strasbourg rendered it a European Constitutional Court enforcing Convention law with direct effect and primacy over national law, they argue.[168] In other words, the European court had finally fully embraced conventionality control in line with its Inter-American counterpart.[169] The Convention underpinning the *jus constitutionale commune* in Europe, 'the Council of Europe may put forward a strong European constitutional claim, if need be, against any contradicting domestic constitutional claim, regardless of the size of the supporting political majority'.[170] In short, a supranational unconstitutional constitutional amendment doctrine was, to at least two Strasbourg judges, the logical (and desirable) consequence of a finding of violation against a state on account of their constitutional provisions breaching the Convention.

The *Baka* case has at least one precursor outside of Europe.[171] When the Nicaraguan parliament attempted to amend the constitution to remove certain presidential powers in 2004, it did so following the procedure for partial revision of the constitution. According to Articles 192 and 194 of the Nicaraguan Constitution, the procedure required validation by a special commission, debate in two legislative sessions, and a 60 per cent majority of votes to pass. The sitting president contested the move, arguing that because the changes would effectively transform the Nicaraguan system of government from a presidential to a parliamentary one, it constituted a total revision of the constitution. Such revisions needed to be passed through the more onerous procedure stipulated by Articles 193 and 194 requiring

[165] *Baka* v. *Hungary* (Application No. 20261/12), Grand Chamber Judgment, 23 June 2016, Joint concurring opinion of Judges Pinto de Albuquerque and Dedov, para. 11.

[166] Ibid., para. 7. The concurring judges explicitly cite scholarship on unconstitutional constitutional amendment doctrines.

[167] Ibid., para. 21.

[168] Ibid., para. 23.

[169] Ibid.

[170] Ibid., para. 25.

[171] Stephen J. Schnably, 'Emerging International Law Constraints on Constitutional Structure and Revision: A Preliminary Appraisal', *University of Miami Law Review* 62 (2008) 417. See also discussion in Marco Antonio Simonelli, 'Towards a Theory of "Unconventional Constitutional Amendments": Some Lessons from the *Baka* Case', *DPCE Online* 39:2 (2019) 1561, 1574–5.

setting up a constituent assembly and a two-thirds majority vote in parliament to adopt the revisions. He filed petitions with both the Nicaraguan Supreme Court and the Central American Court of Justice, the latter having jurisdiction, inter alia, over disputes between government organs within its member states.

The Central American Court issued its judgment in March 2005,[172] finding that the amendments in question did amount to a total revision of the constitution. The court stated that they altered the balance of powers and the executive's independence and thereby undermined the principles of the separation of powers and democracy. The court was concerned that by taking powers away from the president, the amendments in effect transformed the Nicaraguan system from a presidential to a parliamentary one and were therefore unconstitutional. On the same day, however, the Nicaraguan Supreme Court also issued a ruling declaring the Central American Court's findings invalid. The president tried to force the implementation of the supranational court's ruling via executive decree, a move that the Supreme Court again rejected. The stand-off was eventually resolved through political dialogue, with the constitutional reforms postponed until 2007 when the incumbent president agreed to leave office.

More significant for our purposes, however, is that the Nicaraguan case illustrates the potential clashes between supranational and domestic institutions when the former attempt to intervene in national inter-branch conflicts, in particular constitutional reform processes. The Central American Court of Justice has encountered resistance from other member states' supreme courts, including those of Costa Rica, Guatemala, and Panama.[173] I already noted the pushback against conventionality control in the Inter-American system above. The European Court of Human Rights is also experiencing growing resistance and even backlash, ranging from British rejection of its so-called mission creep to the Russian Constitutional Court's developing of a doctrine of constitutional supremacy over decisions of the Strasbourg court.[174] In some instances, the backlash has gone hand in hand with abusive constitutionalism, with captured courts refusing to follow Strasbourg case law.[175] Importantly, however, the resistance is not just due to domestic actors displaying bad faith and seeking to eschew their international obligations. At least some of the resistance has also been principled and is the result of 'inter-layer irritation' between the different levels of constitutional governance involved in rights

[172] Corte Centroamericana de Justicia, *Caso de Conflicto entre Poderes en Nicaragua*, Sentencia, 29 March 2005.

[173] Salvatore Caserta, 'Regional Integration through Law and International Courts—the Interplay between De Jure and De Facto Supranationality in Central America and the Caribbean', *Leiden Journal of International Law* 30 (2017) 579, 594.

[174] Marten Breuer, ed., *Principled Resistance to ECtHR Judgments—A New Paradigm?* (Springer 2019).

[175] David Kosař et al., *Domestic Judicial Treatment of European Court of Human Rights Case Law* (Routledge 2020), 245–51.

protection, both domestic and international.[176] Or, to revisit Vicki Jackson's terminology, we find engagement with the transnational in the human rights sphere to run the gamut from convergence to outright resistance.

5.3 Conclusion

The transnational embeddedness of constitutional rules, including of principles declared to be unamendable, is not automatically problematic from the point of view of democratic constitutionalism. Indeed, in numerous instances the influence of transnational norms has been on balance positive, such as in promoting the adoption of principles of democratic governance, non-discrimination, and minority rights. However, transnational embeddedness has also sometimes come at the expense of democratic control over institutional choices, such as when international loan conditionality led to the constitutional entrenchment of technocratic rule or when the Venice Commission promoted narrower policy choices in the name of broad normative commitments to democracy, human rights, and the rule of law. In instances where the very process of constitution-making has been internationalized, there are strong reasons to question the understanding of constitutional unamendability as the expression of a single, unified, and knowable constituent power. Transnational engagement means both the *who* and the *what* of constitutions can no longer be understood solely within national bounds.

This chapter has sought not only to raise awareness about this growing internationalization of constitutional authorship and content, but also to caution against assumptions that transnational engagement will necessarily rest on norm convergence and good faith cooperation. Norm contestation, partial or outright flawed comparative methodologies, and divergence from or open opposition to the transnational are equally likely. Any argument about the supranational illegality of constitutional amendments must take these factors into account. The growing backlash against the supranational, including in the realm of human rights law and regional integration, has seen unamendability itself used as an anchor for transnational resistance.

[176] Colm O'Cinneide, 'Human Rights within Multi-Layered Systems of Constitutional Governance: Rights Cosmopolitanism and Domestic Particularism in Tension', *Irish Yearbook of International Law* 3 (2010) 19.

6

Eternity Faces 'the People'

Unamendability and Participatory Constitutional Change

This chapter juxtaposes the increased recourse to constitutional unamendability with a seemingly contradictory trend: the rise of popular participation in constitution-making and reform, such as through referendums, public consultations, and citizen assembly-style constitutional conventions. Such participation is increasingly promoted by constitutional experts and international institutions involved in constitution building throughout the world, not least as a means to achieve enduring constitutional legitimacy.[1] This chapter explores whether unamendability is compatible with this shift towards participation or whether it is part of a counter-current. The chapter thus seeks an answer to the question of popular participation's relationship to eternity clauses: is it a justification for, an alternative to, or otherwise closely linked to unamendable provisions? More broadly, are eternity clauses the high point of the battle between rigidity and openness in constitutional design today or are they merely a distraction?

This chapter places the discussion of eternity clauses in the wider context of advancements in constitution-making and asks whether they are compatible. It focuses on the trend towards encouraging popular participation during constituent moments as evidence of the enriched notion of democracy—and constitutionalism—which constitution-makers increasingly strive for. The participatory pull is both normatively and empirically attractive. Scholars of participatory democracy extol its capacity to create a better informed, empowered citizenry ready to more closely engage in the business of governance. Democratic constitutionalists build on these insights and combine them with their belief in popular sovereignty as a reality and not mere rhetoric. They believe that harnessing participation's potential will enhance constitutionalism and therefore search for concrete institutions and decision-making strategies that would bring popular participation to constitutional politics. By taking their efforts seriously, this chapter

[1] Cheryl Saunders, 'Constitution Making in the 21st Century', *International Review of Law* 1:4 (2012) 1; Silvia Suteu, 'Constitutional Conventions in the Digital Era: Lessons from Iceland and Ireland', *Boston College International & Comparative Law Review* 38:2 (2015) 251; Abrak Saati, 'Participatory Constitution-Making as a Transnational Legal Norm: Why Does It Stick in Some Contexts and Not in Others', *UC Irvine Journal of International, Transnational and Comparative Law* 2 (2017a) 113.

Eternity Clauses in Democratic Constitutionalism. Silvia Suteu, Oxford University Press. © Silvia Suteu 2021.
DOI: 10.1093/oso/9780198858867.003.0007

sets out to explore whether unamendability is compatible with this shift towards participation or whether it is a potentially costly anachronism.

The chapter proceeds as follows. It first discusses the rise of participation in constitution-making and presents the advantages as well as the drawbacks or uncertain consequences of promoting such public input. It briefly lists two mechanisms as examples of this trend: constitutional referendums and citizen assembly-style constitutional conventions. Both are instruments that have been used with increased frequency to encourage and manage popular involvement in fundamental constitutional change. The reason such institutional innovations are important to constitutional theory is that, in different ways, they seek to give weight to the commitment of letting the people speak on matters of constitutional change. In other words, they are potential answers to the question of how, precisely, to approximate the popular voice in constitution-making. These mechanisms will be imperfect as is unavoidably true of any purported institutionalization of constituent power. Nevertheless, at their best, they can result in a better representation of popular will than purely elite-driven processes. As such, the chapter argues that they deserve our attention particularly when seeking the type of enduring constitutional legitimacy which eternity clauses also pursue.

The chapter then explores the relationship between constitutional rigidity in the form of eternity clauses and participation. The chapter maps out both instances of popular constitution-making having resulted in constitutional texts without an unamendable provision and those wherein such a provision was included. Case studies discussed include South Africa, Kenya, Iceland, and Tunisia. This empirical investigation tests out two possible interplays between participation and unamendability. The first, that participation in the constituent moment will result in a more participatory, flexible constitution and therefore a rejection of unamendability. Iceland's 'crowdsourced' 2011 draft would seem to confirm this hypothesis, as it not only did not contain an eternity clause but it also enshrined numerous provisions on direct democracy. However, Tunisia's example is sobering insofar as it opted for unamendability in the context of a participatory foundational moment, as well as for not constitutionally enshrining guarantees of future participation in constitutional reform. The second possible interplay is that constitutional courts might be less willing to embrace unamendability doctrines when guarding basic laws drafted with substantive popular input. Here again the evidence is mixed. While Kenya's Constitutional Court has subscribed to the protection of the constitution's identity and restricted its fundamental alteration to a new exercise in constituent power only, South Africa's court appears more ambivalent. The same court which certified the country's 1996 Constitution based on pre-agreed substantive fundamental principles later found textual barriers to the embrace of a doctrine of unconstitutional constitutional amendment.

The evidence indicates that we should not assume that popular authorship automatically correlates with a flexible constitution, or with constitutional adjudication that resists the development of an unconstitutional constitutional amendment doctrine. The chapter concludes that the interplay between the rise of unamendability and the rise of participation in constitutional change processes is best characterized not by opposition, but by ambiguity. At the very least, this chapter serves to signal to drafters the need to be aware of the possible tension between mechanisms for rigidity and those for openness in the final constitutional text, and to adjust constitutional design in light of this interplay.

6.1 The rise of participation in constitutional change

While calls to take popular participation seriously in constitutional decision-making are more numerous today, they have not occurred in a theoretical vacuum. Their debt to democratic theory is further explored shortly. However, there are also echoes here of older scholarship on responsive constitutionalism. A. V. Dicey explained that responsive constitutionalism, such as he found in England, and irresponsive constitutionalism, which he exemplified by the United States, should not be assumed to neatly correspond to democratic versus non-democratic, nor to flexible versus rigid constitutionalism.[2] What mattered according to Dicey was the speed and ease with which 'expression can be . . . given to the wishes, feelings, or opinions of the citizens of a given country'.[3] A different understanding of responsive constitutionalism emphasizes empathy to those who are subordinated and the explicit incorporation of lessons from the past into the constitution (on the model of South Africa).[4] Underlying both these positions is a positive expectation that the constitutional practice and text would correlate with public opinion and the wider community, respectively. Promoters of participatory democracy in constitution-making have presented it as the tool with which to ensure this tight bond.

The promises of participatory constitutional change

We can group into four clusters the arguments for why we should care about processes of constitution-making, as follows.[5]

[2] Albert V. Dicey, *Comparative Constitutionalism* (John W. F. Allison ed., Oxford University Press 2013), 243–8.
[3] Ibid., 243.
[4] Peggy Cooper Davis, 'Responsive Constitutionalism and the Idea of Dignity', *Journal of Constitutional Law* 11:5 (2009) 1373.
[5] For a more in-depth analysis of this turn to participation in recent constitution-making, see Suteu (2015).

The first rests on a correlation between the legitimacy of the process and that of the resulting constitutional order. While constitutional legitimacy depends on a series of factors, the process of its creation is often central. Cheryl Saunders has identified four common features of twenty-first-century constitution-making, of which two are distinctly relevant here. The first has to do with popular participation in constitution-making: 'there is now, effectively, universal acceptance that the authority for a Constitution must derive, in one way or another, from the people of the state concerned'.[6] She argues that we may broadly identify a trend 'towards openness, inclusivity and the active involvement of the people of a state at all stages of the process through participation, rather than mere consultation'.[7] Others have echoed this view,[8] even going so far as to identify a right to participate in democratic governance in international law which extends to constitution-making.[9] An inclusive and open process of constitutional change gives weight to ideas of self-government and public engagement in politics. As we saw in Chapter 4, the inclusiveness of the amendment process has also been interpreted as relevant for the scope of unconstitutional constitutional amendment doctrines: the more participatory the amendment, the argument went, the less intrusive judicial control should be.[10]

The other common feature Saunders identifies is an emphasis on process:

> Process can underpin the legitimacy of a Constitution, increase public knowledge of it, instil a sense of public ownership and create an expectation that the Constitution will be observed, in spirit as well as form. A constitution-making process may assist to set the tone for ordinary politics, including the peaceful transfer of power in accordance with constitutional rules.[11]

In other words, there is an educational element involved in having a 'good' constitution-making process, as it can serve as model for subsequent political interactions. There is also a link to public ownership and increased vigilance: an informed public will know when the constitution has been transgressed and demand accountability.[12]

[6] Saunders (2012), 2–3.

[7] Ibid., 9.

[8] Claude Klein and András Sajó, 'Constitution-Making: Process and Substance' in Michel Rosenfeld and András Sajó, eds., *The Oxford Handbook of Comparative Constitutional Law* (Oxford University Press 2012) 419, 435–6.

[9] Vivien Hart, 'Democratic Constitution Making', United States Institute of Peace Special Report 107 (July 2003) 1, http://www.usip.org/sites/default/files/resources/sr107.pdf.

[10] Yaniv Roznai, *Unconstitutional Constitutional Amendments: The Limits of Amendment Powers* (Oxford University Press 2017), 219–20.

[11] Saunders (2012), 5.

[12] See also Jennifer Widner, 'Constitution-Writing in Post-Conflict Settings: An Overview', *William and Mary Law Review* 49:4 (2008) 1513, 1519.

A second argument in favour of caring about participatory constitution-making rests on a possible link between it and having more mechanisms of popular involvement included in the new or revised constitution.[13] There is evidence suggesting that more inclusive constitutional moments lead to more democratic politics, to more constraints on government authority, and to stronger, and thus more durable, constitutions.[14] These findings would seem to confirm that 'the content of constitutions depends on who sits at the table to hammer out their provisions': the more inclusive the drafting and negotiation of the content of constitutions, the greater the benefits for democracy and constitutional stability.[15] The case studies examined later in this chapter partially endorse this conclusion, but the relationship between a participatory process and the adoption of more direct democratic mechanisms is not straightforward.

A third point has been briefly touched upon above and has to do with the correlation between inclusion during constitution-making and constitutional longevity. In their empirical study of constitutions, Elkins et al. have identified inclusion—the breadth of participation in both formulating and subsequently enforcing constitutional agreements—as one of the key factors ensuring constitutional survival.[16] The common knowledge created when the constitution is publicly formulated and debated, they argue, leads to attachment to the constitutional project, which results in self-enforcement and in turn in its longevity.[17] It is hardly surprising, then, that the same authors praised the Icelandic process when reviewing the 2011 draft constitution.[18]

A final perspective on the benefits of participatory constitutional change links it to the crisis of democracy and the latter's turn to deliberation. In an age where citizens feel detached from regular politics, deliberative forms of engagement may yet resurrect their interest. As some scholars have noted, '[a]lthough electoral participation is generally declining, participation is expanding into new forms of action', with citizens seeking a more active role and 'prepared to challenge (and thereby engage with) existing systems and norms'.[19] A 'new model of democracy' is said to

[13] For an early study on the link between public participation in constitutional promulgation and the content of the constitutional text, see Zachary Elkins, Tom Ginsburg, and Justin Blunt, 'The Citizen as Founder: Public Participation in Constitutional Approval', *Temple Law Review* 81:2 (2008) 361.

[14] John M. Carey, 'Does It Matter How a Constitution Is Created?' in Zoltan Barany and Robert G. Moser, eds., *Is Democracy Exportable?* (Cambridge University Press 2009) 155, 159–60.

[15] Ibid., 177.

[16] Elkins et al. (2009), 78.

[17] Ibid., 78–9.

[18] Zachary Elkins, Tom Ginsburg, and James Melton, 'A Review of Iceland's Draft Constitution', Comparative Constitutions Project, 14 October 2012, http://comparativeconstitutionsproject.org/wp-content/uploads/CCP-Iceland-Report.pdf.

[19] David M. Farrell, Eoin O'Malley, and Jane Suiter, 'Deliberative Democracy in Action Irish-Style: The 2011 *We the Citizens* Pilot Citizens' Assembly', *Irish Political Studies* 28:1 (2013) 100, citing Russell J. Dalton, *The Good Citizen: How a Younger Generation Is Reshaping American Politics* (2nd ed., Congressional Quarterly Press 2009), 1. See also Silvia Suteu, 'The Populist Turn in Central and Eastern Europe: Is Deliberative Democracy Part of the Solution?', *European Constitutional Law Review* 15:3 (2019) 488, arguing that in Central and Eastern Europe, popular disenchantment with traditional

be evolving, one which requires more from its citizens.[20] Perhaps it is not unrelated that these mechanisms have been called for in the aftermath of economic crises (as the constitutional conventions set up in Iceland and Ireland were) or of 'once in a generation' decisions (as the 2014 independence referendum was in Scotland). The advantages promised by deliberative democracy—creativity, openness, and consensus-based (rather than adversarial) politics among them—are that much more attractive when confronted with constitutional failure and stale institutions. Moreover, there is no reason to consider this a trade-off: representative institutions can coexist with such innovations, and may in fact be developed and improved alongside them.[21]

The limits of participatory constitutional change

The narrative centred on the benefits of increased participation in constitution-making requires at least two significant caveats. The first deals with the dangers of 'overselling' the benefits of participation and its effects on legitimacy. Such concerns are expressed in two forms. They focus either on counter-examples to prove participation is not necessary—cases where non-participatory processes still led to constitutions accepted as legitimate (such as Germany or Japan)—or on cases where participation backfired. Examples include Chad's 1996 constitutional conference increasing francophone–Arab tensions and Nicaragua's 1987 process with doubts over the fairness of canvassing local opinion.[22] These examples serve to remind advocates of participation, including international NGOs involved in advising governments and providing expertise such as the US Institute for Peace (USIP), Interpeace, and International IDEA,[23] that local conditions should

forms of representative democracy coexists with democratic vibrancy in informal spheres such as social protests.

[20] Ibid.

[21] Peter Vermeersch, 'Innovating Democracy in Times of Crisis: Solution or Utopia?', *Open Citizenship* 4:1 (2013) 66; David M. Farrell, 'The Irish Constitutional Convention: A Bold Step or a Damp Squib?' in John O'Dowd and Giuseppe Ferrari, eds., *75 Years of the Constitution of Ireland: An Irish–Italian Dialogue* (Clarus Press 2014) 191, arguing that innovative mechanisms such as the Irish constitutional convention are a complement to other representative institutions.

[22] Alicia L. Bannon, 'Designing a Constitution-Drafting Process: Lessons from Kenya', *Yale Law Journal* 116:8 (2007) 1824, 1843–4. See also Richard Stacey, 'Constituent Power and Carl Schmitt's Theory of Constitution in Kenya's Constitution-making Process', *International Journal of Constitutional Law* 9:3–4 (2011) 587, arguing that participation is not a *sine qua non* for constitutional efficacy.

[23] For an example of USIP calling for participation in constitution-making, see Jason Gluck and Michele Brandt, *Participatory and Inclusive Constitution Making: Giving Voice to the Demands of Citizens in the Wake of the Arab Spring* (United States Institute of Peace 2015), 18, http://www.usip.org/publications/participatory-and-inclusive-constitution-making. For an example of Interpeace doing so, see Michele Brandt, Jill Cottrell, Yash Ghai, and Anthony Regan, *Constitution-Making and Reform: Options for the Process* (Interpeace 2011), http://www.constitutionmakingforpeace.org/sites/default/files/Constitution-Making-Handbook.pdf. For an example of the same from International

determine the degree to which popular involvement is appropriate in any given context. Participation is not a panacea for constitutional legitimacy, as Kenya's example below also illustrates. Nevertheless, the evidence on necessary local preconditions for participation to be effective is growing.[24] The myriad forms participation can take also means its impact on the final constitution can be scaled up or down.

A second, related, caveat is that it is possible that in societies emerging from conflict, or where there is a strong possibility that the constitution-making process would be subverted if fully participatory, considerations such as those presented above may have more limited relevance. In other words, indiscriminately opening up constitution-making in conflict-affected or fragile democracies can have deleterious effects. One study has in fact indicated that the representativeness of constitutional assemblies in post-conflict situations might not be very important.[25] David Landau has also recently cautioned against idealizing constitution-making moments. He has noted that there is in some contexts a real danger of unilateral exercises of power diverting the constitutional process.[26] These are valid concerns in need of further exploration. They alert us to the fact that the essentially positive, respectful, and consensus-seeking nature of experiences such as Iceland's may have masked crucial preconditions for their success. Nevertheless, the inclusion of participatory elements in several transitional contexts such as in South Africa, Kenya, and Tunisia tempers this pessimism. These experiences show that we should not too hastily discard avenues for popular involvement in constitutional drafting and that this openness may actually aid conflict resolution.[27]

Examples of participation in constitutional change: referendums and constitutional conventions

There has been much recent interest in mechanisms for achieving constitutional change. In-depth comparative legal work has helped paint a complex picture of the varied tools, both formal and informal, which countries around the world use to

IDEA, see Markus Böckenförde, Nora Hedling, and Winluck Wahiu, *A Practical Guide to Constitution Building* (International IDEA 2011) 16–18, http://www.idea.int/publications/pgcb/.

[24] See Suteu (2015), 276; Bannon (2007), 1844.

[25] Widner (2008), 1533. See also Fernando Mendez and Jonathan Wheatley, eds., *Patterns of Constitutional Design: The Role of Citizens and Elites in Constitution-making* (Ashgate 2013), 13.

[26] David Landau, 'Constitution-Making Gone Wrong', *Alabama Law Review* 64:5 (2013) 923.

[27] For even more optimistic views on the prospects of participatory democracy in post-conflict and deeply divided societies, see Ron Levy, 'Shotgun Referendums: Popular Deliberation and Constitutional Settlement in Conflict Societies', *Melbourne University Law Review* 41 (2018) 1237; Ian O'Flynn and Ron Levy, 'Deliberative Constitutional Referendums in Deeply Divided Societies', *UBC Law Review* 53 (2020) 205.

achieve constitutional reform.[28] This interest has been matched in the field of political theory, wherein scholars have tried to incorporate democratic innovations into theories of institutional design.[29] While authors have put forth typologies of participatory constitution-making instruments,[30] distinguishing between forms as disparate as constituent assemblies, round tables, constitutional conventions, or peace negotiations, only constitutional referendums and conventions modelled on citizen assemblies will be analysed here.[31] These are by no means the sole innovative mechanisms of participatory decision-making, which also include citizen juries, deliberative polls and participatory budgeting. Indeed, one study listed over 100 different types of participation mechanisms.[32] Such mechanisms are especially promising advancements in constitutional theory and comparative constitutional design when it comes to giving voice to 'the people' in whose name the constitution will be written. Scholarship on mechanisms for the expression of constituent power has too long remained uninterested in institutions other than constituent assemblies or roundtables.[33] While these still hold promise for certain situations—indeed, the Tunisian process discussed below involved the creation of a constituent assembly—there are advantages to enlarging our constitutional imagination.

The first example of the participatory trend is the rise in recourse to constitutional referendums, understood as referendums which bring to the voting public questions of constitutional significance.[34] Scotland and Catalonia are only the

[28] See, e.g., Mads Andenas, ed., *The Creation and Amendment of Constitutional Norms* (British Institute of International and Comparative Law 2000); Dawn Oliver and Carlo Fusaro, eds., *How Constitutions Change: A Comparative Study* (Hart 2011); Xenophon Contiades, ed., *Engineering Constitutional Change: A Comparative Perspective on Europe, Canada and the USA* (Routledge 2012); Richard Albert, Xenophon Contiades, and Alkmene Fotiadou, eds., *The Foundations and Traditions of Constitutional Amendment* (Hart 2017); Xenophon Contiades and Alkmene Fotiadou, eds., *Routledge Handbook of Comparative Constitutional Change* (Routledge 2020).

[29] See, among others, Graham Smith, *Democratic Innovations: Designing Institutions for Citizen Participation* (Cambridge University Press 2009).

[30] See Andrew Arato, 'Conventions, Constituent Assemblies, and Round Tables: Models, Principles and Elements of Democratic Constitution-Making', *Global Constitutionalism* 1:1 (2012) 173; Andrew Arato, 'Forms of Constitution Making and Theories of Democracy', *Cardozo Law Review* 17:2 (1995) 191; Xenophon Contiades and Alkmene Fotiadou, eds., *Participatory Constitutional Change: The People as Amenders of the Constitution* (Routledge 2017). See also Michel Rosenfeld, *The Identity of the Constitutional Subject: Selfhood, Citizenship, Culture, and Community* (Routledge 2010), 185–209 for typologies of constitution-making more broadly.

[31] In what follows, I analyse their separate use, although arguments have been put forward that combining micro- and macro-deliberative instruments may maximize democratic input into processes of constitutional change. See Silvia Suteu and Stephen Tierney, 'Squaring the Circle? Bringing Deliberation and Participation Together in Processes of Constitution-Making' in Ron Levy, Hoi Kong, Graeme Orr, and Jeff King, eds., *The Cambridge Handbook of Deliberative Constitutionalism* (Cambridge University Press 2018) 282.

[32] Gene Rowe and Lynn J. Frewer, 'A Typology of Public Engagement Mechanisms', *Science, Technology, & Human Values* 30:2 (2005) 257.

[33] See Arato (2012); Jon Elster, 'Ways of Constitution-Making' in Axel Hadenius, ed., *Democracy's Victory and Crisis* (Cambridge University Press 1997) 123; Arato (1995); Jon Elster, 'Forces and Mechanisms in the Constitution-Making Process', *Duke Law Journal* 45 (1995) 364.

[34] Stephen Tierney, *Constitutional Referendums: The Theory and Practice of Republican Deliberation* (Oxford University Press 2012).

most recent and visible instances of what has been called Europe entering the 'age of referendums'.[35] Such cases, with Quebec's 1995 referendum as another example, bring to the voting public the issue of sovereignty of a subnational unit and its relationship to the plurinational state. As Stephen Tierney has argued, they challenge contemporary assumptions about the waning of nationalism (whether at the state or substate levels) and about the unitary character of constituent power, understood as the embodiment of a unified demos.[36]

In the cases discussed below, however, referendums appear at the end of constitutional drafting as mechanisms for garnering a popular stamp of approval on the final text. Such instances can be more or less inclusive and thus achieve a higher or more limited degree of legitimation of the new constitution. Tierney is again our guide when searching for principles of good practice to help ensure such referendums return a close approximation of popular will rather than becoming exercises in populism.[37] Among the goals he identifies as key to a democratic, deliberative, and inclusive referendum are: maximizing popular participation (including via voter registration and regulating the franchise); ensuring an environment where meaningful public reasoning can take place (including outreach to ensure the people understand the options before them); inclusion and parity of esteem (bridging societal divides so as to ensure widespread assent to the referendum's result, but also setting out balanced funding and spending rules to ensure a level playing field); and transparent rules for measuring consent (agreeing on the majority requirements for referendum success). These are the preconditions to public deliberation which arguments that unamendability is itself deliberation-inducing have failed to articulate.

Of the case studies below, only Kenya and Iceland held referendums to validate the outcomes of their participatory processes of constitutional reform. In Kenya, a number of factors likely precluded the processes in question from rising to the high threshold for democratic legitimacy identified by Tierney and argued by him to have characterized the 2014 Scottish referendum,[38] not least among them the post-conflict nature of the Kenyan context. However imperfect, the recourse to national referendums played an important symbolic role in these processes of constitutional renewal. Moreover, as will be seen, the referendum was used in conjunction with other participatory mechanisms.

[35] Stephen Tierney, 'Europe Is Entering the "Age of the Referendum", But There Is Nothing to Fear for European Democracy If Referendums Are Properly Regulated', *Democratic Audit*, 22 October 2014, http://www.democraticaudit.com/?p=8777.

[36] Stephen Tierney, '"We the Peoples": Constituent Power and Constitutionalism in Plurinational States' in Martin Loughlin and Neil Walker, eds., *The Paradox of Constitutionalism: Constituent Power and Constitutional Form* (Oxford University Press 2008) 229.

[37] Tierney (2012).

[38] Stephen Tierney, '"And the Winner is … the Referendum": Scottish Independence and the Deliberative Participation of Citizens', *I-CONnect Blog*, 26 September 2014, http://www.iconnectblog.com/2014/09/and-the-winner-is-the-referendum-scottish-independence-and-the-deliberative-participation-of-citizens/.

Another innovation in institutional design of constitution-making bodies is the citizen assembly-style constitutional convention of the type used in Iceland and discussed below. Such conventions have been deemed to stand out as 'the most extensive modern form of collective decision-making by common folk' and as representing 'the only method of citizen policymaking that combines all the following characteristics: a relatively large group of ordinary people, lengthy periods of learning and deliberation, and a collective decision with important political consequences for an entire political system'.[39] Moreover, citizen assemblies have been said to amount to 'a litmus test for the consequences of deliberation'.[40] Constitutional conventions of this type—termed by some 'people's conventions'[41]—are united by several traits, including the centrality of randomly selected (in Iceland's case, elected) citizens tasked with deciding important constitutional reforms in a deliberative setting. When it comes to experiments with deliberative mini-publics, understood as 'forums, usually organised by policy-makers, where citizens representing different viewpoints are gathered together to deliberate on a particular issue in small-N groups',[42] British Columbia, the Netherlands, and Ontario are Iceland's precursors. British Columbia in particular was a groundbreaking experiment with a citizen assembly, sparking a 'demonstration effect' in other contexts.[43] These earlier examples were all aimed at effecting electoral reform and not far-reaching constitutional change. Nevertheless, they also shared a commitment to participatory and deliberative democracy aimed at 'inject[ing] some popular legitimacy into policymaking'.[44]

Such considerations were at the heart of resorting to a people-driven constitutional convention in the Icelandic and later Irish contexts.[45] Scholars have seen the Icelandic experiment in particular as playing on 'the idea of self-governance and a perception of constitutionalism which understands civic participation as a necessity in order for a constitution to become a vibrant reflection of a political community's political imagery and self-understanding'.[46] Similar arguments have underpinned arguments for a constitutional convention as one possible

[39] Patrick Fournier, Henk van der Kolk, R. Kenneth Carty, André Blais, and Jonathan Rose, *When Citizens Decide: Lessons from Citizen Assemblies on Electoral Reform* (Oxford University Press 2011), 10.

[40] Ibid., 13.

[41] Farrell (2013).

[42] Kimmo Grönlund, André Bächtiger, and Maija Setälä, eds., *Deliberative Mini-Publics: Involving Citizens in the Democratic Process* (ECPR Press 2014), 1.

[43] Fournier et al. (2011), 28. For more on the experience of British Columbia, see Mark E. Warren and Hilary Pearse, eds., *Designing Deliberative Democracy: The British Columbia Citizens' Assembly* (Cambridge University Press 2008).

[44] Fournier et al. (2011), 18.

[45] For more on the Irish constitutional convention set up in 2012 and tasked with making recommendations for constitutional reform, see Farrell (2014); Suteu (2015).

[46] Baldvin Thor Bergsson and Paul Blokker, 'The Constitutional Experiment in Iceland' in Kálmán Pócza, ed., *Verfassunggebung in konsolidierten Demokratien: Neubeginn oder Verfall eines Systems?* (Nomos Verlag 2014) 155, 159–60.

mechanism for effectuating needed changes to the UK constitution.[47] Advocates there also believe such a convention to be the only way to achieve both comprehensive constitutional change and democratic legitimacy. The normative assumption behind such arguments has been that direct citizen engagement in constitutional revision processes can supplement or even replace traditional political institutions and thereby invigorate democracy. Involving the people in constitution-drafting, the argument goes, actualizes the hitherto mythical 'people' and turns self-government into an empirical reality.

The case of Iceland is discussed below as the only instance where such a convention has been set up and entrusted with the task of drafting a completely new constitution. That said, an important caveat is in order. There is a difference in the way citizen assembly-style constitutional conventions have been conceptualized, in contrast with their cousins, constituent assemblies in the tradition of eighteenth-century France and the United States. The latter have long been seen as being formed in the aftermath of constitutional upheaval and as fully embodying popular sovereignty; as such, they have been seen as omnipotent in discarding prior constitutions, making their own procedural rules, and deciding on the content of the basic law they would produce.[48] That is also the model on which most modern constitutional theorists have constructed their notions of constituent power. If our starting point is an understanding of constituent power as resisting any institutionalization within the constitution, a constitutional convention in the form discussed here carries no greater legitimacy than would a national opinion poll. However, as has been argued by democratic constitutionalists such as Joel Colón-Riós and throughout this book, a robust commitment to giving voice to the constituent power can coexist with designing institutions for its expression as part of the current constitutional order.[49] An example would be the constitutionalization of the constituent assembly as a mechanism of constitutional change in the Colombian constitution (see Title XIII on constitutional reform in the constitution of Colombia). Thus, conventions as analysed here can come close to approximating (but never fully embodying) constituent will; when set up properly, they certainly are no less entitled to claiming they do so than would be a constituent assembly of more traditional ilk. The truth of this claim, however, depends on careful design of such conventions and can only be confirmed retroactively.[50]

[47] For a more in-depth discussion of calls for the establishment of a constitutional convention in the UK in the aftermath of the Scottish independence referendum, see Silvia Suteu, 'The Scottish Independence Referendum and the Participatory Turn in UK Constitution-Making: The Move towards a Constitutional Convention', *Global Constitutionalism* 6:2 (2017c) 184.

[48] See Andreas Auer, 'L'institution de la constituante: traits caractéristiques, naissance et développement', Centre for Research on Direct Democracy (C2D) Working Paper Series 37/2011 (2011), http://www.c2d.ch/files/C2D_WP37.pdf.

[49] Joel Colón-Ríos, *Constituent Power and the Law* (Oxford University Press 2020).

[50] Vicki C. Jackson, '"Constituent Power" or Degrees of Legitimacy?', *Vienna Journal of International Constitutional Law* 12:3 (2018) 319.

6.2 Case studies: unamendability and participation in constitutional change

The purpose of this section is to investigate concrete cases of participatory constitution-making in an effort to ascertain the answers to three sets of questions. The first asks in what way these processes were participatory, what forms this participation took, and if known, to what extent it influenced the content of the final product. A second set of questions is whether an eternity clause was explicitly incorporated in the resulting drafts. If it was, its content and fit within the larger constitutional architecture is analysed, including provisions on constitutional review. Even where such a clause was not formally adopted as part of the constitution, the examination here extends to whether a judicial doctrine of substantive limitations on amendments was subsequently developed and if so in what context. Note is also briefly made of what if any provisions on direct democracy were incorporated into these basic laws in an effort to ascertain whether the hypothesis of openness of process triggering a more open result (in this case, the constitutional text) actually holds. Table 1 illustrates these different interplays. I will then build on these insights in order to assess the relationship between the rise of constitutional rigidity and the trend towards participatory constitutional change.

South Africa's 1996 Constitution: tiered amendment and the rejection of unamendability

South Africa's Constitution and constitution-making process have become a model for post-conflict societies drafting transformative and inclusive basic laws. Political negotiations during the country's transition took place against a backdrop of political violence and resulted in a two-stage process: an interim constitution was agreed upon in 1993, followed by the adoption of the permanent constitution

Table 1. The interplay between participatory constitutional change and unamendability

Constitution resulting from a participatory process	Unamendable provision adopted	Doctrine of implied limits on amendment developed
South Africa 1996	No	No
Kenya 2010	No	Yes
Iceland 2011	No	N/A
Tunisia 2014	Yes	N/A

in 1996.[51] The former set up a government of national unity and made provisions for a constituent assembly tasked with adopting a new constitution. It also incorporated a set of constitutional principles emerging from multi-party talks which were to guide the constitution-making process, among them commitments to a democratic system of government, equality between the genders and races, human rights, and non-discrimination.[52] The new constitution was to be certified by the Constitutional Court, which initially rejected the draft before confirming a modified version's compliance with these principles.[53] The success of this process, particularly in a post-conflict context and in a society struggling to overcome a long period of racist oppression, has been heralded as nothing short of a miracle.[54] It has also led some scholars to view multi-stage constitution-making as the ideal model of bringing about a new constitutional order.[55] The constitution's endurance in spite of continued deep divisions in society and inequality is taken as proof of this success.

The South African process was notable for a different reason as well: it strove for public participation, both in terms of outreach to the population to have it be informed of ongoing developments and in terms of substantive input on drafting. Heinz Klug places this emphasis on inclusiveness in the larger context of a 'new international moment', one 'marked ... by the increasing politicization of constitutional change accompanied by demands for greater participation', including by the re-emergence of elected constituent assemblies.[56] Thus, he sees the constitution-making effort in South Africa as a mix of polar opposites: elite-pacting constrained by limits of local and international imperatives and multi-party negotiations and public debate.[57] The latter took the form of vast publicity exercises, public meetings around the country, workshops run by the constituent assembly, a dedicated weekly television programme focusing on constitutional issues, a regular assembly

[51] For fuller accounts of the various steps in the process, see Lauren Segal and Sharon Cort, *One Law, One Nation: The Making of the South African Constitution* (Jacana Media 2011); Hassen Ebrahim, *The Soul of a Nation: Constitution-Making in South Africa* (Oxford University Press 1999).

[52] (Interim) Constitution of the Republic of South Africa, Act 200 of 1993, Schedule 4.

[53] Certification of the Constitution of the Republic of South Africa, 1996 (CCT 23/96) [1996] ZACC 26; 1996 (4) SA 744 (CC); 1996 (10) BCLR 1253 (CC), 6 September 1996 (hereafter 'First Certification Judgment') and *Certification of the Amended Text of the Constitution of the Republic of South Africa*, 1996 (CCT37/96) [1996] ZACC 24; 1997 (1) BCLR 1; 1997 (2) SA 97, 4 December 1996.

[54] Hugh Corder, 'The Republic of South Africa' in Dawn Oliver and Carlo Fusaro, eds., *How Constitutions Change: A Comparative Study* (Hart 2011) 261; Steven Friedman and Doreen Atkinson, *The Small Miracle: South Africa's Negotiated Settlement* (Ravan Press 1995).

[55] Andrew Arato, *Post Sovereign Constitution Making: Learning and Legitimacy* (Oxford University Press 2016); Andrew Arato, 'Multi-Track Constitutionalism beyond Carl Schmitt', *Constellations* 18:3 (2011) 324.

[56] Heinz Klug, 'Participating in the Design: Constitution-Making in South Africa', *Review of Constitutional Studies* 3:1 (1996) 18, 31.

[57] Ibid., 19–20. Abrak Saati mentions the sequencing in the South African process—the fact that public participation was preceded by elite negotiations—as an oft-forgotten but significant reason for the success of participation in that context. See Abrak Saati, 'Constitution-Building Bodies and the Sequencing of Public Participation: A Comparison of Seven Empirical Cases', *Journal of Politics and Law* 10:3 (2017b) 13.

publication, and a dedicated telephone service and website.[58] These efforts were that much more impressive given the high level of illiteracy in the country, which constitution-makers made real efforts to address.[59] Even before the first draft was made public, the assembly had received over two million submissions from the public.[60] Thus, if the period before the establishment of the constituent assembly was marked by mass actions, demonstrations, and petitions which gave way to various claims and frustrations,[61] the creation of the constituent assembly changed the nature of participation to 'a more individualistic, yet equally active, form of participation in the attendance of discussion-meetings and the making of formal submissions'.[62] The final draft was adopted in December 1996 and came into force in February 1997.

Perhaps surprisingly given this emphasis on popular inclusion during the drafting period, the text of the constitution does not make much room for public involvement in constitutional change. Legislative initiative is vested in the National Assembly, the National Council of Provinces, cabinet members, and the president, depending also on the nature of the law in question (Articles 55(1), 68, 73, and 85(2), respectively). The president is also empowered to call a national referendum 'in terms of an Act of Parliament' (Article 84(2)(g)), but no further language was included in the constitution to specify the conditions for this to take place. The amendment procedure, however, is comprehensively described. It includes different majority requirements depending on the object of change in the constitution and the interests affected by the amendment, as well as detailed procedural steps (Article 74). Amendment power is vested in the National Assembly, with the participation of the National Council of Provinces when provincial interests are at stake (Article 44(1)). A two-thirds majority in the National Assembly is required for the adoption of constitutional amendments, with the obligatory or optional vote of the provinces depending on the subject matter of the amendment (Article 74(2) and (3)). A higher threshold of 75 per cent is set out in Article 74(1). This covers changes to Article 1 of the constitution, which lists the values underpinning the state, the supremacy of the constitution, citizenship, the national anthem and flag, and the official languages; it similarly entrenches Article 74 itself. As one author has noted, however, there is 'significant difference' between these principles and the values which have come to underpin the 1996 document.[63]

One of the most important innovations of the 1996 Constitution was the establishment of a constitutional court with wide-ranging powers of review. The

[58] Klug (1996), 56.

[59] Thomas M. Franck and Arun K. Thiruvengadam, 'Norms of International Law Relating to the Constitution-Making Process' in Laurel E. Miller and Louis Aucoin, eds., *Framing the State in Times of Transition: Case Studies in Constitution Making* (United States Institute for Peace 2010), 9.

[60] Klug (1996), 56.

[61] Ibid., 42–3.

[62] Ibid., 57.

[63] Heinz Klug, *The Constitution of South Africa: A Contextual Analysis* (Hart 2010), 110.

South African Constitutional Court gets to decide on constitutional matters and, since an amendment in 2012, on 'any other matter of general public importance' (Article 167(3)). Its jurisdiction extends to, among others, disputes between organs of state, reviewing bills of the national parliament or provinces, and, explicitly, to deciding on the constitutionality of any amendment to the constitution (Article 167(4)). The court also certifies orders of invalidity of laws by other higher courts (Article 167(5)). Through a series of adjudicative strategies, the court has established its reputation as a guarantor of rights and democracy both in South Africa and internationally, and has gained institutional stability.[64] It has achieved this despite great early pressures. For instance, it abolished the death penalty on human rights grounds in one of its earliest judgments despite public support for capital punishment.[65] With regard to its duty to certify the permanent constitution, many had expected this to be an exercise in rubber-stamping the result of years of protracted negotiations. The court instead accepted challenges from minority political parties and other interest groups and found the initial draft not in compliance with the pre-agreed constitutional principles.[66] Despite the unpopularity of these two decisions, they were unquestionably followed.[67]

The South African situation is an interesting example of innovative popular involvement in constitution-making mixed with textual entrenchment guarded by a powerful constitutional court. The 1996 Constitution insulates core values by way of a high threshold for constitutional amendment but stops short of incorporating an eternity clause. This despite previous experience with such a mechanism, such as Section 74 of the interim 1993 Constitution. The latter sought to protect the pre-agreed constitutional principles, as well as the requirement for the permanent text to comply with these principles and for Constitutional Court certification, for the duration of the ensuing negotiations. One can go even further back in South Africa's history to find another fraught example of constitutional entrenchment, in the South Africa Act 1909.[68]

Most relevant for the present inquiry, however, is the fact that the South African Constitutional Court has on several occasions come close to embracing a doctrine of substantive limits on amendment similar to the Indian basic structure one. In a case involving questions of limits to parliament's power to delegate its authority, Sachs J found limitations on this power to be inherent in the very nature of parliament's

[64] See Theunis Roux, 'Principle and Pragmatism on the Constitutional Court of South Africa', *International Journal of Constitutional Law* 7:1 (2009) 106; Theunis Roux, *The Politics of Principle: The First South African Constitutional Court, 1995–2005* (Cambridge University Press 2013).

[65] *S v. Makwanyane and Another* (CCT3/94) [1995] ZACC 3; 1995 (6) BCLR 665; 1995 (3) SA 391; [1996] 2 CHRLD 164; 1995 (2) SACR 1, 6 June 1995.

[66] Roux (2013), 35.

[67] Ibid.

[68] The Act had sought to entrench voting rights in the Cape Province, including those of 'Coloureds', and led to a constitutional crisis in the 1950s when the Senate was packed in order to overcome the obstacles to amendment. See also Erwin N. Griswold, 'The "Coloured Vote Case" in South Africa', *Harvard Law Review* 65:8 (1952) 1361.

role in a democracy: 'There are certain fundamental features of Parliamentary democracy which are not spelt out in the Constitution but which are inherent in its very nature, design and purpose.'[69] Another case concerned an amendment to the 1993 Constitution having the effect of delaying the elections in the province of KwaZulu-Natal by three days, in which the court responded to the argument 'that amendments to the Constitution had to be made within the "spirit" of the Constitution.'[70] Mahomed DP writing for the majority opined:

> The reliance upon the 'spirit' of the Constitution is, in my view, misconceived. There is a procedure which is prescribed for amendments to the Constitution and this procedure has to be followed. If that is properly done, the amendment is constitutionally unassailable. It may perhaps be that a purported amendment to the Constitution, following the formal procedures prescribed by the Constitution, but radically and fundamentally restructuring and re-organizing the fundamental premises of the Constitution, might not qualify as an 'amendment' at all.[71]

While the court did not do so in that case, such language and positive references to Indian case law appeared to leave open the possibility of adopting a version of the basic structure doctrine.[72] In the *United Democratic Movement (UDM)* case of 2002, however, this possibility seems to have been rendered more remote.[73] The case involved two amendments and two statutes which together were meant to overcome the ban on political 'floor-crossing' in legislatures at the national, provincial, and local levels. The prohibition had been adopted and constitutionalized as corollary to South Africa's closed-list proportional representation system.[74] The ban had been contested as part of the certification procedure on the 1996 Constitution, with the Constitutional Court rejecting its incompatibility with the constitutional commitment to multi-party democracy.[75] The response of the court in *UDM* was to hold that it was

> not necessary to address problems of amendments that would undermine democracy itself, and in effect abrogate or destroy the Constitution. The electoral system adopted in our Constitution is one of many that are consistent with democracy,

[69] *Executive Council of the Western Cape Legislature and Others* v. *President of the Republic of South Africa and Others* (CCT27/95) [1995] ZACC 8; 1995 (10) BCLR 1289; 1995 (4) SA 877, 22 September 1995, para. 204.

[70] *Premier of Kwazulu-Natal and Others* v. *President of the Republic of South Africa and Others* (CCT36/95) [1995] ZACC 10; 1995 (12) BCLR 1561; 1996 (1) SA 769, 29 November 1995, para. 45.

[71] Ibid., para. 47.

[72] See Andrew Henderson, 'Cry, the Beloved Constitution: Constitutional Amendment, the Vanished Imperative of the Constitutional Principles and the Controlling Values of Section 1', *South African Law Journal* 114 (1997) 542, 553, fn. 89.

[73] *United Democratic Movement* v. *President of the Republic of South Africa and Others* (No. 2) (CCT23/02) [2002] ZACC 21; 2003 (1) SA 495; 2002 (11) BCLR 1179, 4 October 2002.

[74] For a more in-depth analysis of the case, see Roux (2013), 351–62.

[75] First Certification Judgment, paras. 180–8.

> some containing anti-defection clauses, others not; some proportional, others not. It cannot be said that proportional representation, and the anti-defection provisions which support it, are so fundamental to our constitutional order as to preclude any amendment of their provisions.[76]

A different argument brought by the applicant was that proportional representation was to be inferred in the constitutional principles of Article 1 of the 1996 Constitution and as such that its amendment should have been passed with the highest threshold as set out by Article 74(1). To this, judges retorted that the absence of any explicit mention of proportional representation in Article 1 meant it could not be inferred as a fundamental value in the same vein and reiterated that a commitment to democracy was compatible with a multitude of electoral systems.[77] It has been argued that this was an 'unusually deferential and unconvincing' judgment of the court, which misrepresented the applicant's case and was overly influenced by institutional reasons such as the reluctance of the court 'to pierce the veil of South Africa's dominant-party democracy'.[78]

In light of this fraught case law, evaluations of the South African Constitutional Court's relationship to the basic structure doctrine have differed. Some have described the precise status of the basic structure doctrine in South Africa as 'ambiguous'.[79] Others have seen the jurisprudence in this area as one of avoidance, moderation, and concern for other branches of government.[80] Most persuasive appear to be those interpretations which more clearly view the court's stance as one of rejection.[81] They view its refusal to embrace a basic structure doctrine on both formal and contextual grounds: the former have to do with the explicit entrenchment of values in the 1996 Constitution, which is interpreted as excluding others; the latter refer to unease about the doctrine's origins in land redistribution and property rights cases.[82] As noted, the reasons for this stance may be found in the court's own strategic positioning as a player within South Africa's democracy.[83] Nevertheless, a multi-tiered amendment procedure and a Constitutional Court unwilling to formally embrace a basic structure doctrine together mean that South Africa may not (yet) be included on the map of constitutional orders embracing substantive limits on amendment.

76 *United Democratic Movement*, para. 17.

77 Ibid., para. 29.

78 Roux (2013), 362.

79 Roznai (2017), 62.

80 Michael Freitas Mohallem, 'Immutable Clauses and Judicial Review in India, Brazil and South Africa: Expanding Constitutional Courts' Authority', *International Journal of Human Rights* 15:5 (2010) 765, 779 and 781.

81 Sujit Choudhry, '"He Had a Mandate": The South African Constitutional Court and the African National Congress in a Dominant Party Democracy', *Constitutional Court Review* 2:1 (2009) 1, 45.

82 Ibid., 47–8.

83 Roux (2013), 362.

Kenya's 2010 Constitution: implied limits on constitutional amendment and court-mandated participation in constitutional change

Kenya's current constitution was adopted in 2010 and represents the culmination of a protracted, hard-fought process. It began in 2002, when an act of parliament set out the legal framework for the process of constitutional review and created the Constitution of Kenya Review Commission (CKRC); the Commission was tasked with preparing a draft later to be submitted to the larger National Constitutional Conference ('the Bomas').[84] The latter comprised over 600 members, including all members of parliament and representatives from political parties, from each district, religious groups, women's groups, youth groups, the disabled, trade unions, and NGOs.[85] The Bomas draft, which included significant checks on executive power, was rejected by the government, which instead put its own modified draft ('the Wako draft') to a referendum in 2005. The people rejected the new draft. The December 2007 elections followed, infamously resulting in political violence across the country. Violence subsided once a Government of National Unity was formed brokered by Kofi Anan under the auspices of the African Union. A Commission of Experts was also set up in accordance with the Constitution of Kenya Review Act (2008). Its task was 'to identify and resolve outstanding constitutional issues',[86] with the review process having to 'provide[] the people of Kenya with an opportunity to actively, freely and meaningfully participate in generating and debating proposals to review and replace the Constitution'.[87]

The post-2008 process was characterized by a diversity of outreach efforts. These comprised general debates, dissemination campaigns including via the media and the training of civic educators, and consultations with various stakeholders, with special efforts made to overcome poverty and illiteracy.[88] The Commission collected over 26,400 memoranda and presentations from members of the public in eight months, including from political parties, religious organizations, statutory bodies, and civil society.[89] Efforts were also made to show to the public that its input had been acknowledged and possibly also incorporated into the working draft.[90] The process was not without faults, however, among which were political capture

[84] For overviews of this process, see Christina Murray, 'Political Elites and the People: Kenya's Decade Long Constitution-Making Process' in Gabriel L. Negretto, ed., *Redrafting Constitutions in Democratic Regimes: Theoretical and Comparative Perspective* (Cambridge University Press 2020) 190; Kibet A. Ngetich, 'Toward a People-Driven Constitution: Opportunities, Constraints, and Challenges of the Kenyan Example' in Said Adejumobi, ed., *Democratic Renewal in Africa: Trends and Discourses* (Palgrave Macmillan 2015) 133, 135–8; Stacey (2011), 594–8.

[85] Ngetich (2015), 136; Bannon (2007), 1860.

[86] Ngetich (2015), 137.

[87] Constitution of Kenya Review Act (2008), Article 4(6)(d)(i)).

[88] Ngetich (2015), 137–8.

[89] Ibid., 138.

[90] Ibid., 144.

of certain forms of participation and the influence of sectoral interests on delegates.[91] Despite these shortcomings, there seems to be agreement among commentators that, '[o]n balance, Kenya's highly participatory process was likely "worth" the cost'.[92] In August 2010, the new draft was approved in a national referendum.[93]

Criticism does remain, however, of the underlying understanding of the process of constitutional reform as one of amendment rather than an exercise of constituent power.[94] The issue goes back to the pre-2005 referendum period, when a cleric, Timothy Njoya, challenged the Bomas draft before the High Court of Kenya arguing that the constitutional reform process was unconstitutional because it amounted to constitutional replacement and not mere amendment, as the then constitution would have permitted.[95] Interestingly, his argument drew explicit analogies to India's basic structure doctrine. The judges agreed that the draft could only become the new constitution if given the imprimatur of an exercise of constituent power, i.e. a referendum. The alternative would have seen the parliament exercising unlimited powers and thus amounted to a subversion of the supremacy of the constitution. The Review Act was subsequently amended,[96] and the referendum was held.

It is fascinating to note how the same decision has been interpreted by scholars both as a repudiation of Kelsenian positivism and as its clearest instantiation. Richard Stacey, as a proponent of the former, has found the High Court's opinion congruent with Schmittian notions of constituent power even while accepting that the post-2008 process involved severe limits on its exercise.[97] Conversely, James Thuo Gathii has seen in the *Njoya* case the court's subscribing to a purely Kelsenian world view: it wanted to base the rule of recognition for a new constitutional order on the pre-existing norm of popular sovereignty as recognized by the constitution then in force.[98] In other words, as a positive norm rather than an inherent power of self-government. This was troubling given the colonial roots of Kenya's basic law and, Gathii argues, possibly fetishized popular authorship.[99] The divergence between the two views seems to rest on how one ultimately legitimizes participation in the Kenyan constitution-making process. If one follows the High Court's reasoning, then Gathii's apprehension at formally basing popular involvement in the previous constitution is justified. However, if one accepts the existence of a norm

[91] See Ngetich (2015), 143; Bannon (2007), 1841–58.

[92] Bannon (2007), 1844.

[93] Ngetich (2015), 139.

[94] Ibid., 145.

[95] *Njoya and Six Others* v. *Attorney General and Another* [2004] 1 KLR, 3 March 2004. See also discussion in Stacey (2011), 597ff.

[96] Constitution of Kenya Review Act 13 of 1997 (as amended), Section 26. See also discussion in Stacey (2011), 597.

[97] Stacey (2011), 606.

[98] James Thuo Gathii, 'Popular Authorship and Constitution Making: Comparing and Contrasting the DRC and Kenya', *William & Mary Law Review* 49:4 (2008) 1109, 1130.

[99] Ibid., 1131.

of popular participation inherent in the notion of constituent power irrespective of the language of Kenya's former constitution, this should alleviate such anxieties.

In terms of the resulting text, it included no eternity clause.[100] It did introduce profound changes to Kenya's system of government, including the creation of national and county governments; checks and balances between the branches of government; principles of good governance; and a bill of rights and provisions for socio-economic rights protection.[101] The 2010 Constitution vests amendment power in the parliament (Article 94(3)), but also stipulates the option of popular initiative (Article 257). A popular initiative requires at least one million signatures for 'a general suggestion or a formulated draft Bill', which is first submitted for verification by the electoral commission and, if approved, to each county assembly for consideration within three months; if a majority of county assemblies approve the bill, it is submitted to parliament and then follows the regular amendment procedure. The latter, detailed in Article 255, differentiates between amendments to certain substantive elements of the constitution and other amendments. Thus, according to Article 255(1), a mandatory referendum is required in the case of a bill amending: the supremacy of this constitution; the territory of Kenya; the sovereignty of the people; the national values and principles of governance mentioned in Article 10(2)(a) to (d); the Bill of Rights; the term of office of the president; the independence of the judiciary and the commissions and independent offices to which Chapter Fifteen applies; and the functions of parliament. Article 10(2) includes democracy and participation of the people alongside such principles as national unity, human rights, inclusiveness, and non-discrimination. These values are meant to govern the application and interpretation of the constitution, but also the adoption and interpretation of laws and public policy decisions (Article 10(1)).

The lack of further provisions on popular involvement in constitutional matters has been noted as 'paradoxical', given that 'while Kenya went through a unique and historical process that was participatory and all-inclusive by design, it resulted in a largely constitutional outcome without a participatory outlook'.[102] What has become increasingly uncontested, however, is the significance of this highly participatory process in the Kenyan context. It provided a sharp contrast with the fact that Kenyans had never had a post-independence participatory opportunity to exercise constituent power, previous constitutions having been negotiated by

[100] This has not precluded the question of whether an unconstitutional constitutional amendment doctrine should nevertheless be recognized by Kenyan courts. A petition to the High Court lodged in September 2020 sought to have that court embrace precisely such a doctrine. The petitioners argued that five chapters in the constitution were substantively protected from amendment, under either Article 256 (legislative amendment) or 257 (popular initiative). As of the time of writing, the court had not yet ruled on the petition. See Jeremiah Wakaya, 'Kenya: Petitioners Seek Court's Interpretation on Constitutional Amendment Limitations', *CapitalFM*, 16 September 2020, https://allafrica.com/stories/202009160840.html.

[101] Ngetich (2015), 139.

[102] Ibid., 145.

elites and amended without referendums.[103] Popular participation in Kenyan constitutional reform has been described as an outgrowth of a larger democratization (and decolonization) movement and as such equated with a normative and logical imperative.[104] Thus, despite failings, participation seems to have been a necessary legitimizing force for Kenyan constitutionalism.

Iceland's 2011 draft constitution: 'crowdsourcing' constitutional openness

Iceland's attempt at constitutional reform came in the aftermath of the country's financial crash in 2008 and the so-called pots and pans revolution which followed. Calls for constitutional change had existed for a long time, although they had not managed to garner enough support to gain traction.[105] Following the crash, however, a constitutional assembly was set up and tasked with recommending changes to the constitution.[106] The twenty-five-member elected assembly ('Constitutional Council') would deliberate based on a report produced by a 950-strong national forum of randomly selected citizens. The Council sought both to inform citizens of its progress, as well as to have them participate and make suggestions along the way. It set up various social media platforms for this purpose, posted meeting schedules and minutes online, and updated its website with news and a weekly newsletter. Advertisements encouraging the public to become involved in the process were also published in the media. By the end of the Council's work, the public had made some 360 proposals and more than 3,600 comments on the various available platforms.[107] The process was not without its flaws, with some delays in publicizing materials, a lack of resources and institutionalization of feedback-giving, and with the 'crowd' not truly authoring the draft constitution, despite the result being subsequently lauded as the 'world's first crowdsourced constitution'.[108]

[103] Stacey (2011), 595. For more on the role of constitutions as sites of authority in Kenya's political culture, see Mateo Taussig-Rubbo, 'From the "Stranger King" to the "Stranger Constitution": Domesticating Sovereignty in Kenya', *Constellations* 19:2 (2012) 248.

[104] Bannon (2007), 1844.

[105] For more on the build-up to the 'constitutional moment' following the 2008 financial crisis, see Anne Meuwese, 'Popular Constitution-Making: The Case of Iceland' in Denis J. Galligan and Mila Versteeg, eds., *Social and Political Foundations of Constitutions* (Cambridge University Press 2013) 469, 472–6.

[106] Act on a Constitutional Assembly No. 90/2010.

[107] Hélène Landemore, 'Inclusive Constitution-Making: The Icelandic Experiment', *Journal of Political Philosophy* 23:2 (2015) 166, 182. On assessing whether these public interventions were consequential, see Alexander Hudson, 'When Does Public Participation Make a Difference? Evidence from Iceland's Crowdsourced Constitution', *Policy & Internet* 10:2 (2018) 185.

[108] For a more in-depth critique of the Icelandic process, see Suteu (2015).

The Council unanimously adopted the bill it was to present to parliament in July 2011.[109] The main themes observed during its work had been distribution of power, transparency, and responsibility, which were reflected in its draft. With regard to the amendment procedure, the draft Article 113 stipulated that a bill passed by the parliament required approval in a national referendum, unless it had been passed with more than a five-sixths majority, in which case it became law automatically. Interesting for the aims of the present discussion was also the inclusion of several items related to democratic participation in decision-making. Thus, provisions were made for public input such as on bills returned to parliament by the president (Article 60) and on approving the removal of the president from office (Article 84). The more radical provisions were Article 65, which stipulated that 'Ten per cent of voters may demand a national referendum on laws passed by *Althingi* [the Parliament]', and Article 66, which stated that 'Two per cent of voters may present an issue to *Althingi*. Ten per cent of voters may present a bill to *Althingi*', the latter of which was then to be submitted to a referendum. The draft also mentioned the Supreme Court (Article 101), a court of final appeal which had previously been instituted by ordinary legislation only, but did not stipulate any powers of constitutional review. No formal eternity clause was included.

The picture emerging from this brief analysis is of a draft with innovative elements for direct democracy and thus in many ways quite flexible. Commentaries on the draft constitution have noted that '[o]ne of the most salient features of the Icelandic Constitutional Bill is its open approach to the direct participation of citizens, through referendums, in government business and legislation'.[110] The Venice Commission was more ambivalent in its appraisal of the draft's direct democracy elements, noting their lack of clarity and of necessary technical detail.[111] Others regretted that such a radical process of constitution-making did not result in 'a radically participatory form of democracy in constitutional terms'.[112] There have been those who were very enthusiastic, however, finding 'that Iceland's [draft] constitution comes in as one of the most inclusive in history and well-above the mean of contemporary constitutions'.[113]

In many ways, the Icelandic experience confirmed the presuppositions of participatory democrats. The constitutional convention and public consultation both appeared to have worked well and, while inclusiveness was not perfect, the end result was widely lauded as a triumph of citizen engagement in constitution-making. The process of constitutional renewal has fizzled out, however. The work of the

[109] See 'A Proposal for a New Constitution for the Republic of Iceland, Drafted by Stjórnlagaráð, a Constitutional Council, appointed by an Althingi resolution on March 24th 2011' (English translation), http://www.stjornlagarad.is/other_files/stjornlagarad/Frumvarp-enska.pdf.

[110] European Commission for Democracy Through Law (Venice Commission), *Opinion on the Draft New Constitution of Iceland*, CDL-AD(2013)010-e, 11 March 2013, para. 116.

[111] Ibid., paras. 116–30.

[112] Bergsson and Blokker (2014), 162.

[113] Elkins et al. (2012), 3.

Council was to 'form the basis of a new draft Constitution' following approval in a national (advisory) referendum in October 2012.[114] Political parties were unable to fully consider the draft before the general elections in April 2013 and a new bill introduced a novel procedure to amend the constitution by 2017, combining legislative initiative and a threshold referendum.[115] During the 2013 general elections, the constitution was not high on voters' priority lists and, although all parties agreed that constitutional change was necessary, it seems support for a completely new constitution had waned.[116] Despite this, we may still look at the Icelandic participatory process for lessons on how and when popular involvement in constitution-making may succeed, as well as draw cautionary tales about the fate of such a process.

Tunisia's 2014 Constitution: participatory constitutional change embracing unamendability

Tunisia's 2014 Constitution is one of several recently adopted basic laws incorporating a formal eternity clause (another is Nepal's Constitution, ratified in September 2015).[117] It was drafted during an intensive and prolonged process, following the ousting of President Ben Ali and the so-called Jasmine Revolution in 2011. Heavy expectations loomed over the constitutional assembly elected in October 2011, which simultaneously had to draft a new fundamental law and act as transitional legislative body.[118] Opinions differed widely on how long the assembly had to deliberate,[119] though in the end it completed its work in two years. The final constitution was adopted in January 2014 by a two-thirds majority of the assembly but was not submitted to popular referendum. It would bring to an end what some

[114] Other questions asked about national ownership over natural resources, the establishment of a national church, the election of individuals to parliament, and the weight of votes cast in different parts of the country. See 'Questions on the Ballot: Discussion and Clarification', Thjodaratkvaedi.is (website for the general referendum in Iceland), 20 October 2012, http://www.thjodaratkvaedi.is/2012/en/question_on_the_ballot.html.

[115] Bergsson and Blokker (2014), 166–7.

[116] Ibid., 169–71.

[117] On negotiations surrounding unamendability in the Tunisian constitution, see Silvia Suteu, 'Eternity Clauses in Post-Conflict and Post-Authoritarian Constitution-Making: Promise and Limits', *Global Constitutionalism* 6:1 (2017b) 63. On Nepal's experience with two participatory constitution-making processes, see Abrak Saati, 'Participatory Constitution-Building in Nepal—A Comparison of the 2008–2012 and the 2013–2015 Process', *Journal of Politics and Law* 10:4 (2017c) 29.

[118] See Loi Constituante no. 2011-6 du 16 décembre 2011, portant organisation provisoire des pouvoirs publics and Décret-loi no. 2011-14 du 23 mars 2011, portant organisation provisoire des pouvoirs publics.

[119] Eymen Gamha, 'Tunisia's Constituent Assembly: How Long Will It Last?', *Tunisia Live*, 10 October 2011, available at http://www.tunisia-live.net/2011/10/10/constituent-assembly-what-about-its-duration/.

have seen as a period of 'extraordinary politics' whereby the Tunisian people actively reconstituted society.[120]

Among other elements, the drafting process was notable due to the efforts to involve the public. Focus groups conducted before the assembly began deliberating warned that it needed to 'listen to the people' and 'should not forget what happened to [ousted President] Ben Ali; the Tunisian people revolted once and can do so again'.[121] Moreover, a February 2013 poll 'showed that 80 percent of Tunisians wanted to be able to vote on the constitution at referendum, a contingency that was available only if the Constituent Assembly failed to approve the draft by a two-thirds majority vote'.[122] The initial drafting stages were less inclusive, but transparency and public involvement were pursued following the publication of the first draft in August 2012.[123] Once a second draft was published, these efforts intensified. A two-month outreach campaign was launched that included public meetings in the assembly members' constituencies, hearings with interest groups, and television broadcasts of most assembly proceedings, and the United Nations supported a dialogue between assembly members and citizens and civil society organizations in all of Tunisia's governorates.[124] Estimates are of 6,000 citizens, 300 civil society organizations, and 320 university representatives having provided input directly to assembly members.[125] This input seems to have had a direct bearing on certain changes to the text, including on issues such as guarantees of the separation of powers and of the right to vote, state involvement in religious practice, and constitutional language on women.[126] Moreover, civil society representatives were involved in brokering compromise between political parties and thereby overcoming a majoritarian political dynamic in the assembly.[127] However, poor planning, inadequate resources, and to an extent a lack of understanding of the role public participation could play also led to failings in the process, particularly in its early months.[128]

The new constitution's substantive provisions on amendment allocate amendment initiative to the president or to one-third of the members of parliament (Article 143) and stipulate that proposed amendments must obtain a two-thirds

[120] Sami Zemni, 'The Extraordinary Politics of the Tunisian Revolution: The Process of Constitution Making', *Mediterranean Politics* 20:1 (2015) 1, 2. See also Nimer Sultany, *Law and Revolution: Legitimacy and Constitutionalism after the Arab Spring* (Oxford University Press 2017), 213, arguing that this reconstitution of the polity entailed reclaiming notions of popular sovereignty previously denied under authoritarian rule.

[121] Gluck and Brandt (2015), 7.

[122] Ibid.

[123] Ibid., 8.

[124] Ibid., 10.

[125] Ibid.

[126] Ibid., fn. 44–5.

[127] Ibid., 10.

[128] *The Constitution-Making Process in Tunisia: Final Report 2011–2014*, Carter Center, 15 April 2015, 68–71, http://www.cartercenter.org/news/publications/peace/democracy_publications/tunisia-peace-reports.html.

majority in parliament and may be submitted to a referendum by the president (Article 144). Provisions on unamendability are scattered throughout the text: in Article 1 which declares the characteristics of the Tunisian state ('Tunisia is a free, independent, sovereign state; its religion is Islam, its language Arabic, and its system is republican');[129] in Article 2 on the civil nature of the state ('Tunisia is a civil state based on citizenship, the will of the people, and the supremacy of law'); in Article 49, the constitution's general limitation clause on rights ('There can be no amendment to the Constitution that undermines the human rights and freedoms guaranteed in this Constitution'); and finally in Article 75, banning amendments that would increase the number or the length of presidential terms. In previous drafts, these had been collated in a single eternity clause, and the language used was of precluding amendments that 'may be prejudicial to' these guarantees.[130] Interestingly, one draft had included a sunset clause alongside an unamendability provision, banning amendments for a period of five years after the constitution would enter into force.[131] Entrenching the hard-fought gains of the drafting process was clearly on the minds of its architects.

Another important concern for drafters was instituting a well-functioning, independent judiciary. A Constitutional Court with extensive competencies is to be set up (Title V. Part II of the constitution). Its mandate is to include *ex ante* and *ex post* constitutional review (Article 120), reviewing presidential impeachment (Article 88) and declarations of states of emergency (Article 80), and playing the role of arbiter in disputes over executive powers (Article 101). The new court, which was to replace the previous, weaker Constitutional Council, was strongly advocated by international actors as 'a step towards establishing effective democratic institutions'[132] and as constituting now 'a standard component of a democracy'.[133] Previous drafts had narrower provisions on access to the Court, for instance, only permitting the president to call for *ex ante* review.[134] The Venice Commission, in

[129] This article mirrors Article 1 of Tunisia's previous Constitution of 1959. The latter, however, only precluded amendments of the republican form of state (Article 72), in the tradition of French constitutional law.

[130] Article 9.3 of Draft of the Constitution of the Republic of Tunisia, 14 August 2012, http://www.constitutionnet.org/files/2012.08.14_-_draft_constitution_english.pdf; Article 148 of the Draft Constitution of the Republic of Tunisia, 14 December 2012, http://www.constitutionnet.org/files/tunistian_consititution14_dec_2012-english-undp.pdf; Article 136 of the Draft Constitution of the Tunisian Republic, 22 April 2013, http://www.constitutionnet.org/files/2013_04_23_-_third_draft_english_idea_3.pdf (unofficial translations).

[131] Article 147 of the Draft Constitution of the Republic of Tunisia, 14 December 2012.

[132] *Enhancing the Rule of Law and Guaranteeing Human Rights in the Constitution: A Report on the Constitutional Reform Process in Tunisia*, International Commission of Jurists, 2013, http://icj.wpengine.netdna-cdn.com/wp-content/uploads/2013/02/TUNISIA-CONSTITUTION-REPORT-FINAL.pdf.

[133] *Constitutional Review in New Democracies*, Center for Constitutional Transitions and Democracy Reporting International, Briefing Paper No. 40, September 2013, 1, http://constitutionaltransitions.org/wp-content/uploads/2013/10/CT-DRI-BP-EN_Constitutional_Review_in_New_Democracies_2013.pdf.

[134] Article 114(1) of the Draft Constitution of the Tunisian Republic, 22 April 2013.

an opinion on the draft constitution, welcomed the creation of the new court and its extensive competences but encouraged wider access to initiating constitutional review procedures.[135] As of the time of writing, however, appointments to the Constitutional Court have yet to be made, far exceeding the deadline imposed by the constitution for the establishment of the institution (within one year of the first legislative elections, held in 2014 (Article 148)).

With regard to provisions on direct democracy, the Tunisian text is rather less embracing. The president has the power to submit to a referendum 'the draft laws related to the ratification of treaties, to freedoms and human rights, or personal status' passed by the parliament (Article 82). As already noted above, calling a referendum on constitutional amendments, also among the powers of the president, is optional. Legislative initiative belongs exclusively to members of parliament, the president, and the head of government (Article 62). Thus, and despite Article 3's declaration that 'The people are sovereign and the source of authority, which is exercised through the peoples' representatives and by referendum', the Tunisian Constitution cannot be said to have formalized any of the participatory elements of its drafting process. More will depend on ensuing constitutional practice, of course. For now and on the face of it, the text itself seems more preoccupied with preventing any erosion of the difficult compromise achieved than with instituting mechanisms of flexibility and openness.[136] The reliance on entrenchment, including via unamendable provisions, goes hand in hand with the creation of a strong constitutional court. The latter has been entrusted with a key role in consolidating Tunisian democracy but several years since the entry into force of the new basic law, the court is still not operational.

6.3 Conclusion

These forays into the practice of participatory constitution-making allow for more informed speculation about its potential relationship to mechanisms of rigidity in constitutions such as eternity clauses. One conclusion to be drawn based on these case studies is that participation and unamendability can and do coexist. Tunisia's constitution is proof of this. The various drafts made public in that process show an early concern with rendering certain principles unamendable. The fact that the previous constitution also had an eternity clause in the French tradition of protecting the republican nature of the state, a provision again found in the 2014 text, may have meant that unamendability was always going to be present in drafters'

[135] European Commission for Democracy Through Law (Venice Commission), *Opinion on the Final Draft Constitution of the Republic of Tunisia*, CDL-AD(2013)032, 17 October 2013, paras. 165–82.

[136] On the Tunisian constitution's unamendable provisions being an instance of unamendability facilitating political settlement, see Suteu (2017b).

constitutional imaginations. It appears undeniable, however, that the tense context in which Tunisian constitutional negotiations took place, with the very real possibility of the country sliding into violence, also explains this focus on taking certain principles off the table. The content of these principles is similar to other eternity clauses discussed in this book, including state characteristics, executive term limits, and a minimum standard of human rights protection.

At the other pole is Iceland's 2011 draft, which not only did not contain an eternity clause but also seems to have confirmed predictions about highly participatory processes resulting in inclusive constitutions with more numerous provisions on direct democracy. South Africa's case is different, in that while the constitution did not formally incorporate an eternity clause, the South African Constitutional Court has come close to embracing a basic structure doctrine. Judges on several occasions indicated that they saw value in arguments that certain constitutional changes should not be permitted even if procedurally irreproachable, even while in the end they did not go as far as to expound an unconstitutional constitutional doctrine outright.

Kenya's case is in many ways the most challenging for this investigation. On the one hand, its participatory process, for all its flaws, produced a draft which received the popular stamp of approval in a national referendum and which has since remained in place without significant contestation. On the other hand, the High Court intervened in the process in 2004 with a decision which purported to define the legitimacy boundaries of the constitution-making process. Was this judicial intervention justified from a democratic point of view because it triggered legislative change to formalize popular involvement in the process? Or, in line with Gathii's arguments above, should we nonetheless be sceptical of this judicial need to control and ground the process in a prior norm? Kenya's case forces us to consider the normative basis for calls for participation in constitutional drafting. It is not the same to find this basis in an emerging international norm of democratic governance (as discussed in Chapter 5 in this book) or intrinsic in the constitutional order (as examined in Part II). In the latter case, it is again different whether we link participation to an inherent openness of any constitution to manifestations of constituent power or to a positive commitment to popular sovereignty. The former is similar to Akhil Reed Amar's argument that Article V of the US Constitution does not exhaust the popular sovereign's right to amendment;[137] the latter seems to have been the Kenyan High Court's interpretation and is more formalist, giving some credence to Gathii's analysis. The court's intervention can be cautiously welcomed insofar as it encouraged increased democratic participation in the process, even while the grounds on which it did this were dubious. As we saw

[137] Akhil Reed Amar, 'Popular Sovereignty and Constitutional Amendment' in Sanford Levinson, ed., *Responding to Imperfection: The Theory and Practice of Constitutional Amendment* (Princeton University Press, 1995) 89.

above, the unamendability question has returned in Kenya, with continued appeals for Kenyan courts to embrace an unconstitutional constitutional amendment doctrine that safeguards key elements of the 2010 Constitution.

There are other conclusions emerging from these case studies, beyond those about the links between unamendability and participation. One has to do with the nature and mechanisms of participation and how widely these have differed from case to case.[138] The type and level of participation in these processes reflected, first, the state of constitution-making practice and knowledge at the time. Thus, South Africa's inclusiveness efforts were groundbreaking and farsighted even while they may seem limited when looking at a case such as Iceland's. Second, local contexts and capacities severely affected participatory possibilities: the complex diversity, economic, and literacy challenges present in South Africa, Kenya, and to an extent Tunisia were not there in the highly industrialized, homogeneous Iceland. Nevertheless, there are sufficient similarities between these cases—at the level of the aims of resorting to participation if not at that of implementation—to reassure us that these are instances of the same broad phenomenon.

What of the initial assumptions about the benefits and limitations of participatory constitution-making? First, it would appear that fears about citizen apathy and/or inability to take part in such processes may be overblown. These four cases further show that such anxieties applied distinctly to post-conflict or divided societies may be similarly exaggerated. South Africa, Kenya, and Tunisia were all contexts in which deep divisions in society and the threat of violence could have derailed the entire constitution-making endeavour, not just its participatory elements. They nevertheless produced results, raising the prospect that a well-designed and implemented process may overcome even such challenging conditions. Second, the four constitutional texts examined only partially support the hypothesis of a correlation between participatory drafting and a participation-friendly constitution. Third, the question of whether participation breeds higher levels of legitimacy and thus greater constitutional longevity cannot be definitively answered on the basis of this succinct investigation. The adoption and consolidation of the South African Constitution have been heralded as nothing short of miraculous and are likely to have triggered the turn to participation in conflict-affected constitution-building. Kenya's Constitution likewise seems to have managed to unify the country at the same time as it has transformed its system of government. Tunisia's fundamental law is thus far the only instance of a continuing democratic transition amidst the

[138] Saati also calls for more analytical sharpness in distinguishing degrees of participation in constitution-making. See Abrak Saati, 'Different Types of Participation in Constitution Making Processes: Towards a Conceptualization', *Southern African Journal of Policy and Development* 2:2 (2016) 18.

Arab Spring countries, and is being promoted as a model as a consequence.[139] Only time will tell whether and how these basic laws will survive.

The bigger question of the place of eternity clauses within the battle between constitutional rigidity and openness has also been partially answered. The cases discussed in this chapter are not sufficient to decisively declare popular participation and unamendability as incompatible. On the contrary, they seem bound to continue to coexist, in particular as part of constitutions in conflict-affected and transitional settings—the majority of new constitutions written today.[140] There is value, however, in having identified the macro-phenomena of unamendability and popular participation as occasionally occurring simultaneously and possibly being in contradiction with each other. The analysis here may thus be seen as an initial investigation into this potential clash in constitution-making, to which future research will hopefully add further insights.

Also obvious from the discussion in this chapter is the presence of transnational forces at play in these constitution-making processes.[141] In the case of the four countries discussed, these forces have taken different forms. In South Africa, as Klug and others have argued, there was from the very beginning international pressure for the political settlement to be achieved in an inclusive manner.[142] While the impact and precise contours of such changes in international political culture may be vague, other examples of international intervention in the cases discussed are unambiguous. Thus, the involvement of the Venice Commission in the Icelandic and Tunisian processes took the form of reports on constitutional drafts. In these, the Commission evaluated substantive provisions against what it considered transnational norms of constitution-making good practice. Its report on Tunisia is that much more far-reaching when remembering that the country is not a member of the Council of Europe.[143]

Such interventions—which also include the presence as advisers of foreign experts, international NGOs, and representatives of transnational professional bodies—hark back to the discussion in Chapter 5 in this book, in particular calls to pluralize and internationalize notions of constituent power to take into account the myriad forces at play in constitution-making considered legitimate today. International standards in this area are still in flux, although there is at least one set of norms with which participation is potentially in tension: the area of minority protection. Fears of majoritarian takeover of a participatory process (which are

[139] Scott Stearns, 'Kerry: Tunisia's New Constitution Is Model for Arab World', *Voice of America*, 18 February 2014, http://www.voanews.com/content/kerry-visits-tunisia-amid-democratic-transition/1853607.html.

[140] See further Chapter 2 in this book.

[141] See further Chapter 5 in this book.

[142] Klug (1996), 22–9; Franck and Thiruvengadam (2010), 7–10.

[143] While not a member, Tunisia has ratified several instruments of the Council of Europe and joined the Venice Commission in 2010.

no less present in elite-driven processes)[144] appear not to have been borne out in the four cases discussed in this chapter. They all produced basic laws with bills of rights and protections against discrimination, in all four cases with clear awareness of the country's international human rights obligations in this respect. In at least one case, Iceland's, there even seems to be evidence that the citizen-drafted constitution was more sophisticated and liberal in protecting religious freedom than competing, expert-drafted texts.[145] Beyond rights protections, however, the internationalization of constitution-making as discussed in this chapter raises the question of whether even the most highly participatory drafting processes today can escape some form of transnational certification.

[144] Ulrich K. Preuss, 'The Implications of "Eternity Clauses": The German Experience', *Israel Law Review* 44 (2011) 429, 447.

[145] Hélène Landemore, 'Inclusive Constitution Making and Religious Rights: Lessons from the Icelandic Experiment', *Journal of Politics* 79:3 (2017) 762.

7
Relinquishing Eternity
Amending Unamendability Out of the Constitution

This chapter looks at what has happened, or what might happen, when an eternity clause is called into question. The latter may amount to calls for it to be repealed entirely or else for its content to be renegotiated, whether this results in different principles being enshrined or in formalizing a judicial doctrine into a positive constitutional provision. The desire to relinquish or adjust an unamendable provision or doctrine may be triggered by the need to adapt the constitution to evolving standards and expectations in society. On a more abstract level, it may also be seen as an important inquiry into the nature of unamendable constitutions and whether eternity clauses can truly forestall change, short of revolution.

There are several ways in which to assess such reform attempts. The first might be to hold that, where there is a formal eternity clause in the constitution, efforts to remove or change it are by definition illegal, as the very point of enshrining such a provision was to take the matters it addresses off the table at least until a new constitution-making moment (and possibly forever, if taken to enshrine principles which also bind the constituent power). This illegality is sometimes rendered explicit, such as when proposals to amend the eternity clause are outright prohibited. The most extreme example of this is criminalizing any such attempts as in the case of Honduras (discussed in detail in Chapter 2). Increasingly, however, even where such explicit illegality is not present, it is taken as a logical precondition of unamendable provisions.

In the case of judicial doctrines of unamendability such as the basic structure doctrine in India, the path towards repeal is presumably easier: the court having first expounded it may at any subsequent point denounce it and simply reverse itself. However, this is an unlikely course of events, for several reasons. On the one hand, where the doctrines are built around core elements of constitutionalism itself, such as the rule of law or judicial independence, a well-meaning court will neither denounce them nor be likely to refrain from enforcing them after already having done so. On the other hand, where unconstitutional constitutional amendment doctrines extend beyond relatively uncontroversial commitments and encompass substantive values, such as secularism in both India and Turkey, they afford great power and flexibility to courts. Moreover, as in the case of India, such a doctrine may come to be seen as a distinct method of judicial interpretation rather

Eternity Clauses in Democratic Constitutionalism. Silvia Suteu, Oxford University Press. © Silvia Suteu 2021.
DOI: 10.1093/oso/9780198858867.003.0008

than a purely judicial artefact, gaining legitimacy with each uncontested application in a case. Judges are therefore not likely to part lightly with so powerful a weapon in their arsenal.

A separate view, applicable to both formal provisions and judicially created doctrines, would hold that, despite their language, unamendability cannot realistically aspire to true eternity and is instead best read as an obstacle to radical constitutional change. Thus, according to this line of reasoning, while it cannot forever forestall change, unamendability encourages deliberation around certain core values of the polity, ensures a higher threshold of agreement for their alteration, and serves to attach a stigma of illegality where reform is brought about in a non-deliberative, non-consensual manner. This is primarily applicable to eternity clauses in the form of formal constitutional provisions, around which it is perhaps easier to focus constitutional debates.

A final aspect discussed in this chapter is the difficulty of distinguishing between permitted amendments to the constitution and reforms which amount to illegitimate constitutional replacement or repeal. The problem here is not new in constitutional scholarship. It is nevertheless of special relevance in the case of eternity clauses, particularly when discussing their own amendment. Often interpretations of eternity clauses posit that their modification would constitute an alteration of the basic law of such magnitude as to effectively amount to constitutional replacement. However, the neat distinctions upon which such arguments rest—between permissible and impermissible amendments of certain values, between legislating around the limits of a right and abolishing it etc.—are not very neat after all. As such, relying on a discrete constitutional provision in order to identify transgressions of the constitutional order in its entirety may simply not be feasible. This raises doubts as to the viability of invoking unamendable constitutional amendment doctrines in the face of incremental and informal changes such as those adopted by would-be autocrats in power.

7.1 Case studies: eternity clauses in constitutional reform processes

Before proceeding to examine the substantive arguments surrounding the defensibility of eternity clause amendment, let us pause to explore whether this is a real problem. Two concrete cases of constitutional reform wherein unamendability was involved will be useful illustrations: Turkey and India. They can help us shed light on whether the problem at the heart of this chapter—discovering how eternity clauses help or hinder otherwise legitimate calls for constitutional change—actually occurs in processes of constitutional transformation and if it does, its centrality to these processes. These two jurisdictions have undergone or attempted constitutional reform processes involving both a formal unamendable provision and a judicial doctrine, respectively. Where appropriate, cases invoked in previous chapters, such as Honduras and Bosnia and Herzegovina, will also be discussed.

Turkey's constitutional review process

Let us begin with Turkey. The country was embroiled in a protracted process of constitutional revision from the summer of 2007, when the ruling Justice and Development Party (AKP) party of then Prime Minister and current President Erdoğan initiated it, until the April 2017 highly controversial referendum approving a set of amendments that increased the powers of the president and removed important checks and balances.[1] These efforts came after a tripartite constitutional crisis in 2007, which saw bitter disputes over the election of a new president, the Constitutional Court's headscarf decision, and a party ban case brought against the majority AKP itself (the latter two discussed in Chapter 1).[2] Previous attempts at elite convergence and cooperation surrounding reforms were reversed by these developments and led to 2010, when a package of amendments was passed by parliament and endorsed by a popular referendum. While that referendum passed with a comfortable majority, the Turkish constitutional reform process was still not complete. A new constitution remained one of President Erdoğan's key objectives and, in 2017, he achieved his wish to change the country's parliamentary system into a presidential one and to remove important limits on executive power.[3] However, the following discussion focuses on the reforms debated before Erdoğan introduced his eighteen amendments (designed to alter seventy-six existing constitutional provisions) in 2016. This is to highlight the role of the Turkish eternity clause within that democratic reform process.

The post-2007 changes were aimed at removing protections for military coup leaders as enshrined in the 1982 constitution, at enhancing the protection of certain economic and social rights and individual freedoms, as well as at judicial

[1] This was not the first time the Turkish Constitution underwent change, however. Some have estimated that over 70 per cent of the text has been altered since adoption, particularly in efforts towards European Union accession. See Patrick Sharfe, 'Erdoğan's Presidential Dreams, Turkey's Constitutional Politics', *Origins* 8:5 (2015) 1. Such alterations had been piecemeal, however.

[2] For overviews of the reform process, see Andrew Arato, *Post Sovereign Constitution Making: Learning and Legitimacy* (Oxford University Press 2016), 223–66; Ersin Kalaycıoğlu, '*Kulturkampf* in Turkey: The Constitutional Referendum of 12 September 2010', *South European Society and Politics* 17:1 (2012) 1; Ergun Özbudun, 'Turkey's Search for a New Constitution', *Insight Turkey* 14:1 (2012) 39; Andrew Arato, 'The Constitutional Reform Proposal of the Turkish Government: The Return of Majority Imposition', *Constellations* 17:2 (2010) 345; Ergun Özbudun, 'Turkey's Constitutional Reform and the 2010 Constitutional Referendum', *Mediterranean Politics* (2011), http://www.iemed.org/observatori-en/arees-danalisi/arxius-adjunts/anuari/med.2011/Ozbudun_en.pdf; Felix Petersen and Zeynep Yanaşmayan, eds., *The Failure of Popular Constitution Making in Turkey: Regressing Towards Autocracy* (Cambridge University Press 2019).

[3] 'Turkey's Erdogan Says New Constitution Priority after 2015 Election', *Reuters* (1 October 2014), http://www.reuters.com/article/2014/10/01/us-turkey-constitution-idUSKCN0HQ47H20141001.

reform. There were also amendments aimed at reforming the Constitutional Court, including by introducing individual complaints, stricter rules in party ban cases, new election rules for judges, and twelve-year term limits.[4] Not everyone saw the reform as an attempt to eliminate 'the authoritarian, statist, and tutelary features of the 1982 Constitution'[5] and reign in 'juristocracy'.[6] Opposition parties suspected the reforms of masking AKP's Islamist intentions and being aimed at the politicization of the judiciary and the packing of the Constitutional Court.[7]

Sources of deep divisions were also the first four, unamendable articles of the Turkish Constitution, with opinion split as to whether they could be altered by reforms.[8] Such divisions were not limited to political parties accusing the AKP of an Islamist agenda, however. A split existed within civil society groups as well, which were divided between those seeing these unamendable clauses as red lines and those for whom a new constitution by necessity had to involve the renegotiation of the constitution's very foundations.[9] These entrenched differences between various sectors of society have led some to describe Turkey as a deeply divided society and the debates surrounding the 2010 referendum as 'a long-running *kulturkampf* between the secularists and the Islamic revivalists'.[10] Rather than provide the contours of deliberation, unamendability appears to have become the site of intractable struggle over deep-seated differences.

The struggle over constitutional reform reverberated beyond Turkey's borders. The Venice Commission, through its president, initially welcomed the process of constitutional change, including of the eternity clause, which he termed '[t]he cornerstone of the tutelary system, established by the 1982 Constitution'.[11] While admitting that other European constitutions also included such clauses, he expressed concern at their broad and 'unparalleled' enforcement in Turkey.[12] The

[4] Kalaycıoğlu (2012), 5

[5] Özbudun (2011), 193.

[6] Özbudun (2012), 49.

[7] Kalaycıoğlu (2012), 6.

[8] For a breakdown of the different parties' views, see Oya Yegen, 'Debating Unamendability: Deadlock in Turkey's Constitution-Making Process' in Richard Albert and Bertil Emrah Oder, eds., *An Unamendable Constitution? Unamendability in Constitutional Democracies* (Springer 2018) 281.

[9] Ferhat Kentel, Levent Köker, Mehmet Uçum, and Özge Genç, 'Making of a New Constitution in Turkey: Monitoring Report October 2011–January 2012', TESEV Democratization Programme, July 2012, 15.

[10] Kalaycıoğlu (2012), 2.

[11] 'Democratisation Process in Turkey in the Light of a New Constitution', 'Turkey in Europe' conference, keynote speech by Mr Gianni Buquicchio, President of the Venice Commission of the Council of Europe (2 November 2010), http://www.venice.coe.int/Newsletter/NEWSLETTER_2010_04/8_Speech_TUR_EN.html. For the Venice Commission's (critical) opinion on the 2016 amendment package, see European Commission for Democracy Through Law (Venice Commission), *Turkey: Opinion on the Amendments to the Constitution Adopted by the Grand National Assembly on 21 January 2017 and to Be Submitted to a National Referendum on 16 April 2017*, CDL-AD(2017)005, 13 March 2017.

[12] Buquicchio (2010).

president of the Venice Commission expressed the institution's outright preference for the provisions to be amended out of the Turkish text:

> This may mean, for example, that it might be wise not to open the issue of the three unamendable articles of the Constitution if, in the public perception, this would be linked to a desire to abandon the secular character of the State. If interpreted in a different manner, these articles seem to be compatible with a modern liberal democracy. Our preference would certainly be not to keep these articles as they are. But if keeping these articles is necessary to get a consensus on a new Constitution within society, this may be a price worth paying.[13]

The statement not only leaves little doubt as to the Commission's stance on the direction Turkish reform needed to take, but appears to have disregarded the actual reasons for opposition to amendment of Turkey's eternity clause. As Andrew Arato had noted, it was not any one amendment package which was seen as the problem; instead, such a package was worrisome if it was the first in a two-step plan to remove obstacles to governmental constitution-making.[14] Buquicchio's statement, however, seemed more focused on how unamendable commitments had played out judicially than in the full complexity of constitutional politics surrounding them.

Turkey's case is at first glance paradoxical: here was a society that to a large extent (but for very different reasons) agreed that a new constitution was needed but that could not come together, despite years of initiatives, to bring it about. The evidence for popular support for constitutional renewal lay in the continued electoral victories of the AKP, in the successful referendum in 2010, as well as in the fact that both in 2011 and in 2015 elections, all parties had promised a new constitution. If everybody agreed that the 1982 Constitution's authoritarian and tutelary features should have been done away with, why did it prove so difficult to make this a reality? The answers are to be found in deep suspicions about the AKP's, and in particular Erdoğan's, reformist push, as well as in the different interpretations given to the unamendable provisions in the constitution. The latter, and secularism in particular, is to some coextensive with the identity of modern Turkey and to alter it would amount to constitutional revolution. To others, however, the secular commitment has become an unduly oppressive mechanism of (secular) elite control. The two positions appear irreconcilable. The slight waning of AKP's hold on power in the June 2015 elections appeared to have pried open the door for a more inclusive process of constitutional change,[15] but this optimism was thwarted by

[13] Ibid.

[14] Arato (2010), 348.

[15] Yüksel Sezgin, 'Could Erdogan Lose Turkey's Upcoming Election?', *Washington Post*, 19 May 2015, https://www.washingtonpost.com/blogs/monkey-cage/wp/2015/05/19/could-erdogan-lose-turkeys-upcoming-election/.

the gains made by the AKP in the November 2015 early elections.[16] The constitutional change process was newly energized by these gains, but the prospects for it being more broad-based went from slim to zero following the failed military coup in 2016.

Calls for renouncing India's basic structure doctrine

Turning now to India, the parameters of the discussion change. Calls for altering or doing away with the basic structure doctrine are inevitably different from a formal process of constitutional amendment. The Indian Constitution has been amended on several occasions, tallying up 104 amendments as of the time of writing. As was discussed in previous chapters of this book, several of these amendments came up for review before the Supreme Court, which evaluated their conformity with the basic structure of the constitution. Also seen in Chapter 4, the doctrine has undergone numerous adjustments and additions over the years and a serious effort in reconstruction is needed for one to have a full picture of its elements today.

As Sudhir Krishnaswamy has argued, the basic structure doctrine has never attained unanimous acceptance and its sociological legitimacy can only be evaluated at a given point in time.[17] The doctrine received harsh criticism in its early years, gained in legitimacy during and after the 1975 emergency, and again came under fire at the turn of the century.[18] The latter round of contestation came when the National Commission to Review the Working of the Constitution was established by the Bharatiya Janata Party (BJP)-led coalition government in 2000.[19] According to its terms of reference:

> The Commission shall examine, in the light of the experience of the past 50 years, as to how best the Constitution can respond to the changing needs of [an] efficient, smooth and effective system of governance and socio-economic development of modern India within the framework of Parliamentary democracy and to recommend changes, if any, that are required in the provisions of the Constitution without interfering with its basic structure or features.[20]

[16] Jon Henley et al., 'Turkey Election: Erdoğan and AKP Return to Power with Outright Majority', *The Guardian*, 2 November 2015, http://www.theguardian.com/world/2015/nov/01/turkish-election-akp-set-for-majority-with-90-of-vote-counted.

[17] Sudhir Krishnaswamy *Democracy and Constitutionalism in India* (Oxford University Press 2009), 226–7.

[18] Ibid.

[19] Cabinet Resolution No. A-45012(2)/98-ADmn.III(LA), New Delhi, 22 February 2000.

[20] Ibid., para. 2.

The Commission was to fulfil the BJP's election promises and long-standing advocacy for radical change to the constitution, which it claimed needed 'to reflect political indigenous institutions and values'.[21] Despite the Commission's terms of reference explicitly mentioning the basic structure doctrine as the red line at which constitutional change would stop, opposition parties criticized the Commission on various grounds.[22] They deplored what they saw as an attempt to bring about comprehensive constitutional change by way of an executive decision which circumvented parliament. They also disagreed with the government's intentions to replace the vote of no confidence with one of constructive confidence modelled on Germany's, which they saw as a ploy by the ruling coalition to ensure it remained in power. The government offered reassurances that the Commission's recommendations would be aimed at bringing constitutional institutions closer to their actual operation and at correcting regional and social imbalances. The opposition retorted that the bypassing of parliament on such important matters was unconstitutional. Moreover, they feared that, given the ideological commitments of the coalition parties, the rights of *dalits* and minorities would be eroded without the ability of parliament to exercise oversight. In the end, the Commission's report received little attention when it was published in 2002.[23]

The doctrine has always had its most ardent detractors among academics and legal professionals. Objections do not just focus on the doctrine's lack of textual basis or on its unpredictable application by the Supreme Court (both objections discussed at length in Chapter 4 in this book), but also on its appropriateness for India's democratic constitutional order. For example, writing two decades ago, Raju Ramachandran argued that 'the doctrine can now stand in the way of political and economic changes which may be felt necessary'[24] and that its time had passed:

> The basic structure doctrine has served a certain purpose: it has warned a fledgling democracy of the perils of brute majoritarianism. Those days are however gone. Coalitions can only bring about major changes through consensus. The doctrine must now be buried. The nation must be given an opportunity to put half a century's experience of politics and economics into the Constitution.[25]

[21] Krishnaswamy (2009), xii.

[22] See overview of these arguments in *Genesis of the Review Commission*, Commonwealth Human Rights Institute [undated], 17–19, http://www.humanrightsinitiative.org/publications/const/review_of_the_indian_constitution.pdf.

[23] National Commission to Review the Working of the Constitution, *Final Report*, 2002, http://lawmin.nic.in/ncrwc/ncrwcreport.htm.

[24] Raju Ramachandran, 'The Supreme Court and the Basic Structure Doctrine' in B. N. Kirpal, Ashok H. Desai, Gopal Subramanian, Rajeev Dhavan, and Raju Ramchandran, eds., *Supreme But Not Infallible: Essays in Honour of the Supreme Court of India* (Oxford University Press 2000) 107, 108.

[25] Ibid., 130.

This mirrors empirical findings in militant democracy literature that the force of militant measures, including judicial interventions, is higher the newer the democratic order and wanes with democratic consolidation.[26] This might support the view that, once democratic security concerns diminish, unamendability's attractiveness could follow suit.

Other advocates of radical change also argue that the 'basic dichotomy between the constitutional values and the superstructure of the political system' would need to be addressed by constitutional reform.[27] Sceptics of such calls see behind them efforts to create the 'political space for manoeuvre' to entirely reconstruct the doctrine[28] or as amounting to 'elite flirtations with an authoritarian government'.[29] Ramachandran himself has since wondered whether his initial assessment was naive in light of the unprecedented majority gained by the BJP in the 2014 elections and the possibility of its pursuit of a majoritarian Hindu state.[30]

What is striking about these debates is the degree to which they are reminiscent of arguments in favour of constitutional reform in places such as Bosnia and Herzegovina or Honduras. There too advocates of change thought the time was ripe for previously entrenched commitments, once thought to be crucial for the survival of the polity, to be set aside in the name of progress. As was seen in previous chapters, such arguments may have been more persuasive in the case of Bosnia's power-sharing system of government, which has been blamed for the political stalemate in the country. Less persuasive were arguments in Honduras claiming that its unamendable presidential term limit rule was no longer needed as Honduran democracy had consolidated.

Where India's debates are different from these, however, is in the disputed nature of the type of change needed were the basic structure doctrine to be reformed. To the extent that the creation of the doctrine is considered an amendment to the constitution by way of judicial overreach, the parliament may attempt to reverse it through legislative constitutional amendment.[31] This was precisely what Indira Gandhi's government had attempted to do following the *Kesavananda* decision: it adopted the Forty-Second Amendment,[32] in which it tried to reduce the powers

[26] Angela K. Bourne and Fernando Casal Bértoa, 'Mapping "Militant Democracy": Variation in Party Ban Practices in European Democracies (1945–2015)', *European Constitutional Law Review* 13:2 (2017) 221.

[27] Subhash C. Kashyap et al., *Need to Review the Working of the Constitution* (Shipra 2004), 6, cited in Krishnaswamy (2009), xiv.

[28] Upendra Baxi, 'Kar Seva of the Indian Constitution? Reflection on Proposals for Review of the Constitution', *Economics and Political Weekly* 35 (2000) 891, cited in Krishnaswamy (2009), xiv.

[29] Krishnaswamy (2008), xiv, referencing Manoranjan Mohanty, 'Does India Need a New Constitution?' in Surya Narayan Misra, Subhas Chandra Hazary, and Amareswar Mishra, eds., *Constitution and Constitutionalism in India* (APH Publishing Corporation 1999), 1.

[30] Raju Ramachandran, 'The Quest and the Questions', *Outlook India*, 25 August 2014, http://www.outlookindia.com/article/the-quest-and-the-questions/291655.

[31] See discussion in Krishnaswamy (2008), 183–9.

[32] Constitution (Forty-second amendment) Act, 1976, 28 August 1976.

of review of the Supreme Court and to eliminate limitations on the amendment powers of parliament. The Supreme Court struck down these parts of the amendment as unconstitutional on the grounds, among others, that parliament could not enlarge the scope of its own limited powers.[33] That judgment has attained a certain level of approval, rendered as it was during a time of national emergency when constitutionalism was perceived to be under threat. Nevertheless, the question remains as to whether and how it would be possible to alter, if not do away with, the Supreme Court's powers of substantive review of amendments. Were there to be societal agreement behind significant changes to the elements of the doctrine or even its elimination, how could they ever carry the day? I return to these questions shortly, in the context of investigating options for reversing unconstitutional constitutional amendment doctrines.

7.2 Repealing eternity clauses as by definition illegal

The obvious answer to a desire to repeal a formal eternity clause might be to attempt to amend it out of the constitution. As will be seen, however, this is not straightforward, whether because of an explicit or an implicit prohibition on such change. The alternative in such instances, it has been argued, would be to resort to a new constitution-making moment.[34] The novel constitution would then either incorporate a changed eternity clause or else renounce unamendability entirely. This option would amount to a Kelsenian iteration of eternities, in the sense that each new basic law would assume as eternal those commitments declared as such and would ignore the possibility of constitutional revolution. This section focuses on the first option—of amending an eternity clause out of the constitution—and highlights the problematic aspects, both practical and theoretical, with this approach. I will discuss the challenging notion of constitutional revolution later in this chapter.

As a matter of practice, there has been at least one instance in which an unamendable provision has itself been amended. In 1989, Article 288 of the Portuguese Constitution was altered to remove the reference to an unamendable principle of collective ownership of means of production and to repeal the constitutional clause that had originally declared the irreversibility of nationalizations undertaken between 1974 and 1976.[35] This double change, done in order to bring the Portuguese economic system in line with European Community requirements and to permit the government to embark on a privatization programme, was not

[33] *Minerva Mills* v. *Union of India*, AIR 1980 SC 1789.

[34] Yaniv Roznai, *Unconstitutional Constitutional Amendments: The Limits of Amendment Powers* (Oxford University Press 2017), 129–33.

[35] Víctor Ferreres Comella, *Constitutional Courts and Democratic Values: A European Perspective* (Yale University Press 2009), 207, fn. 39.

challenged before the Constitutional Court.[36] While this amendment has been taken as proof that Article 288 can be amended, Portuguese scholars have drawn distinctions among its components, arguing that some principles are too fundamental and close to the identity of the constitution for them to be altered.[37] Thus, the 1989 amendment seems to represent an exception rather than the rule, brought about by the unique circumstances of the fall of communism which rendered many provisions of the Portuguese Constitution irrelevant.[38] Such entrenchment of the specific economic organisation of the state had already been criticized as inappropriate for constitutionalization.[39] Article 288 is still said to require a revolution or some type of constitutional moment in order to be amended.[40]

The Portuguese example illustrates this first possibility of eliminating or altering unamendable commitments in constitutions: by amending the eternity clause itself. Whether done in a single amendment as in Portugal, or else via a procedure of double amendment (amending the eternity clause first, followed by the desired change to a previously entrenched principle), this option has been advocated as an acceptable solution to the danger of 'fossilising the constitution'.[41] However, critics have argued that such escape by double amendment is 'sleazy'[42] and amounts to a 'fraud upon the constitution'.[43] Some value may still be found in the two-step process of amendment, in the form of the deliberations it triggers around fundamental constitutional change (more on this below). Double amendment may also be appealing insofar as it remains within the realm of legality, whereas the alternative—constitutional revolution—would likely escape it.[44] More often, however, eternity clauses are taken to be implicitly entrenched even absent any language to this effect.

Before discussing arguments in favour of such implicit entrenchment, however, I wish to address the immediate obstacle to amending constitutional amendment provisions, including eternity clauses, represented by language explicitly prohibiting such a change or else rendering it very difficult. An example of a deeply entrenched amendment procedure is contained in Article 74(1) of South Africa's Constitution, which sets out a higher threshold for amending certain principles in the constitution as well as for amending the amendment formula itself. Examples

[36] Ibid.

[37] Ibid. See also Catarina Santos Botelho, 'Constitutional Narcissism on the Couch of Psychoanalysis: Constitutional Unamendability in Portugal and Spain', *European Journal of Law Reform* 21:3 (2019) 346, 364–65.

[38] Jonatas E. M. Machado, 'The Portuguese Constitution of 1976: Half-life and Decay' in Xenophon Contiades, ed., *Engineering Constitutional Change: A Comparative Perspective on Europe, Canada and the USA* (Routledge 2012) 286.

[39] Ibid.

[40] Ibid., 283.

[41] See proponents of this view discussed by Virgílio Afonso da Silva, 'A Fossilised Constitution?', *Ratio Juris* 17:4 (2004) 454.

[42] Walter F. Murphy, *Constitutional Democracy: Creating and Maintaining a Just Political Order* (Johns Hopkins University Press 2007), 504, fn. 24.

[43] Roznai (2017), 140.

[44] Santos Botelho (2019), 359.

of unamendable eternity clauses include Article 114 of the Armenian Constitution, Article X(2) of the Constitution of Bosnia and Herzegovina, Article 153 in the Constitution of the Central African Republic, and Article 175 in Niger's. The 2015 Constitution of Nepal also includes such a protection for its eternity clause in Article 274, the latter prohibiting amendments contrary to the 'self-rule of Nepal, sovereignty, territorial integrity and sovereignty vested in people'. Article 374 in the Honduran Constitution also contains a ban on amending the article itself. As was seen in Chapter 2, the case of Honduras is an extreme one, in that alongside an unamendable provision on presidential terms, the basic law also attached sanctions of loss of citizenship and political rights to the initiation or support of executive term limit extension.

In the scenario discussed in this section—one in which formal unamendability is respected as an impediment to constitutional change—such entrenchment of the eternity clause appears unassailable, short of revolution. This problem is not limited to explicit bans on modifying the eternity clause, however. Often, even in the absence of language to this effect, courts have interpreted unamendable provisions as themselves protected. For instance, Germany's *Ewigkeitsklausel* has been interpreted as itself among the principles not open to change as a matter of logic.[45] Thus, even though the 'right of resistance' (*Widerstandsrecht*) was added to Article 20(4) of the German Basic Law in 1968, it is not considered as part of the eternity clause, 'as otherwise [the clause's] modification through the elimination of some original principles would also be facilitated, which would put the effective protection provided by the provision at risk'.[46] The only alternative remains the revolutionary one mandated by Article 146 of the *Grundgesetz*, though its interaction with Article 79(3) is not straightforward. This reasoning is distinct from arguments about certain constitutional provisions having become de facto unamendable as a matter of constitutional practice, such as have been adduced in the case of the American First Amendment.[47] It rests instead on an acceptance of eternity clauses as binding and as the source of real obligations, irrespective of whether they are themselves formally entrenched.[48] As Hans Kelsen has argued, if we accept the validity of higher amendment threshold norms, we must also accept the validity of those prohibiting amendment altogether.[49] In other words, an earnest reading of formal unamendable clauses accepts their effect upon constitutional change and takes seriously their claim to eternity.

[45] Jens Woelk, 'Germany' in Dawn Oliver and Carlo Fusaro, eds., *How Constitutions Change: A Comparative Study* (Hart 2011) 143, 153.

[46] Ibid.

[47] See Richard Albert, 'The Unamendable Core of the United States Constitution' in András Koltay, ed., *Comparative Perspectives on the Fundamental Freedom of Expression* (Wolters Kluwer 2015a) 13. See more broadly Douglas Linder, 'What in the Constitution Cannot Be Amended?', *Arizona Law Review* 23 (1981) 717. See also discussion in Chapter 4 in this book.

[48] Melissa Schwartzenberg, *Democracy and Legal Change* (Cambridge University Press 2009), 9, fn. 9.

[49] Hans Kelsen, *General Theory of Law and State* (Lawbook Exchange 2009), 259.

What the analysis in this section has shown is that undoing formal unamendability is often impossible without a new constituent moment. Whether formally entrenched or not, eternity clauses have been interpreted as being themselves immune to change. As I will discuss further below, this is an understanding which also results in a static and reactionary solution to radical change and does not take into account how constitution-making occurs today.

7.3 Reversing judicial doctrines of unamendability

The previous discussion referred to instances of eternity clauses formally incorporated into the constitutional text, but what of judicial doctrines of unamendability? Two options for reversing such doctrines present themselves: either the parliament explicitly legislates against them, or somehow restricts the court's powers of constitutional review, or else the court itself backtracks. I address both scenarios in what follows, primarily referring to the Indian experience already discussed above.

The first alternative implies that parliament would have the power to push back against judicial pronouncements of a basic structure doctrine. This is precisely what was attempted during the emergency period in India, via constitutional amendments that would have rendered parliament's power of constitutional amendment limitless. In more recent years, the Supreme Court has been said to have developed remedies allowing for some institutional dialogue with parliament.[50] However, the evidence for the latter is flimsy and revolves around one example: the case of *Indra Sawhney* v. *Union of India*,[51] in which the Supreme Court found certain reservations for backward classes to be in violation of equality as a basic feature of the constitution. Amendments to the impugned legislation were later upheld and not found in breach of the basic structure doctrine.[52] This has been taken as evidence of inter-institutional dialogue and the court shying away from having the last word in basic structure matters.[53] It is scholarly commentators who have put forward such (re)interpretations of this Supreme Court case law, however. The court has not itself hinted at any renunciation of its judicial supremacy in this area, quite on the contrary.[54] In fact, scholars have even read basic structure doctrines as being even more rigid than eternity clauses insofar as they remove any possibility of reversal via formal amendment by parliament; the final word always rests with the court.[55]

[50] Krishnaswamy (2009), 219.

[51] *Indra Sawhney v. Union of India*, AIR 1993 SC 477.

[52] *M. Nagaraj v. Union of India*, AIR 2007 SC 71.

[53] Krishnaswamy (2009), 213–15.

[54] See discussion of its reading of judicial supremacy in the judicial appointments procedure as part of the basic structure doctrine in Chapter 4.

[55] Joel Colón-Ríos, 'A New Typology of Judicial Review of Legislation', *Global Constitutionalism* 3:2 (2014) 143, 153–4.

It is useful to ponder here the nature of the basic structure doctrine. Its detractors, finding no textual basis for the doctrine, have accused the Supreme Court of effectively amending the Indian constitution.[56] This, authors like Krishnaswamy have retorted, is to misunderstand the nature of the doctrine.[57] He draws analogies with the doctrine of separation of powers and the doctrine of pith and substance ('which assists the court to determine the zones of legislative and executive competence between state and union governments'), both of which similarly lack a textual basis.[58] Their force is not lessened, Krishnaswamy argues, for this absence of a textual hook in the constitution.[59] As a consequence, '[a]ny constitutionally and politically nuanced project of radical constitutional change must integrate the pronouncements of the Supreme Court on the basic structure doctrine'.[60] According to this view, then, constraints such as those identified as part of the basic structure not only cannot be amended out of the constitution, but presumably would also substantively limit future exercises of constituent power.

There are two problems with this view, however. The first is that, even accepting the basic structure doctrine as a separate doctrine of legal interpretation, it does not follow that it should take precedence over others. Absent language to the contrary, constitutional systems including India's accept a variety of cannons of interpretation without a hierarchy established among them; as such, neither canon may be regarded as the 'true' one.[61] A second problem is that we are not dealing with abstract commitments to uncontested values of constitutionalism. Instead, the basic structure protected by the doctrine has come to be identified with a concrete list of principles, declared and ordered by the Indian Supreme Court in concrete cases. As Chapter 3 in this book has argued, eternity clauses do not merely express a set of values considered essential to the polity, but also effectively impose a hierarchy of norms within the constitution. Judicial pronouncements on the basic structure doctrine may similarly be said to have altered the hierarchy of commitments in the Indian constitution, not all of which are *sine qua nons* of constitutionalism. The separation of powers and even federalism and secularism may be uncontroversial in the abstract; their narrower understandings as given by the Supreme Court, however, are not. They are instead permeated by value judgments and as such can

[56] Ibid., xv. See full discussion in Chapter 4 in this book.

[57] Ibid. Madhav Khosla agrees, viewing textual imprecision as inevitable and arguing that: 'The text itself could not unpack the distinction between legitimate and illegitimate constitutional change. This task could only be achieved by turning to two or three fixed values around which the Constitution was to be anchored' (Madhav Khosla, 'Constitutional Amendment' in Sujit Choudhry, Madhav Khosla, and Pratap Bhanu Mehta, eds., *The Oxford Handbook of the Indian Constitution* (Oxford University Press 2016) 232, 241).

[58] Krishnaswamy (2009), 169.

[59] Ibid.

[60] Ibid., xv.

[61] See Andrea Dolcetti and Giovanni Battista Ratti, 'Legal Disagreements and the Dual Nature of Law' in Wil Waluchow and Stefan Sciaraffa, eds., *Philosophical Foundations of the Nature of Law* (Oxford University Press 2013) 314.

and have led to contestation.[62] Thus, even if we agreed on a set of abstract higher values underpinning the constitutional order, a judicial doctrine for their enforcement cannot preclude reasonable disagreement over their interpretation in concrete cases.

A second alternative for doing away with judicial doctrines of unamendability would be for the issuing court itself to bring this about. It could do so either by reversing itself or by declaring, as some have called upon the Indian Supreme Court to do, that the doctrine is no longer needed to protect the constitutional order. There is no evidence of courts with basic structure doctrines having backtracked in this manner. On the contrary, as shown in Chapter 4, it appears as though the doctrine continues to migrate to new jurisdictions. Even if these courts wished to exercise judicial restraint, it is unlikely that this would come in the form of a repudiation of the basic structure doctrine. It would be odd to find a court having linked such a doctrine to the core elements of constitutionalism either denounce these or deny itself the role of their guardian. At most, judges may exercise restraint by keeping the number of basic structure decisions—and certainly of those striking down amendments—low, as the Indian Supreme Court has seemingly done.[63] However, arguing for courts to take a further step back and revert to a political question doctrine with regard to issues previously decided on basic structure grounds seems futile. Not only would it require them to give up an instrument affording them great flexibility, but it would place these courts in the unlikely situation of curtailing their own powers of review. As has been argued more generally in the context of the rise of strong forms of constitutional review, it is improbable that the direction be other than towards increased judicial power.[64] The discussion on unamendability review of purported attacks on judicial independence in Chapter 4 provides evidence for this.

A final option briefly considered is the possibility of formalizing judicial doctrines as discrete constitutional provisions. In other words, of amending the constitution itself so as to codify an eternity clause mirroring the basic structure doctrine developed by the judiciary. This would present a variety of novel problems, however, not least among them potential incongruities between constitutional text, judicial pronouncements pre- and post-adoption, and framer intent. It would also not solve the difficulties of repeal: even if the constitutional clause were open to amendment and successfully changed, courts could nonetheless continue

[62] See discussion in Chapter 4 in this book.

[63] Krishnaswamy (2009), 212–13, although the 2016 judicial appointments judgment has reignited debates as to the illegitimate expansion of the doctrine. See *Supreme Court Advocates-on-Record Association* v. *Union of India*, (2016) 4 SCC 1. For a critique of the judgment, and an assessment of its unprecedented nature both in India and comparatively, see Rehan Abeyratne, 'Upholding Judicial Supremacy in India: The NJAC Judgment in Comparative Perspective', *George Washington International Law Review* 49 (2017): 569–613; Chapter 4 in this book.

[64] Mark Tushnet, *Weak Courts, Strong Rights: Judicial Review and Social Welfare Rights in Comparative Constitutional Law* (Princeton University Press 2009), 254.

to consider the basic structure doctrine binding in its judicial formulation. The one instance where a constitutional amendment has sought to formalize a judicially created basic structure doctrine occurred in Bangladesh with the passing of the Fifteenth Amendment Act in 2011. The Bangladeshi constitution now lists 'the basic provisions of the constitution' that 'shall not be amendable by way of insertion, modification, substitution, repeal or by any other means' (Article 7B). Ambiguities have nevertheless remained about the relationship between the constitutional provision and the basic structure doctrine, as well as about how to reconcile unamendable elements in Article 7B such as dual commitments to Islam and secularism.

7.4 Eternity clauses as a tool encouraging deliberation

A separate line of argument justifying eternity clauses in democratic constitutions does so by describing them as deliberation-inducing. More specifically, proponents of this view argue that rather than ensuring eternal unamendability, eternity clauses impose an added procedural hurdle to radical constitutional change which plays the role of a trigger for a society-wide debate on the proposed reform. Authors subscribing to this view include Tom Ginsburg, Jason Mazzone, and Yaniv Roznai.

Unamendability's chilling effect

Ginsburg, writing on Honduras's 2009 constitutional crisis triggered by the ban on a presidential third term and the criminal penalties attached to calls for reform of this provision, questions the wisdom of entrenching such 'second-order proscriptions on debate or proposal of amendments'.[65] He finds these to be 'of more serious concern, as they freeze the deliberative process that the constitution may be designed to encourage'; he also argues the ban on debate 'may conflict with other parts of the constitution that are of equivalent normative authority, in particular a right to free speech'.[66]

Beyond these outright prohibitions on debating reform, however, Ginsburg sees the potential value on having certain issues taken off the table, particularly of those he considers uncontroversial such as certain state characteristics. He nonetheless calls for caution:

[65] Tom Ginsburg, 'The Puzzle of Unamendable Provisions: Debate-Impairing Rules vs. Substantive Entrenchment', I-CONnect Blog, 13 August 2009, http://www.iconnectblog.com/2009/08/the-puzzle-of-unamendable-provisions-debate-impairing-rules-vs-sub. For a more in-depth discussion of the Honduran case, see discussion in Chapter 2 of this book.

[66] Ginsburg (2009).

> On the other hand, a substantive prohibition on amendment may perhaps be best effectuated by nipping proposals in the bud. And some issues such as the religious or republican character of the state may indeed be best handled by removing them completely from ordinary or constitutional politics. But others, in particular the issue of term limits, do not seem so contentious as to prohibit all discussion of them. Term limits, after all, restrict democratic choice. Perhaps the only conclusion then, is that constitution-makers should tread cautiously when purporting to make some provisions unamendable: different issues seem differentially suited to this approach, and second-order prohibitions on debate risk the unintended consequence of premature constitutional death.[67]

Ginsburg is thus prudently not endorsing unamendability in all situations. He also acknowledges its potential chilling effect on debate, but sees this as beneficial with regard to some principles, notably fundamental state features.

Ginsburg's approach finds echoes in those of Mazzone and Roznai. In discussing the problem posed by un-entrenched eternity clauses—the possibility of the unamendable provision being itself amended out of the constitution—Mazzone finds such a two-step process to preserve some value for entrenchment. He writes:

> Entrenchment is therefore a meaningful restriction, because the first step invites deliberation on why the constitutional rule was entrenched in the first place. Repeal of an entrenched clause also might prove more difficult than other kinds of amendments just because it involves two stages: Some number of people might be opposed to taking the first step, out of special respect for entrenched provisions, even if they would quite happily take the second step if the objectionable provision were not entrenched.[68]

Roznai similarly defends eternity clauses on deliberative grounds. He views unamendability as important even if eventually removed 'because its removal would still necessitate political and public deliberations regarding the protected constitutional subject. Such deliberations grant the unamendable provision [an] important role.'[69] He goes on to argue that the additional procedural hurdle unamendability interposes in the amendment process offers increased protection, in the form of the double amendment required to do away with an eternity clause, and is a valuable democratic safeguard.[70] He also assesses positively the 'chilling effect' an

[67] Ibid.
[68] Jason Mazzone, 'Unamendments', *Iowa Law Review* 90 (2005b) 1747, 1818.
[69] Roznai (2017), 141.
[70] Ibid.

unamendable provision might have, 'leading to hesitation before repealing the so-called unamendable subject'.[71]

The tenuous link between unamendability and deliberation

These three arguments are worthy of being addressed separately. First, Mazzone and Roznai do not expand any further on how, precisely, such deliberations are to take place ideally or how they have occurred in practice. They seem to base this point on similar arguments about the deliberative character of constitutional amendment rules more generally.[72] The latter view supermajority rules or two-stage amendment processes as 'additional filters designed to approximate the will of the people as a whole and reduce the effect of factions'.[73] In this vein, Richard Albert has discussed mechanisms such as temporal limits on amendment or requirements of institutional dialogue during constitutional change as 'deliberation requirements'.[74]

All of these accounts seem to refer to deliberation in the broad sense of public discussion rather than the narrower sense of deliberative democratic theory as applied to the constitutional field.[75] Indeed, as Simone Chambers has argued, 'nearly everybody these days endorses deliberation in some form or other'[76] and these authors' use of the term is no exception. While there is value in this generic type of public debate, something is nevertheless lost in diluting the concept of deliberation to mean just any form of discussion in the public arena. Understood in this broad sense, the normatively attractive features of the concept are missing—the conditions of equality, inclusiveness, openness, and reflexivity (to name but a few) which are key to real deliberation fall out of sight. Constitutional theorists have recently begun to fine-tune these principles as they apply to various processes of constitutional change, arguing that it is possible to build on deliberative insights in order to achieve a more robust constitutional democracy.[77] Compared to these

[71] Ibid. Mark Tushnet has also defended the chilling effect of unamendability (Mark Tushnet, 'Amendment Theory and Constituent Power' in Gary J. Jacobsohn and Miguel Schor, eds., *Comparative Constitutional Theory* (Edward Elgar 2018) 317, 332).

[72] See Richard Albert, 'The Structure of Constitutional Amendment Rules', *Wake Forrest Law Review* 49 (2014a) 913. See also Mazzone (2005b), 1818.

[73] Raymond Ku, 'Consensus of the Governed: The Legitimacy of Constitutional Change', *Fordham Law Review*, 64:2 (1995) 535, 571.

[74] Albert (2014a), 952. See also Kristian Skagen Ekeli, 'How Difficult Should It Be to Amend Constitutional Laws?', *Scandinavian Studies in Law* 52 (2007) 79.

[75] For an example of the latter, see Ron Levy, 'The Law of Deliberative Democracy: Seeding the Field', *Election Law Journal* 12:4 (2013) 355.

[76] Simone Chambers, 'Deliberative Democratic Theory', *Annual Review of Political Science* 6 (2003) 307, 308.

[77] For an argument in favour of constitutional referendums as potentially deliberative exercises, see Stephen Tierney, *Constitutional Referendums: The Theory and Practice of Republican Deliberation* (Oxford University Press 2012). See also Ron Levy, 'Deliberative Constitutional Change in a Polarised

advances, deliberative arguments in favour of eternity clauses appear at best underdeveloped.[78] They also ignore the counter-current, discussed more in depth in Chapter 6 in this book, of increased popular participation and deliberation in constitutional change. As such, these arguments miss the importance of the conditions necessary for deliberation and merely assume that it will occur when unamendable provisions are called into question. As the Turkish example discussed above shows, often constitutional deliberations—including on the possible revision of eternity clauses—are path dependent and reflect past disagreement and polarization; within such processes, eternity clauses may act more as obstacles rather than facilitators of deliberative consensus-building.

To the second step of the argument put forth by Mazzone and Roznai, that the extra procedural hurdle adds a better protection of the unamendable principles in question, one can retort that this added protection is only effective so long as there is parliamentary balance of power. Hungary's 2011 adoption of a new Fundamental Law has proven that even seemingly consolidated constitutional democracies may slide into authoritarianism when an illiberal supermajority exists in parliament.[79] This is not so much a counter-argument as a qualification of the two authors' point, however. Its aim is to reiterate that there is no guarantee that a procedural hurdle in the form of an unamendable provision, or of a multi-tiered amendment process for that matter, would be able to forestall constitutional change. As was argued in Part I of this book, however, eternity clauses are most necessary, and common, in places where constitutional contestation *as well as* democratic fragility are likely to be high. As such, the success of the eternity clause as a stalling mechanism will depend directly on the strength and democratic commitments of other key players in the constitutional order, notably the legislature and the courts.

Finally and similarly to Ginsburg, Roznai concludes his defence of amendable unamendable provisions on the grounds of their inhibitive function. This is

Federation' in Paul Kildea, Andrew Lynch, and George Williams, eds., *Tomorrow's Federation: Reforming Australian Government* (Federation Press 2012) 350, arguing that deliberative values can be incorporated into constitutional change processes with a view to narrowing the latter's 'democratic gap'. See also Ron Levy, Hoi Kong, Graeme Orr, and Jeff King, eds., *The Cambridge Handbook of Deliberative Constitutionalism* (Cambridge University Press 2018); Hoi Kong, 'Deliberative Constitutional Amendments', *Queen's Law Journal* 41:1 (2015) 105; Ron Levy and Graeme Orr, eds., 'Symposium: The Law of Deliberative Democracy', *Election Law Journal* 12:4 (2013) 355.

[78] An exception is Joel Colón-Ríos, who has also found deliberative claims about unamendability unconvincing. He argues that institutional innovations in amendment rules may be possible to achieve truly deliberative processes of constitutional change. See Joel Colón-Ríos, 'Deliberative Democracy and the Doctrine of Unconstitutional Constitutional Amendments' in Ron Levy, Hoi Kong, Graeme Orr, and Jeff King, eds., *The Cambridge Handbook of Deliberative Constitutionalism* (Cambridge University Press 2018) 271.

[79] See discussion in Miklós Bánkuti, Gábor Halmai, and Kim Lane Scheppele, 'Hungary's Illiberal Turn: Disabling the Constitution', *Journal of Democracy* 23:3 (2012) 138; Gábor Halmai, 'Unconstitutional Constitutional Amendments: Constitutional Courts as Guardians of the Constitution?', *Constellations* 19:2 (2012) 182.

somewhat ironic in the context of an overall argument about the deliberation-inducing qualities of eternity clauses. The 'hesitation' Roznai speaks of may be seen as the silencing of dissent. The technique of taking certain agreements off the table in a nascent constitution has long been employed as a mechanism of constitutional design in post-conflict situations.[80] As Chapter 2 in this book has argued, in such contexts, the hard-fought political agreement is especially fragile and as such insulated from amendment, at least temporarily via a sunset clause, for the sake of preserving peace and preventing a return to conflict. An example typical of such post-conflict situations is the constitutionalization of amnesties, which occasionally also takes the form of unamendable provisions such as in the 1999 Constitution of Niger or the 2013 Fijian basic law.

Beyond the immediate aftermath of conflict, however, the chilling effect on public discussion of constitutional fundamentals begins to lose its appeal. The message sent to citizens is one of distrust in their capacity to debate the fundamentals of their own constitutional order, and more broadly of lack of confidence in the prospects of democracy. As Chapter 6 has argued, there is growing evidence that citizens can and do engage effectively in processes of constitutional change when given the opportunity and adequate resources. A model of democracy built around permanently distrusting their ability to do so is not the most robust. When we further factor in the exclusionary nature of unamendable provisions in a number of instances, discussed in Chapter 3 of this book with reference to Romania and Israel, the inhibitory nature of unamendability becomes a tool of continued oppression. In other words, how we assess the obstructionist effects of eternity clauses should take seriously the possibility that they insulate majoritarian projects against minorities seeking reasonable change.

There is another dimension to the effect of eternity clauses on public deliberation. This book has sought to show that the consequences of unamendability may be to preclude certain constitutional renegotiation entirely, or more likely to shift the locus of such debates to the judiciary. This results in constitutional courts playing the role of final arbiter in first order matters of the constitutional order, a task for which, as Samuel Issacharoff reminds us, they may be distinctly ill-suited, particularly in newer democracies.[81] In some instances, courts may even seek to referee the very possibility of legislative deliberation surrounding an unamendable provision. In a 1980 decision reviewing a proposed amendment to the 1967 Constitution, the Brazilian Federal Supreme Court dismissed the change (in that instance, to the

[80] Louis Aucoin, 'Introduction' in Laurel E. Miller and Louis Aucoin, eds., *Framing the State in Times of Transition: Case Studies in Constitution Making* (United States Institute for Peace, 2010) xviii.

[81] Samuel Issacharoff, *Fragile Democracies: Contested Power in the Era of Constitutional Courts* (Cambridge University Press 2011), 971.

republican character of the state) and argued that such a proposal could not even be subject to deliberations in Congress.[82] In that case, the court reasoned that:

> In such cases, the unconstitutionality pertains to the very progress of the legislative proceedings, and this is because the Constitution does not want—in view of the seriousness of these deliberations, if consummated—that it even reaches deliberation, forbidding it explicitly. The unconstitutionality, if occurring, already exists before the bill or the proposal turns into law or constitutional amendment, because the very proceeding already frontally disrespects the Constitution.[83]

Writing on the danger which judicialization represents for deliberation, Ron Levy gives the example of the Australian High Court 'second-guess[ing] parliamentary choices about democratic design trade-offs' in a case involving publicly funded broadcast airtime for political parties.[84] He sees the court in that case as engaging in rights reasoning and as such imposing a coercive outcome upon the dispute.[85] Although that case involved the interpretation of electoral law, cases involving eternity clauses may prove an even more contentious site for court involvement. Indeed, the examples drawn from German, Indian, Turkish, Bosnian, and other jurisprudence in previous chapters are all instances in which reasonable disagreement about essentially political questions was resolved by apex courts. What Levy identified as the threat of codification of rules of good practice in the arena of political law—'a self-perpetuating process of juridification and judicialisation' which only 'shift[s] the site of political contestation to the courts'[86]—is thus even more likely to occur in the case of substantive limits on constitutional change which by their very nature require courts to engage in value adjudication. The process of rationalizing values said to be at the core of deliberative democracy[87] is thus funnelled to constitutional courts to the exclusion of competing deliberative arenas such as parliament or the wider public sphere.

The link between eternity clauses and juridification is by now inescapable. Juridification in the field of constitutional change is thus aided by unamendability and goes beyond the expansion of legal norms and the increased pursuit of conflict-solving with reference to law.[88] It should also be understood

[82] Juliano Zaiden Benvindo, 'Brazil in the Context of the Debate over Unamendability in Latin America' in Richard Albert and Bertil Emrah Oder, eds., *An Unamendable Constitution? Unamendability in Constitutional Democracies* (Springer 2018) 345, 358.
[83] Cited in ibid.
[84] Ron Levy, 'Deliberative Democracy and Political Law: The Coercion Problem' (2014), 14, https://papers.ssrn.com/sol3/papers.cfm?abstract_id=2490239.
[85] Ibid.
[86] Ibid., 16.
[87] Ibid., 5.
[88] Lars Blichner and Anders Molander, 'What Is Juridification?', Centre for European Studies, University of Oslo Working Paper No. 14, March 2005, 5.

as augmented judicial power or, as Alec Stone Sweet views it, 'as shorthand for . . . the construction of judicial power'.[89] The notion that courts, and constitutional courts in particular, may themselves act as deliberative forums has recently been advanced by scholars,[90] but it does not alleviate the concerns expressed here. Rather, these concerns should be viewed in the larger context of critiques of the rise of 'strong' versions of constitutional review and of an impoverishment of constitutional experiences correlated to the advent of legal constitutionalism. This has been observed for decades in the case of American constitutional discourse,[91] and is now also noted in other countries having followed the legal constitutionalist model.[92]

7.5 The difficult distinction between amendment and repeal

Let us now also unpack some of the assumptions underlying arguments about constitutional renewal. One such assumption is that we may neatly, or at least convincingly, be able to distinguish between constitutional amendment and other instances of constitutional change, including via judicial interpretation. An ability to distinguish between 'ordinary' and 'fundamental' change, and between substantively permissible and impermissible variants of the latter, underpins all unconstitutional constitutional amendment doctrines. A second set of assumptions believes in a revolutionary solution to impulses for radical change. Those who argue for revolution as the only alternative to an eternity clause appear to trust that this is both a feasible and a desirable, or at least not an inordinately costly, way out of unamendability. These assumptions must be tested and placed in the context of processes of constitutional change as they occur today.

[89] Alec Stone Sweet, 'Judicialization and the Construction of Governance' in Martin Shapiro and Alec Stone Sweet, *On Law, Politics and Judicialization* (Oxford University Press 2002), 71.

[90] Conrado Hübner Mendes, *Constitutional Courts and Deliberative Democracy* (Oxford University Press 2013).

[91] See, *inter alia*, Gerhard Casper, 'Guardians of the Constitution', *Southern California Law Review* 53 (1980) 773, 783, stating:

> The American legal culture's fixation on the courts, which accords the Supreme Court its monopoly on constitutional interpretation, results in a rather sharp division between constitutional law and politics which, unlike the Federal Republic, makes the bounds of constitutional law coextensive with the limits of justiciability. This American approach exacts a cost: the impoverishment of general constitutional thinking and scholarship.

[92] See Paul Blokker's comments on Central and Eastern Europe in Paul Blokker, *New Democracies in Crisis? A Comparative Constitutional Study of the Czech Republic, Hungary, Poland, Romania and Slovakia* (Routledge 2014), 5.

Defining amendment

We encounter a first hurdle when attempting to conceptualize constitutional amendment as distinct from other mechanisms through which constitutional meaning is changed.[93] Sanford Levinson has defined amendments as 'a legal invention not derivable from the existing body of accepted legal materials'.[94] He has identified five levels at which constitutional change may come about: interpretation of what was already immanent within the existing body of legal materials; interpretation of the powers allowed governmental actors by the constitution; amendment; revision; and, finally, revolution.[95] Laurence Tribe has spoken of the 'quasi-revolutionary process of constitutional amendment'[96] and has explained the resort to it as resulting from a breakdown in the evolutionary possibilities of ordinary lawmaking:

> The resort to amendment—to constitutional *politics* as opposed to constitutional *law*—should be taken as a sign that the legal system has come to a point of discontinuity, a point at which something less radical than revolution but distinctly more radical than ordinary legal evolution is called for.[97]

American constitutional discourse has also highlighted the differences in tone when speaking of amendments. The positive language associated with amendments may be exemplified by Walter Murphy's understanding of them as a correction of the system, 'operat[ing] within the theoretical parameters of the existing Constitution'.[98] Furthermore, the desirability of some degree of constitutional flexibility is broadly accepted. A variety of reasons exist for wanting to be able to fine-tune the political system, and in turn the constitution.[99] However, amendment

[93] On this point, see Sanford Levinson, 'How Many Times Has the United States Constitution Been Amended? (A) < 26; (B) 26; (c) 27; (D) > 27: Accounting for Constitutional Change' in Sanford Levinson, ed., *Responding to Imperfection: The Theory and Practice of Constitutional Amendment* (Princeton University Press 1995) 13, 20–1; Walter F. Murphy, 'Merlin's Memory: The Past and Future Imperfect of the Once and Future Polity' in Sanford Levinson, ed., *Responding to Imperfection: The Theory and Practice of Constitutional Amendment* (Princeton University Press 1995) 163, 177; Michel Rosenfeld, *The Identity of the Constitutional Subject: Selfhood, Citizenship, Culture, and Community* (Routledge 2009), 30–1.

[94] Levinson (1995), 16.

[95] Ibid., 20–1.

[96] Laurence H. Tribe, 'A *Constitution* We Are Amending: In Defense of a Restrained Judicial Role', *Harvard Law Review* 97:2 (1983) 433, 436, fn. 13.

[97] Ibid., 436.

[98] Walter F. Murphy, 'Constitutions, Constitutionalism, and Democracy' in Douglas Greenberg, Stanley N. Katz, and Melanie Beth Oliviero, eds., *Constitutionalism and Democracy: Transitions in the Contemporary World* (Oxford University Press 1993) 3, 14.

[99] A good round-up of these possible reasons comes from Donald Lutz in his study of empirical patterns of amendment across constitutions:

> Every political system needs to be modified over time as a result of some combination of (1) changes in the environment within which the political system operates (including economics, technology, foreign relations, demographics, etc.); (2) changes in the value system

triggers are not only varied, they relate differently to the original text: they may be correlated to a lacuna in the constitutional text, to a discontinuity akin to a small revolution, or indeed, to an invention that, if adopted via unorthodox means, may be illegitimate.[100] Levinson, describing how amendment is often pitted against interpretation as a means of innovation, also brings to the fore a particularly negative connotation of the use of the term:

> In many contexts ... to describe something as an amendment is at the same time to proclaim its status as a legal invention and its putative illegitimacy as an interpretation of the preexisting legal materials.[101]

Designating something as interpretation would seem to carry with it 'a certain legal dignity', provided it had been exercised in good faith.[102] Scholars such as Bruce Ackerman have not only come to defend such amendment mechanisms lacking in textual basis, but even to praise them as a means of 'using old institutions in new ways' and of thereby gaining in popular legitimacy.[103]

We thus speak of different things, and with vastly different tones, when discussing amendments. One of the thorniest distinctions in this discourse as it applies to eternity clause remains the one between permissible and impermissible interpretation of unamendable principles and whether it amounts to a de facto amendment. Given the open-ended nature of unamendable provisions, these boundaries are hazy, and possibly even blurrier in cases of evolving judicial doctrines of unamendability. As discussed previously in this book with regard to theories of multitrack constitution-making, discriminating between an ordinary versus a fundamental change may not always be straightforward. It may also not always allow for constitutional contestation. Indeed, the recent erosion of rule of law and democratic institutions in Poland has been that much more effective the more insidiously it has come about. The Polish government, enjoying a broad majority in the legislature, has been able to dismantle judicial independence and other

> distributed across the population; (3) unwanted or unexpected institutional effects; and (4) the cumulative effect of the decisions made by the legislature, executive and judiciary.

Donald S. Lutz, 'Toward a Theory of Constitutional Amendment', *American Political Science Review* 88:2 (1994) 355, 357.

[100] See also Rosalind Dixon, 'Constitutional Amendment Rules: A Comparative Perspective' in Tom Ginsburg and Rosalind Dixon, eds., *Comparative Constitutional Law* (Edward Elgar 2011) 96.

[101] Levinson (1995), 17.

[102] Ibid.

[103] Bruce Ackerman, 'Higher Lawmaking' in Sanford Levinson, ed., *Responding to Imperfection: The Theory and Practice of Constitutional Amendment* (Princeton University Press 1995) 63, 69. A more in-depth look at Ackerman's theory of the evolution of American constitutional law via non-Article V amendments is found in Bruce Ackerman, *We the People, Vol. 1, Foundations* (Belknap Press of the Harvard University Press 1991) and *We the People, Vol. 2, Transformations* (Belknap Press of the Harvard University Press 1998).

checks and balances not via fundamental constitutional upheaval, but via ordinary legislation—what Wojciech Sadurski has termed 'statutory amendments'.[104] Thus, tinkering with judicial appointments, term limits, retirement ages, etc. was enough to paralyse and then capture the Polish Constitutional Tribunal; restricting rights to assembly and privacy further weakened the tools of democratic opposition to the government's agenda. Even had the Polish Constitution included a lengthy eternity clause, or else had the Polish Constitutional Tribunal developed a robust unamendable constitutional amendment doctrine, it is doubtful they would have been able to stop such a multidirectional attack.

A further question, of whether courts themselves may be bound by eternity clauses, had initially received only academic interest.[105] However, there has been a rise in clashes between constitutional courts and supranational institutions as in Bosnia's *Sejdić and Finci* and Germany's *Lisbon* cases and as part of the defence of particularistic values such as the Hungarian Constitutional Court developing its own constitutional identity review to uphold government policy.[106] Implied in all these cases has been the question of who has ultimate authority to decide on first order issues for the polity, including as they are protected via eternity clauses. They are indicators of where unamendability jurisprudence is heading: towards ever-stronger judicial doctrines rooted in identitarian claims that may well oppose supranational forces or universal values.

Amendment and judicial interpretation

Even outside the area of constitutional review of unamendability, however, identifying the proper judicial role in amendment processes is not easy. Opinions vary concerning the proper role of courts in steering, or even taking over, constitutional change. Some authors are staunch defenders of such a proactive role,[107] while others urge more caution.[108] Even terminology differs, ranging from calling certain judicial interventions 'virtual amendments' to the constitutional text[109] to naming them outright 'usurpation'.[110] There is no denying, however, that courts have played a significant role in constitutional change even in the absence of eternity clauses. As was discussed in Chapter 6 in this book, the Constitutional

[104] Wojciech Sadurski, *Poland's Constitutional Breakdown* (Oxford University Press 2020), vi.

[105] Maartje de Visser, *Constitutional Review in Europe: A Comparative Analysis* (Hart 2014), 371, fn. 204.

[106] These decisions are discussed in more depth in Chapters 3 and 5 of this book.

[107] Walter Dellinger, 'The Legitimacy of Constitutional Change: Rethinking the Amendment Process', *Harvard Law Review* 97:2 (1983) 386.

[108] Tribe (1983). See also Elai Katz, 'On Amending Constitutions: The Legality and Legitimacy of Constitutional Entrenchment', *Columbia Journal of Law and Social Problems* 29 (1996) 251, 290.

[109] Peter Suber, *The Paradox of Self-Amendment: A Study of Law, Logic, Omnipotence, and Change* (Peter Lang 1990), 199. See full discussion at 197–206 and also 415.

[110] Abraham Lincoln cited in Levinson (1995), 69.

Court of South Africa was called upon to certify the entirety of the country's 1996 Constitution. Perhaps the epitome of 'activist' courts, the Israeli Supreme Court is another example here. Its expansion of its own powers of review and declaration of a 'constitutional revolution' resulted in Israel's shift

> from a state with no written constitution or judicial review to a state that, at least from the Court's perspective, transitioned almost overnight to a full-blown constitutional regime complete with judicial review, with very little public engagement, deliberation, or intention.[111]

A more recent example may be found in Canada, which has been said to have one of the most difficult constitutions to formally amend.[112] Despite or likely because of this rigidity, the Canadian Constitution has undergone a remaking at the hands of its Supreme Court judges which in the course of one year has included the constitutionalization of provisions in the Supreme Court Act and the introduction of a right to strike and of a right to assisted suicide.[113] How one views these judicial innovations depends on one's notions of the proper judicial role in a democracy and perhaps on how desirable one finds these changes. It can hardly be denied, however, that such interventions have radically altered their respective constitutional landscapes, to no less a degree than a formal amendment would have done.

Informal amendment

A corresponding discussion, beyond one over the benefits and vices of judicial review generally, touches upon the desirability of adhering to a more formalist amendment procedure. After all, one answer to the occurrence of constitutional amendment by judicial review could be to add to or clarify the constitutional text. The virtues of formalism would be that it gives fair notice to constitutional actors and signals to them 'the point at which a particular exercise in constitutional law-making comes to an end'.[114] It thus breeds legal certainty.[115] As was seen in Chapter 1, this positivist preference was a central concern for drafters of the German Basic Law's amendment procedure.[116]

[111] Adam Shinar, 'Accidental Constitutionalism: The Political Foundations and Implications of Constitution-Making in Israel' in Denis J. Galligan and Mila Versteeg, eds., *Social and Political Foundations of Constitutions* (Cambridge University Press 2013) 207, 217.

[112] Richard Albert, *Constitutional Amendments: Making, Breaking, and Changing Constitutions* (Oxford University Press 2019), 105.

[113] Grégoire Webber, 'The Remaking of the Constitution of Canada', *UK Constitutional Law Blog*, 1 July 2015, https://ukconstitutionallaw.org/2015/07/01/gregoire-webber-the-remaking-of-the-constitution-of-canada/.

[114] Ackerman (1995), 84.

[115] Dellinger (1983), 389.

[116] See also discussion in Woelk (2011), 145–7.

Detractors of such formalism, however, point to the risk of '*presuming* the existence of a mobilized and considered popular judgment by pointing to some readily observable institutional criteria'.[117] In other words, assuming higher legitimacy for formal amendments may be erroneous in cases where the process of constitutional change can be manipulated. Elai Katz gives the hypothetical example of a vast majority of the French population seeking to change the republican nature of their state, entrenched as immutable in the 1958 French Constitution, finding that such an act, though illegal, 'may be legitimate in terms of popular consent or popular sovereignty'.[118] Even as a matter of political opportunity, it is not clear that a deliberate circumvention of formal amendment rules (what Richard Albert has called 'amendment by stealth')[119] can easily be prevented. Moreover, other types of informal amendment may affect eternity clauses, such as constitutional desuetude—the falling into disuse of certain constitutional provisions[120]—or amendment by custom. The latter may take the form of an unwritten constitutional convention contradicting one of the unamendable principles. Given that such conventions are not binding and their scope is not fixed, it is unlikely that they would be interpreted to contravene a textual provision; they are also open to be overridden by a formal amendment.

Amendment and revolution

The last strand of arguments advocates revolution as a possible way around eternity clauses. Proponents of this view argue that there is nothing which ultimately prevents a new constitution-making moment from occurring during which unamendability is to be renounced or its contours modified.[121] Such views echo theories of a right to amendment as corollary to the concept of popular sovereignty such as Akhil Reed Amar's, who views this right as 'preexisting' and founded on 'first principles' of the American Constitution.[122] While Amar sees this right as one capable of being employed *within* the current constitutional order, the view

[117] Ackerman (1995), 85. He goes on to call this the 'theory of institutional resistance': 'Institutional resistance . . . will frustrate the cynical manipulation of the idea of a higher law by coalitions of narrow pressure groups' (ibid.).

[118] Katz (1996), 265.

[119] Richard Albert, 'Constitutional Amendment by Stealth', *McGill Law Journal* 60:4 (2015b) 673.

[120] For an argument that Article V in the US Constitution has fallen into desuetude, see Albert (2019), 100.

[121] See, inter alia, Roznai (2017), 130; Woelk (2011), 154; Markus Kotzur, 'Constitutional Amendments and Constitutional Changes in Germany' in Xenophon Contiades, ed., *Engineering Constitutional Change: A Comparative Perspective on Europe, Canada and the USA* (Routledge 2012) 125, 131.

[122] Akhil Reed Amar, 'Popular Sovereignty and Constitutional Amendment' in Levinson (1995), 97. Richard Albert has accused eternity clauses of 'deny[ing] citizens the democratic right to amend their own constitution'. Richard Albert, 'Constitutional Handcuffs', *Arizona State Law Journal* 42:3 (2010) 663, 667.

discussed here refers to a distinct legal rupture as the means of changing eternity clauses.

Revolutions domesticated

Such ruptures may take the form of revolution in the classical sense of the French and American revolutions of the eighteenth century, completely breaking the legal order. However, even these may not conform neatly to notions of revolutions as violent events. As Frederick Schauer has argued, debates on the initial illegality of the US Constitution are 'premised on the mistaken supposition that the only options are violent and armed revolution, on the one hand, and legal continuity, on the other'.[123] He has explained instead that, 'if we accept the fact that there can be peaceful, orderly, and deliberative revolutions', then we could also view the American framers as not acting lawlessly in the violent sense of that term.[124] In post-war constitution-making in the twentieth century, talk of constitutional ruptures has been further domesticated. Article 146 in the German Basic Law has already been mentioned as one instance where drafters envisioned a constitutional transition, justified by the initial provisional character of the text. Furthermore, the post-1989 constitution-making episodes in Central and Eastern Europe were considered cases of partial transformation of the legal order, or instances of 'rebuilding the ship at sea'.[125] These examples would seem to fit Stephen Gardbaum's category of 'revolutionary constitutionalism', understood as 'essentially connected to constitutional*ist* revolution: a revolution aimed at bringing about the radical transformation of the political order from the old non-constitutionalist regime to a new constitutionalist one'.[126] In his view, therefore, the new political order we are witnessing is characterized by its ultimate constitutionalist objective.

More recently as well, polities in transition have employed mechanisms to reach constitutional settlements without interruptions in legality.[127] Nimer Sultany's examination of constitutional change processes after the Arab Spring reveals a further insight: several of these regimes responded to crisis by adopting orderly constitutional amendments without actually transforming the

[123] Frederick Schauer, 'Amending the Presuppositions of a Constitution' in Sanford Levinson, ed., *Responding to Imperfection: The Theory and Practice of Constitutional Amendment* (Princeton University Press 1995) 145, 154, fn. 20. On the illegality of the American founding, see Bruce Ackerman, 'Storrs Lecture: Discovering the Constitution', *Yale Law Journal* 93 (1984) 1013, 1058 and Richard S. Kay, 'The Illegality of the Constitution', *Constitutional Commentary* 4 (1987) 57.

[124] Schauer (1995), 154, fn. 20.

[125] Jon Elster, Claus Offe, and Ulrich K. Preuss, *Institutional Design in Post-Communist Societies: Rebuilding the Ship at Sea* (Cambridge University Press 1998). See also Ulrich K. Preuss, *Constitutional Revolution: The Link between Constitutionalism and Progress* (Humanities Press International 1995).

[126] Stephen Gardbaum, 'Revolutionary Constitutionalism', *International Journal of Constitutional Law* 15:1 (2017) 173, 178.

[127] Arato (2016).

polity at all.[128] Thus, the regimes in question (Morocco, Jordan, Bahrain, Oman, and Algeria) 'primarily sought to appease the protesters and stabilize the regime through limited change that would reproduce the status quo and reaffirm its legitimacy'.[129] These constitutional amendments were thus meant to provide a veneer of reform while retrenching the status quo, a move nowhere more obvious than in denying any popular participation in the process and in rendering the hereditary monarchy unamendable.[130]

To these we may add the transnational embeddedness of processes of constitution-making discussed in Chapter 5. We found there that the scope of acceptable constitutional reform and drafting is also constrained by transnational norms, diffused in both soft form, such as through international constitutional assistance, and in harder forms, such as through conditionality and even linking state recognition to certain value commitments.

If revolution has or may become domesticated, has our core concern been solved? Are eternity clauses democratically acceptable in conjunction with this domestication of radical change? In fact, democratic problems linger despite the most optimistic scenarios in which an eternity clause is to be replaced in a new act of constitution-writing. First, not all constitutions are open to their own replacement. Perhaps an extreme example of this is the Mexican Constitution, which in Article 136 expressly declares the continuation in force of the constitution in spite of rebellion. Ginsburg et al. have traced similar provisions in a number of constitutions and explain the presence of such constitutional 'rights to resist' according to context: either as retroactive legitimizing tools for coup makers or as insurance against democratic backsliding.[131] One can easily imagine such clauses being invoked in order to delegitimize calls for the change of an unamendable provision.

Unamendable limits on revolution

A second potential obstacle to unamendability repeal via a novel episode of constitution-making is the advent of judicial pronouncements that constituent power is itself substantively limited. As was discussed in Chapter 3, Germany's Constitutional Court has hinted that the limitations of Article 79(3) of the German Basic Law would also apply to a new exercise of constituent power.[132] Similar questions were raised within the Turkish constitutional renewal debates, asking whether the reform commission could even consider altering

[128] Nimer Sultany, *Law and Revolution: Legitimacy and Constitutionalism after the Arab Spring* (Oxford University Press 2017), 263.

[129] Ibid.

[130] Ibid., 263–4.

[131] Tom Ginsburg, Daniel Lansberg-Rodriguez, and Mila Versteeg, 'When to Overthrow Your Government: The Right to Resist in the World's Constitutions', *UCLA Law Review* 60 (2013) 1184.

[132] See also Woelk (2011), 154.

the constitution's unamendable provisions.[133] Gardbaum sees those constitutions embodying both a transformative spirit and, simultaneously, resistance to change in the form of an eternity clause as the highpoint of the paradoxical tension between transformation and continuity in revolutionary constitutionalism. He also discards the ' "formal" solution of distinguishing between the constitution as a tool for, rather than an object of, radical change' as merely 'restat[ing] the tension'.[134] Moreover, the internationalized environment in which constitutional drafting takes place today places very real constraints on the constituent power.[135] Such interpretations only leave room for constitutional change within ever-narrower boundaries, possibly including those of present-day eternity clauses. Thus, one increasingly finds little reassurance in calls to seek revolution if dissatisfied with a given unamendable provision.

The high cost of revolution

Similar frustration may come from a third problem with advocating constitutional replacement: the potentially high costs of this solution. Particularly in conflict-affected and deeply divided societies, the political settlement embodied in the constitution may be fragile and the prospect of its unravelling, including by way of too much constitutional flexibility, is feared by drafters. Indeed, that is one of the main justifications for adopting eternity clauses in such settings. Nevertheless, these societies also evolve and their constitutional arrangements need to be able to evolve with them. The same is true for changing conditions in other societies as well, potentially resulting in clashes over unamendable principles. The case of Turkey discussed at the start of this chapter amply illustrated this. One cannot estimate in the abstract whether the costs of opening up a particular constitution for renegotiation would be preferable to carrying on with a dysfunctional or unpopular unamendable commitment. There is some evidence that in cases where deferral—understood as the deliberate choice of drafters to postpone deciding on certain contentious elements of constitutional design—was not embraced in the constitutional design, the likelihood of 'significant pressures for whole-scale constitutional replacement, as opposed to amendment' increases.[136] Applying this to eternity clauses which were adopted in a non-inclusive, contested manner, one can expect them to be the source of

[133] Oya Yegen, 'Debating the Amendment-Making Rule: The Rigidity vs. Flexibility Debate in the Turkish Constitution-Making Process' in Felix Petersen and Zeynep Yanaşmayan, eds., *The Failure of Popular Constitution Making in Turkey: Regressing Towards Autocracy* (Cambridge University Press 2019) 249, 268.

[134] Gardbaum (2017), 183.

[135] See more in Chapter 5 in this book.

[136] Rosalind Dixon and Tom Ginsburg, 'Deciding Not to Decide: Deferral in Constitutional Design', *Journal of International Constitutional Law* 9: 3–4 (2011) 636, 645. On incrementalism as a useful mechanism of constitutional design in divided societies, see Hanna Lerner, *Making Constitutions in Deeply Divided Societies* (Cambridge University Press 2011). See also the discussion in Chapter 2 of this book.

continued instability in the polity and potentially to trigger early constitutional replacement.

7.6 Conclusion

This chapter has shown that the repeal of eternity clauses poses challenging theoretical problems as well as difficulties of implementation. While the trend still appears to be toward the expansion rather than the repeal of unconstitutional constitutional amendment doctrines, the concrete cases of attempted reform of unamendable provisions discussed here have shown that such attempts are likely to become battlegrounds once they do occur. Any pushback against unamendability seems to only be possible via revolution. However, this chapter has also shown how complicated and costly such revolution may be, particularly in societies where the constitution reflects delicate post-conflict balances. Chapter 6 discussed the adoption of eternity clauses in several participatory constitution-making processes. These last two chapters of the book thus reinforce each other by presenting the promises and limits of process-based solutions to the democratic shortcomings of eternity clauses.

Conclusion

In the face of an explosion of interest in the study of constitutional amendments, eternity clauses and doctrines of unconstitutional constitutional amendments, this book is an invitation to reorient our attention to the most troubling aspect of unamendability: its deep tension with democratic constitutionalism. By taking this democratic challenge seriously, studies of eternity clauses come face to face with the darker reality of constitutional unamendability: its origin in often fraught, deeply contested, externally conditioned processes of constitution-making; its use as vehicle for judicial self-empowerment to block democratically legitimate constitutional change; and its irrelevance when democratic backsliding actually occurs. Less an attempt to argue for or against the adoption of unamendable provisions or the judicial development of doctrines of implicit unamendability in the abstract, this book is a warning about the very real dangers of constitutional eternity in practice.

The book also seeks to correct certain persisting assumptions in the now rich body of literature on constitutional unamendability. Viewing eternity clauses as repositories of constituent will or else of constitutional expressiveness oversimplifies both the processes behind their adoption and how they are operationalized by courts. Eternity clauses are not the product of a unified, pacified constituent will that has manifested during a nationally owned process of constitution-building, committed itself to liberal constitutionalism, imposed material limits on the amendment power, and then exited the constitutional order, not to re-emerge until revolutionary times. Democratic accounts of constitution-making tell a different story. This constituent will is actually a composite, a chorus of divergent voices that may or may not find expression in the constitutional text. The latter also lies and distorts in an effort of constitutional myth creation. Participatory constitution-making does not definitively show an affinity between popular input in constitution-building and either constitutional flexibility or rigidity. Furthermore, because of the global diffusion of constitutional values and the transnational embeddedness of both constitution-making processes and constitutional adjudication, unamendability has moved beyond the state. Our constitutional imaginary has not followed suit with these insights, however. This book is an attempt to move us in this direction.

Unamendability remains deeply problematic at the level of adjudication as well. Its tension with democratic constitutionalism goes much beyond the familiar democratic anxieties about strong forms of judicial review and judicial expansion

Eternity Clauses in Democratic Constitutionalism. Silvia Suteu, Oxford University Press. © Silvia Suteu 2021.
DOI: 10.1093/oso/9780198858867.003.0009

of constitutional review powers. Instead, and precisely because of its claims to protect constitutional identities, basic structures, or substantive cores, the lure of unamendability is undeniable for the constitutional judge, and the scope of the power it entrusts them with great. Despite tenuous theoretical and doctrinal foundations, adopting unconstitutional constitutional amendment doctrines is resisted less and less, even in jurisdictions that previously subscribed to notions of parliamentary sovereignty with which the idea of substantive limits on constitutional amendment would have been inconsistent. In several European jurisdictions, eternity clauses have been read into doctrines of constitutional identity review meant to limit European integration. Whether read as a form of turf protection (national constitutional courts seeking to reclaim the final word from their supranational counterparts) or as a new type of judicial review of international treaties (developed in light of the democratic deficit at the supranational level), unamendability has come to be associated with sovereigntist claims it was never envisioned as encompassing. Moreover, constitutional courts such as Germany's have at least entertained the possibility of expanding the reach of eternity clauses to new processes of constitution-making. In other words, expanding the reach of unamendability—understood as supra-constitutional limits, grounded in some version of natural law—to constitutional revolution. To some, the revolution *will* be juridified.

Even if we adopt a thinner, procedural understanding of democratic constitutionalism, the material review of constitutional amendments is revealed to be problematic. On the one hand, the book shows that neither formal nor implicit unamendability is necessarily interpreted as limited to fundamentals of constitutional democracy. In some instances, eternity clauses and the constitutional basic structure are interpreted as demanding specific legislative choices, with possible anti-democratic results. This can take the form of exclusionary constitution-building being reinforced via unamendability, such as in Romania and Israel. It can also take the form of electoral competition being skewed in the name of protecting secularism or territorial integrity, as was seen in Turkey. Finally, we have seen courts from India to Slovakia developing unconstitutional constitutional amendment doctrines, of which judicial independence and the separation of powers are central elements, in order to guard judicial supremacy in judicial appointments processes and prevent any restriction of constitutional review powers.

We have now also accumulated sufficient comparative practice to understand just how limited the promise of unamendability is when faced with democratic backsliding. Expectations that unconstitutional constitutional amendment doctrines will enter the arsenal of militant democracy and help protect against abusive constitutional amendments have been dashed by the reality of democratic erosion in a number of constitutional contexts. As the instructive example of Hungary has shown, not only was a previously strong constitutional court unable to intervene to prevent constitutional replacement and abusive amendments. It itself became an early victim of the slide into autocracy and, once captured, developed its own anti-democratic notion of constitutional identity. The abundance of cases of term limit removal and amendment in Latin American and African countries is further evidence of how difficult it is to rely on a single constitutional mechanism to protect democratic constitutionalism. Even the unamendable term limit in Honduras, extreme in criminalizing even proposing an amendment regarding the presidential term and doubly entrenched, was no match for political forces bent on constitutional reform. The judicial endorsement of the change in the name of international human rights was another irony in the story of the troubled adjudication of unamendable provisions.

The committed democratic constitutionalist will thus not ignore the threat of closing off democratic avenues for constitutional change in the name of judicially enforced constitutional rigidity. She will be mindful of the possibility that constitutional entrenchment and its enforcement shield elitist, contested, and exclusionary values. She will also be aware of the danger of unamendability backfiring, such as when it is used by courts to undermine democratic constitutional commitments and to reduce rather than enhance democratic pluralism. Anxious to prevent democratic erosion realised through legal means, she will look to the entirety of the constitutional architecture in her search for a democratic constitutional response to backsliding. This will likely include: rules safeguarding electoral competition; constitutional protection for the rights of the political opposition; consensus-building tools in legislative and constitutional reform processes; rules protecting a democratic media; a variety of democratic accountability mechanisms beyond courts such as ombudspersons, electoral commissions, electoral management bodies and more. The task will not be easy. However, the answer to democratic backsliding will need to match the complexity of attacks on democratic constitutionalism. Even if we were to ignore its underlying democratic deficiencies, unamendability would be neither panacea nor likely effective in such scenarios.

This book is, in many ways, a triple call: for more critical engagement with the deep-seated and, I have argued, foundational democratic problems raised by constitutional unamendability; for more modesty in our expectations of its ability to act as effective democratic safeguard precisely in the fragile contexts for which it has been designed; and for grounding our study of eternity clauses and unconstitutional constitutional amendment doctrines in constitutional politics alongside constitutional doctrine. The latter correlates to a broader realization in comparative constitutional law that unamendability exceeds the bounds of legal constitutionalism and may even reveal its shortcomings:

> If courts rely on some implicit limits to constitutional change or even establish so-called 'basic structure' to which the power of constitutional amendment must yield, the confrontation will not stay just between political majority and minority, but will extend further between political branches and the judiciary … Legal constitutionalism, the reliance on constitutions as legal texts in codifying and

> entrenching transformative politics, has seen broken promises. Constitutional politics escapes from legal confinement. As the stories of unconstitutional constitutional amendments across jurisdictions illustrate, the more constitutional laws are to confine constitutional politics, the more constitutional laws become part of constitutional politics.[1]

Our object of study thus straddles the space between law and politics. It may well be that eternity clauses and unamendability more generally are part of a broader story of the inadequacy of strongly legalistic versions of liberal constitutionalism to respond to contemporary constitutional challenges. A deeper soul-searching is then in order, one that includes a re-evaluation of our substantive democratic commitments as well.[2]

[1] Wen-Chen Chang, 'Back into the Political? Rethinking Judicial, Legal, and Transnational Constitutionalism', *International Journal of Constitutional Law* 17:2 (2019) 453, 459.

[2] For one such argument, see Silvia Suteu, 'The Populist Turn in Central and Eastern Europe: Is Deliberative Democracy Part of the Solution?', *European Constitutional Law Review* 15:3 (2019) 488.

Bibliography

Abeyratne, R., 'Upholding Judicial Supremacy in India: The *NJAC* Judgment in Comparative Perspective', *George Washington International Law Review* 49 (2017) 569.

Ackerman, B., 'Storrs Lecture: Discovering the Constitution', *Yale Law Journal* 93 (1984) 1013.

Ackerman, B., 'Higher Lawmaking' in S. Levinson (ed.), *Responding to Imperfection: The Theory and Practice of Constitutional Amendment* (Princeton University Press 1995) 63.

Ackerman, B., *We the People, Vol. 1, Foundations* (The Belknap Press of the Harvard University Press 1991).

Ackerman, B., *We the People, Vol. 2, Transformations* (The Belknap Press of the Harvard University Press 1998).

Agne, H., 'Democratic Founding: We the People and the Others', *International Journal of Constitutional Law* 10:3 (2012) 836.

Ahmed, D.I., and T. Ginsburg, 'Constitutional Islamization and Human Rights: The Surprising Origin and Spread of Islamic Supremacy in Constitutions', *Virginia Journal of International Law* 54:3 (2013) 615.

Al-Ali, Z., 'Constitutional Drafting and External Influence' in T. Ginsburg and R. Dixon (eds.), *Comparative Constitutional Law* (Edward Elgar 2011) 77.

Albert, R., 'Constitutional Handcuffs', *Arizona State Law Journal* 42:3 (2010) 663.

Albert, R., 'The Expressive Function of Constitutional Amendment Rules', *McGill Law Journal* 59:2 (2013) 225.

Albert, A., 'The Structure of Constitutional Amendment Rules', *Wake Forrest Law Review* 49 (2014) 913.

Albert, R., 'The Unamendable Core of the United States Constitution' in A. Koltay (ed.), *Comparative Perspectives on the Fundamental Freedom of Expression* (Wolters Kluwer 2015a) 13.

Albert, R., 'Constitutional Amendment by Stealth', *McGill Law Journal* 60:4 (2015b) 673.

Albert, R., 'Four Unconstitutional Constitutions and Their Democratic Foundations' 50:2 (2017) *Cornell International Law Journal* 169.

Albert, R., *Constitutional Amendments: Making, Breaking, and Changing Constitutions* (Oxford University Press 2019).

Albert, R., X. Contiades, and A. Fotiadou (eds.), *The Foundations and Traditions of Constitutional Amendment* (Hart 2017).

Albert, R., X. Contiades, and A. Fotiadou (eds.), *The Law and Legitimacy of Imposed Constitutions* (Routledge 2019).

Albert, R., M. Nakashidze, and T. Olcay, 'The Formalist Resistance to Unconstitutional Constitutional Amendments', *Hastings Law Journal* 70 (2019) 639.

Albert, R. and B.E. Oder (eds.), *An Unamendable Constitution? Unamendability in Constitutional Democracies* (Springer 2018).

Albert, R. and Y. Roznai, 'Religion, Secularism and Limitations on Constitutional Amendment' in R. Ahdar (ed.), *Research Handbook on Law and Religion* (Edward Elgar 2018) 154.

Alviar García, H., 'Neoliberalism as a Form of Authoritarian Constitutionalism' in H. Alviar García and G. Frankenberg (eds.), *Authoritarian Constitutionalism: Comparative Analysis and Critique* (Edward Elgar 2019) 37.

Amar, A.K., 'Popular Sovereignty and Constitutional Amendment', in S. Levinson (ed.), *Responding to Imperfection: The Theory and Practice of Constitutional Amendment* (Princeton University Press 1995) 89.

Amara, T., 'Tunisia Parliament Approves Controversial Amnesty for Ben Ali-era Corruption', *Reuters*, 13 September 2017, https://uk.reuters.com/article/uk-tunisia-politics-corruption/tunisia-parliament-approves-controversial-amnesty-for-ben-ali-era-corruption-idUKKCN1BO2KY.

Andenas, M. (ed.), *The Creation and Amendment of Constitutional Norms* (British Institute of International and Comparative Law 2000).

Arantes, R.B. and C.G. Couto, 'Constitutionalizing Policy: The Brazilian Constitution of 1988 and Its Impact on Governance' in D. Nolte and A. Schilling-Vacaflor (eds.), *New Constitutionalism in Latin America: Promises and Practices* (Routledge 2012) 203.

Arato, A., 'Forms of Constitution Making and Theories of Democracy', *Cardozo Law Review* 17:2 (1995) 191.

Arato, A., *Constitution Making Under Occupation: The Politics of Imposed Revolution in Iraq* (Columbia University Press 2009).

Arato, A., 'The Constitutional Reform Proposal of the Turkish Government: The Return of Majority Imposition', *Constellations* 17:2 (2010) 345.

Arato, A., 'Multi-Track Constitutionalism Beyond Carl Schmitt', *Constellations* 18:3 (2011) 324.

Arato, A., 'Conventions, Constituent Assemblies, and Round Tables: Models, Principles and Elements of Democratic Constitution-Making', *Global Constitutionalism* 1:1 (2012) 173.

Arato, A., *Post Sovereign Constitution Making: Learning and Legitimacy* (Oxford University Press 2016).

Arato, A., *The Adventures of the Constituent Power: Beyond Revolutions?* (Cambridge University Press 2017).

Arold Lorenz, N.-L., X. Groussot, and G.T. Petursson, *The European Human Rights Culture—A Paradox of Human Rights Protection in Europe?* (Martinus Nijhoff 2013).

Asociația Pro Democrația, *Raportul Forumului Constituțional 2013*, Bucharest, 2013, http://www.apd.ro/wp-content/uploads/2015/03/Raport-Forumul-Constitutional-2015.pdf.

Aucoin, L., 'Introduction' in L.E. Miller and L. Aucoin (eds.), *Framing the State in Times of Transition: Case Studies in Constitution Making* (United States Institute for Peace 2010) xiii.

Auer, A., 'L'institution de la constituante: traits caractéristiques, naissance et développement', Centre for Research on Direct Democracy (C2D) Working Paper Series 37/2011 (2011), http://www.c2d.ch/files/C2D_WP37.pdf.

Austin, G., *The Indian Constitution: Cornerstone of a Nation* (Clarendon Press 1966).

Austin, G., *Working a Democratic Constitution: A History of the Indian Experience* (Oxford University Press 2003).

Badri, B. and A.M. Tripp (eds.), *Women's Activism in Africa: Struggles for Rights and Representation* (Zed Books 2017).

Bakk, M., 'Comunitate politică, comunitate națională, comunități teritoriale' in G. Andreescu, M. Bakk, L. Bojin, and V. Constantin (eds.), *Comentarii la Constituția României* (Editura Polirom 2010) 87.

Bannon, A.L., 'Designing a Constitution-Drafting Process: Lessons from Kenya', *Yale Law Journal* 116:8 (2007) 1824.

Baquero Cruz, J., 'The Legacy of the Maastricht-Urteil and the Pluralist Movement', *European Law Journal* 14:4 (2008) 389.

Barak, A., 'Unconstitutional Constitutional Amendments', *Israel Law Review* 44 (2011) 321.

Baranger, D., 'The Language of Eternity: Judicial Review of the Amending Power in France (or the Absence Thereof)', *Israeli Law Review* 44 (2011) 389.

Bašić, A., '*Sejdić-Finci* and *Pilav*: Bosnia-Hercegovina's Road to Implementation of the European Convention on Human Rights', *Transnational Law & Contemporary Problems* 29:1 (2019) 569.

Baxi, U., 'The Constitutional Quicksands of Kesavananda Bharati and the Twenty-Fifth Amendment', Supreme Court Cases 1 (1974) 45.

Baxi, U., 'Some Reflections on the Nature of Constituent Power' in R. Dhavan and A. Jacob (eds.), *Indian Constitution: Trends and Issues* (N.M. Tripathi 1978) 122.

Baxi, U., 'Taking Suffering Seriously: Social Action Litigation in the Supreme Court of India', *Third World Legal Studies* 4 (1985) 107.

Baxi, U., 'Kar Seva of the Indian Constitution? Reflection on Proposals for Review of the Constitution', *Economics and Political Weekly* 35 (2000) 891.

Bánkuti, M., G. Halmai, and K.L. Scheppele, 'Hungary's Illiberal Turn: Disabling the Constitution', *Journal of Democracy* 23:3 (2012) 138.

Begić, Z., and Z. Delić, 'Constituency of Peoples in the Constitutional System of Bosnia and Herzegovina: Chasing fair Solutions', *International Journal of Constitutional Law* 11:2 (2013) 447.

Bell, C., *Peace Agreements and Human Rights* (Oxford University Press 2003).

Bell, C., *On the Law of Peace: Peace Agreements and the Lex Pacificatoria* (Oxford University Press 2008).

Bell, C., 'What We Talk about When We Talk about International Constitutional Law', *Transnational Legal Theory* 5:2 (2014) 241.

Bell, C., 'Litigating Constituent Power: The International Law of Constitutional Transitions', Paper presented at the International Society of Public Law (ICON-S) Annual Conference, New York, 1–3 July 2015 (on file with author).

Bell, C., 'Introduction: Bargaining on Constitutions—Political Settlements and Constitutional State-Building', *Global Constitutionalism* 6:1 (2017) 13.

Benvindo, J.Z., 'Brazil in the Context of the Debate over Unamendability in Latin America' in R. Albert and B.E. Oder (eds.), *An Unamendable Constitution? Unamendability in Constitutional Democracies* (Springer 2018) 345.

Bergsson, B.T. and P. Blokker, 'The Constitutional Experiment in Iceland' in K. Pócza (ed.), *Verfassunggebung in konsolidierten Demokratien: Neubeginn oder Verfall eines Systems?* (Nomos 2014) 155.

Bernal, C., 'Unconstitutional Constitutional Amendments in the Case Study of Colombia: An Analysis of the Justification and Meaning of the Constitutional Replacement Doctrine', *International Journal of Constitutional Law* 11:2 (2013) 339.

Besbes, S., 'L'ONU—Acteur du Processus Transitionnel en Tunisie', Tunisia in Transition: German–Arab Research Group, Working Paper (December 2013).

Bieber, F., 'The Balkans: The Promotion of Power-Sharing by Outsiders' in J. McEvoy and B. O'Leary (eds.), *Power-Sharing in Deeply Divided Places* (University of Pennsylvania Press 2013) 312.

Bin Haris, I., 'Judicial Review of Constitutional Amendments—Pakistan's Uneasy Subscription to the Basic Structure Doctrine', UK Constitutional Law Blog, 24 September 2015, https://ukconstitutionallaw.org/2015/09/24/isaam-bin-haris-judicial-review-of-constitutional-amendments-pakistans-uneasy-subscription-to-the-basic-structure-doctrine/.

Blichner, L., and A. Molander, 'What Is Juridification?', Centre for European Studies, University of Oslo Working Paper No. 14, March 2005.

Blokker, P., 'Dilemmas of Democratisation from Legal Revolutions to Democratic Constitutionalism?', *Nordic Journal of International Law* 81 (2012) 437.

Blokker, P., *New Democracies in Crisis? A Comparative Constitutional Study of the Czech Republic, Hungary, Poland, Romania and Slovakia* (Routledge 2014).

Blokker, P., 'Constitutional Reform in Europe and Recourse to the People' in X. Contiades and A. Fotiadou (eds.), *Participatory Constitutional Change: The People as Amenders of the Constitution* (Routledge 2017) 31.

Bogaards, M., M. Basedau, and C. Hartmann, 'Ethnic Party Bans in Africa: An Introduction', *Democratization* 17:4 (2010) 599.

Bose, S., 'The Bosnian State a Decade after Dayton', *International Peacekeeping* 12:3 (2005) 322.

Bourne, A.K., 'Democratization and the Illegalization of Political Parties in Europe', *Democratization* 19:6 (2012) 1065.

Bourne, A.K. and F. Casal Bértoa, 'Mapping "Militant Democracy": Variation in Party Ban Practices in European Democracies (1945–2015)', *European Constitutional Law Review* 13:2 (2017) 221.

Böcü, G. and F. Petersen, 'Debating State Organization Principles in the Constitutional Conciliation Commission' in F. Petersen and Z. Yanaşmayan (eds.), *The Failure of Popular Constitution Making in Turkey: Regressing Towards Autocracy* (Cambridge University Press 2019) 150.

Böckenförde, E.-W., *Constitutional and Political Theory: Selected Writings* (Mirjam Künkler and Tine Stein eds., Oxford University Press 2017).

Böckenförde, M., N. Hedling, and W. Wahiu, *A Practical Guide to Constitution Building*, International IDEA (2011), http://www.idea.int/publications/pgcb/.

Böckenförde, M., and D. Sabsay, 'Supranational Organizations and Their Impact on National Constitutions' in M. Tushnet, T. Fleiner, and C. Saunders (eds.), *Routledge Handbook of Constitutional Law* (Routledge 2013) 469.

Brandt, M., J. Cottrell, Y. Ghai, and A. Regan, *Constitution-making Making and Reform: Options for the Process*, Interpeace (November 2011), http://www.constitutionmakingforpeace.org/sites/default/files/Constitution-Making-Handbook.pdf.

Breslin, B., *From Words to Worlds: Exploring Constitutional Functionality* (Johns Hopkins University Press 2008).

Breuer, M. (ed.), *Principled Resistance to ECtHR Judgments—A New Paradigm?* (Springer 2019).

Brodeala, E. and S. Suteu, 'Women and Constitution-Making in Post-Communist Romania' in R. Rubio-Marin and H. Irving (eds.), *Women as Constitution-Makers: Case Studies from the New Democratic Era* (Cambridge University Press 2019) 81.

Brumberg, D. and M. Ben Salem, 'Tunisia's Endless Transition?', *Journal of Democracy* 31:2 (2020) 110.

Bříza, P., 'The Czech Constitutional Court on the Lisbon Treaty', *European Constitutional Law Review* 5:1 (2009) 143.

Bui, N.S., *Constitutional Change in the Contemporary Socialist World* (Oxford University Press 2020).

Bui, N.S., 'Politics of Unconstitutional Constitutional Amendments: The Case of Thailand' in H. Glaser (ed.), *Identity and Change–The Basic Structure in Asian Constitutional Orders The Law and Politics of Unconstitutional Constitutional Amendments in Asia* (Nomos forthcoming).

Buquicchio, G., 'Democratisation Process in Turkey in the Light of a New Constitution', 'Turkey in Europe' Conference keynote speech by Mr Gianni Buquicchio, President of the

Venice Commission of the Council of Europe, 2 November 2010, http://www.venice.coe.int/Newsletter/NEWSLETTER_2010_04/8_Speech_TUR_EN.html.

Cajas-Sarria, M.A., 'Judicial Review of Constitutional Amendments in Colombia: A Political and Historical Perspective, 1955–2016', *The Theory and Practice of Legislation* 5:3 (2017) 245.

Calliess, C., 'Constitutional Identity in Germany: One for Three or Three in One?' in C. Calliess and G. van der Schyff (eds.), *Constitutional Identity in a Europe of Multilevel Constitutionalism* (Cambridge University Press 2019) 153.

Carey, J.M., 'Does It Matter How a Constitution Is Created?' in Z. Barany and R.G. Moser (eds.), *Is Democracy Exportable?* (Cambridge University Press 2009) 155.

The Carter Center, *The Constitution-Making Process in Tunisia: Final Report 2011–2014*, 15 April 2015, http://www.cartercenter.org/news/publications/peace/democracy_publications/tunisia-peace-reports.html.

Casañas Adam, E., 'The Constitutional Court of Spain: From System Balancer to Polarizing Centralist' in N. Aroney and J. Kinkaid (eds.), *Courts in Federal Countries: Federalists or Unitarists?* (University of Toronto Press 2017) 367.

Caserta, S., 'Regional Integration through Law and International Courts—the Interplay between *De Jure* and *De Facto* Supranationality in Central America and the Caribbean', *Leiden Journal of International Law* 30 (2017) 579.

Casper, G., 'Guardians of the Constitution', *Southern California Law Review* 53 (1980) 773.

Cassel, D., 'Honduras: Coup d'Etat in Constitutional Clothing?', *ASIL* 13:9, (15 October 2009).

The Center for Constitutional Transitions and Democracy Reporting International, *Constitutional Review in New Democracies*, Briefing Paper No. 40, September 2013, http://constitutionaltransitions.org/wp-content/uploads/2013/10/CT-DRI-BP-EN_Constitutional_Review_in_New_Democracies_2013.pdf.

Chambers, S., 'Deliberative Democratic Theory', *Annual Review of Political Science* 6 (2003) 307.

Chang, W.-C., 'Back into the Political? Rethinking Judicial, Legal, and Transnational Constitutionalism', *International Journal of Constitutional Law* 17:2 (2019) 453.

Cheema, M.H., 'Beyond Beliefs: Deconstructing the Dominant Narratives of the Islamization of Pakistan's Law', *American Journal of Comparative Law* 60:4 (2012) 875.

Cheema, M.H., 'The '"Chaudhry Court": Deconstructing the "Judicialization of Politics" in Pakistan', *Washington International Law Journal* 25:3 (2016) 447.

Cheema, M.H., 'Two Steps Forward One Step Back: The Non-linear Expansion of Judicial Power in Pakistan', *International Journal of Constitutional Law* 16:2 (2018) 503.

Chinnappa Reddy, O., *The Court and the Constitution of India: Summit and Shallows* (Oxford University Press 2010).

Chng, K., 'The Theoretical Foundations of Judicial Review in Singapore', *Singapore Journal of Legal Studies* [2019] 294.

Chou, M., *Democracy Against Itself: Sustaining an Unsustainable Idea* (Edinburgh University Press 2014).

Choudhry, S., '"He Had a Mandate": The South African Constitutional Court and the African National Congress in a Dominant Party Democracy', *Constitutional Court Review* 2:1 (2009) 1.

Choudhry, S. (ed.), *Constitutional Design for Divided Societies: Integration or Accommodation?* (Oxford University Press 2008).

Choudhry, S. 'Transnational Constitutionalism and a Limited Doctrine of Unconstitutional Constitutional Amendment: A Reply to Rosalind Dixon and David Landau', *International Journal of Constitutional Law* 15:3 (2017) 826.

Chowdhury, R., 'The Doctrine of Basic Structure in Bangladesh: From "Calfpath" to Matryoshka Dolls', *Bangladesh Journal of Law* 14:1–2 (2014) 43.

Cloots, E., *National Identity in EU Law* (Oxford University Press 2015).

Colburn, F.D., and A. Trejos, 'Democracy Undermined: Constitutional Subterfuge in Latin America', *Dissent* 57:3 (2010) 11.

Colón-Ríos, J., 'Carl Schmitt and Constituent Power in Latin American Courts: The Cases of Venezuela and Colombia', *Constellations*, 18:3 (2011) 365.

Colón-Ríos, J., *Weak Constitutionalism: Democratic Legitimacy and the Question of Constituent Power* (Routledge 2012).

Colón-Ríos, J., 'A New Typology of Judicial Review of Legislation', *Global Constitutionalism* 3:2 (2014) 143.

Colón-Ríos, J., 'Deliberative Democracy and the Doctrine of Unconstitutional Constitutional Amendments' in Levy, R., H. Kong, G. Orr, and J. King (eds.), *The Cambridge Handbook of Deliberative Constitutionalism* (Cambridge University Press 2018) 271.

Colón-Ríos, J., *Constituent Power and the Law* (Oxford University Press 2020).

Comisión de la Verdad y la Reconciliación (CVR), 'Hallazgos y recomendaciones Para que los hechos no se repitan', July 2011, https://www.oas.org/es/sap/docs/DSDME/2011/CVR/Honduras%20-%20Informe%20CVR%20-%20RECOMENDACIONES.pdf.

Commonwealth Human Rights Institute, *Genesis of the Review Commission*, [undated], http://www.humanrightsinitiative.org/publications/const/review_of_the_indian_constitution.pdf.

'Confronting Memories: Constitutionalization after Bitter Experiences' special issue, *German Law Journal* 6:2 (2005).

Contesse, J., 'The International Authority of the Inter-American Court of Human Rights: A Critique of the Conventionality Control Doctrine', *International Journal of Human Rights* 22:9 (2018) 1168.

Contiades, X. (ed.), *Engineering Constitutional Change: A Comparative Perspective on Europe, Canada and the USA* (Routledge 2012).

Contiades, X. and A. Fotiadou (eds.), *Participatory Constitutional Change: The People as Amenders of the Constitution* (Routledge 2017).

Contiades, X., and A. Fotiadou, 'Imposed Constitutions: Heteronomy and (Un) amendability' in R. Albert, X. Contiades, and A. Fotiadou (eds.), *The Law and Legitimacy of Imposed Constitutions* (Routledge 2019) 15.

Contiades, X. and A. Fotiadou (eds.), *Routledge Handbook of Comparative Constitutional Change* (Routledge 2020).

Cooper Davis, P., 'Responsive Constitutionalism and the Idea of Dignity', *Journal of Constitutional Law* 11:5 (2009) 1373.

Corder, H., 'The Republic of South Africa' in D. Oliver and C. Fusaro (eds.), *How Constitutions Change: A Comparative Study* (Hart 2011) 261.

Cox, N., *Behind the Veil: A Critical Analysis of European Veiling Laws* (Edward Elgar 2019).

Craig, P., 'Transnational Constitution-Making: The Contribution of the Venice Commission on Law and Democracy', *UC Irvine Journal of International, Transnational and Comparative Law* 2 (2017) 57.

Daly, E., 'Translating Popular Sovereignty as Unfettered Constitutional Amendability', *European Constitutional Law Review* 15 (2019) 619.

da Silva, V.A., 'A Fossilised Constitution?', *Ratio Juris* 17:4 (2004) 454.

de Ridder, E. and D. Kochenov, 'Democratic Conditionality in the Eastern Enlargement: Ambitious Window Dressing', *European Foreign Affairs Review* 16 (2011) 589.

de Visser, M., *Constitutional Review in Europe: A Comparative Analysis* (Hart 2014).

de Visser, M., 'A Critical Assessment of the Role of the Venice Commission in Processes of Domestic Constitutional Reform', *American Journal of Comparative Law* 63 (2015) 963.

Dalton, R.J., *The Good Citizen: How a Younger Generation Is Reshaping American Politics* (2nd ed., Congressional Quarterly Press 2009).

Dann, P. and Z. Al-Ali, 'The Internationalized *Pouvoir Constituant*—Constitution-Making under External Influence in Iraq, Sudan and East Timor', *Max Plank Yearbook of UN Law* 10 (2006) 423.

Davis, D., A. Richter, and C. Saunders (eds.), *An Inquiry into the Existence of Global Values: Through the Lens of Comparative Constitutional Law* (Hart 2015).

'Dealing with Populists in Government' special issue, *Democratization* 23:2 (2016).

Dellinger, W., 'The Legitimacy of Constitutional Change: Rethinking the Amendment Process', *Harvard Law Review* 97:2 (1983) 386.

Desai, A., 'Constitutional Amendments and the "Basic Structure" Doctrine' in V. Iyer (ed.), *Democracy, Human Rights and the Rule of Law* (Butterworths India 2000) 90.

Dicey, A.V., *Comparative Constitutionalism* (John W. F. Allison ed., Oxford University Press 2013).

Dietze, G., 'Unconstitutional Constitutional Norms: Constitutional Development in Postwar Germany', *Virginia Law Review* 42:1 (1956) 1.

Dixon, R., 'A Democratic Theory of Constitutional Comparison', *American Journal of Comparative Law* 56:4 (2008) 947.

Dixon, R., 'Constitutional Amendment Rules: A Comparative Perspective' in T. Ginsburg and R. Dixon (eds.), *Comparative Constitutional Law* (Edward Elgar 2011) 96.

Dixon, R., 'Amending Constitutional Identity', *Cardozo Law Review* 33:5 (2012) 1847.

Dixon, R. and T. Ginsburg, 'Deciding Not to Decide: Deferral in Constitutional Design', *Journal of International Constitutional Law* 9: 3–4 (2011) 636.

Dixon, R. and T. Ginsburg, 'The Forms and Limits of Constitutions as Political Insurance', *International Journal of Constitutional Law* 15:4 (2017) 988.

Dixon, R. and S. Issacharoff, 'Living to Fight Another Day: Judicial Deferral in Defense of Democracy', *Wisconsin Law Review* (2016) 683.

Dixon, R. and D. Landau, 'Transnational Constitutionalism and a Limited Doctrine of Unconstitutional Constitutional Amendment', *International Journal of Constitutional Law* 13:3 (2015) 606.

Dixon, R. and D. Landau, 'Competitive Democracy and the Constitutional Minimum Core' in T. Ginsburg and A.Z. Huq (eds.), *Assessing Constitutional Performance* (Cambridge University Press 2016) 268.

Dixon, R. and D. Landau, 'Transnational Constitutionalism and a Limited Doctrine of Unconstitutional Constitutional Amendment: A Rejoinder to Sujit Choudhry', *International Journal of Constitutional Law* 15:3 (2017) 833.

Dixon, R. and D. Landau, 'Tiered Constitutional Design', *George Washington Law Review* 86:2 (2018) 438.

Dixon, R. and D. Landau, 'Abusive Judicial Review: Courts against Democracy', 53 *UC Davis Law Review* (2020) 1313.

Dixon, R. and A. Stone, *The Invisible Constitution in Comparative Perspective* (Cambridge University Press 2018).

Dixon, R. and F. Uhlman, 'The Swiss Constitution and a Weak-form Form Unconstitutional Amendment Doctrine?', *International Journal of Constitutional Law* 16:1 (2018) 54.

Dolcetti, A. and G. Battista Ratti, 'Legal Disagreements and the Dual Nature of Law' in W. Waluchow and S. Sciaraffa (eds.), *Philosophical Foundations of the Nature of Law* (Oxford University Press 2013) 301.

Domin, M., 'A Part of the Constitution Is Unconstitutional, the Slovak Constitutional Court Has Ruled', Verfassungsblog, 8 February 2019, https://verfassungsblog.de/

a-part-of-the-constitution-is-unconstitutional-the-slovak-constitutional-court-has-ruled/.

Dragomaca, R., 'Constitutional Amendments and the Limits of Judicial Activism: The Case of the Czech Republic' in W. Witteveen and M. de Visser (eds.), *The Jurisprudence of Aharon Barak: Views from Europe* (Wolf Legal Publishers 2011) 198.

Drugda, S., 'Slovak Constitutional Court Strikes Down a Constitutional Amendment—But the Amendment Remains Valid', ICONnect Blog, 25 April 2019, http://www.iconnectblog.com/2019/04/slovak-constitutional-court-strikes-down-a-constitutional-amendment-but-the-amendment-remains-valid/.

Dulitzky, A.E., 'An Inter-American Constitutional Court? The Invention of the Conventionality Control by the Inter-American Court of Human Rights', *Texas International Law Journal* 50:1 (2015) 45.

Eberle, E.J., 'Human Dignity, Privacy, and Personality in German and American Constitutional Law', *Utah Law Review* (1997), 963.

Ebrahim, H., *The Soul of a Nation: Constitution-making Making in South Africa* (Oxford University Press 1999).

Ekeli, K.S., 'How Difficult Should It Be to Amend Constitutional Laws?', *Scandinavian Studies in Law* 52 (2007) 79.

Elías, J.S., 'Constitutional Changes, Transitional Justice, and Legitimacy: The Life and Death of Argentina's "Amnesty" Laws', *Hastings International & Comparative Law Review* 31:2 (2008) 587.

Elkins, Z., T. Ginsburg, and J. Blunt, 'The Citizen as Founder: Public Participation in Constitutional Approval', *Temple Law Review* 81:2 (2008) 361.

Elkins, Z., T. Ginsburg, and J. Melton, 'A Review of Iceland's Draft Constitution', The Comparative Constitutions Project, 14 October 2012, http://comparativeconstitutionsproject.org/wp-content/uploads/CCP-Iceland-Report.pdf.

Elkins, Z., T. Ginsburg, and B. Simmons, 'Getting to Rights: Treaty Ratification, Constitutional Convergence and International Law', *Harvard International Law Journal* 54:1 (2013) 61.

Elster, J., 'Consequences of Constitutional Choice: Reflections on Tocqueville' in J. Elster and R. Slagstad (eds.), *Constitutionalism and Democracy* (Cambridge University Press 1988) 81.

Elster, J., 'Constitutionalism in Eastern Europe: An Introduction', *The University of Chicago Law Review* 58:2 (1991) 447.

Elster, J., 'Forces and Mechanisms in the Constitution-Making Process', *Duke Law Journal* 45 (1995) 364.

Elster, J., 'Ways of Constitution-making' Making' in A. Hadenius (ed.), *Democracy's Victory and Crisis* (Cambridge University Press 1997) 123.

Elster, J., *Ulysses Unbound: Studies in Rationality, Precommitment, and Constraints* (Cambridge University Press 2000).

Elster, J., 'Majority Rule and Individual Rights' in O. Savić (ed.), *The Politics of Human Rights* (Verso 2002) 120.

Elster, J., C. Offe, and U.K. Preuss, *Institutional Design in Post-Communist Societies: Rebuilding the Ship at Sea* (Cambridge University Press 1998).

Ely, J.H., *Democracy and Distrust: A Theory of Judicial Review* (Harvard University Press 1980).

Eriksen, E.O. and J.E. Fossum, 'Bringing European Democracy Back In—Or How to Read the German Constitutional Court's Lisbon Treaty Ruling', *European Law Journal* 17:2 (2011) 153.

'Ethnic Party Bans in Africa' special issue, *Democratization* 17:4 (2010).

European Commission for Democracy Through Law (Venice Commission), *Self-Determination and Secession in Constitutional Law*, CDL-INF (2000) 2, 12 January 2000.

European Commission for Democracy Through Law (Venice Commission), *Opinion on the Constitutional and Legal Provisions Relevant to the Prohibition of Political Parties in Turkey*, CDL-AD (2009) 006, 13 March 2009.

European Commission for Democracy through Law (Venice Commission), *Final Draft Report: On Constitutional Amendment Procedures*, CDL(2009)168, 4 December 2009.

European Commission for Democracy through Law (Venice Commission), *Report on Constitutional Amendment*, CDL-AD(2010)001, 19 January 2010.

European Commission for Democracy Through Law (Venice Commission), *Opinion on the Draft New Constitution of Iceland*, CDL-AD(2013)010-e, 11 March 2013.

European Commission for Democracy Through Law (Venice Commission), *Opinion on the Final Draft Constitution of the Republic of Tunisia Adopted by the Venice Commission at its 96th Plenary Session (Venice, 11--12 October 2013)*, CDL-AD(2013)032, 17 October 2013.

European Commission for Democracy through Law (Venice Commission), *Compilation of Venice Commission Opinions Concerning Constitutional Provisions for Amending the Constitution*, CDL-PI(2015)023*, 22 December 2015.

European Commission for Democracy Through Law (Venice Commission), *Turkey: Opinion on the Amendments to the Constitution Adopted by the Grand National Assembly on 21 January 2017 and to Be Submitted to a National Referendum on 16 April 2017*, CDL-AD(2017)005, 13 March 2017.

European Commission for Democracy through Law (Venice Commission), *Ukraine Opinion on the Draft Law on Anti-Corruption Courts*, CDL-AD(2017)020, 9 October 2017.

European Commission for Democracy through Law (Venice Commission), *Armenia: Opinion on Three Legal Questions in the Context of Draft Constitutional Amendments Concerning the Mandate of the Judges of the Constitutional Court*, CDL-AD(2020)016, 22 June 2020.

Fabbrini, F. and O. Pollicino, 'Constitutional Identity in Italy' in C. Calliess and G. van der Schyff (eds.), *Constitutional Identity in a Europe of Multilevel Constitutionalism* (Cambridge University Press 2019) 201.

Fabbrini, F. and A. Sajó, 'The Dangers of Constitutional Identity', *European Law Journal* 25 (2019) 457.

Faraguna, P., 'Constitutional Identity in the EU—A Shield or a Sword?', *German Law Journal* 18:7 (2017) 1617.

Faraguna, P., 'Unamendability and Constitutional Identity in the Italian Constitutional Experience', *European Journal of Law Reform* 21 (2019) 329.

Farrell, D.M., 'The Irish Constitutional Convention: A Bold Step or a Damp Squib?' in J. O'Dowd and G. Ferrari (eds.), *75 Years of the Constitution of Ireland: An Irish–Italian Dialogue* (Clarus Press 2014) 191.

Farrell, D.M., E. O'Malley, and J. Suiter, 'Deliberative Democracy in Action Irish-Style: The 2011 We the Citizens Pilot Citizens' Assembly', *Irish Political Studies* 28:1 (2013) 100.

Fassbender, B., 'We the Peoples of the United Nations: Constituent Power and Constitutional Form in International Law' in M. Loughlin and N. Walker (eds.), *The Paradox of Constitutionalism: Constituent Power and Constitutional Form* (Oxford University Press 2008) 269.

Feldman, D., 'The Nature and Effects of Constitutional Rights in Post-conflict Bosnia and Herzegovina' in C. Harvey and A. Schwartz (eds.), *Rights in Divided Societies* (Hart 2012) 151.

Ferejohn, J., J.N. Rakove, and J. Riley (eds.), *Constitutional Culture and Democratic Rule* (Cambridge University Press 2001).
Ferreres Comella, V., *Constitutional Courts and Democratic Values: A European Perspective* (Yale University Press 2009).
Fierro, E., *European Union's Approach to Human Rights Conditionality in Practice* (Martinus Nijhoff 2003).
Fombad, C.M., 'Problematising the Issue of Constitutional Implementation in Africa' in C.M. Fombad (ed.), *The Implementation of Modern African Constitutions: Challenges and Prospects* (University of Pretoria Press 2016) 10.
Fombad, C.M. and E. Nwauche, 'Africa's Imperial Presidents: Immunity, Impunity and Accountability' *African Journal of Legal Studies* 5 (2012) 91.
Fournier, P., H. van der Kolk, R.K. Carty, A. Blais, and J. Rose, *When Citizens Decide: Lessons from Citizen Assemblies on Electoral Reform* (Oxford University Press 2011).
Fox, G.H. and G. Nolte, 'Intolerant Democracies', *Harvard Journal of International Law* 36:1 (1995) 1.
Franck, T.M., and A.K. Thiruvengadam, 'Norms of International Law Relating to the Constitution-Making Process' in L.E. Miller and L. Aucoin (eds.), *Framing the State in Times of Transition: Case Studies in Constitution Making* (United States Institute for Peace 2010).
Freeman, M., *Necessary Evils: Amnesties and the Search for Justice* (Cambridge University Press 2009).
Friedman, S., and D. Atkinson, *The Small Miracle: South Africa's Negotiated Settlement* (Ravan Press 1995).
Frosini, J.O., 'Constitutional Preambles: More than Just a Narration of History', *University of Illinois Law Review* (2017) 603.
Gajendragadkar, P.B., *The Constitution of India: Its Philosophy and Basic Postulates* (Oxford University Press 1969).
Galligan, D.J., and M. Versteeg (eds.), *Social and Political Foundations of Constitutions* (Cambridge University Press 2013).
Gamha, E., 'Tunisia's Constituent Assembly: How Long Will It Last?', *Tunisia Live*, 10 October 2011, available at http://www.tunisia-live.net/2011/10/10/constituent-assembly-what-about-its-duration/.
Ganguly, S., 'Six Decades of Independence', *Journal of Democracy* 18:2 (2007) 30.
Gardbaum, S., 'Are Strong Constitutional Courts Always a Good Thing for New Democracies?', *Columbia Journal of Transnational Law* 53 (2015) 285.
Gardbaum, S., 'Revolutionary Constitutionalism', *International Journal of Constitutional Law* 15:1 (2017) 173.
Gardbaum, S., 'The Counter-playbook: Resisting the Populist Assault on Separation of Powers', *Columbia Journal of Transnational Law* 59:1 (2020 forthcoming).
Gargarella, R., 'Towards a Typology of Latin American Constitutionalism, 1810–60', *Latin American Research Review* 39:2 (2004) 141.
Garlicki, L. and Z.A. Garlicka, 'External Review of Constitutional Amendments? International Law as a Norm of Reference', *Israel Law Review* 44 (2011) 343.
Garlicki, L. and Z.A. Garlicka-Sowers, 'Unconstitutional Constitutional Amendments', *Vienna Journal of International Constitutional Law* 12:3 (2018) 307.
Gathii, J.T., 'Popular Authorship and Constitution Making: Comparing and Contrasting the DRC and Kenya', *William & Mary Law Review* 49:4 (2008) 1109.
Gárdos-Orosz, F., 'Unamendability as a Judicial Discovery? Inductive Learning Lessons from Hungary' in R. Albert and B.E. Oder (eds.), *An Unamendable Constitution? Unamendability in Constitutional Democracies* (Springer 2018) 231.

Geertjes, G.J. and J. Uzman, 'Conventions of Unamendability: Covert Constitutional Unamendability in (Two) Politically Enforced Constitutions' in A. Albert and B.E. Oder (eds.), *An Unamendable Constitution? Unamendability in Constitutional Democracies* (Springer 2018) 89.

Ghai, Y., 'Ethnicity and Competing Nations of Rights' in C. Harvey and A. Schwartz (eds.), *Rights in Divided Societies* (Hart 2012) 62.

Ghai, Y. and J. Cottrell, 'A Tale of Three Constitutions: Ethnicity and Politics in Fiji' in S. Choudhry (ed.) *Constitutional Design for Divided Societies: Integration or Accommodation?* (Oxford University Press 2008) 287.

Gilmartin, D., 'Election Law and the "People" in Colonial and Postcolonial India' in D. Chakrabarty, R. Majumdar, and A. Sartori (eds.), *From the Colonial to the Postcolonial: India and Pakistan in Transition* (Oxford University Press 2007) 55.

Ginsburg, T., *Judicial Review in New Democracies: Constitutional Courts in Asian Cases* (Cambridge University Press 2003).

Ginsburg, T., 'The Puzzle of Unamendable Provisions: Debate-Impairing Rules vs. Substantive Entrenchment', I-CONnect Blog, 13 August 2009, http://www.iconnectblog.com/2009/08/the-puzzle-of-unamendable-provisions-debate-impairing-rules-vs-substantive-entrenchment/.

Ginsburg, T., Z. Elkins, and J. Melton, 'Do Executive Term Limits Cause Constitutional Crises?' in T. Ginsburg (ed.), *Comparative Constitutional Design* (Cambridge University Press 2012) 350.

Ginsburg, T., N. Foti, and D. Rockmore, "We the Peoples": The Global Origins of Constitutional Preambles', *George Washington International Law Review* 46:2 (2014) 305.

Ginsburg, T., D. Lansberg-Rodriguez, and M. Versteeg, 'When to Overthrow Your Government: The Right to Resist in the World's Constitutions', *UCLA Law Review* 60 (2013) 1184.

Ginsburg, T., J. Melton, and Z. Elkins, 'On the Evasion of Executive Term Limits', *William and Mary Law Review* 52 (2011) 1807.

Ginsburg, T., and Y. Ngenge, 'The Judiciary and Constitution Building in 2013' in S. Bisarya (ed.), *Constitution Building: A Global Review (2013)*, International IDEA, 2014, 32.

Ginsburg, T., D. Rockmore, and N. Foti, '"We the Peoples": The Global Origins of Constitutional Preamble', *George Washington International Law Review* 46 (2014) 305.

Gluck, J., and M. Brandt, *Participatory and Inclusive Constitution Making: Giving Voice to the Demands of Citizens in the Wake of the Arab Spring*, United States Institute of Peace (2015), http://www.usip.org/publications/participatory-and-inclusive-constitution-making.

Gomien, D., 'Human Rights in Bosnia and Herzegovina: European Practice, Fraught Federalism and the Future' in W. Benedek (ed.), *Human Rights in Bosnia and Herzegovina after Dayton: From Theory to Practice* (Kluwer Law International 1999) 107.

Goodman, J., and B. Schmidt, 'Honduras Supreme Court Judge Defends President Ouster (Update1)', *Bloomberg*, 1 July 2009, http://www.bloomberg.com/apps/news?pid=newsarchive&sid=axGENUiy9yKs.

Govindjee, A., and R. Kruger, 'The Basic Structure Doctrine Debate: South African Explorations' in S.S. Jain and S. Narayan (eds.), *Basic Structure Constitutionalism: Revisiting Kesavananda Bharti* (Eastern Book Company 2011) 209.

Gözler, K., *Judicial Review of Constitutional Amendments: A Comparative Study* (Ekin Press 2008).

Grimm, D., 'Defending Sovereign Statehood against Transforming the Union into a State', *European Constitutional Law Review* 5:3 (2009) 353

Grimm, D., *Constitutionalism: Past, Present, and Future* (Oxford University Press 2016).

Griswold, E.N., 'The "Coloured Vote Case" in South Africa', *Harvard Law Review* 65:8 (1952) 1361.

Groppi, T., and M.-C. Ponthoreau (eds.), *The Use of Foreign Precedents by Constitutional Judges* (Hart 2013).

Grönlund, K., A. Bächtiger, and M. Setälä (eds.), *Deliberative Mini-Publics: Involving Citizens in the Democratic Process* (ECPR Press 2014).

Guastaferro, B. and L. Payero, 'Devolution and Secession in Comparative Perspective: The Case of Spain and Italy' in R. Schütze and S. Tierney (eds.), *The United Kingdom and the Federal Idea* (Hart 2018) 123.

Gustavsson, S., 'The Need for Legitimate Opposition and Protectionism' in O. Cramme and S.B. Hobolt (eds.), *Democratic Politics in a European Union Under Stress* (Oxford University Press 2014) 236.

Halmai, G., 'Unconstitutional Constitutional Amendments: Constitutional Courts as Guardians of the Constitution?', *Constellations* 19:2 (2012) 182.

Halmai, G., 'The Early Retirement Age of the Hungarian Judges' in F. Nicola and B. Davies (eds.), *EU Law Stories: Contextual and Critical Histories of European Jurisprudence* (Cambridge University Press 2017) 471.

Halmai, G., 'Abuse of Constitutional Identity. : The Hungarian Constitutional Court on Interpretation of Article E) (2) of the Fundamental Law', *Review of Central and East European Law* 43 (2018a) 23.

Halmai, G., 'Silence of Transitional Constitutions: The "Invisible Constitution" Concept of the Hungarian Constitutional Court', *International Journal of Constitutional Law* 16:3 (2018b) 969.

Halmai, G., 'Transitional Constitutional Unamendability?', *European Journal of Law Reform* 21:3 (2019) 259.

Hart, V., 'Democratic Constitution Making', United States Institute of Peace Special Report 107, July 2003, http://www.usip.org/sites/default/files/resources/sr107.pdf.

Hein, M., 'Do Constitutional Entrenchment Clauses Matter? Constitutional Review of Constitutional Amendments in Europe', *International Journal of Constitutional Law* 18:1 (2020) 78.

Henderson, A., 'Cry, the Beloved Constitution: Constitutional Amendment, the Vanished Imperative of the Constitutional Principles and the Controlling Values of Section 1', *South African Law Journal* 114 (1997) 542.

Hendricks, C. and G.N. Kiven, 'Presidential Term Limits: Slippery Slope Back to Authoritarianism in Africa', *The Conversation*, 17 May 2018, https://theconversation.com/presidential-term-limits-slippery-slope-back-to-authoritarianism-in-africa-96796.

Henley, J., K. Shaheen, and C. Letsch, 'Turkey Election: Erdoğan and AKP Return to Power with Outright Majority', *The Guardian*, 2 November 2015, http://www.theguardian.com/world/2015/nov/01/turkish-election-akp-set-for-majority-with-90-of-vote-counted.

Heun, W., *The Constitution of Germany: A Contextual Analysis* (Hart 2011).

Hickman, T., 'Problems for Proportionality', *New Zealand Law Review* (2010) 303.

Hirschl, R., *Towards Juristocracy: The Origins and Consequences of the New Constitutionalism* (Harvard University Press 2007).

Hirschl, R., 'The Theocratic Challenge to Constitution Drafting in Post-conflict Conflict States', *William and Mary Law Review* 49:4 (2008) 1179.

Hirschl, R., *Constitutional Theocracy* (Harvard University Press 2010).

Hirschl, R., *Comparative Matters: The Renaissance of Comparative Constitutional Law* (Oxford University Press 2014).

Holmes, S., *Passions and Constraint: On the Theory of Liberal Democracy* (University of Chicago Press 1995).

Holmes, S., 'Precommitment and the Paradox of Democracy' in J. Elster and R. Slagstad (eds.), *Constitutionalism and Democracy* (Cambridge University Press 1988) 195.

Hoque, R., 'Constitutionalism and the Judiciary in Bangladesh' in S. Khilnani, V. Raghavan, and A.K. Thiruvengadam (eds.), *Comparative Constitutionalism in South Asia* (Oxford University Press 2014) 303.

Hoque, R., 'The Judicialization of Politics in Bangladesh: Pragmatism, Legitimacy, and Consequences' in M. Tushnet and M. Khosla (eds.), *Unstable Constitutionalism: Law and Politics in South Asia* (Cambridge University Press 2015) 261.

Hoque, R., 'Developments in Bangladeshi Constitutional Law: The Year 2016 in Review', ICONnect Blog, 12 October 2017, http://www.iconnectblog.com/2017/10/developments-in-bangladeshi-constitutional-law-the-year-2016-in-review/.

Horowitz, D.L., 'Conciliatory Institutions and Constitutional Processes in Post-Conflict States', *William and Mary Law Review* 49:4 (2008) 1213.

Hostovsky Brandes, T., 'Basic Law: Israel as the Nation State of the Jewish People: Implications for Equality, Self-Determination and Social Solidarity', *Minnesota Journal of International Law* 29:1 (2020) 65.

Hucko, E.M., *The Democratic Tradition: Four German Constitutions* (Berg Publishers 1987).

Hudson, A., 'When Does Public Participation Make a Difference? Evidence from Iceland's Crowdsourced Constitution', *Policy & Internet* 10:2 (2018) 185.

Huneeus, A., 'When Illiberals Embrace Human Rights', *AJIL Unbound* 113 (2019) 380.

Hutchinson, A.C. and J. Colón-Ríos, 'Democracy and Constitutional Change', Osgoode Hall Law School Research Paper No. 48/2010 6:11 (2010).

Hübner Mendes, C., 'Judicial Review of Constitutional Amendments in the Brazilian Supreme Court', *Florida Journal of International Law* 17:3 (2005) 449.

Hübner Mendes, C., *Constitutional Courts and Deliberative Democracy* (Oxford University Press 2013).

Iancu, B., '*Quod licet Jovi non licet bovi?*: The Venice Commission as Norm Entrepreneur', *Hague Journal on the Rule of Law* 11 (2019) 189.

Inclusive Security, *How Women Influence Constitution Making after Conflict and Unrest* (2018).

Inter-American Commission of Human Rights, *Guarantees for the Independence of Justice Operators*, OEA/Ser.L/V/II.Doc. 44, 5 December 2013.

International Commission of Jurists, *International Standards on the Independence and Accountability of Judges, Lawyers and Prosecutors*, https://www.icj.org/themes/centre-for-the-independence-of-judges-and-lawyers/international-standards/.

International Commission of Jurists, *Enhancing the Rule of Law and Guaranteeing Human Rights in the Constitution: A Report on the Constitutional Reform Process in Tunisia* (2013), http://icj.wpengine.netdna-cdn.com/wp-content/uploads/2013/02/TUNISIA-CONSTITUTION-REPORT-FINAL.pdf.

International IDEA, *Constitution Building after Conflict: External Support to a Sovereign Process* (2011).

International IDEA, *Interim Constitutions: Peacekeeping and Democracy-Building Tools* (2015).

International IDEA, *Sequencing Peace Agreements and Constitutions in the Political Settlement Process* (2016).

Irving, H., 'Constitutional Identity Theory and Gender: The Missing Referent', Sydney Law School Research Paper No. 17/56 (2017).

Issacharoff, S., 'Constitutional Courts and Democratic Hedging', *Georgetown Law Journal* 99 (2011) 961.

Issacharoff, S., *Fragile Democracies: Contested Power in the Era of Constitutional Courts* (Cambridge University Press 2015).

Iyer, V., 'The Supreme Court of India' in B. Dickson (ed.), *Judicial Activism in Common Law Supreme Courts* (Oxford University Press 2007) 121.

Jackson, V.C., 'Holistic Interpretation: *Fitzpatrick v. Bitzer* and Our Bifurcated Constitution', *Stanford Law Review* 53:5 (2001) 1259.

Jackson, V.C., 'What's in a Name? Reflections on Timing, Naming, and Constitution-making', *William and Mary Law Review* 49:4 (2008) 1249.

Jackson, V.C., *Constitutional Engagement in a Transnational Era* (Oxford University Press 2010).

Jackson, V.C., 'Comparative Constitutional Law: Methodologies' in M. Rosenfeld and A. Sajó (eds.), *The Oxford Handbook of Comparative Constitutional Law* (Oxford University Press 2012) 54.

Jackson, V.C., 'The (Myth of Un)amendability of the US Constitution and the Democratic Component of Constitutionalism', *International Journal of Constitutional Law* 13:3 (2015) 575.

Jackson, V.C., '"Constituent Power" or Degrees of Legitimacy?', *Vienna Journal of International Constitutional Law* 12:3 (2018) 319.

Jacobsohn, G.J., *The Wheel of Law: India's Secularism in Comparative Constitutional Context* (Princeton University Press 2003).

Jacobsohn, G.J., *Constitutional Identity* (Harvard University Press 2010).

Jacobsohn, G.J., 'The Formation of Constitutional Identities' in T. Ginsburg and R. Dixon (eds.), *Comparative Constitutional Law* (Edward Elgar 2011) 129.

Jacobsohn, Gary J. and S. Shankar, 'Constitutional Borrowing in South Asia: India, Sri Lanka, and Secular Constitutional Identity' in S. Khilnani, V. Raghavan, and A.K. Thiruvengadam (eds.), *Comparative Constitutionalism in South Asia* (Oxford University Press 2014) 180.

Jefferson, T., *Letter to James Madison*, 6 September 1789.

Kahn, J., *Federalism, Democratization, and the Rule of Law in Russia* (Oxford University Press 2002), 52.

Kalaycıoğlu, E., 'Kulturkampf in Turkey: The Constitutional Referendum of 12 September 2010', *South European Society and Politics* 17:1 (2012) 1.

Kapiszewski, D., *High Courts and Economic Governance in Argentina and Brazil* (Cambridge University Press 2012).

Kashyap, S.C., D.D. Khanna, and G.W. Kueck, *Need to Review the Working of the Constitution* (Shipra Publishers 2004).

Katz, E., 'On Amending Constitutions: The Legality and Legitimacy of Constitutional Entrenchment', *Columbia Journal of Law and Social Problems* 29 (1996) 251.

Kay, R.S., 'The Illegality of the Constitution', *Constitutional Commentary* 4 (1987) 57.

Kelemen, R.D. and L. Pech, 'The Uses and Abuses of Constitutional Pluralism: Undermining the Rule of Law in the Name of Constitutional Identity in Hungary and Poland', *Cambridge Yearbook of European Legal Studies* 21 (2019) 59.

Kelley, J.G., *Ethnic Politics in Europe: The Power of Norms and Incentives* (Princeton University Press 2004).

Kelsen, H., *General Theory of Law and State* (The Lawbook Exchange 2009).

Kentel, F., L. Köker, M. Uçum, and Ö. Genç, 'Making of a New Constitution in Turkey: Monitoring Report October 2011--January 2012', TESEV Democratization Programme, July 2012.

Kettley, C., 'Ethnicity, Language and Transition Politics in Romania: The Hungarian Minority in Context' in F. Daftary and F. Grin (eds.), *Nation-building, Ethnicity and*

Language Politics in Transition Countries (Local Government and Public Service Reform Initiative, Open Society Institute 2003) 243.

Khosla, M., 'Inclusive Constitutional Comparison: Reflections on India's Sodomy Decision', *American Journal of Comparative Law* 59:4 (2011) 909.

Khosla, M., 'Constitutional Amendment' in S. Choudhry, M. Khosla, and P.B. Mehta (eds.), *The Oxford Handbook of the Indian Constitution* (Oxford University Press 2016) 232.

Kiiver, P., 'The Lisbon Judgment of the German Constitutional Court: A Court-Ordered Strengthening of the National Legislature in the EU', *European Law Journal* 16:5 (2010) 578.

King, J., 'Proportionality: A Halfway House', *New Zealand Law Review* (2010) 327.

Kirkby, C., 'Analysis: Constitution of Fiji', IACL–AIDC Blog, 14 September 2015, https://blog-iacl-aidc.org/new-blog/2018/5/27/analysis-constitution-of-fiji.

Kirkby, C., 'A Cure for Coups: The South African Influence on Fijian Constitutionalism' in R. Dixon and T. Roux (eds.), *Constitutional Triumphs, Constitutional Disappointments: A Critical Assessment of the 1996 South African Constitution's Local and International Influence* (Cambridge University Press 2018) 312.

Klein, C. and A. Sajó, 'Constitution-Making: Process and Substance' in M. Rosenfeld and A. Sajó (eds.), *The Oxford Handbook of Comparative Constitutional Law* (Oxford University Press 2012) 419.

Klug, H., 'Participating in the Design: Constitution-Making in South Africa', *Review of Constitutional Studies* 3:1 (1996) 18.

Klug, H., *Constituting Democracy: Law, Globalism and South Africa's Political Reconstruction* (Cambridge University Press 2000).

Klug, H., *The Constitution of South Africa: A Contextual Analysis* (Hart 2010).

Klug, H., 'Constitution Making and Social Transformation' in D. Landau and H. Lerner (eds.), *Comparative Constitution Making* (Edward Elgar 2019) 47.

Koch, H.W., *A Constitutional History of Germany* (Longman 1984).

Kochenov, D., 'Overestimating Conditionality' in I. Govaere, E. Lannon, P. van Elsuwege, and S. Adam (eds.), *The European Union in the World Essays in Honour of Marc Maresceau* (Brill Nijhoff 2014) 541.

Koertvelyesi, Z., and B. Majtenyi, 'Game of Values: The Threat of Exclusive Constitutional Identity, the EU and Hungary', *German Law Journal* 18:7 (2017) 1721.

Koğacıoğlu, D., 'Progress, Unity, and Democracy: Dissolving Political Parties in Turkey', *Law & Society Review* 38:3 (2004) 433.

Kommers, D.P., 'Germany: Balancing Rights and Duties' in J. Goldsworthy (ed.), *Interpreting Constitutions: A Comparative Study* (Oxford University Press 2007) 161.

Kommers, D.P. and R.A. Miller, *The Constitutional Jurisprudence of the Federal Republic of Germany* (Duke University Press 2012).

Kong, H., 'Deliberative Constitutional Amendments', *Queen's Law Journal* 41:1 (2015) 105.

Korenica, F. and D. Doli, 'The Politics of Constitutional Design in Divided Societies: The Case of Kosovo', *Croatian Yearbook of European Law and Policy* 6:6 (2010) 265.

Kosař, D., *Perils of Judicial Self-Government in Transitional Societies* (Cambridge University Press 2016).

Kosař, D., J. Petrov, K. Šipulová, H. Smekal, L. Vyhnánek, and J. Janovský, *Domestic Judicial Treatment of European Court of Human Rights Case Law* (Routledge 2020).

Kosař, D. and K. Šipulová, 'The Strasbourg Court Meets Abusive Constitutionalism: *Baka v. Hungary* and the Rule of Law', *Hague Journal on the Rule of Law* 10 (2017) 83.

Kosař, D. and L. Vyhnánek, 'Constitutional Identity in the Czech Republic': A New Twist on an Old Fashioned Idea' in C. Calliess and G. van der Schyff (eds.), *Constitutional Identity in a Europe of Multilevel Constitutionalism* (Cambridge University Press 2019) 85.

Kotzur, M., 'Constitutional Amendments and Constitutional Changes in Germany' in X. Contiades (ed.), *Engineering Constitutional Change: A Comparative Perspective on Europe, Canada and the USA* (Routledge 2012) 125.

Kovacs, K., 'The Rise of an Ethnocultural Constitutional Identity in the Jurisprudence of the East Central European Courts', *German Law Journal* 18:7 (2017) 703.

Krisch, N., '*Pouvoir Constituant* and *Pouvoir Irritant* in the Postnational Order', *International Journal of Constitutional Law* 14:3 (2016) 657.

Krishna, S., 'Constitutionalism, Democracy and Political Culture in India' in D.P. Franklin and M.J. Braun (eds.), *Political Culture and Constitutionalism: A Comparative Approach* (M.E. Sharpe 1995) 161.

Krishnamurthy, V., 'Colonial Cousins: Explaining India and Canada's Unwritten Constitutional Principles', *Yale Journal of International Law* 34:1 (2009) 207.

Krishnaswamy, S., *Democracy and Constitutionalism in India* (Oxford University Press 2009).

Ku, R., 'Consensus of the Governed: The Legitimacy of Constitutional Change', *Fordham Law Review*, 64:2 (1995) 535.

Kuo, M.-S., 'Moving Towards a Nominal Constitutional Court? Critical Reflections on the Shift from Judicial Activism to Constitutional Irrelevance in Taiwan's Constitutional Politics', *Washington International Law Journal* 25:3 (2016) 597.

Landau, D., 'Abusive Constitutionalism', *UC Davis Law Review* 47 (2013a) 189.

Landau, D., 'Constitution-Making Gone Wrong', *Alabama Law Review* 64:5 (2013b) 923.

Landau, D., 'The Honduran Constitutional Chamber's Decision Erasing Presidential Term Limits: Abusive Constitutionalism by Judiciary?', I-CONnect Blog, 6 May 2015, http://www.iconnectblog.com/2015/05/the-honduran-constitutional-chambers-decision-erasing-presidential-term-limits-abusive-constitutionalism-by-judiciary/.

Landau, D., 'Presidential Term Limits in Latin America: A Critical Analysis of the Migration of the Unconstitutional Constitutional Amendment Doctrine', *Law & Ethics of Human Rights* 12:2 (2018a) 225.

Landau, D., 'Institutional Failure and Intertemporal Theories of Judicial Role in the Global South' in D. Bilchitz and D. Landau (eds.), *The Evolution of the Separation of Powers: Between the Global North and the Global South* (Edward Elgar 2018b) 31.

Landau, D., Dixon, R., and Roznai, Y., 'From an Unconstitutional Constitutional Amendment to an Unconstitutional Constitution? Lessons from Honduras', *Global Constitutionalism* 8:1 (2019) 40.

Landemore, H., 'Inclusive Constitution-Making: The Icelandic Experiment', *Journal of Political Philosophy* 23:2 (2015) 166.

Landemore, H., 'Inclusive Constitution Making and Religious Rights: Lessons from the Icelandic Experiment', *Journal of Politics* 79:3 (2017) 762.

Law, D.S., 'Globalization and the Future of Constitutional Rights', *Northwestern University Law Review* 102 (2008) 1277.

Law, D.S., 'Constitutional Archetypes', *Texas Law Review* 95:2 (2016) 153.

Law, D.S., 'The Global Language of Human Rights: A Computational Linguistic Analysis', *Law & Ethics of Human Rights* 12:1 (2018) 111.

Law, D.S., 'Constitutional Dialects: The Language of Transnational Legal Orders' in G. Shaffer, T. Ginsburg, and T.C. Halliday (eds.), *Constitution-Making and Transnational Legal Order* (Cambridge University Press 2019) 110.

Law, D.S. and M. Versteeg, 'The Evolution and Ideology of Global Constitutionalism', *California Law Review* 99 (2011) 1163.

Law, D.S. and M. Versteeg, 'Sham Constitutions', *California Law Review* 101 (2013) 863.

Leibholz, G., 'The Federal Constitutional Court in Germany and the "Southwest Case"', *The American Political Science Review* 46:3 (1952) 723.

Lerner, H., *Making Constitutions in Deeply Divided Societies* (Cambridge University Press 2011).

Lessa, F. and L.A. Payne, *Amnesty in the Age of Human Rights Accountability* (Cambridge University Press 2012).

Levinson, S., 'How Many Times Has the United States Constitution Been Amended? (A) < 26; (B) 26; (c) 27; (D) > 27: Accounting for Constitutional Change' in S. Levinson (ed.), *Responding to Imperfection: The Theory and Practice of Constitutional Amendment* (Princeton University Press 1995) 13.

Levinson, S., 'Do Constitutions Have a Point? Reflections on "Parchment Barriers" and Preambles' in E. Frankel Paul, F.D. Miller, Jr, and J. Paul (eds.), *What Should Constitutions Do?* (Cambridge University Press 2011) 150.

Levy, R., 'Deliberative Constitutional Change in a Polarised Federation' in P. Kildea, A. Lynch, and G. Williams (eds.), *Tomorrow's Federation: Reforming Australian Government* (The Federation Press 2012) 350.

Levy, R., 'The Law of Deliberative Democracy: Seeding the Field', *Election Law Journal* 12:4 (2013) 355.

Levy, R., 'Deliberative Democracy and Political Law: The Coercion Problem' (2014), https://papers.ssrn.com/sol3/papers.cfm?abstract_id=2490239.

Levy, R., 'Shotgun Referendums: Popular Deliberation and Constitutional Settlement in Conflict Societies', *Melbourne University Law Review* 41 (2018) 1237.

Levy, R., H. Kong, G. Orr, and J. King (eds.), *The Cambridge Handbook of Deliberative Constitutionalism* (Cambridge University Press 2018).

Levy, R. and G. Orr (eds.), 'Symposium: The Law of Deliberative Democracy', *Election Law Journal* 12:4 (2013) 355.

Linder, D., 'What in the Constitution Cannot Be Amended?', *Arizona Law Review* 23 (1981) 717.

Llanos, M., and L. Marsteintredet, 'Epilogue: The Breakdown of Zelaya's Presidency: Honduras in Comparative Perspective' in M. Llanos and L. Marsteintredet (eds.), *Presidential Breakdowns in Latin America: Causes and Outcomes of Executive Instability in Developing Democracies* (Palgrave Macmillan 2010) 229.

Loewenstein, K., 'Militant Democracy and Fundamental Rights I', *The American Political Science Review*, 31:3 (1937) 424.

Loughlin, M., *The Idea of Public Law* (Oxford University Press 2003).

Loughlin, M. and N. Walker (eds.), *The Paradox of Constitutionalism: Constituent Power and Constitutional Form* (Oxford University Press 2008).

Lutz, D.S., 'Toward a Theory of Constitutional Amendment', *American Political Science Review* 88:2 (1994) 355.

Machado, J.E.M., 'The Portuguese Constitution of 1976: Half-life and Decay' in X. Contiades (ed.), *Engineering Constitutional Change: A Comparative Perspective on Europe, Canada and the USA* (Routledge 2012) 286.

Macklem, P., 'Militant Democracy, Legal Pluralism, and the Paradox of Self-determination', *International Journal of Constitutional Law* 4:3 (2006), 488.

Madison, J. *Federalist No. 49*, 5 February 1788.

Mahmoudi, S., 'The Shari'a in the New Afghan Constitution: Contradiction or Compliment?', *Zeitschrift für ausländisches öffentliches Recht und Völkerrecht* 64 (2004) 867.

Malagodi, M., *Constitutional Nationalism and Legal Exclusion: Equality, Identity Politics, and Democracy in Nepal (1990–2007)* (Oxford University Press 2013).

Maltz, G., 'The Case for Presidential Term Limits', *Journal of Democracy* 18:1 (2007) 128.

Mancini, S., 'The Tempting of Europe, the Political Seduction of the Cross: A Schmittian Reading of Christianity and Islam in European Constitutionalism', in S. Mancini and M. Rosenfeld (eds.), *Constitutional Secularism in an Age of Religious Revival* (Oxford University Press 2014) 111.

Marsteintredet, L., 'The Honduran Supreme Court Renders Inapplicable Unamendable Constitutional Provisions', I-CONnect Blog, 2 May 2015, http://www.iconnectblog.com/2015/05/marsteintredet-on-honduras/.

Masri, M., *The Dynamics of Exclusionary Constitutionalism: Israel as a Jewish and Democratic State* (Hart 2017).

Masri, M., 'Unamendability in Israel: A Critical Perspective' in R. Albert and B.E. Oder (eds.), *An Unamendable Constitution? Unamendability in Constitutional Democracies* (Springer 2018) 169.

Mate, M.S., 'Two Paths to Judicial Power: The Basic Structure Doctrine and Public Interest Litigation in Comparative Perspective', *San Diego International Law Journal* 12 (2010) 175.

Mate, M., 'Judicial Supremacy in Comparative Constitutional Law', *Tulane Law Review* 92:2 (2017) 393.

Mayer, F.C., 'Rashomon in Karlsruhe: A Reflection on Democracy and Identity in the European Union', *International Journal of Constitutional Law* 9:3–4 (2011) 757.

Mazzone, J., 'The Creation of a Constitutional Culture', *Tulsa Law Review* 40 (2005a) 671.

Mazzone, J., 'Unamendments', *Iowa Law Review* 90 (2005b) 1747.

McCrudden, C., and B. O'Leary, 'Courts and Consociations, or How Human Rights Courts May Destabilize Power-Sharing Settlements', *European Journal of International Law* 24:2 (2013a) 477.

McCrudden, C., and B. O'Leary, *Courts and Consociations: Human Rights versus Power-Sharing* (Oxford University Press 2013b).

Mehta, P.B., 'The Inner Conflict of Constitutionalism: Judicial Review and the "Basic Structure"', in Z. Hasan, E. Sridharan, and R. Sudarshan (eds.), *India's Living Constitution: Ideas, Practices, Controversies* (Permanent Black 2002) 179.

Mehta, P.B., 'India's Unlikely Democracy: The Rise of Judicial Sovereignty', *Journal of Democracy* 18:2 (2007) 70.

Mehta, P.B., 'The Indian Supreme Court and the Art of Democratic Positioning' in M. Tushnet and M. Khosla (eds.), *Unstable Constitutionalism: Law and Politics in South Asia* (Cambridge University Press 2015) 233.

Mekonnen, D.R., and S.M. Weldehaimanot, 'Transitional Constitutionalism: Comparing the Eritrean and South African Experience', Paper paper presented at ANCL--RADC annual conference, on 'The Internationalisation of Constitutional Law', Rabat, Morocco, 2–5 February 2011.

Mendez, F., and J. Wheatley (eds.), *Patterns of Constitutional Design: The Role of Citizens and Elites in Constitution-Making* (Ashgate 2013).

Mendonça Bertotti, B., '(Un)Constitutional Amendment No. 95/2016 and the Limit for Public Expenses in Brazil: Amendment or Dismemberment?', ICONnect Blog, 24 August 2018, http://www.iconnectblog.com/2018/08/unconstitutional-amendment-no-95-2016-and-the-limit-for-public-expenses-in-brazil-amendment-or-dismemberment/.

Meuwese, A., 'Popular Constitution-Making: The Case of Iceland' in D.J. Galligan and M. Versteeg (eds.), *Social and Political Foundations of Constitutions* (Cambridge University Press 2013) 469.

'Military Coup Ousts Niger president President Mamadou Tandja', *BBC News*, 19 February 2010, http://news.bbc.co.uk/1/hi/world/africa/8523196.stm.

Ministerio de Relaciones Exteriores y Culto s/ informe sentencia dictada en el caso 'Fontevecchia y D'Amico vs. Argentina' por la Corte Interamericana de Derechos Humanos, Sentencia, 14 February 2017.

Minkenberg, M., 'Repression and Reaction: Militant Democracy and the Radical Right in Germany and France', *Patterns of Prejudice* 40:1 (2006) 25.

Mohallem, M.F., 'Immutable Clauses and Judicial Review in India, Brazil and South Africa: Expanding Constitutional Courts' Authority', *International Journal of Human Rights* 15:5 (2010) 765.

Mohanty, M., 'Does India Need a New Constitution?' in S.N. Misra, S.C. Hazary, and A. Mishra, eds., *Constitution and Constitutionalism in India* (APH Publishing Corporation 1999), 1.

Morina, V., F. Korenica and D. Doli, 'The Relationship between International Law and National Law in the Case of Kosovo: A Constitutional Perspective', *International Journal of Constitutional Law* 9:1 (2011) 274.

Moschtaghi, R.S., 'Constitutionalism in an Islamic Republic: The Principles of the Afghan Constitution and the Conflicts between Them' in R. Grote and T. Röder (eds.), *Constitutionalism in Islamic Countries: Between Upheaval and Continuity* (Oxford University Press 2012) 683.

Möllers, C., '"We Are (Afraid of) the People": Constituent Power in German Constitutionalism' in M. Loughlin and N. Walker (eds.), *The Paradox of Constitutionalism: Constituent Power and Constitutional Form* (Oxford University Press 2008) 87.

Murkens, J., *From Empire to Union: Conceptions of German Constitutional Law since 1871* (Oxford University Press 2013).

Murphy, W.F., 'An Ordering of Constitutional Values', *South California Law Review* 53 (1980) 703.

Murphy, W.F., 'Constitutions, Constitutionalism, and Democracy' in D. Greenberg, S.N. Katz, and M.B. Oliviero (eds.), *Constitutionalism and Democracy: Transitions in the Contemporary World* (Oxford University Press 1993) 3.

Murphy, W.F., 'Merlin's Memory: The Past and Future Imperfect of the Once and Future Polity' in S. Levinson (ed.), *Responding to Imperfection: The Theory and Practice of Constitutional Amendment* (Princeton University Press 1995) 163.

Murphy, W.F., *Constitutional Democracy: Creating and Maintaining a Just Political Order* (Johns Hopkins University Press 2007).

Murray, C., 'Political Elites and the People: Kenya's Decade Long Constitution-Making Process' in G.L. Negretto (ed.), *Redrafting Constitutions in Democratic Regimes: Theoretical and Comparative Perspective* (Cambridge University Press 2020) 190.

Mutua, M., *Human Rights: A Political and Cultural Critique* (University of Pennsylvania Press 2002).

Müller, J.-W., *Constitutional Patriotism* (Princeton University Press 2007).

Müller, J-W., *Contesting Democracy: Political Ideas in Twentieth-Century Europe* (Yale University Press 2011).

National Commission to Review the Working of the Constitution, Final Report, 2002, http://lawmin.nic.in/ncrwc/ncrwcreport.htm.

'National Identity and Constitutionalism in Europe' special issue, *Nations and Nationalism* 16:1 (2010).

Nelson, M.J., 'Indian Basic Structure Jurisprudence in the Islamic Republic of Pakistan: Reconfiguring the Constitutional Politics of Religion', *Asian Journal of Comparative Law* 13:2 (2018) 333.

Neo, J.L., 'A Contextual Approach to Unconstitutional Constitutional Amendments: Judicial Power and the Basic Structure Doctrine in Malaysia', *Asian Journal of Comparative Law* 15 (2020) 69.

Neuborne, B., 'Constitutional Court Profile: The Supreme Court of India', *International Journal of Constitutional Law* 1:3 (2003) 476.

Ngetich, K.A., 'Toward a People-Driven Constitution: Opportunities, Constraints, and Challenges of the Kenyan Example', in S. Adejumobi (ed.), *Democratic Renewal in Africa: Trends and Discourses* (Palgrave Macmillan 2015) 133.

Nicolaïdis, K., 'Germany as Europe: How the Constitutional Court Unwittingly Embraced EU Demoi-cracy', *International Journal of Constitutional Law* 9:3–4 (2011) 786.

Niesen, P., 'Constituent Power in Global Constitutionalism' in A.F. Lang and A. Wiener (eds.), *Handbook on Global Constitutionalism* (Edward Elgar 2017) 222.

Nolte, D. and A. Schilling-Vacaflor (eds.), *New Constitutionalism in Latin America: Promises and Practices* (Routledge 2012).

O'Cinneide, C., 'Human Rights within Multi-Layered Systems of Constitutional Governance: Rights Cosmopolitanism and Domestic Particularism in Tension', *Irish Yearbook of International Law* 3 (2010) 19.

O'Cinneide, C., 'Rights under Pressure', *European Human Rights Law Review* 1 (2017) 43.

O'Connell, R., 'Militant Democracy and Human Rights Principles', *Constitutional Law Review* 5:1 (2009) 84.

O'Donoghue, A., *Constitutionalism in Global Constitutionalisation* (Cambridge University Press 2014).

O'Flynn, I. and R. Levy, 'Deliberative Constitutional Referendums in Deeply Divided Societies', *UBC Law Review* 53 (2020) 205.

Oberndörfer, D., 'Freedom of Speech Through Constitutional Provisions: History and Overall Record' in D. Kretzmer and F. Kershman Hazan (eds.), *Freedom of Speech and Incitement Against Democracy* (Kluwer Law International 2000) 240.

Oklopcic, Z., 'Constitutional (Re)Vision: Sovereign Peoples, New Constituent Powers, and the Formation of Constitutional Orders in the Balkans', *Constellations* 19:1 (2012) 81.

Oklopcic, Z., 'Constitutional Theory and Cognitive Estrangement: Beyond Revolutions, Amendments and Constitutional Moments' in R. Albert, X. Contiades, and A. Fotiadou (eds.), *The Foundations and Traditions of Constitutional Amendment* (Hart 2017) 51.

Oklopcic, Z., *Beyond the People: Social Imaginary and Constituent Imagination* (Oxford University Press 2018).

Olinga, A.D., 'La promotion de la démocratie et d'un ordre constitutionnel de qualité par le système africain des droits fondamentaux: entre acquis et défis', *Annuaire Africain des Droits de l'Homme* 1 (2017) 239.

Oliver, D. and C. Fusaro (eds.), *How Constitutions Change: A Comparative Study* (Hart 2011).

Orford, A., 'Feminism, Imperialism and the Mission of International Law', *Nordic Journal of International Law* 71:2 (2002) 275.

Orgad, L., 'The Preamble in Constitutional Interpretation', *International Journal of Constitutional Law* 8:4 (2010) 714.

Özbudun, E., 'Turkey's Constitutional Reform and the 2010 Constitutional Referendum', *Mediterranean Politics*, 2011, http://www.iemed.org/observatori-en/arees-danalisi/arxius-adjunts/anuari/med.2011/Ozbudun_en.pdf.

Özbudun, E., 'Turkey's Search for a New Constitution', *Insight Turkey* 14:1 (2012) 39.

Özbudun, E., 'Democracy, Tutelarism and the Search for a New Constitution', in C. Rodríguez, A. Ávalos, H. Yılmaz, and A.I. Planet (eds.), *Turkey's Democratization Process* (Routledge 2014) 274.

Pajic, Z., 'A Critical Appraisal of Human Rights Provisions of the Dayton Constitution of Bosnia and Herzegovina', *Human Rights Quarterly* 20:1 (1998) 125.

Palombella, G., 'Structures and Process in the Constitutional Self: Coping with the Future?', *International Journal of Constitutional Law* 8:3 (2010) 656.

Pap, A.L., *Democratic Decline in Hungary: Law and Society in an Illiberal Democracy* (Routledge 2018).

Patberg, M., 'Constituent Power beyond the State: An Emerging Debate in International Political Theory', *Millennium Journal of International Studies* 42:1 (2013) 224.

Pernice, I., 'Artikel 23: Europäische Union', in H. Dreier (ed.), *Grundgesetz: Kommentar (Band II)* (Mohr Siebeck 1998).

Perritt, Jr., H.H., *The Road to Independence for Kosovo: A Chronicle of the Ahtisaari Plan* (Cambridge University Press 2010).

Perry, V., 'Constitutional Reform Processes in Bosnia and Herzegovina' in S. Keil and V. Perry (eds.), *State-Building and Democratization in Bosnia and Herzegovina* (Routledge 2015) 15.

Peters, A., 'Supremacy Lost: International Law Meets Domestic Constitutional Law', *Vienna Journal on International Constitutional Law* 3:3 (2009) 170.

Petersen, F. and Z. Yanaşmayan (eds.), *The Failure of Popular Constitution Making in Turkey: Regressing Towards Autocracy* (Cambridge University Press 2019).

Pildes, R., 'Political Parties and Constitutionalism' in T. Ginsburg and R. Dixon (eds.), *Comparative Constitutional Law* (Edward Elgar 2011) 254.

Polzin, M., 'Constitutional Identity, Unconstitutional Amendments and the Idea of Constituent Power: The Development of the Doctrine of Constitutional Identity in German Constitutional Law', *International Journal of Constitutional Law* 14:2 (2016) 411.

Polzin, M., 'Constitutional Identity as a Constructed Reality and a Restless Soul', *German Law Journal* 18:7 (2017) 1595.

'Ponta, despre monarhie: Viitorul şef al statului are obligaţia de a organiza un referendum privind forma de guvernământ', *Mediafax*, 20 October 2014, http://www.gandul.info/politica/ponta-despre-monarhie-viitorul-sef-al-statului-are-obligatia-de-a-organiza-un-referendum-privind-forma-de-guvernamant-13422241.

Popova, M., *Politicized Justice in Emerging Democracies: A Study of Courts in Russia and Ukraine* (Cambridge University Press 2012).

Preuss, U.K., *Constitutional Revolution: The Link between Constitutionalism and Progress* (Humanities Press International 1995).

Preuss, U.K., 'Perspectives on Post-Conflict Constitutionalism: Reflections on Regime Change through External Constitutionalization', *New York Law School Law Review* 51 (2006) 467.

Preuss, U.K., 'The Implications of "Eternity Clauses": The German Experience', *Israel Law Review* 44 (2011) 429.

'Questions on the Ballot: Discussion and Clarification', Thjodaratkvaedi.is (website for the general referendum in Iceland), 20 October 2012, http://www.thjodaratkvaedi.is/2012/en/question_on_the_ballot.html.

Ramachandran, R., 'The Supreme Court and the Basic Structure Doctrine' in B.N. Kirpal, A.H. Desai, G. Subramanian, R. Dhavan, and R. Ramchandran (eds.), *Supreme But Not Infallible: Essays in Honour of the Supreme Court of India* (Oxford University Press 2000) 107.

Ramachandran, R., 'The Quest and the Questions', *Outlook India*, 25 August 2014, http://www.outlookindia.com/article/the-quest-and-the-questions/291655.

Ramnath, K., '"We the People": Seamless Webs and Social Revolution in India's Constituent Assembly Debates', *South Asia Research* 32:1 (2012) 57.

Ress, G., 'The Constitution and the Requirements of Democracy in Germany' in C. Starck (ed.), *New Challenges to the German Basic Law: The German Contributions to the Third World Congress of the International Association of Constitutional Law* (Nomos 1991) 123.

Riegner, M., 'The Two Faces of the Internationalized *Pouvoir Constituant*: Independence and Constitution-Making under External Influence in Kosovo', *Goettingen Journal of International Law* 2:3 (2010) 1035.

Rosenfeld, M., The *Identity of the Constitutional Subject: Selfhood, Citizenship, Culture, and Community* (Routledge 2009).

Rosenfeld, M., 'Constitutional Identity' in M. Rosenfeld and A. Sajó, eds., *The Oxford Handbook of Comparative Constitutional Law* (Oxford University Press 2012) 757.

Roux, T., 'Principle and Pragmatism on the Constitutional Court of South Africa', *International Journal of Constitutional Law* 7:1 (2009) 106.

Roux, T., *The Politics of Principle: The First South African Constitutional Court, 1995–2005* (Cambridge University Press 2013).

Rowe, G., and L.J. Frewer, 'A Typology of Public Engagement Mechanisms', *Science, Technology, & Human Values* 30:2 (2005) 257.

Roznai, Y., 'Unconstitutional Constitutional Amendments—The Migration and Success of a Constitutional Idea', *American Journal of Comparative Law* 61 (2013) 657.

Roznai, Y., 'Legisprudence Limitations on Constitutional Amendments? Reflections on the Czech Constitutional Court's Declaration of Unconstitutional Constitutional Act', *Vienna Journal on International Constitutional Law* 8:1 (2014) 29.

Roznai, Y., 'Unamendability and the Genetic Code of the Constitution', *European Review of Public Law* 27:2 (2015) 775.

Roznai, Y., *Unconstitutional Constitutional Amendments: The Limits of Amendment Powers* (Oxford University Press 2017).

Roznai, R. and L.R. Camargo Kreuz, 'Conventionality Control and Amendment 95/2016—A Brazilian Case of Unconstitutional Constitutional Amendment' *Revista de Investigações Constitucionais* 5:2 (2018) 35.

Roznai, Y. and S. Suteu, 'The Eternal Territory? The Crimean Crisis and Ukraine's Territorial Integrity as an Unamendable Constitutional Principle', *German Law Journal* 16:3 (2015) 542.

Roznai, Y. and S. Yolcu, 'An Unconstitutional Constitutional Amendment—The Turkish Perspective: A Comment on the Turkish Constitutional Court's Headscarf Decision', *International Journal of Constitutional Law* 10:1 (2012) 175.

Rubin, B.R., 'Crafting a Constitution for Afghanistan', *Journal of Democracy* 15:3 (2004) 5.

Ruhl, J.M., 'Honduras Unravels', *Journal of Democracy* 21:2 (2010) 93.

Saati, A., 'Different Types of Participation in Constitution Making Processes: Towards a Conceptualization', *Southern African Journal of Policy and Development* 2:2 (2016) 18.

Saati, A., 'Participatory Constitution-Making as a Transnational Legal Norm: Why Does It Stick in Some Contexts and Not in Others', *UC Irvine Journal of International, Transnational and Comparative Law* 2 (2017a) 113.

Saati, A., 'Constitution-building Building Bodies and the Sequencing of Public Participation: A Comparison of Seven Empirical Cases', *Journal of Politics and Law* 10:3 (2017b) 13.

Saati, A., 'Participatory Constitution-Building in Nepal—A Comparison of the 2008–2012 and the 2013–2015 Process', *Journal of Politics and Law* 10:4 (2017c) 29.

Saati, A., 'Participatory Constitution-Building in Fiji: A Comparison of the 1993–1997 and the 2012–2013 Processes', *International Journal of Constitutional Law* 18:1 (2020) 260.

Sadurski, W., 'Transitional Constitutionalism: Simplistic and Fancy Theories' in A.W. Czarnota, M. Krygier, and W. Sadurski (eds.), *Rethinking the Rule of Law After Communism* (CEU Press 2005) 9.

Sadurski, W., *Constitutionalism and the Enlargement of Europe* (Oxford University Press 2012).

Sadurski, W., *Poland's Constitutional Breakdown* (Oxford University Press 2019).

Saiz Arnaiz, A., and C. Alcoberro Llivina (eds.), *National Constitutional Identity and European Integration* (Intersentia 2013).

Sajó, A., 'Preliminaries to a Concept of Constitutional Secularism', in S. Mancini and M. Rosenfeld, eds., *Constitutional Secularism in an Age of Religious Revival* (Oxford University Press 2014) 54.

Samuels, D.J. and S. Mainwaring, 'Strong Federalism, Constraints on Central Government, and Economic Reform in Brazil' in E.L. Gibson (ed.), *Federalism and Democracy in Latin America* (Johns Hopkins University Press 2004) 85.

Santos Botelho, C., 'Constitutional Narcissism on the Couch of Psychoanalysis: Constitutional Unamendability in Portugal and Spain', *European Journal of Law Reform* 21:3 (2019) 346.

Sasse, G., 'The European Neighbourhood Policy: Conditionality Revisited for the EU's Eastern Neighbours', *Europe-Asia Studies* 60:2 (2008a) 295.

Sasse, G., 'The Politics of EU Conditionality: The Norm of Minority Protection During and Beyond beyond EU Accession', *Journal of European Public Policy* 15:6 (2008b) 842.

Sasse, G., 'The Council of Europe as a Norm Entrepreneur: The Political Strengths of a Weak International Institution' in N. Walker, J. Shaw, and S. Tierney (eds.), *Europe's Constitutional Mosaic* (Hart 2011) 171.

Sathe, S.P., *Judicial Activism in India: Transgressing Borders and Enforcing Limits* (Oxford University Press 2002).

Saunders, C., 'Constitution Making in the 21st Century', *International Review of Law* 1:4 (2012) 1.

Saunders, C., 'Designing and Operating Constitutions in Global Context' in M. Elliott and D. Feldman (eds.), *The Cambridge Companion to Public Law* (Cambridge University Press 2015) 256.

Sayarı, S., 'Party System and Democratic Consolidation in Turkey: Problems and Prospects' in C. Rodríguez, A. Ávalos, H. Yılmaz , and A.I. Planet (eds.), *Turkey's Democratization Process* (Routledge 2014) 89.

Schauer, F., 'Amending the Presuppositions of a Constitution' in S. Levinson (ed.), *Responding to Imperfection: The Theory and Practice of Constitutional Amendment* (Princeton University Press 1995) 145.

Scheppele, K.L., 'The Rule of Law and the Frankenstate: Why Governance Checklists Do Not Work', *Governance* 26:4 (2013) 559.

Scheppele, K.L., 'Autocratic Legalism', *University of Chicago Law Review* 85 (2018) 545.

Schnably, S.J., 'Emerging International Law Constraints on Constitutional Structure and Revision: A Preliminary Appraisal', *University of Miami Law Review* 62 (2008) 417.

Schneiderman, D., *Constitutionalizing Economic Globalization Investment Rules and Democracy's Promise* (Cambridge University Press 2008).

Schonthal, B., *Buddhism, Politics and the Limits of Law: The Pyrrhic Constitutionalism of Sri Lanka* (Cambridge University Press 2016).

Schönberger, C., 'Lisbon in Karlsruhe: Maastricht's Epigones At Sea', *German Law Journal* 10:8 (2009) 1201.

Schwartzberg, M., *Democracy and Legal Change* (Cambridge University Press 2009).

Scwellnus, G., 'The Adoption of Nondiscrimination and Minority Protection Rules in Romania, Hungary, and Poland' in F. Schimmelfennig and U. Sedelmeier (eds.), *The Europeanization of Central and Eastern Europe* (Cornell University Press 2005) 51.

Segal, L., and S. Cort, One Law, *One Nation: The Making of the South African Constitution* (Jacana Media 2011).

Sekulić, T., *The European Union and the Paradox of Enlargement: The Complex Accession of the Western Balkans* (Palgrave Macmillan 2020).

Selejan-Guţan, B., 'The Constitutional Court and Others in Romanian Constitutionalism—25 Years After', *Vienna Journal of International Constitutional Law* 11:4 (2017) 565.

Sen, S., *The Constitution of India: Popular Sovereignty and Democratic Transformations* (Oxford University Press 2007).

Sezgin, Y., 'Could Erdogan Lose Turkey's Upcoming Election?', *Washington Post*, 19 May 2015, https://www.washingtonpost.com/blogs/monkey-cage/wp/2015/05/19/could-erdogan-lose-turkeys-upcoming-election/.

Shachar, A., 'The Return of the Repressed: Constitutionalism, Religion, and Political Pluralism', *International Journal of Constitutional Law* 8:3 (2010) 665.

Shaffer, G., T. Ginsburg, and T.C. Halliday (eds.), *Constitution-Making and Transnational Legal Order* (Cambridge University Press 2019).

Shafir, M., 'Mişcările xenofobe şi dilemele "„includerii" şi "„excluderii": cazul minorităţii maghiare din România', *Altera* 6:15 (2000a) 159.

Shafir, M., 'The Political Party as National Holding Company: The Hungarian Democratic Federation of Romania' in J. Stein (ed.), *The Politics of National Minority Participation in Post-Communist Europe: State Building, Democracy and Ethnic Mobilization* (M.E. Sharpe 2000b) 101.

Sharfe, P., 'Erdoğan's Presidential Dreams, Turkey's Constitutional Politics', *Origins* 8:5 (2015) 1.

Shinar, A., 'Accidental Constitutionalism: The Political Foundations and Implications of Constitution-Making in Israel' in D.J. Galligan and M. Versteeg (eds.), *Social and Political Foundations of Constitutions* (Cambridge University Press 2013) 207.

Siddique, O., 'The Judicialization of Politics in Pakistan: The Supreme Court after the Lawyers' Movement' in M. Tushnet and M. Khosla (eds.), *Unstable Constitutionalism: Law and Politics in South Asia* (Cambridge University Press 2015) 159.

Simonelli, M.A., 'Towards a Theory of "Unconventional Constitutional Amendments": Some Lessons from the Baka Case', *DPCE Online* 39:2 (2019) 1561.

Simović, D., 'Constitutional Rigidity and Aporias of the Amendment Procedure in the Republic of Serbia', *Fondacija Centar za javno pravo* (2017).

Singh, M.P., 'India' in D. Oliver and C. Fusaro (eds.), *How Constitutions Change: A Comparative Study* (Hart 2011) 169.

Skach, C., *Borrowing Constitutional Designs: Constitutional Law in Weimar Germany and the French Fifth Republic* (Princeton University Press 2005).

Skach, C., 'Şahin v. Turkey. App. no. 44774/98; "Teacher Headscarf". Case no. 2BvR 1436/02', *American Journal of International Law* 100:1 (2006) 186.

Skach, C., 'Political Parties and the Constitution' in M. Rosenfeld and A. Sajó (eds.), *The Oxford Handbook of Comparative Constitutional Law* (Oxford University Press 2012) 874.

Smith, E., 'Old and Protected? On the "Supra-Constitutional" Clause in the Constitution of Norway', *Israel Law Review* 44 (2011) 369

Smith, G., *Democratic Innovations: Designing Institutions for Citizen Participation* (Cambridge University Press 2009).

Somek, A., 'The Constituent Power in a Transnational Context', *Transnational Legal Theory* 3:1 (2012) 31.

Sonnevend, P., A. Jakab, and L. Csink, 'The Constitution as an Instrument of Everyday Party Politics: The Basic Law of Hungary' in A. von Bogdandy and P. Sonnevend (eds.), *Constitutional Crisis in the European Constitutional Area: Theory, Law and Politics in Hungary and Romania* (Hart 2015) 33.

Sorabjee, S., 'The Ideal Remedy: A Valediction' in P. Chopra (ed.), *The Supreme Court versus the Constitution* (Sage Publications 2006) 199.

Souza, C., 'Brazil: From "Isolated" Federalism to Hybridity' in J. Loughlin, J. Kincaid, and W. Swenden (eds.), *Routledge Handbook of Regionalism & Federalism* (Routledge 2013) 457.

Special Envoy of the Secretary-General for Kosovo, *Report of the Special Envoy of the Secretary-General on Kosovo's Future Status*, S/2007/168, 27 March 2001.

Squires, J., 'Liberal Constitutionalism, Identity and Difference' in R. Bellamy and D. Castiglione (eds.), *Constitutionalism in Transformation: European and Theoretical Perspectives* (Blackwell Publishers 1996) 208.

Sripati, V., *Constitution-Making under UN Auspices: Fostering Dependency in Sovereign Lands* (Oxford University Press 2020).

Stacey, R., 'Constituent Power and Carl Schmitt's Theory of Constitution in Kenya's Constitution-making Process', *International Journal of Constitutional Law* 9:3–4 (2011) 587.

Stearns, S., 'Kerry: Tunisia's New Constitution Is Model for Arab World', *Voice of America*, 18 February 2014, http://www.voanews.com/content/kerry-visits-tunisia-amid-democratic-transition/1853607.html.

Stjórnlagaráð, 'A Proposal for a New Constitution for the Republic of Iceland, Drafted by Stjórnlagaráð, a Constitutional Council, appointed by an Althingi resolution on March 24th 2011' (English translation), http://www.stjornlagarad.is/other_files/stjornlagarad/Frumvarp-enska.pdf.

Stone Sweet, A., 'Judicialization and the Construction of Governance', in M. Shapiro and A. Stone Sweet, *On Law, Politics and Judicialization* (Oxford University Press 2002) 55.

Stone Sweet, A., 'On the Constitutionalisation of the Convention: The European Court of Human Rights as a Constitutional Court', *Revue Trimestrielle des Droits de l'Homme* 80 (2009) 923.

Suber, P., *The Paradox of Self-Amendment: A Study of Law, Logic, Omnipotence, and Change* (Peter Lang 1990).

Sudarshan, R., '"Stateness" and Democracy in India's Constitution' in Z. Hasan, E. Sridharan, and R. Sudarshan (eds.), *India's Living Constitution: Ideas, Practices, Controversies* (Permanent Black 2002) 159.

Sultany, N., *Law and Revolution: Legitimacy and Constitutionalism After the Arab Spring* (Oxford University Press 2017).

Sunstein, C.R., 'Constitutions and Democracies: An Epilogue' in J. Elster and R. Slagstad (eds.), *Constitutionalism and Democracy* (Cambridge University Press 1988) 327.

Suteu, S., 'Constitutional Conventions in the Digital Era: Lessons from Iceland and Ireland', *Boston College International & Comparative Law Review* 38:2 (2015) 251.

Suteu, S., 'The Multinational State That Wasn't: The Constitutional Definition of Romania as a National State', Vienna Journal on International Constitutional Law 11:3 (2017a) 413.

Suteu, S. 'Eternity Clauses in Post-conflict Conflict and Post-authoritarian Authoritarian Constitution-Making: Promise and Limits', *Global Constitutionalism* 6:1 (2017b) 63.

Suteu, S., 'The Scottish Independence Referendum and the Participatory Turn in UK Constitution-Making: The Move towards a Constitutional Convention', *Global Constitutionalism* 6:2 (2017c) 184.

Suteu, S., 'The Populist Turn in Central and Eastern Europe: Is Deliberative Democracy Part of the Solution?', *European Constitutional Law Review* 15:3 (2019) 488.

Suteu, S. and S. Tierney, 'Squaring the Circle? Bringing Deliberation and Participation Together in Processes of Constitution-Making' in R. Levy, H. Kong, G. Orr, and J. King (eds.), *The Cambridge Handbook of Deliberative Constitutionalism* (Cambridge University Press 2018) 282.

'Symposium on the Proposed European Constitution' special issue, *International Journal of Constitutional Law* 3: 2–3 (2005).

Szasz, P.C., 'The Protection of Human Rights through the Dayton/Paris Peace Agreement on Bosnia', *American Journal of International Law* 90:2 (1996) 301.

Śledzińska-Simon, A., 'A Model of Individual, Relational, and Collective Self and Its Application in Poland', *International Journal of Constitutional Law* 13:1 (2015) 124.

Taussig-Rubbo, M., 'From the "Stranger King" to the "Stranger Constitution": Domesticating Sovereignty in Kenya', *Constellations* 19:2 (2012) 248.

Tănăsescu, S., 'Despre Identitatea Constituţională şi Rolul Integrator al Constituţiei', *Curierul Judiciar* 5 (2017) 243.

Tew, Y., *Constitutional Statecraft in Asian Courts* (Oxford University Press 2020).

Theil, S., 'What Red Lines, If Any, Do the Lisbon Judgments of European Constitutional Courts Draw for Future EU Integration?', *German Law Journal* 15:4 (2014) 599.

Tierney, S., '"We the Peoples": Constituent Power and Constitutionalism in Plurinational States' in M. Loughlin and N. Walker (eds.), *The Paradox of Constitutionalism: Constituent Power and Constitutional Form* (Oxford University Press 2008) 229.

Tierney, S., *Constitutional Referendums: The Theory and Practice of Republican Deliberation* (Oxford University Press 2012).

Tierney, S., 'Europe Is Entering the "Age of the Referendum", But There Is Nothing to Fear for European Democracy If Referendums Are Properly Regulated', Democratic Audit, 22 October 2014a, http://www.democraticaudit.com/?p=8777.

Tierney, S., '"And the Winner Is ... the Referendum": Scottish Independence and the Deliberative Participation of Citizens', I-CONnect Blog, 26 September 2014b, http://www.iconnectblog.com/2014/09/and-the-winner-is-the-referendum-scottish-independence-and-the-deliberative-participation-of-citizens/.

Tomoszek, M., 'The Czech Republic' in D. Oliver and C. Fusaro (eds.), *How Constitutions Change: A Comparative Study* (Hart 2011) 41.

Toplak, J., and Đ. Gardašević, 'Concepts of National and Constitutional Identity in Croatian Constitutional Law', *Review of Central and East European Law* 42 (2017) 263.

Torelly, M., 'Transnational Legal Process and Fundamental Rights in Latin America: How Does the Inter-American Human Rights System Reshape Domestic Constitutional Rights?' in P. Rubim Borges Fortes, L. Verri Bortti, A. Palacios Lleras, and T.G. Daly (eds.), *Law and Policy in Latin America: Transforming Courts, Institutions, and Rights* (Springer 2016) 21.

Torres Pérez, A., 'Judicial Self-Government and Judicial Independence: The Political Capture of the General Council of the Judiciary in Spain', *German Law Journal* 19:7 (2018) 1769.

Tóth, G.A., 'Lost in Transition: Invisible Constitutionalism in Hungary' in R. Dixon and A. Stone (eds.), *The Invisible Constitution in Comparative Perspective* (Cambridge University Press 2018) 541.

Tribe, L.H., 'A Constitution We Are Amending: In Defense of a Restrained Judicial Role', *Harvard Law Review* 97:2 (1983) 433.

Tribe, L., *The Invisible Constitution* (Oxford University Press 2008).

Tripathi, P.K., 'Perspectives on the American Influence on the Constitution of India', in L.W. Beer (ed.), *Constitutionalism in Asia: Views of the American Influence* (University of California Press 1979) 59.

Tripkovic, B., *The Metaethics of Constitutional Adjudication* (Oxford University Press 2018).

Trochev, A., *Judging Russia: The Role of the Constitutional Court in Russian Politics 1990–2006* (Cambridge University Press 2008).

Tsakyrakis, S., 'Proportionality: An Assault on Human Rights?', *International Journal of Constitutional Law* 7:3 (2009) 468.

'Turkey's Erdogan Says New Constitution Priority after 2015 Election', *Reuters*, 1 October 2014, http://www.reuters.com/article/2014/10/01/us-turkey-constitution-idUSKCN0HQ47H20141001.

Tushnet, M., 'Some Reflections on Method in Comparative Constitutional Law' in S. Choudhry (ed.), *The Migration of Constitutional Ideas* (Cambridge University Press 2007) 67.

Tushnet, M., *Weak Courts, Strong Rights: Judicial Review and Social Welfare Rights in Comparative Constitutional Law* (Princeton University Press 2009).

Tushnet, M., 'Constitution-Making: An Introduction', *Texas Law Review* 91 (2013) 1983.

Tushnet, M., 'Amendment Theory and Constituent Power' in G.J. Jacobsohn and M. Schor (eds.), *Comparative Constitutional Theory* (Edward Elgar 2018) 317.

Tushnet, M., 'The Globalisation of Constitutional Law as a Weakly Neo-liberal Project', *Global Constitutionalism* 8:1 (2019) 29.

Tyulkina, T., *Militant Democracy: Undemocratic Political Parties and Beyond* (Routledge 2015).

Uitz, R., 'Expelling Dissent: On Account of the ECtHR Judgment in *Baka v Hungary*', Verfassungsblog, 3 June 2014, https://verfassungsblog.de/expelling-dissent-account-ecthr-judgment-baka-v-hungary-2/.

Uitz, R., 'Can You Tell When an Illiberal Democracy Is in the Making? An Appeal to Comparative Constitutional Scholarship from Hungary', *International Journal of Constitutional Law* 13:1 (2015) 279.

Uitz, R., 'National Constitutional Identity in the European Constitutional Project: A Recipe for Exposing Cover Ups and Masquerades', Verfassungsblog, 11 November 2016, https://verfassungsblog.de/national-constitutional-identity-in-the-european-constitutional-project-a-recipe-for-exposing-cover-ups-and-masquerades/.

The UN Constitutional: A Newsletter on United Nations Constitutional Support, Issue 2: spring/summer (2014), 16–17.

Urbina, F.J., *A Critique of Proportionality and Balancing* (Cambridge University Press 2017).

Varshney, A., 'Why Democracy Survives', *Journal of Democracy* 9:3 (1998) 36.

Vassilev, R., 'Will Bulgaria Become [a] Monarchy Again?', *Southeast European Politics* 4:2-3 (2003) 157.

Vermeersch, P., 'Innovating Democracy in Times of Crisis: Solution or Utopia?', *Open Citizenship* 4:1 (2013) 66.

Voermans, W., M. Stremler, and P. Cliteur, *Constitutional Preambles: A Comparative Analysis* (Edward Elgar 2017).

Vinx, L., 'The Incoherence of Strong Popular Sovereignty', *International Journal of Constitutional Law* 11:1 (2013) 101.

Wakaya, J., 'Kenya: Petitioners Seek Court's Interpretation on Constitutional Amendment Limitations', *CapitalFM*, 16 September 2020, https://allafrica.com/stories/202009160840.html.

Waldron, J., *Law and Disagreement* (Oxford University Press 1999).

Wallis, J., *Constitution Making during State Building* (Cambridge University Press 2014).

Walker, N., 'Post-Constituent Constitutionalism? The Case of the European Union' in M. Loughlin and N. Walker (eds.), *The Paradox of Constitutionalism: Constituent Power and Constitutional Form* (Oxford University Press 2008) 247.

Walker, N., 'Rosenfeld's Plural Constitutionalism', *International Journal of Constitutional Law* 8:3 (2010) 677.

Walsh, F.M., 'The Honduran Constitution Is Not a Suicide Pact: The Legality of Honduran President Manuel Zelaya's Removal', *Georgia Journal of International and Comparative Law*, 38 (2010) 339.

Warren, M.E., and H. Pearse (eds.), *Designing Deliberative Democracy: The British Columbia Citizens' Assembly* (Cambridge University Press 2008).

Webber, G., 'The Remaking of the Constitution of Canada', UK Constitutional Law Blog, 1 July 2015, https://ukconstitutionallaw.org/2015/07/01/gregoire-webber-the-remaking-of-the-constitution-of-canada/.

Weil, R., 'On the Nexus of Eternity Clauses, Proportional Representation, and Banned Political Parties', *Election Law Journal* 16:2 (2017) 237.

Weiler, J.H.H., 'Federalism without Constitutionalism: Europe's Sonderweg' in K. Nicolaïdis and R. Howse (eds.), *The Federal Vision: Legitimacy and Levels of Governance in the United States and the European Union* (Oxford University Press 2001) 54.

Weiler, J.H.H., 'The "Lisbon Urteil" and the Fast Food Culture', *European Journal of International Law* 20:3 (2009) 505.

Weintal, S., 'The Challenge of Reconciling Constitutional Eternity Clauses with Popular Sovereignty: Toward Three-track Democracy in Israel as a Universal Holistic Constitutional System and Theory', *Israel Law Review* 44 (2011) 449.

Welikala, A., 'Southphalia or Southfailure? National Pluralism and the State in South Asia' in S. Tierney (ed.), *Nationalism and Globalisation* (Hart 2015) 93.

Wendel, M., 'Judicial Restraint and the Return to Openness: The Decision of the German Federal Constitutional Court on the ESM and the Fiscal Treaty of 12 September 2012', *German Law Journal* 14:1 (2013) 21.

'West African Leaders Shelves Third-term Ban Proposal', *BBC News*, 20 May 2015, https://www.bbc.co.uk/news/world-africa-32808685.

Widner, J., 'Constitution-Writing in Post-conflict Conflict Settings: An Overview', *William and Mary Law Review* 49:4 (2008) 1513.

Wiebusch, M., 'The Role of Regional Organizations in the Protection of Constitutionalism', International IDEA Discussion Paper 17/2016, 24 August 2016.

Wiebush, M., and C. Murray, 'Presidential Term Limits and the African Union', *Journal of African Law* 63:1 (2019) 131.

Wilkinson, M.A., 'Authoritarian Liberalism in the European Constitutional Imagination: Second Time as Farce?', *European Law Journal* 21:3 (2015) 313.

Wilkinson, M.A., 'Authoritarian Liberalism as Authoritarian Constitutionalism' in H. Alviar García and G. Frankenberg (eds.), *Authoritarian Constitutionalism: Comparative Analysis and Critique* (Edward Elgar 2019) 317.

Williams, K., 'Judicial Review of Electoral Thresholds in Germany, Russia and the Czech Republic', *Election Law Journal* 4:3 (2005), 191.

Williams, K., 'When a Constitutional Amendment Violates the "Substantive Core": The Czech Constitutional Court's September 2009 Early Elections Decision', *Review of Central and Eastern European Law* 36 (2011) 33.

Woelk, J., 'Germany' in D. Oliver and C. Fusaro (eds.), *How Constitutions Change: A Comparative Study* (Hart 2011) 143.

Yap, P.J., 'The Conundrum of Unconstitutional Constitutional Amendments', *Global Constitutionalism* 4:1 (2015) 114.

Yap, P.J., *Courts and Democracies in Asia* (Cambridge University Press 2017).

Yegen, O., 'Debating Unamendability: Deadlock in Turkey's Constitution-Making Process' in R. Albert and B.E. Oder (eds.), *An Unamendable Constitution? Unamendability in Constitutional Democracies* (Springer 2018) 281.

Yegen, O., 'Debating the Amendment-Making Rule: The Rigidity vs. Flexibility Debate in the Turkish Constitution-Making Process' in F. Petersen and Z. Yanaşmayan (eds.), *The Failure of Popular Constitution Making in Turkey: Regressing Towards Autocracy* (Cambridge University Press 2019) 249.

Zemni, S., 'The Extraordinary Politics of the Tunisian Revolution: The Process of Constitution Making', *Mediterranean Politics* 20:1 (2015) 1.

Index

For the benefit of digital users, indexed terms that span two pages (e.g., 52–53) may, on occasion, appear on only one of those pages.